DOCTRINE
— AND —
COVENANTS

A COMMENTARY ON THE

DOCTRINE

— AND —

COVENANTS

VOLUME TWO

Stephen E. Robinson

H. Dean Garrett

DESERET BOOK COMPANY

SALT LAKE CITY, UTAH

Library of Congress Cataloging-in-Publication Data

Robinson, Stephen Edward.

A commentary on the Doctrine and Covenants / Stephen E. Robinson and
     H. Dean Garrett.

p.   cm.

Includes bibliographical references.

ISBN-10 1-57345-851-1 (hardback)
ISBN-13 978-1-57345-851-1 (hardback)
ISBN-13 978-1-62972-841-4 (paperback)

1. Doctrine and Covenants—Commentaries.   I. Garrett, H. Dean.
     II. Title
BX8628 .R65   2000
289.3'2—dc21

                                                        00-040441

Printed in the United States of America
Brigham Young University Press, Provo, UT

10 9   8   7   6   5   4   3   2   1

CONTENTS

CONTENTS

DOCTRINE AND COVENANTS

41

BACKGROUND

Even before their conversion to the gospel, some of the Saints in the Kirtland area had been trying, under the leadership of Sidney Rigdon, to live primitive Christianity—the pure and original Christianity of the New Testament—by following the teachings of the New Testament and nothing else. When they read in Acts 2:44–45; 4:32–35 that the ancient Saints "were together, and had all things common," they formed a communal society called "the family" and practiced group ownership of all individual resources. They called this arrangement having "common stock." When Sidney Rigdon joined the Church, he went to Fayette and invited the Prophet to Kirtland, but Joseph sent John Whitmer instead, and Sidney stayed in Fayette to act as scribe for the Prophet. Though most of "the family" in Kirtland had since joined the Church, they were still involved in living with "common stock" when John Whitmer arrived from Fayette to preside over the community. John, seeing the problems created by common stock, wrote to the Prophet and requested that he come to Kirtland. Joseph inquired of the Lord and was told to go quickly.

According to Joseph Smith's account in *History of the Church,* he and Emma, in company with Sidney Rigdon and Edward Partridge, arrived in Kirtland, Ohio, around 1 February 1831, and perhaps as early as 30 January.[1] Emma was then six months

1

pregnant with twins, and the Smiths moved temporarily into the home of Newel K. and Elizabeth Whitney. On his arrival, Joseph Smith found a young, enthusiastic, branch of the Church in Kirtland. His own observation was that the members were "striving to do the will of God, so far as they knew it, though some strange notions and false spirits had crept in among them. With a little caution and some wisdom, I soon assisted the brethren and sisters to overcome them. The plan of 'common stock,' which had existed in what was called 'the family,' whose members generally had embraced the everlasting Gospel, was readily abandoned for the more perfect law of the Lord; and the false spirits were easily discerned and rejected by the light of revelation."[2]

John Whitmer added the following information to Joseph's account: "About these days Joseph and Sidney arrived at Kirtland to the joy and satisfaction of the Saints. The disciples had all things common, and were going to destruction very fast as to temporal things; for they considered from reading the scripture that what belonged to a brother, belonged to any of the brethren. Therefore they would take each other's clothes and other property and use it without leave which brought on confusion and disappointment, for they did not understand the scripture."[3] For example, when Levi Hancock was visiting "the family," Heman Bassett, one of its members, took Levi's pocket watch and sold it. He later explained that he had thought "it was all in the family."[4]

For the Lord to give the true law of consecration to the Church and thus to correct the "common stock" ideas of the members of "the family," he needed someone to act as his agent in administering properties according to his law. Consequently, Edward Partridge was called to become the first bishop in the latter-day Church.

Doctrine and Covenants 41 was the first revelation received in Ohio. Its purpose was essentially to prepare the Saints for Doctrine and Covenants 42, which was received five days later, on 9 February 1831.

COMMENTARY

1. Greatest of all blessings. Being a member of the Church magnifies the possible consequences of our actions in life. By keeping the commandments of the gospel, members are candidates for the greatest of all blessings—exaltation in the celestial kingdom. By disobedience to the commandments of the gospel, however, we might conceivably become candidates for the greatest of God's cursings. Those who have received the fulness of the gospel in mortality will be judged according to a different standard from those who were ignorant—this standard will allow them to rise higher or sink lower than they could otherwise have done. There is no blessing higher than that received by faithful Saints, and no cursing harsher than that received by wilful apostates. Certainly those Saints who profess the name of Christ but who will not obey his commandments should reexamine their future in light of this verse.

1. Hear me; . . . hear me not. The verb *to hear* is used here in its sense of "hearken" or "obey."

2. Assemble yourselves together. In Doctrine and Covenants 38:32 the Lord told the Saints in New York that if they would go to Ohio, he would reveal his law to them. Here one further requirement is given. There was to be a special meeting of the elders in Kirtland to hear and ratify the Lord's law. This meeting took place five days later, on 9 February 1831, and the law was given to the Church at that time.[5]

2. Agree upon my word. According to the law of common consent (see D&C 26:2), the elders must collectively agree to accept their responsibilities under the law of the Church by their sustaining vote.

3. By the prayer of your faith. The Saints had prayed in great faith to be given the further knowledge contained in the Lord's law. The elders gathered together in obedience to the command in verse 2, knowing that if they would petition the Lord in faithful prayer, they would receive the law they sought.

3. Receive my law. Beyond the articles and covenants of the

Church (Doctrine and Covenants 20), which state the duties of the members and the policies and practices of the Church, the "law" of the Church (Doctrine and Covenants 42) states the standards of personal behavior and social organization upon which membership and fellowship in the Church and kingdom depends. This law of personal righteousness and consecration directly prepares Church members to establish a Zion society, for if they live this law, they will be of one heart and one mind, will dwell in righteousness, and will have no poor among them (see Moses 7:18). Receiving and living this law of the Church, including the law of consecration, is a necessary step, and a very large one, in establishing Zion then or now.

3. Ye may know how to govern. The law given is for the governance of the Church and for judging its members. It was given specifically to the elders, whose place it was, at that time at least, to govern and judge the Church, because the first high priests were not ordained until 3 June 1831.

5. The same is my disciple. It is typical of modern thought to define discipleship in terms of beliefs. When we want to know what this or that religion is, we ask, "What do you believe?" The Lord does not define discipleship in this way. Those who *do* the Lord's will are his disciples. Those who profess belief in the gospel but will not live it are to be cast out, or excommunicated. True discipleship is determined by our actions, not just by our words or beliefs. In fact, believing the gospel and not living it will bring the greater condemnation upon us (see v. 1). In this verse, "my law" refers to the commandments contained in section 42, which is the "law of the Church."

6. It is not meet. The word *meet* has an archaic meaning of "right, fitting, appropriate, or proper." Because the Church was about to receive the law of consecration, it was not right that those who would not make the sacrifices of discipleship should reap the rewards of faithful members' consecration. Right now in the Church we have room for "inactive" members. But when the Church as a whole begins again to live the law of consecration institutionally instead of individually as we now do, and we begin to establish Zion, there will quickly be no more middle ground for the passive and lukewarm to stand upon. Since Zion is a community of Saints who are of one heart and one mind, who dwell in righteousness, and have no poor among them, the less active who will not dwell in righteousness, or who are not of one heart and one mind with the Saints, must either repent or leave—otherwise Zion cannot be established.

Diversity is not necessarily a virtue in Zion, nor is Zion a pluralistic society. There will certainly be diversity of races and to a degree a diversity of cultures, of personalities, of interests, and of wants. But there will be no diversity of values, ethics, morals, or of religious beliefs and doctrine, for Zion will be of one heart and one mind in these essentials and will dwell in righteousness according to one law—the heart and mind of the Savior, which is the law of the Church.

7. Have a house built. Joseph Smith had just arrived ten days earlier from New York and had no lodging for his family. "In response to the Lord's instruction a small home (either a log cabin or a frame house) was built on the [Isaac] Morley farm for Joseph and Emma, where they lived for six months."[6] By fall of 1832, the upper floor of Newel K. Whitney's store had also been provided as living quarters for the Prophet and his family.

8. Live as seemeth him good. As a Protestant minister, Sidney Rigdon had had a fine home built for him by the several congregations he ministered to. When he joined the LDS Church, however, the majority in those congregations requested that he leave the home they had built. Consequently, Sidney had no place for his family. The Lord instructed Sidney to take whatever measures he must in order to provide for his family, as long as he kept the commandments.

9. Edward Partridge. See Background to Doctrine and Covenants 36.

9. Appointed by the voice of the church. This verse reveals how a bishop is called in the Church. Even though the Lord revealed to the Prophet who should be the bishop, Edward Partridge could not be ordained until the collective voice of the Church sustained him, according to the law of common consent (see D&C 26) and the express instructions of the Lord. Only then, after being designated by revelation, called by those in authority, and sustained publicly by the voice of the membership, could Edward be ordained.

Today the procedure is essentially the same. A stake president seeks revelation to nominate a person to be bishop and sends that nomination to the First Presidency, who, in consultation with the Quorum of the Twelve, seek the Lord's approval and then issue a call through the stake president. After a public, sustaining vote of the ward members, the stake presidency, with approval of the First Presidency, ordains the individual to the office of bishop and sets him apart to preside over a particular ward.

10. Edward Partridge was to be made bishop to the whole Church to prepare to administer the law of the Church and other laws of God that had not yet been given. The law of the Church, section 42, was given five days later, and other laws followed thereafter.

11. Like unto Nathanael of old, in whom there is no guile. See John 1:47. What a compliment was paid here to Edward Partridge! Guile is any form of deceit, fraud, hypocrisy, two-facedness, or otherwise presenting things as they are not. To be without guile is to be totally open and honest.

12. They are pure before me. God's word is pure and holy in all its many forms, whether as scripture, as prophetic utterance, or as personal revelation. Saints who are under covenant to obey God's word must be careful not to take it lightly, as some do. We will be judged on how we treat God's holy word—with reverence, respect, and obedience, or with carelessness.

---

1. See 1:145; see also Cook, *Revelations of the Prophet Joseph Smith,* 131, n. 1.
2. *History of the Church,* 1:146–47.
3. Whitmer, *Early Latter Day Saint History,* 37.

---

4. Whitmer, *Early Latter Day Saint History*, 37.

5. See *History of the Church*, 1:148–54.

6. See Dahl, "Joseph Smith Translation and the Doctrine and Covenants," 107; esp. Dahl's extensive sources on 129–30, n. 6.

DOCTRINE AND COVENANTS

4 2

BACKGROUND

When Joseph Smith arrived in Kirtland, Ohio, from Fayette, New York, he found the Saints there willing to serve the Lord but, of course, unskilled in the doctrines and policies of the Church. He first had to bring closure to the communal "family" and end its system of common stock. Then he had to put a stop to a sort of spiritual hysteria he found among some of the Kirtland Saints. These excesses were of the sort that happen when people insist on increasing the intensity of their religious experience but lack the Spirit of God: false spirits and human deceivers are only too happy to accommodate them.[1]

Before the Saints could seriously prepare to establish Zion, they had to be given the law of the Church, which, besides a high personal morality, included the celestial principles of sacrifice and consecration. Those who could not accept the laws and principles given in Kirtland would probably not move on to Zion in Missouri.

Joseph had been in Kirtland only about five days, since 4 February 1831, when the Lord gave Doctrine and Covenants 41 to the Church as a preliminary step to revealing the law of the Church, Doctrine and Covenants 42 (promised in D&C 38:32). As instructed in Doctrine and Covenants 41:9–10, Joseph had called Edward Partridge to be the new bishop to the Church, because a bishop would be needed to implement and administer the social and economic policies and principles of section 42 when it came. The law of the Church would also establish standards of personal behavior by which the Saints would be judged by their new bishop, the common judge in Israel.

Joseph began planning for the growth of the Church in Kirtland, knowing that converts from the eastern United States and Canada would soon be flowing in, for Kirtland was to be the central staging area for establishing Zion further west "on the borders by the Lamanites" (D&C 28:9). The growth of the Church in Kirtland would also bring some tensions between old and new members or between local and eastern members. The problems of getting along in a rapidly growing community that was trying to live the law of consecration intensified as new arrivals came in from New York and elsewhere, and as more of those who had been prepared for the gospel by the preaching of Sidney Rigdon (see D&C 35:4) were converted in the Kirtland area. Notice that most of the next fifteen revelations deal with better organizing the Church, resolving disputes between members, and combating the influence of false spirits and deceivers among the members.

In preparation for receiving the law of the Church, as instructed by the Lord in Doctrine and Covenants 41:2–3, Joseph gathered twelve elders together on 9 February 1831. John Whitmer recorded what happened on this occasion: "Behold, after this revelation [D&C 41] was received the Elders were called together, and united in mighty [prayer] and were agreed, as touching the reception of the Law; therefore, thus saith the Lord your God"[2]—followed by Doctrine and Covenants 42:1–73. Concerning the reaction of the Church to the new law, John Whitmer also stated: "After the above law or revelation was received, the elders went forth to proclaim repentance according to commandment, and there were members added to the church. Though Bishop Edward Partridge visited the church in its several branches, there were some that would not receive the Law. The time has not yet come that the law can be fully established, for the disciples live scattered abroad and are not organized, our [numbers] are small and the disciples untaught, consequently they understand not the things of the Kingdom. There were some of the disciples who were flattered into the church because they thought that all things were to be common, therefore they thought to glut themselves upon the labors of others."[3]

Joseph Smith's own description of receiving section 42 simply states: "On the 9th of February, 1831, at Kirtland, in the presence of twelve Elders, and according to the promise heretofore made [D&C 38:32; 41:3], the Lord gave the following revelation, embracing the law of the Church"[4]—followed by Doctrine and Covenants 42. Concerning the reception of the law by the Church, Joseph noted in a letter to Martin Harris: "We have received the laws of the Kingdom since we came here and the Disciples in these parts have received them gladly."[5]

Doctrine and Covenants 42, the law of the Church, is actually a series of laws received in three different parts on two different dates. The first part, verses 1–73, was received at the 9 February meeting of the elders, as described above. Verses 74–77 and verses 78–93 were received two weeks later on 23 February. Verses 74–77, however, were recorded separately in the *Kirtland Revelation Book*,[6] where they stand alone as a single revelation. Later, verses 1–73 appeared in the 1833 Book of Commandments as chapter 44, while verses 78–93 appeared separately as chapter 47. It also seems that some portions of Doctrine and Covenants 42 may once have been introduced by specific questions asked of the Lord, much like we see in Doctrine and Covenants 77 or 113. These questions and some other verses found in a few early copies do not now appear in section 42.[7] All of these changes—the combining of originally separate parts and the omission of some elements—were made under the direction of Joseph Smith in the 1835 Doctrine and Covenants.[8]

It should perhaps be noted again that Latter-day Saints understand inspiration to lie primarily in the Prophet Joseph rather than in the text. That is, the divine revelation was given *through* the

Prophet and was often shaped by his vocabulary, thinking, and ability to express himself (see D&C 1:24). As the Prophet's skills or understanding increased, he could edit and revise what had been written earlier as he saw ways of expressing the intent of the revelation more clearly or more exactly, and this has the effect of making such revisions even *more* inspired than the original—as, for example, in the Joseph Smith Translation. Uneasiness over these types of changes is a typically Protestant reaction, because Protestant thinking generally attributes inspiration primarily to the text. Thus, Protestants want to find the "earliest" text or the "most faithful" copies, while Latter-day Saints want to know the Prophet's latest and most mature judgment on how a revelation should be understood or expressed. The latest and most mature judgment of the Prophet Joseph Smith and his successors on these early revelations is found in the present text of the Doctrine and Covenants.

COMMENTARY

3. According to the commandment. The commandment found in Doctrine and Covenants 41:2–3.

3. And are agreed. According to the law of common consent, the twelve elders present agreed in advance to accept and live the law that the Lord would give them. It was an exercise of faith in God to agree to live a covenant before the Lord revealed exactly what it was. A modern parallel may be found in going to the temple for the first time, when we commit ourselves in principle to receive certain covenants even before the Lord reveals to us exactly what they are.

3. Have asked the Father in my name. Even though the Lord wanted and intended to give the Church his law, he still required that they ask him for it before it would be given to them. The lesson here is the importance and efficacy of our petitions to our Heavenly Father. Even though we may need some blessing, and even though he may want to give it to us, we might not get it until we finally *ask* him directly in fervent prayer.

4. Every one of you. This phrase refers specifically to the twelve elders who were present when this revelation was received. They were commanded to go immediately on missions to the West.

5. I give unto them. To Joseph and Sidney. They were also to go on missions at this time, but were to stay out only a short time until the Spirit indicated they should return to Kirtland.

6. Ye shall go forth. The instructions given here in verses 6–7 are still basic principles of missionary work. Missionaries are to have the gift and power of the Holy Ghost; they are to travel in pairs, probably for safety and to fulfill the law of witnesses (see D&C 6:28; Deuteronomy 19:15; Matthew 18:16; 2 Corinthians 13:1); and they are to preach vocally and publicly the gospel of repentance and baptism (see Matthew 3:2; 4:17; Alma 10:20; Helaman 5:32). In this they are to be like the angels, who are also messengers of God (see D&C 133:36).

8. The regions westward. Missouri is west of Ohio, and the elders were to pursue their missions in that direction, apparently in order to help prepare for the future gathering to Missouri.

9. The city of the New Jerusalem. This is the first use of this phrase in the Doctrine and Covenants and refers here to the Zion to be established in Missouri, to which the Saints of this dispensation will be gathered (see vv. 35, 62, 67; D&C 45:64–66; 84:2, 4; Articles of Faith 1:10). That city will be called New Jerusalem (see Ether 13:3–8; D&C 133:53–56; Revelation 3:12; 21:2), and it will be built upon the American continent by the descendants of Joseph who was sold into Egypt, with its center in Jackson County, Missouri (see D&C 84:2–4; 3 Nephi 20:22; 21:23–24; Ether 13:4). The Lord promised here that the location of the New Jerusalem would be revealed in the future, a promise fulfilled in Doctrine and Covenants 57:2–3 (see also D&C 28:9; 45:64–66). Though the ancient Jerusalem, the city from which Lehi fled, will also eventually be built up, it will not be called "New" Jerusalem because it has existed from ancient times (see Ether 13:5).

11. It shall not be given. No one can preach the gospel as a missionary for the Church ("go forth to preach") or as a teacher in the Church ("build up my church") without having first been called, ordained, and set apart by the recognized authorities of the Church and sustained publicly by the membership. There are no secret callings or ordinations in the kingdom of God. This policy provides great protection against deception by those who have no authority. As President Harold B. Lee taught: "Now, if one comes claiming that he has authority, ask him, 'Where do you get your authority? Have you been ordained by someone who has author-ity, who is known to the Church, that you have authority and have been regularly ordained by the heads of the Church?' If the answer is no, you may know that he is an imposter. This is the test that our people should always apply when some imposter comes try-ing to lead them astray."[9]

12. The principles of my gospel, which are in the Bible and the Book of Mormon. At the time this revelation was received, the Pearl of Great Price had not yet been published. Those portions of the present Doctrine and Covenants known to the Church at that time were also implicitly included by the word-ing of verse 13, since both the "covenants" and the "articles" that were to be taught by the Spirit refer specifically to the revelations of Joseph Smith. The term *covenants* was often used to mean "rev-elations," as in the later title, Doctrine and Covenants, and "Church articles" refers specifically to Doctrine and Covenants 20.

It is common in the Church to use the phrase "the fulness of the gospel" to mean all the revelations, principles, covenants, and knowledge the Lord has revealed in the latter days (see D&C 14:10; 20:9; 27:5).[10] But notice the more technical and specific definition used here and elsewhere in scripture. Here "the fulness of the gospel" consists very specifically of faith in Christ, repentance, baptism, and the gift of the Holy Ghost (see D&C 33:12; 39:6; 3 Nephi 27:20–21; Hebrews 6:1–2). These basic principles are all found in the Bible, Book of Mormon, Doctrine and Covenants, and Pearl of Great Price—the standard works of the Church.

Once we have accepted the gospel, or "good news," about Jesus Christ and our redemption from the Fall, there are additional covenants and principles belonging to the new and everlasting covenant that are designed to bring us to exaltation—for example, the ordinances of the temple. The Book of Mormon, "in the which is the fulness of the gospel," does not, however, explicitly teach these additional covenants and principles. Thus, we should keep clear in our minds the distinction between the basic gospel, which is designed to bring us to Christ, to redeem from the Fall, and to save us in his kingdom, and those additional principles and ordinances of the new and everlasting covenant, revealed *after* the publication of the Book of Mormon, which are designed to take the redeemed and saved onward to full exaltation.[11]

Those who preach and teach with authority are to do so according to the fulness of the gospel as found in the standard works. Understanding that the "fulness of the gospel" in this context is the basic message of redemption in Christ—faith, repentance, baptism, and receiving the gift of the Holy Ghost—eliminates the possibility of inappropriately teaching investigators doctrines they will not be prepared for until a proper foundation has been laid.

13. Observe the covenants. The term *covenants* was probably used here to indicate the various commandments found in individual revelations of the Doctrine and Covenants. This is, after all, how the term *covenants* is used in the title "Doctrine and Covenants." All commandments are also covenants because there is a promise and blessing attached to each.

13. Church articles. This phrase is a reference to the rules and policies found in Doctrine and Covenants 20, the articles and covenants of the Church of Christ.[12]

14. Ye shall not teach. Any teaching of the gospel that will have power to convert or have a lasting effect for good must be accomplished by the Spirit of the Lord. Teaching and learning spiritual truth can be done only spirit to spirit, as a three-cornered transaction between the spirit of the teacher, the spirit of the student, and the Spirit of the Holy Ghost. The inspiration of the Spirit is to be obtained by personally living the principles of the gospel and keeping the commandments, and by the fervent prayer of faith. Even righteous teachers must pray for the Spirit to be with them and to confirm what they teach to their students. If we do not so live and so pray, we can *talk* but we cannot *teach*. There will be no spiritual power in our teaching; and when our students' hearts are left untouched, they may conclude it is the gospel that has no power, rather than just the teacher. Thus, those who have not the Spirit *cannot* teach by the Spirit and *should not* pretend to. The last lines in verse 14 are both a statement of fact and a commandment.

President Heber J. Grant said, "No man can proclaim this Gospel by the Spirit of the Living God unless that man is living his religion."[13] One cannot teach by the Spirit any principle one does not personally live. In order not to be dry wells, teachers must themselves be converted to and be living the principles they teach—they cannot give what they do not have. They can only talk about it. When teachers are unconverted or unworthy, the Holy Ghost will not press their teachings down into the souls of their pupils to change their lives for good.

15. The fulness of my scriptures. This phrase refers to future revelations now recorded in the Doctrine and Covenants, the Pearl of Great Price, and the Joseph Smith Translation, and others yet to come—for example, the sealed portions of the Book of Mormon.

18. Unto the church. At this point the Lord was no longer specifically addressing the elders present on 9 February 1831 but rather the entire Church.

18. Thou shalt not kill. It is common to refer to verses 18–29 as part of the Ten Commandments of the Old Testament, but this is technically incorrect. The distinction here is very fine, but it is also very important in understanding the role of the law of Moses in the restored gospel. The principles embodied in the Ten Commandments are eternal—and God has reiterated those principles from the time of Adam[14]—but as part of the law of Moses, as found in Exodus 20 and Deuteronomy 5, they are part of a legislation that would eventually be done away. The law given to Moses was a preparatory law of carnal commandments given to a rebellious and stiffnecked people to teach them obedience and prepare them for a later reception of the gospel (see D&C 84:23–27).

Joseph Smith's translation of Exodus 34:1–2 explains that when the children of Israel sinned, the higher law previously given to Moses on Sinai (see Exodus 20–31) was changed to a preparatory law. The present Ten Commandments of Moses are a part of that lesser, preparatory law (see Matthew 5:21–22, 27–28; Romans 13:8–10; 2 Corinthians 3:3–8), which is done away in the gospel (see 3 Nephi 9:17; 12:19–22, 27–28; 15:2–9; Romans 6:14; 7:6; 8:2; Galatians 3:24; 5:18).

It is critical to understand, however, that the principles embodied in the Ten Commandments are eternally valid and binding upon the Saints, even though the specific legislation to Moses and Israel in Exodus 20 and Deuteronomy 5 is not. For example, Latter-day Saints must and do observe the *principle* of the Sabbath, but not the Sabbath law of Moses—for that legislation specified Israel should observe the *seventh* day as a Sabbath, and that violators should be put to death. In the restored Church we observe the *first* day, Sunday or the Lord's Day, as the Sabbath. In some countries members of the Church are instructed to observe Saturday, or Friday, as the Sabbath. We keep the eternal principle of Sabbath observance but not the third commandment as given to Moses on Sinai.

It would be correct to say that the principles behind the Ten Commandments of Moses have been given to the Latter-day Saints in a new form, but no part of the "lesser law" as given to Moses is still binding upon those who receive the "higher law" of the gospel (see Romans 6:14; 7:6; 8:1–4). Doctrine and Covenants 42:18–29 is not simply a restatement of part of the law of Moses from ancient times. It is a renewed law, the law of the Church, given to Joseph Smith in 1831, containing many of the same principles as the legislation given Moses, but a *new* legislation nonetheless.

18. Shall not have forgiveness in this world, nor in the world to come. Note that the Lord addresses this part of the revelation to members of the Church. It might not apply to nonmembers.

Forgiveness here means "atonement," or the removal of guilt so that one becomes innocent once again and a candidate for the celestial kingdom. Those who murder, who willingly shed innocent blood, cannot be forgiven in this sense, neither here in mortality nor in the spirit world afterward. They lose the opportunity to repent and be made clean of their sin. Thus, murderers cannot be saved from the pains of hell until the resurrection. Nevertheless, there is a world *after* this world and even after the spirit world to come. This third "world" is the world that begins with resurrection, and the fate of murderers at that time has not been revealed.[15]

Perhaps it should be mentioned here that abortion, although a gravely serious sin, is *not* equal to murder. Those guilty of abortion are not denied the gift of repentance and may, *if they do repent,* receive the full blessings of the Atonement and become once again candidates for the celestial kingdom.[16]

The unforgivable sin of murder should not be confused with the unpardonable sin against the Holy Ghost; murderers, although they cannot be *forgiven,* may be *pardoned.* When, like King David (see Psalm 16:10; Acts 2:27–31), they have suffered for their sin and have paid the full demands of justice to "the uttermost farthing" (Matthew 5:26), they may then confess Christ, turn to him, and through his atonement be pardoned. That is, they will not become innocent, but their suffering will end. As David was promised that his soul would not be left forever in hell—a fate known as perdition—so other murderers who turn to Christ after suffering for their sins will not be left forever in hell. This will allow them to avoid perdition, to be redeemed from the power of Satan, and to receive *some* degree of glory. Just as in our civil courts acquittal means being declared innocent and receiving a pardon means "guilty, but set free," so in eternity to be forgiven means to become innocent through the Atonement, while being pardoned means "guilty, but finally set free." On the other hand, those who commit the sin against the Holy Ghost can neither be forgiven nor pardoned. They are lost (Latin, *perditus*) forever, and hence are called sons of perdition (see D&C 76:25–38, 43–48).[17]

The Prophet Joseph Smith taught: "A murderer, for instance, one that sheds innocent blood, cannot have forgiveness. David sought repentance at the hand of God carefully with tears, for the murder of Uriah; but he could only get it through hell: he got a promise that his soul should not be left in hell. . . . This is the case with murderers."[18]

On another occasion the Prophet stated: "If the ministers of religion had a proper understanding of the doctrine of eternal judgment, they would not be found attending the man who forfeited his life to the injured laws of his country, by shedding innocent blood; for such characters cannot be forgiven, until they have paid the last farthing. The prayers of all the ministers in the world can never close the gates of hell against a murderer."[19]

19. He that killeth shall die. Not by the hand of the Church but by civil authority (see also v. 79). The Lord instructs that those who kill shall be handed over to the law and, if proven guilty, shall be executed according to the law. Obviously, "killing" here excludes killing in self-defense, in national self-defense such as in wars, or in legal executions—circumstances where the bloodshed was not "innocent." These scriptures, part of the law of the Church, lay the foundation for the Church's position on capital punishment. "For remember that he [the killer] hath no forgiveness" (v. 79).

20. He that stealeth and will not repent. Theft is a sin that may be repented of. When members of the Church commit theft, they may remain in the Church on condition of repentance.

20. Shall be cast out. That is, shall be excommunicated.

22. Thou shalt love thy wife with all thy heart. Where all the previous commandments concerning personal behavior have been stated as "thou shalt nots," this commandment is a "thou shalt." "Thou shalt not" commandments may be taken to imply that what is not prohibited is allowed, but "thou shalt" commandments leave no room for guessing. In the law of the Church, all marital conditions *other* than loving "thy wife [or husband] with all thy heart" are prohibited. Men or women who have allowed themselves to fall out of love with faithful, loving spouses are in violation of the law and are under condemnation. Although biological attraction can happen spontaneously, maintaining a long-term, loving relationship in marriage usually does not. It is a goal that must be chosen and diligently pursued, a conscious decision for which husbands and wives may be held accountable. To ignore one's spouse or the relationship that exists between husband and wife is a sin. Sometimes the spouse does not respond to the expression of love, in which case the offending spouse will receive the blame, but for as long as a marriage lasts, true Saints are obligated to love their spouses and maintain a warm and loving relationship to the degree a spouse will allow.

Since exaltation requires that man and wife become one not just in the "bonds of matrimony" but in heart, mind, and spirit, they *must* love one another. If they fail to do this, exaltation must be denied the offender who will not love his or her faithful spouse. Our covenant obligation to be one with our spouse is second only to our obligation to become one with the Lord.

22. And none else. These words leave no room for divided or shared affections. It is a violation of the law of the Church for spouses to let their affections wander or become divided. Elder Spencer W. Kimball explained it this way: "The words *none else* eliminate everyone and everything. The spouse then becomes preeminent in the life of the husband or wife, and neither social life nor occupational life nor political life nor any other interest nor person nor thing shall ever take precedence over the companion spouse. . . .

"Marriage presupposes total allegiance and total fidelity. Each spouse takes the partner with the understanding that he or she gives self totally to the spouse: all the heart, strength, loyalty, honor, and affection with all dignity. Any divergence is sin—any sharing the heart is transgression."[20]

23. Looketh upon a woman to lust after her. There is a difference in degree between carnal-mindedness and looking "upon a woman to lust after her." Both are sins, but the former involves hypothetical thinking or sexual fantasies, while the latter involves intent to commit adultery if given an opportunity. That is why in the latter case the individual has actually committed adultery in his or her heart (see Matthew 5:27–28)—because the act is desired, planned, and intended, though not yet carried out. An individual with such adulterous intent in his or her heart cannot at the same time enjoy the gift of the Holy Ghost and therefore will, without repentance, ultimately deny the faith (see D&C 63:16–17). In such a case, the desired act of adultery has become a personal idol valued more highly than God or the gospel.

24. Thou shalt not commit adultery. Where verses 22–23 involve mental and emotional unfaithfulness, verses 24–26 involve actual physical unfaithfulness. The law of the Church directs that *unrepentant* adulterers be excommunicated from the Church (see 1 Corinthians 5, esp. vv. 9, 11; 6:9).

25–26. Thou shalt/shalt not forgive. These verses emphasize the seriousness of sexual sin. "Adultery is a forgivable sin. However, because of the sacred nature of the procreative powers, repentance is not easy and must be complete. The person must repent with all his or her heart and must totally forsake the sin. If this happens, then the individual will be totally forgiven by the Lord, and the atonement of Christ will pay the full price for the individual."[21] A subsequent return to this sin, however, is usually not to be forgiven by the Church and Church discipline is required. Of course, even in these cases an offender may eventually be baptized again into the Church after showing evidence of genuine repentance and of habitually living the moral law.

27. Thou shalt not speak evil of thy neighbor. Lying, backbiting, gossiping, and bearing false witness are all forbidden by the law of the Church. In fact, any word or deed that would bring injury to the spirit, body, or reputation of another individual is prohibited by the law of the Church.

28. Sinneth and repenteth not. Repeated, blatant sin of any kind where there is no honest attempt at repentance is not to be tolerated in or by the Church.

29. Keep all my commandments. Of course, no one keeps all the commandments all the time, so the safety valve provided in Doctrine and Covenants 46:9 should likely be understood to apply here as well: "and him that seeketh so to do." The Lord does not require absolute personal perfection at this time. The scriptures often use the words "keep all the commandments" when they actually mean *being committed* to keeping all the commandments. This leaves some room for repentance and improvement within the covenant relationship.

30. Consecrate of thy properties. This phrase refers to the law of consecration, which principle as much as anything else prepares the Saints to establish Zion. In principle, consecration means to give all we possess or may possess to The Church of Jesus Christ of Latter-day Saints to administer to the poor and needy and to build Zion, the New Jerusalem (see v. 35). Only those who are willing to *give* everything to the Lord are worthy to *receive* everything from him. All Church members who have been to the temple have covenanted to live the law of consecration, though at present the institutional expectations of the Church require them to live only the law of tithing (see D&C 119) and to accept those demands on their resources that are made in their home wards and branches. Those who have difficulty living the law of tithing, which gives only 10 percent of our increase to the Lord, will undoubtedly have even greater difficulty living the law of consecration, which gives 100 percent to the Lord. Those individuals who have accepted the law of consecration by covenant yet will not observe the law of tithing or make other sacrifices of time or resources requested of them have broken their temple covenants.

Consecration requires faith that the principle will work and unselfishness to give our possessions to help the poor or the cause of Zion. A Zion people eventually will not have any poor among them (see D&C 104:16; 4 Nephi 1:3; Moses 7:18), so implementing the law of consecration is necessary in order to establish Zion.

The principle of consecration can be applied in several different ways. A possible application in the early Church was the system instituted in Ohio and Missouri between 1831 and 1833 (see D&C 51, 56, 72). Another was the united order (see D&C 78:3–12; 92:1; 104:53), and still another was the implementation of various united orders in the Salt Lake Great Basin. But when Zion is established in the last days, the principle of consecration might be applied differently than it has been earlier. The "law of consecration" and the "united order" are not necessarily synonymous terms, and one should recognize the difference between the *principle* of consecration itself and the many different possible systems under which the financial portions of that principle might be implemented.

30. A deed which cannot be broken. Whatever property or other resources a family took with them into the covenant of consecration was to be legally transferred to the Church by deed.[22] Technically, consecrated properties became the Church's and— although this part of the law was not implemented—would not be given back even if an individual changed his mind and wanted to leave.

31. Ye will do it unto me. Resources used to help the poor and the needy are resources given to the Savior (see vv. 37–38; Matthew 25:40, 45; Mosiah 2:17).

31. Or high priests. According to Orson Pratt,[23] these words were added both here and in verse 71 by Joseph Smith several years after Doctrine and Covenants 42 was received. The words referring to a "high council" in verse 34 were also added. In February 1831, when this revelation was first received, there were no high priests or high council in the Church, because the organization of the Church had not yet been fully revealed. Later, after these offices had been revealed, Joseph adjusted verses 31, 34, and 71 to include high priests in their proper places.

32. A steward over his own property. A steward is a manager. The full description of the law given here to the Saints is the law of consecration and the stewardship of property. In this system an individual gives everything to the Church and receives back as his own private property a stewardship, sufficient for his needs, that he is to manage for the Lord for the enrichment of the kingdom.

33. Residue. Stewards are expected to meet their own needs out of the produce of their stewardship. Should a steward or manager produce more than he or she personally needs, the amount left over, or residue, is forwarded to the bishop for the support of the needy.

33. According to his wants. Stewards and their families are not expected to live in poverty. Although personal extravagance would be a violation of principle, stewards are expected to take their just wants from the produce of their stewardships (compare D&C 82:17). It appears that if music is a large part of one's life, or woodworking is a large part of another's, it would be acceptable for the one to have musical instruments and for the other to have woodworking tools. In disputed cases the bishop judges what is a "just" want or desire and what is selfishness or extravagance.

36. For the salvation of my people. If those capable of living a celestial law could gather together and live the law of consecration, they would be both temporally and spiritually better off with consecration in Zion than without it in Babylon. A Zion people need fear no government, no market crash, no wars, no natural disasters. If the Saints would live the law of consecration, cooperate economically, and pool resources, becoming of one heart and one mind and leaving behind the slackers, critics, and the "me-first generation," then the spiritual strength of all members and the temporal circumstances of most members would vastly improve.

39. Among the Gentiles. The prophets mentioned here would include Isaiah (see Isaiah 60:3–7, 16; 61:5–6), who taught that the riches of the Gentiles would be brought to Zion in the last days. This theme is continued in the Epistles of Paul, who insisted that Gentile converts share their wealth with Israel by "contributing" to or "communicating" with the "poor" of Israel (see Acts 24:17; Romans 15:26–27; 1 Corinthians 16:1–3; Galatians 6:6; 1 Timothy 6:18; Hebrews 13:16). The Greek word translated *communicate* in the King James Version of the New Testament is usually some form of *koinoneo,* which means "to have in common." It can also be translated as "share," and from this comes our common sense of "communicate," which is to share ideas by making them common knowledge (apply to Galatians 6:6; 1 Timothy 6:18; Hebrews 13:16).

We now live in the times of the Gentiles, when the gospel is no longer reserved for Israel alone (see Matthew 10:5) but is to be taken to "every nation, kindred, tongue, and people" (see Mosiah 15:28). As the Gentile nations—the United States, Britain, France, and so on—accept missionaries, those Gentiles who are converted will gather to Zion and consecrate their resources to the building of Zion, as they now consecrate their tithing to the building of the Church. Thus, the riches of Gentile converts will contribute to the building of Zion and to the welfare of its inhabitants.

39. The poor of my people. This phrase does not imply that those living the law of consecration will be poverty-stricken; it refers to those in Zion who produce less than they need. Even in Zion there may be needy, but their needs will be met through the consecration of new converts and the surpluses of the more productive stewards (see vv. 33–34; Romans 15:26–27).

40. Let all thy garments be plain. Those who have accepted the law of consecration and received a stewardship by covenant must not expend the resources of their stewardship on unnecessary extravagance such as expensive clothes. To spend thousands of dollars on clothing would be a violation of their covenant to consecrate their riches to the needy rather than enjoy the privileges of wealth. The law of consecration is not intended to subsidize the lifestyles of the rich but to put their surplus resources—beyond what is sufficient for their needs—into the hands of brother and sister Saints who do not have sufficient for their needs. The principle here is that the genuine *needs* of others must have priority over selfish *wants* (see Alma 1:27 for a parallel).

41. In cleanliness. Beauty, simplicity, personal effort, and cleanliness will characterize the Lord's covenant people.[24]

42. Thou shalt not be idle. Just as the covenant of consecration requires us to live simply and without extravagance, so it also requires us to work hard, both for ourselves and for other brothers and sisters in the covenant. A celestial individual can and will work hard without the incentive of direct, personal gain. Those who magnify their callings as bishops, Relief Society presidents, Scoutmasters, nursery leaders, and so on labor very hard indeed for the sake of Christ and his kingdom when they might instead seek their own personal amusement or benefit. Consecration is a celestial law because only the celestial can live it unselfishly, without leaving their share of the work to be done by others. The failure to establish Zion in the past has been largely due to too many in the Church choosing not to live the celestial law of consecration.

42. Shall not eat the bread nor wear the garments of the laborer. It is contrary to the justice of God for those who will not keep their covenants to benefit as though they did. Under the law of consecration this means that those who will not work to support themselves and to help the poor and needy have no claim upon, and must not be given, the fruits of the laborers. Covenant blessings require covenant obedience. In the welfare program of the Church today, this principle is understood to mean that the needy should be faithful to their covenants and first exhaust their own resources, including their own labor, before making a claim on the resources produced by the labor of other Saints. In both cases, the faithful who cannot work, but who would if they could, are entitled to support. Those who are not faithful or who will not work for themselves but expect to be supported by the labor of others must not be allowed to do so.

43. Whosoever among you are sick. Verses 43–52 express the Lord's will concerning the blessing of the sick. There are several main points. First, the Saints are obligated to tenderly care for the sick, even the sick who lack the faith to be healed. Second, it is appropriate to treat the sick with such medicines as are available—in this case herbs and foods. Third, the elders of the Church should be called to bless the sick by the laying on of hands. Fourth, not all of the faithful Saints who are blessed by the elders will recover. Fifth, those who lack the faith to be healed are still candidates for the celestial kingdom, and caring for them is still the responsibility of the members.

44. They shall die/live unto me. To die unto Christ is to be "in Christ" (see 1 Corinthians 1:2, for example) when one dies, to be enduring faithfully in the new and everlasting covenant at the time of one's death. Such will be taken to paradise to await the resurrection of the just. Those who are blessed by the elders and recover from their illness have an obligation to live unto Christ, to be his faithful, covenant sons and daughters in building up his kingdom on the earth.

46. Shall not taste of death. This phrase refers not to dying painlessly but to suffering no pain in the spirit world. Those who die "in Christ," that is, in the gospel covenant, may very well suffer physical pain, even terrible pain, as they die, but being dead will be sweet relief and rest to them, for they will repose in paradise with the certain knowledge that the Lord judges them worthy of celestial glory. On the other hand, the wicked may die peacefully in their beds, but in death they will suffer bitter anguish and the pains of hell with a knowledge of their uncleanness.

48. Not appointed unto death. There is in the natural course of God's plan an appropriate time for each of us to die. This time is not, however, "fated" or "destined." We may by our own disobedience or foolishness cause our own premature death or the premature deaths of others.[25] A drug addict or a sexually promiscuous person may not live as long as the Lord would have allowed had that individual's choices been otherwise. Having our own moral agency in mortality means our choices can accomplish what God might not have wanted—even though he has anticipated and adjusted for all such choices in his great plan. The drunk who runs over a child is not doing God's will but is exercising his own agency in a negligent manner.

Sometimes, however, an individual's time is just up, and it is right and appropriate for the individual to die. Blessing the sick in these cases works only temporarily, even though they and those around them may have great faith.

52. Thou shalt bear their infirmities. Lacking the faith to be healed is not necessarily a sign of a less than celestial character, and in such cases the Lord expects the Saints to support and care for the afflicted under the law of consecration. Having the faith to be healed is, in fact, one of the gifts of the Spirit that is not given to everyone (see D&C 46:19).

53. Stand in the place of thy stewardship. The Saints are to live near and work with the land or other stewardships they have been given. There will be no "absentee" stewards holding a stewardship from the Lord but investing their time or resources elsewhere.

54. Thou shalt pay. One's stewardship under the law of consecration is legally one's own private property, though spiritually held in trust for the Lord, who owns all things. The law of consecration is not a system of common ownership or group ownership as was the system of "common stock." The system of consecration practiced at this time was neither communal nor communistic in the normal sense of those words, but a system of individually controlled and privately owned stewardships working cooperatively toward the same goal—to establish Zion. If a steward needs something from another, he must pay a fair price for it. If he cannot pay, he is to go to the bishop for it, and his needs will be met from the storehouse.

56. My scriptures shall be given. This statement is clearly a reference to the Joseph Smith Translation, which was being worked on at the time this revelation was received.[26] The scriptures here, however, probably also refer to the revelations in the Doctrine and Covenants, since verse 59, "my law to govern my church," likely refers to section 42 itself (see D&C 38:32, 36; 41:3; 43:8).[27]

57. Hold thy peace. The Church was not to use the Joseph Smith Translation and the other new scriptures in preaching publicly until they had been given "in full," or completed. This is perhaps because the Latter-day Saint belief in continuing revelation and in additional scripture may have an inflammatory effect upon non-Latter-day Saints.

It has been claimed that the Joseph Smith Translation was never finished, but Joseph was planning to publish the manuscript during the Nauvoo period, and certainly it adds to our doctrinal and scriptural understanding.[28]

In a letter written by Joseph Smith, Sidney Rigdon, and Frederick G. Williams to the brethren in Zion and dated 2 July 1833, the Prophet said, "We this day finished the translating of the Scriptures, for which we returned gratitude to our Heavenly Father." To this Sidney added, "Having finished the translation of the Bible, a few hours since, and needing some recreation, we know of one way we can spend our time more to divine acceptance than in endeavoring to build up His Zion."[29]

It is likely the word "finished" meant they had made the changes appropriate at that time. Certainly Joseph Smith did not consider 1833 the end of needed changes in the biblical text. We know that Joseph still "worked diligently on it [the Joseph Smith

Translation] during the closing years of his life," and it is clear, at least to Robert J. Matthews, that "the work was not perfected" by that time.[30] Further, "before his death" Joseph had spoken with Brigham Young "about going through the translation of the scriptures again and perfecting it upon points of doctrine which the Lord had restrained him from giving in plainness and fulness at the time of which we write," which was 2 February 1833.[31]

Thus, no specific date can be given for when the Joseph Smith Translation was "finished," or even what the word *finished* might mean in this context. Since Joseph's work is now available to us and is certainly inspired, it would seem foolish not to refer to it for information and insight in addition to that gleaned from the King James text.

59. My law to govern my church. This phrase is a clear reference to Doctrine and Covenants 42, the law of the Church (see the same phrasing in D&C 38:32, 36; 41:3; 43:8—all referring to section 42). Thus the phrase "my scriptures," as used here and in verse 56, obviously includes the Doctrine and Covenants as well as the Joseph Smith Translation.

61. Revelation upon revelation. This is exactly how the Prophet received the Doctrine and Covenants, the Joseph Smith Translation, and other scriptures—successive revisions gradually added here a little and there a little.[32]

61. The mysteries and peaceable things. See Commentary on Doctrine and Covenants 6:7, 11; 8:11; 36:2.

62. Where the New Jerusalem shall be built. This promise was fulfilled in Doctrine and Covenants 57:2.[33]

64. That which is coming. From the perspective of the Kirtland Saints, "that which is coming" would include the Civil War, which would devastate the nation, mark the beginning of "modern war," and probably be the beginning of the wars of the last days (see D&C 87:1–3).

64. And of secret combinations. Evil men would conspire together to victimize and enslave others. As these conspiracies gained power in the world, the only escape from them would be in gathering to Zion.

67. Receive church covenants. More commandments and covenants were yet to be revealed to the Saints in Kirtland, including the sealing power and its ordinances, which helped the Kirtland Saints as well as those who went on to Missouri to establish Zion.

69. The keys of the church. The Church of Jesus Christ of Latter-day Saints is the kingdom of God upon the earth. Therefore, to be given the keys of the Church is to be given possession and control of the earthly kingdom of God.

70–73. All whose labor for the Church prevents them from earning their own livelihood are to be remunerated from the consecrations and surpluses of the Church. Their support shall be administered by the bishop of the Church, who was then Edward Partridge.

74–77. These verses describe the Lord's law to the Church on fidelity and divorce. In the following verses, to "receive" means to receive into full fellowship through baptism. To "cast out" means to cast out of the Church by excommunication.

If an individual divorces his or her spouse because the spouse has committed adultery, that individual is to remain in good standing and fellowship in the Church. Those members who leave their spouse in order to have a sexual relationship with someone else, however, are to be excommunicated. Even a legal divorce and remarriage, if pursued with adulterous motives, is still adultery in the spiritual sense (see Matthew 19:9). Those who are married but are living with someone other than their spouse are not to be received into the Church without repentance. Those who are not married but have been sexually active may also be received into the Church if they will genuinely repent and begin to live chaste lives.

The eternal purposes of sex and marriage are so sacred and such a necessary part of our exaltation that disregard for a loving, faithful, and functional marriage cannot escape the Lord's condemnation. Marriage partners are commanded to love one another and no one else (see v. 22), are not to pursue or even to consider in their hearts any other sexual partners (see v. 23), and may not divorce a faithful spouse and remarry just to get a new partner (see v. 75). Single people are to be faithful to their *future* spouse, whether they marry in this life or the next, and they are to repent of any sexual activity or other sins before being fellowshipped into the Church (see v. 77).

78–87. These verses discuss the relationship of the law of the Church to the law of the land: local, state, and federal courts. If members of the Church break the laws of the land, they are to be turned over to the civil authorities for judgment. Church membership does not protect us from the law of the land and gives us no shield from civil justice.

When individuals break the law of the Church, they are to be dealt with in Church disciplinary councils. Church disciplinary councils cannot impose any penalty or sanction other than loss of membership or fellowship and therefore will not hear cases involving violation of secular law or suits for damages. The Church determines only issues of *sin,* which is violation of God's law (see v. 87). Civil law decides all issues of *crime,* which is violation of civil law, and the Church leaves civil justice to the courts. Thus an individual might be tried in the civil courts and then brought before a Church disciplinary council because the act violated both civil law and the law of God.

88–93. These verses deal with the proper way of handling personal disputes or injuries in the Church. Personal differences are to be taken by the injured party first to the offending party. The assumption is that brothers and sisters in Zion will act in good faith to resolve their differences and remain brothers and sisters. Saints are not to begin by working through third parties or by complaining or making accusations until the offender finally hears about it and comes to them. This approach violates the law of the Church. Instead, the injured party is to go *privately* to the offender, state his or her complaint, and resolve it confidentially. If the offender will not confess and repent, the injured party is to take the matter to proper Church leaders, but *still* privately and confidentially, "not to the members" (v. 89). At this point the Church leaders can decide whether or not an injury can be proved. If the offense can be proved, then the offender will confess and repent or be subject to Church discipline with the possible loss of membership or fellowship.

Private offenses are to be handled by the Church privately, giving the offender the opportunity to make amends to the injured and to God and not to suffer public humiliation for a private fault. "Note the caution that this remedy is to be private—'not before the world.' This is not done in order to hide the facts, but rather to increase the chance that the correction will improve the life of a brother or sister."[34]

Public offenses, however, are generally more high-handed, rebellious, and motivated by pride than private offenses. Therefore, Church discipline for public offenses is to be made public, in order that the offending individuals may be ashamed and curb their pride (see v. 91), thus giving them greater motivation for repentance. Unfortunately, for those whose pride is very great, a public rebuke will often cause them in self-justification to become dissident *former* members, and enemies of the Church.

1. See *History of the Church,* 1:146–47, 154; Whitmer, *Early Latter Day Saint History,* 36.
2. Early Latter Day Saint History, 38.
3. *Early Latter Day Saint History,* 42.
4. *History of the Church,* 1:148.
5. Letter dated 22 February 1831, cited in Woodford, Historical Development, 1:527.
6. See Smith, 117–18.
7. See the excellent summary in Cook, *Revelations of the Prophet Joseph Smith,* 59–61; Whitmer, *Early Latter Day Saint History,* 38–41, n. 6; *Evening and the Morning Star,* Oct. 1832, 9.
8. See Woodford, Historical Development, 1:525–34.
9. In Conference Report, Oct. 1972, 127.
10. See also Commentary on D&C 14:10; 20:9; 27:5.

11. See Millet, *Life in Christ,* 9.

12. See Commentary on v. 12.

13. In Conference Report, Oct. 1937, 130.

14. See Spencer W. Kimball, in Conference Report, Apr. 1975.

15. See Boyd K. Packer, in Conference Report, Sept.–Oct. 1995, 23.

16. See Boyd K. Packer, in Conference Report, Apr. 1992, 95.

17. See also Commentary on D&C 76:26, 32, 34.

18. *Teachings,* 339.

19. *History of the Church,* 4:359.

20. In Conference Report, Oct. 1962, 57.

21. Garrett, *Great Teachings from the Doctrine and Covenants,* 61.

22. See Background to D&C 51.

23. See *History of the Church,* 1:150, 152.

24. See the teaching of President Spencer W. Kimball on cleaning up our homes, farms, and businesses, in Conference Report, Apr. 1975, 5–6.

25. See Kimball, *Tragedy or Destiny,* 9–11.

26. See Dahl, "Joseph Smith Translation and the Doctrine and Covenants," 110.

27. See Smith and Sjodahl, *Doctrine and Covenants Commentary,* 234.

28. See Matthews, "Joseph Smith's Efforts to Publish His Bible Translation," 57–64.

29. *History of the Church,* 1:368–69.

30. "Joseph Smith's Efforts to Publish His Bible Translation," 64.

31. Cannon, *Life of Joseph Smith the Prophet,* 148.

32. See the discussion in Millet, "Joseph Smith Translation," 135–36.

33. See Commentary on v. 9.

34. Oaks, "Speaking Today: Criticism," 72.

DOCTRINE AND COVENANTS

43

BACKGROUND

In September 1830, barely five months before Doctrine and Covenants 43 was received, the Lord had revealed to the Church at Fayette, New York, that *no one* could receive revelation for the Church but the Prophet Joseph Smith (see D&C 28:2). This was in response to the belief of some that God was speaking to the Church through Hiram Page and a certain stone in his possession. The revelation in section 28 was a clear and concise statement of gospel principles: the Prophet reveals the word of God to the Church, no one else does, and there are no exceptions.

In February 1831, a woman known only as Mrs. Hubble arrived in Kirtland declaring that the Church and the Book of Mormon were true and that she was a prophetess receiving revelations from God. John Whitmer recorded the events as follows: "About these days there was a woman by the name of Hubble who professed to be a prophetess of the Lord, and professed to have many revelations, and knew the Book of Mormon was true, and that she should become a teacher in the Church of Christ. She appeared to be very sanctimonious and deceived some who were not able to detect her in her hypocrasy: others however had the spirit of discernment, and her follies and abominations were made manifest. The Lord gave Revelation that the Saints might not be deceived which reads as follows"[1]—Doctrine and Covenants 43.

Apparently, the Hubble affair caused quite a stir. Joseph Smith described the events thus: "Soon after the foregoing revelation [D&C 42] was received, a woman came making great pretensions of revealing commandments, laws and other curious matters; and as almost every person has advocates for both theory and practice, in the various notions and projects of the age, it became necessary to inquire of the Lord [concerning her], when I received the following"[2]—Doctrine and Covenants 43.

In fairness to the Kirtland Saints, two things should be noted. First, Doctrine and Covenants 28, with its clear statement concerning the unique role of the Prophet in receiving revelation for the Church, had been given in Fayette, and very few of the New York Saints had arrived in Kirtland. The revelations did not yet exist in printed form and were accessible to the Kirtland Saints only, if at all, by private, handwritten copies. Most of the Kirtland Saints may therefore have simply been unfamiliar with information in section 28. Second, the Kirtland Saints had come very recently from a Protestant background in which it was believed that any member of a congregation could "get the Spirit" and receive revelation for the congregation. These Protestant churches were very democratic in their structure, working from the bottom up, and the new converts were mostly unfamiliar with the idea of a priesthood order working from the top down or a hierarchy of spiritual authorities over the Church. Thus, the Lord needed to make clear to the Kirtland Saints how he would reveal his will to them in his restored Church.

Doctrine and Covenants 43 was received a few days after Doctrine and Covenants 42 and also in the presence of twelve elders. John Whitmer recorded the effect that this revelation had upon the Kirtland Saints: "After this commandment was received, the saints came to understanding on this subject, and unity and harmony prevailed throughout the church of God: and the Saints began to learn wisdom, and treasure up knowledge which they learned from the word of God, and by experience as they advanced in the way of eternal life."[3]

COMMENTARY

1. Hearken, ye elders. Doctrine and Covenants 43 was delivered to Joseph in response to his inquiry about Mrs. Hubble and her "revelations." It was received in the presence of twelve elders, who represent on this occasion all the elders of the Church and are addressed specifically here.[4]

2. Ye have received a commandment for a law unto my church. Not many days before, the Saints had received through the Prophet Joseph Smith a major revelation known as the law of the Church—Doctrine and Covenants 42. This revelation had come to them through the proper channels, and they had accepted it. Now, just a few days later, they are tempted to follow someone else, Mrs. Hubble, just because she claims to be a prophetess.

3. There is none other. To those Saints—past and present—who so easily become followers of visionaries, scholars, gurus, or any other "alternate voices" speaking to the Church, this verse is particularly instructive. Section 28 tells us that besides the Prophet, "no one shall be appointed to receive commandments and revelations in this church" (D&C 28:2). Section 43 repeats that "there is none other appointed unto you to receive commandments and revelations," and in verse 4 we are told that "none else shall be appointed." Individuals may receive revelation for themselves, parents for their children, bishops for their wards, and so on, but no one but the Prophet can reveal new doctrine or commandments to the Church or its members. Since 1831 there have been hundreds of "Mrs. Hubbles," both females and males, to challenge the leaders of the Church and compete for the loyalty of the members. Always the lesson is the same—only the prophet speaks to the Church for the Lord.

It must be remembered, however, that at this time there was no First Presidency or Quorum of Twelve Apostles to share the keys of the kingdom and to speak to the Church as they might be assigned by the Prophet. Those who hold the apostolic office have the undisputed right to interpret and apply the revelations and commandments authoritatively within their stewardship and even to the whole Church as assigned by the president. But not even apostles can receive *new* revelations, *new* doctrines, or *new* commandments for the Church on their own authority. Only the prophet has the stewardship to receive revelation for the whole Church. This was the lesson even Oliver Cowdery, who held the apostolic office with Joseph, had to learn in Doctrine and Covenants 28:5–7.

4. Except it be through him. In this period before the calling of twelve apostles, the Lord established a very interesting process for the replacement of Joseph Smith if he should fall. As long as Joseph stayed faithful to the Lord, he would have sole power and authority to receive revelations for the Church. Nevertheless, in the event that he fell from his holy calling through iniquity, he alone would have the power to appoint his successor. This provision eliminated the possibility of any outside claim to leadership of the Church, for even if the Prophet did fall, he himself would appoint his own successor. Of course, the Lord knew that Joseph would not fall, but this provision protected the Saints, if they would heed it, from deception by any challenger to Joseph's leadership under any circumstances. It also emphasized again the basic principle: *All* revelation for the Church, even to replace the prophet, comes through the living prophet.

5–6. A law unto you . . . that you may know they are not of me. Not all the Saints realized that the Church had been given this great commandment, a *law* of God, not to accept any teachings from *anyone* who claimed to receive revelations or commandments for the Church other than the Prophet himself. If the source is not the prophet or one appointed by him in the proper line of priesthood authority, we may *know* it is a deception. It doesn't matter how attractive or plausible or persuasive the arguments or claims. We don't even need to know what the claims are to know that they are false, for if it is not the prophet speaking, then it is just one more in a long series of "Mrs. Hubbles," and we are *commanded* not to listen.

7. Ordained of me . . . and be ordained. The first use of the word *ordained* here probably means something like "called," "directed," or "approved." The second use of *ordained* carries the usual meaning. Those who are truly acting under God's direction will come into the Church through the gate of baptism and then be ordained, in the usual, formal sense, to teach what the Lord had already given through the Prophet. President Joseph Fielding Smith explained the order of priesthood succession as follows: "We frequently hear discussions in our classes and between brethren to the effect that any man could be called, if the authorities should choose him, to preside over the Church, and that it is not the fixed order to take the senior apostle to preside, and any member of that quorum could be appointed. The fact is that the senior apostle *automatically* becomes the presiding officer of the Church on the death of the President. If some other man were to be chosen, then the senior would have to receive the revelation setting himself aside"[5] (see v. 4).

8. When ye are assembled together. See Doctrine and Covenants 41:2–3.

8. Instruct and edify each other. *Edify* comes from the same root as *edifice* and means "to build up." "To instruct is one thing, but to instruct and edify is something more. To edify would be to instruct by the power of the Spirit. When a person edifies or teaches by the Spirit, it inspires those who hear to want to do better—to in some way act on what they have been taught."[6] Some ways the modern Church obeys this commandment to instruct and to edify each other is by having Sunday School, priesthood, and Relief Society lessons, Primary, Young Men's and Young Women's classes, sacrament meeting speakers, and the bearing of testimonies on fast Sundays.

12. Appoint ye my servant Joseph Smith, Jun. This is a command for the Church to "provide" for Joseph's temporal support (see v. 13). Larry E. Dahl explains: "Webster's 1828 *American Dictionary of the English Language* and modern dictionaries agree that one of the meanings of the word *appoint* (v. 12) is to 'furnish;

equip with things necessary.' That seems to be the intent of these verses. Joseph Smith needed, in addition to a house, the faith and prayers of Church members, and provisions of 'food and raiment' so that he could accomplish what the Lord had commanded him to do."[7]

12. Uphold him before me by the prayer of faith. The Saints may underestimate the power of their prayers, particularly their prayers in behalf of Church leaders. Besides obtaining blessings for their leaders, the sustaining prayers of the members for the welfare of their leaders increases the members' own standing before God and their power and ability in the world. Daily prayer for Church leaders ought to be part of every Saint's spiritual life "if ye desire the glories of the kingdom"!

13. Provide for him food and raiment. The Kirtland Saints were commanded to contribute to Joseph's temporal support in order to free him to bless them with the revelations, commandments, covenants, ordinances, and scriptures of God (see also v. 14). Sacrifice does bring forth the blessings of heaven, and those who supported Joseph aided materially in the establishment of Zion, while those who neglected this duty were not worthy of Zion. Though many of the Kirtland Saints sacrificed much for Zion, in the long run and as a group they failed to keep this commandment of the Lord. Consequently, the blessings they and the Church after them might have received through Joseph, had he not been forced to stop work on the Joseph Smith Translation in order to support his family, were never received.[8]

15. Ye are not sent forth to be taught. The world has neither the power nor the knowledge to instruct the Latter-day Saints in the gospel of Jesus Christ. Babylon cannot instruct Zion in the things of God. God has called *us* to teach *them,* though in the world's eyes we may seem "weak" and "foolish" (1 Corinthians 1:27). "We are not to be taught of the world. We are the teachers of the world. . . .

" . . . Whatever offering of good the world may make to us, we must use in declaring faith and repentance and the other principles of the Gospel, and the consummation of the purposes of the Lord."[9]

16. Endowed with power. See Commentary on Doctrine and Covenants 38:32.

18. The trump of God. The horn or trumpet that will blow to signal the return of Christ and the resurrection of the just[10] (see 1 Thessalonians 4:16; Alma 29:1).

18. Ye saints arise. At the Second Coming, those who have been born again and sanctified by the gospel covenant will be resurrected to receive the Lord in their glorified flesh. Those who are to receive terrestrial glory will be resurrected sometime *after* the Second Coming (see D&C 45:54; 88:99) but during the Millennium, in what might be called the "afternoon" or "evening" of the first resurrection. The rest of the dead—those who lived wicked lives—will remain where they are until the *end* of the Millennium, when all humanity—celestial, terrestrial, telestial, and sons of perdition—will be brought to the final judgment at the great white throne (see Revelation 20:11–15).

19. Gird up your loins. See Commentary on Doctrine and Covenants 27:15.

20. Call upon the nations. The last dispensation opened with the times of the Gentiles, who make up every nation, kindred, tongue, and people except Israel.[11] Many do not appreciate how remarkable it is for the gospel, which was once restricted to Israel, to be taken to everyone else in the world—*except* Israel. Toward or at the end of this dispensation, the Gentiles will have been taught or at least will have received its opportunity. Then the times of the Gentiles will be over, and the gospel will be taken once more primarily to covenant Israel, the descendants of Jacob.

21. For if I, who am a man. Although Christ, like his Father, is an exalted Man, the colon after the word *saying* in verse 20 indicates that the missionaries of the Church are the speakers here. In essence, missionaries say to the world: "If you hate and reject me, a mere mortal, for saying these things, what will you do when

God himself says them to you with the voice of overwhelming natural disasters until you either repent or die?"

24. Gathered you together. The Lord's desires for the Gentile nations is the same as his desires for Israel—to gather them to Zion for protection from the world of Babylon and its fate.[12]

25. The Lord has approached the Gentile nations before with a desire to convert them; for example, through Abraham, Lot, Jonah, and Paul. His method of calling upon them and getting their attention then was the same as it will be in our dispensation. He did then, and will now, first call them through his servants, by his angels, and even by his own voice. After that he will call to them by the voice of natural forces, such as lightning, tempests, earthquakes, hailstorms, famines and pestilences (see D&C 88:89–92). He has called to them with the inducements of judgment, mercy, and salvation, but the majority of the world would not, and will not, hear him.

26. The cup of the wrath of mine indignation. For those who have repented and come to the Savior, he has already drunk for us the bitter cup of God's wrath.[13] Those who will not repent must drink it themselves at some future time (see D&C 19:16–19).

28. Labor ye in my vineyard for the last time. "As long as the days last, my brethren, we are to thrust in our sickles and reap, and send forth men to discharge this great duty and responsibility; for, when the day cometh that the calamities that are spoken of shall be poured out upon the nations of the earth, let us have no regret that we failed to discharge our duty. Do we rejoice at the prospects of chastisements that shall be ministered to men who do not repent? No, we do not. . . . And if it were in our power to change the conditions we would do it; but we cannot; even God himself cannot change the conditions that will result, except men repent."[14]

29. In mine own due time. No one knows the time of the Lord's coming, nor could they hasten or postpone it if they did.

The Lord will come when he is ready, and many will find his timing inconvenient.

30. The great Millennium. See Doctrine and Covenants 45:45–59; 88:101; Revelation 19:1–20:6.[15]

31. Satan shall be bound. "There are many among us who teach that the binding of Satan will be merely the binding which those dwelling on the earth will place upon him by their refusal to hear his enticings. This is not so. He will not have the privilege during that period of time to tempt any man."[16] Satan will not only be bound by the native righteousness of the millennial Saints, but also by priesthood power that will cast him out and will not allow him the exercise of any influence. He will be *sealed* off from us by the power of God.[17]

31. Loosed again . . . for a little season. When the Millennium is over, Satan will be allowed once more to tempt mortals upon the earth and will have influence again for a short time. There will then be a great last battle, sometimes called the battle of Gog and Magog (see Revelation 20:8) or the battle of the great God (see D&C 88:114), in which Satan and all his servants will be defeated forever. Then the earth will be cleansed once again and will go through a process similar to death and resurrection, at the end of which it will be made a celestial world to be inhabited by all those who lived upon it who were worthy of the celestial kingdom.

32. Changed in the twinkling of an eye. "The twinkling of an eye" is a blink. When mortals die during the Millennium, they will simply pass from mortality to a resurrected state in the twinkling of an eye. At the end of the Millennium, the earth will also "die" and be melted down, so to speak (see 2 Peter 3:10–11), just as raw materials are melted down and made pure in the refiner's fire, and it will then be "resurrected" as a pure, celestial world.

33. The wicked shall go away into unquenchable fire. The term *wicked* here refers to those who are "filthy still" at the resurrection of the unjust after the end of the Millennium. These are the ones who still refuse to repent even after suffering hell in the spirit world and who will not receive any degree of glory. They are the sons of perdition (see D&C 76:31–38, 43–48).

34. The solemnities of eternity. These are the sober facts of eternal life and eternal death. There will be no changes in the conditions and terms of our fate after the resurrection. There will be no additional leniency for those who intentionally were not paying attention or who could not be bothered during the days of their probation. There will be no special arrangements or second chances—not for the wealthy, the pretty, the powerful, the popular, the educated, the spoiled, or for any other class who may think themselves "special." It is up to us now to adapt ourselves to the immovable, unchangeable, nonnegotiable realities of the universe—the solemnities of eternity.

1. *Early Latter Day Saint History,* 42–43.
2. *History of the Church,* 1:154.
3. *Early Latter Day Saint History,* 44.
4. *History of the Church,* 1:148.
5. *Church History and Modern Revelation,* 1:189; emphasis added.
6. Dunn, "Teaching by the Power of the Spirit," 8.
7. "Joseph Smith Translation and the Doctrine and Covenants," 111.
8. See *History of the Church,* 136–37.
9. John A. Widtsoe, in Conference Report, Apr. 1931, 60.
10. See Commentary on D&C 29:13; 88:92.
11. See Commentary on D&C 42:39.
12. See Commentary on D&C 29:2.
13. See Revelation 14:10; Commentary on D&C 29:17.
14. Melvin J. Ballard, in Conference Report, Oct. 1921, 98; see also D&C 39:16; Commentary on D&C 24:19; 33:3–4.
15. See also Commentary on D&C 29:11.
16. Smith, *Church History and Modern Revelation,* 1:192.
17. See Cannon, *Gospel Truth,* 1:86–87.

44

BACKGROUND

The Prophet Joseph Smith gave a very brief introduction to Doctrine and Covenants 44 in *History of the Church*. He simply stated: "The latter part of February [1831] I received the following revelation, which caused the Church to appoint a conference to be held early in the month of June ensuing"[1]—followed immediately by the text of section 44.

In Doctrine and Covenants 20:61 the Lord had instructed the elders of the Church to meet in conference every three months. Thus far, after the founding of the Church on 6 April, they had met on 9 June 1830, 26 September 1830, and 2 January 1831. At the close of the 2 January conference in Fayette, New York, a date was not set for the next conference because the New York Saints would be moving to Ohio in the spring and would thus be prevented from meeting until after that time. Therefore, it was decided that a conference would be scheduled in Kirtland for 3 through 6 June 1831.[2] This allowed time for both the New York Saints and the missionaries, who were particularly instructed to attend (see v. 1), to reach Kirtland.

Some historians have suggested, on the evidence of John Whitmer's history, that a general conference was held in Kirtland on 4 March 1831. The original Whitmer manuscript, however, reads 4 June 1831, a date that was later changed to read 4 March.

No other evidence for a March conference exists, and in a letter to Hyrum dated 3–4 March, Joseph mentioned the Lord's commandment that the elders gather to Kirtland, but he said nothing about a conference then in progress.[3]

By the end of February 1831, there were not enough Ohio Saints to consecrate sufficient land to support all the new converts that would soon be coming to Kirtland expecting to receive stewardships. An obvious solution to this problem was to call the full-time missionaries from their various fields of labor and reassign them to the Kirtland area to increase the number of local converts with local resources to consecrate (see vv. 1–4). Thus, instead of producing converts who left everything somewhere else to come to Kirtland and strain the meager resources there, the elders would find local converts who could provide additional resources for the gathering Saints. The shortage of resources in Kirtland at that time was also one reason why many arriving eastern Saints were sent on to Jackson County, Missouri.[4]

One effect of this intensive proselytizing in Ohio was an increase in the number of converts there who could consecrate their lands. This in turn (1) better met the temporal needs of new converts gathering from the East, (2) enabled the Church to organize according to the law of the Church and the law of the state of Ohio, (3) created a secure base for the whole Church, and (4) provided additional support for the Ohio Saints who had already consecrated their properties and whose personal resources were becoming exhausted (see v. 6).

COMMENTARY

1. My servants. This commandment was directed to Joseph and Sidney rather than to the elders or to the Church. The Lord was instructing them on how to meet the problems of the Church.

1. From the east and from the west. The commanded conference of elders was to include the New York Saints, who were still in New York at this time, the Kirtland Saints, and all the elders previously sent out on missions to various parts of the country. Therefore it would be necessary to hold the conference in the spring after the New York Saints had a chance to gather to Ohio and the missionaries could be contacted and called to Kirtland.

3. Preach repentance. Not *only* repentance, but the gospel of faith, repentance, and so on.[5] The missionaries called to Kirtland from their various mission fields were to be redeployed to preach the gospel around Kirtland, where additional strength was sorely needed.

4. And many shall be converted. The population of the Church in Ohio, and particularly in Kirtland, increased roughly between 50 and 100 percent each year between 1830 and 1838.[6]

4. According to the laws of man. The Church had been legally organized in New York on 6 April 1830 and did not need to be reorganized in every other state. By moving to Ohio, leaving the intense opposition of New York behind, and helping the Church to grow quickly in numbers, Joseph would "obtain power" to implement the law of the Church given in Doctrine and Covenants 42, including the vital law of consecration, in an organized and legally binding manner. Thus, the Saints were "enabled to keep my laws" (v. 5).

5. That your enemies may not have power over you. With less initial opposition, a larger number of members, and legal organization in Ohio, there would be increased protection for the Church from lawsuits and other forms of legal harassment.

President Joseph F. Smith indicated why the Lord concerned himself with observing the laws of the state: "When the Lord restored the Gospel the spirit of gathering came with it. The Lord commanded the people to gather together, and that they should not only be organized as a Church, but that they should be organized under the laws of the land, so that they might not be helpless and dependent and without influence or power; but that by means of united effort and faith they should become a power for the accomplishment of righteousness in the earth."[7] Thus, from then until now, in every country or state that the Church enters, the injunction is given to the Saints to obey the laws of the land and organize themselves as a legal entity.

5. To keep my laws. This phrase refers to the law of the Church that had been given the Saints in Doctrine and Covenants 42.

6. Ye must visit the poor. Joseph and Sidney had to make sure that the poor were taken care of until such time as the law of the Church with its law of consecration and stewardship of property could be fully implemented among the Saints for that same purpose.

1. *History of the Church,* 1:157.
2. See *History of the Church,* 1:157.
3. See Jessee, *Personal Writings of Joseph Smith,* 230–31.
4. See Backman and Perkins, "United under the Laws of the Celestial Kingdom," 173–77.
5. See Commentary on D&C 6:9.
6. See Backman, *Heavens Resound,* 140.
7. In Conference Report, April 1900, 47.

45

BACKGROUND

At the time Doctrine and Covenants 45 was received, Joseph Smith had been in Kirtland scarcely more than a month, and the large majority of the New York Saints were still in New York, not due to arrive in Kirtland for weeks. John Whitmer recorded: "In those days [early March 1831] the Lord blessed his disciples greatly, and he gave Revelation after Revelation [D&C 46 and 47 were received the following day], which contained doctrine, instructions, and prophecies: The word of the Lord came to the Seer as follows"[1]—Doctrine and Covenants 45.

The Prophet Joseph Smith briefly described the setting of section 45 in his *History of the Church*: "At this age of the Church many false reports, lies, and foolish stories, were published in the newspapers, and circulated in every direction, to prevent people from investigating the work, or embracing the faith. . . . But to the joy of the Saints who had to struggle against every thing that prejudice and wickedness could invent, I received the following"[2]— Doctrine and Covenants 45.

In 1831, as now, the exact circumstances and details of the second coming of Christ generated a lot of speculation among the Saints—the type of speculation that is not particularly healthy. In Kirtland during this period, counterfeit spiritual phenomena and false spirits accompanied extreme doctrinal speculations about the

Second Coming and were greatly troubling to the Church. Section 45 may have been given in part to answer some of the questions of the members and to quiet down the extreme speculations and doctrinal hysteria that some were indulging in.

In Church periodicals before 1844, verses 72–75 were not printed with Doctrine and Covenants 45, even though they did appear in the 1833 Book of Commandments and in the 1835 Doctrine and Covenants. This oddity may have been due to an editorial decision not to reproduce a prohibition that was no longer relevant nor to suggest to the Church's enemies that the Saints might be hiding something (see v. 72).

COMMENTARY

1. Hearken. The injunction to listen, hearken, hear, or give ear is repeated ten times in the first fifteen verses of this revelation. The Saints of the Lord are to listen to *his* voice rather than the distorting voice of the world and its fallible media of communication. The strong emphasis on hearing and receiving this information identifies Doctrine and Covenants 45 to be of major doctrinal importance to the Church both in its 1831 context and for us today.

1. O ye people of my church. The designation of this revelation to the whole Church at large, rather than just for the elders or for some individual, further indicates its importance.

2. Lest death shall overtake you. Those who will not listen to the Lord run the risk of being found unredeemed from sin and from the devil when the Lord returns. All who are unprepared on that day will be destroyed. Also, the end of the world comes every day for somebody. When *our* last day arrives we will not be spared the pains of hell if our souls are not yet saved.

2. The summer shall be past. Compare Jeremiah 8:20. Summer is the time to labor and to prepare a harvest with which one may survive the winter. In many times and places those who neglected to work while there was time have found themselves without provisions when winter began and often have died for their foolishness. The Lord here applies this lesson from everyday life to spiritual things. Those who refuse to prepare for his coming while there is time will perish at his coming, and those who have refused to prepare for their own personal "last day" will face a harsher fate than starving.

3. The advocate with the Father. If we must plead our own case to God at the Judgment Day, we will lose, and we will not be allowed into the celestial kingdom of God. There is only one advocate, or spokesman, who can plead our case successfully to the Father, and that is the Son. He has one invincible argument that cannot fail to convince the judge and win our acquittal. That argument is his own voluntary and infinite sacrifice, his incomprehensible agony, the shedding of his *innocent* blood, and his unjust death. He defends us, not by citing the merits of *our* case, not by arguing *our* righteous deeds, but by arguing *his own* merits, his own righteousness, his own perfection, and his own voluntary sacrifice. Nothing can withstand this grand, invincible argument. No other facts, logic, reasoning, or accusations overpower it. His argument cannot be resisted even by the demands of justice—for justice has been satisfied. Jesus will accept our case and plead for us with his grand, invincible argument, however, only if we have become his through sincere repentance (D&C 18:12), if we have entered into his covenant in good faith, and if we have endured in it to the end of our lives.

4–5. Father, behold/spare. These words, spoken by Jesus Christ on behalf of those who are his, will irresistibly and inevitably bring them into celestial glory.

4. That thyself might be glorified. God's glory is the exaltation and eternal life of man. Since Jesus was sent to save and to glorify us, as he accomplishes that task the Father, who sent him and whose plan of salvation it is, also successfully accomplishes *his* work and is himself glorified by our glorification.

6. While it is called today. In the language of scripture, previous ages or dispensations of the gospel are sometimes called "yesterday" (see D&C 20:11–12). "Today," or "the day of this life" in which we are to perform our labors (Alma 34:31–36), is the period of our probation in which repentance and change are possible, that is, the period between our mortal birth and our resurrection. Thus, "tomorrow" would begin at the resurrection, after which change is no longer possible, and when we enter into a "new day" of our eternal existence. "Yesterday" can also be understood, in reference to our own individual existence, as the period of our premortal life. "Today," then, would be our mortal life, including our time in the spirit world, and "tomorrow" would be our resurrected life.

The meaning of "tomorrow" is found in Doctrine and Covenants 64:24, in reference to the Second Coming and the judgment of the wicked.

7. Alpha and Omega. See Commentary on Doctrine and Covenants 19:1.

8. Mine own. This phrase refers to the children of the covenant that Jehovah, or Christ, made with Abraham, Isaac, and Jacob, or Israel—particularly those belonging to Jesus' own tribe of Judah. Since the children belong to the fathers, and the fathers belong to Christ, the children should also be Jesus' own. Jesus is referring here to the generation of Jews who rejected and crucified him. Not all, or even most, Jews of Jesus' day shared responsibility for that crime, nor does any Jew born after that time. To argue that subsequent generations of Jews are guilty of the blood of Christ is to suppose some sort of "original sin" or "inherited guilt" passed from parents to their children. This idea has always been rejected by the Saints (see Articles of Faith 1:2) and is repugnant to the Lord (see Moroni 8:8–9).

8. Gave I power. Those Jews in Jesus' day who received him and his teachings were given the gospel, the priesthood, the new and everlasting covenant, and the fulness of gospel ordinances.

9. I have sent mine everlasting covenant into the world.

This phrase refers to the restoration of the gospel of Jesus Christ in these latter days.

9. Standard. This word is a synonym for an ensign (compare D&C 98:34; 105:39). Both terms refer to a sign, banner, flag, emblem, or other object that can be raised or held aloft to help troops, followers, disciples, or members gather or rally to the right side or the right place, or to help keep them oriented and in their proper place once they've been organized. Ultimately, Jesus Christ himself, raised up on the cross in his sacrificial role as the Lamb of God, is the ensign to the nations, who will gather the faithful to himself and keep them oriented and in their right place in Zion once they have been gathered.

Since Christ is no longer upon the cross, however, the ensign raised up to the nations in the latter days will be his restored gospel, his everlasting covenant, his Zion. To this latter-day ensign the Gentiles will gather, and in so doing they will also gather to the Christ who was crucified and raised up on the cross—the ultimate ensign. Note also that the Church publication most directly responsible for proclaiming the restored gospel of Jesus Christ to the world is appropriately called the *Ensign*.

9. For the Gentiles. Our dispensation begins with the times of the Gentiles (see v. 28)—that period when the gospel is taken and taught first to the Gentiles, and then later to the Jews—just as the preceding dispensation began with the gospel being taken first to the Jews, and then also to the Gentiles (see 1 Nephi 13:42). The Gentiles are the inhabitants of all the nations of the earth, from Albania to Zimbabwe—*every* nation, kindred, tongue, and people. Preaching the gospel to all the world in this manner is a work primarily reserved for our latter-day dispensation.

9. A messenger before my face. Just as John the Baptist was an Elias who prepared the way for Christ, so the latter-day Church prepares the way for the millennial kingdom of God that will be established at the second coming of Christ. The Restoration prepares a people to receive Christ in righteousness, knowing and practicing celestial principles lest at his coming the "earth be smitten with a curse" (see D&C 110:15; 138:48).

10. I will reason. See Isaiah 1:18.

11. The God of Enoch, and his brethren. At the time this revelation was given, the Prophet Joseph Smith had already translated what is now Moses 7 in the Pearl of Great Price. The mention of Enoch and his brethren reminds the reader of the establishment of Zion in Enoch's day by the same celestial principles the Lord revealed to the Latter-day Saints. The Lord is just as able to lead us to Zion today and will do so if members of the Church will keep his commandments.

12. Who were separated from the earth, and were received unto myself. According to Moses 7:21, the Zion of Enoch and its people were taken physically off the earth before the Flood, just as the future inhabitants of Zion will be taken physically off the earth before the burning (see D&C 88:96–98; 1 Thessalonians 4:17; 1 Nephi 13:37). Joseph Smith explained that the people of Enoch were not taken to the direct presence of God, but were translated to a terrestrial order.[3] This would be roughly the same level of glory as found in Eden before the Fall and which will exist during the Millennium after the earth receives its paradisiacal glory (see Articles of Faith 1:10, where the "paradise" of "paradisiacal" is Eden). Joseph further stated that God "appointed unto him [Enoch] a ministry unto terrestrial bodies," and that Enoch's Saints are "held in reserve to be ministering angels unto many planets."[4] When this earth has been raised to a terrestrial glory during the Millennium, then the Zion of Enoch shall be physically returned to the earth (see D&C 133:24; Moses 7:63).[5]

12. A city reserved until a day of righteousness. The Zion of Enoch will stay where it is until righteousness again reigns upon the earth. This will be during the Millennium, when the earth has been raised to a terrestrial glory.

13. Strangers and pilgrims. This phrase is a commonly recurring theme in scripture (see Hebrews 11:13–16; 1 Peter 2:11; see also Ephesians 2:19). In the Bible, the word *stranger* most often means a resident alien, someone who lives in a foreign land though his citizenship is somewhere else. A *pilgrim* is someone on a journey—just passing through. Those who look for the establishment of righteousness upon the earth and long to be citizens of Christ's kingdom when he returns must not feel too much at home in this telestial or fallen world. By virtue of the Atonement and our commitment to the new and everlasting covenant, we are already citizens of a better country than any now found upon the earth, and in the telestial realm of Babylon we are pilgrims just passing through—citizens of a better world forced to wait and dwell in Babylon until Zion is established.

14. Obtained a promise. God promised many ancient Saints, including Abraham, Isaac, and Jacob, that they and their children, if they were faithful, would inherit the millennial kingdom and that they would see it in their resurrected flesh at the second coming of Christ. All who have received the fulness of the gospel and its ordinances have received this same promise made to the patriarchs. We are the "children of the promise" made to the fathers.

15. As unto men in days of old. God is willing to give us the same covenant promises and the same gospel that he gave to Adam, Enoch, Noah, Abraham, and so on. If we are faithful to our covenants, we will, according to the promises of God, be like the ancient saints—patriarchs and matriarchs of an innumerable posterity in a glorious promised land, the celestial kingdom. This promise is guaranteed to us by the same gospel covenants that were given to them. God is willing, even anxious, to treat us all as Adam and Eve, or as Abraham and Sarah, or as the twelve ancient apostles and their wives (see 1 Corinthians 9:5), and to deal with us on the same terms by which he dealt with them. All that was ever available to them is available to us through the Restoration. Thus, God is the same in his dealings with human beings yesterday, today, and forever.

16. I will show it plainly. Beginning with verse 16, the Lord begins to tell the latter-day Church what he told his ancient disciples when they asked him about the details of his second coming. The "it" the Lord will show us is the "day of righteousness" (v. 12) that will begin with his return to the earth at his second coming.

16. Saying. What follows the colon in verse 16 are the words of Jesus to his disciples on the Mount of Olives near Jerusalem in the first century A.D. It is important to bear this in mind while reading these verses in order to place the information in proper historical context. The quotation extends through verse 59, excepting the editorial comment in verse 34 and the first five words of verse 35 (compare Joseph Smith–Matthew in the Pearl of Great Price).

16. In the clouds of heaven. This phrase is a reference to the prophecy in Daniel 7:13, where Daniel saw in a dream the end of the world and the second coming of Christ.

16. To fulfill the promises. All the promises of the gospel will be fulfilled for the righteous at their glorious resurrection, which takes place at the Lord's second coming.

17. Absence of your spirits from your bodies. Compare Doctrine and Covenants 138:50. By the end of the world, the righteous dead, including many of Jesus' ancient disciples, will look upon their time in the spirit world without their bodies as a severe limitation. While spirits in paradise are without pain, they cannot accomplish many things that can be done only with a body. A body of flesh and bones is not, as the hellenistic Greeks thought, a limitation. Rather, it is an enabling factor. It is ability, potency, and power, and we will dearly miss its use in the spirit world where we will be temporarily deprived of that means to effect, to create, and to accomplish.

17. The day of redemption. This phrase refers to the day when we actually return to our physical bodies and receive celestial, terrestrial, or telestial glory. Ultimately, redemption is being "bought back" from all obligations, bondage, and servitude except our obligation to Jesus Christ, who bought us with his agony and blood from death, from hell, from Satan, and from the demands of justice.[6] This final redemption is linked to, simultaneous with, and brought about by the resurrection (see, for example, D&C 76:39–40, 85; 88:14, 16; Jacob 6:9), which alone puts us beyond the reach of all our enemies.

17. Restoration of the scattered Israel. Individual death and resurrection are symbolic of the scattering and restoration of all Israel. Just as one hair of our head shall not be lost in individual resurrection, so not a single branch or twig of the family will be lost or forgotten when the Lord gathers Israel and reconstitutes its tribes and their heritage in the latter days.

18–24. Jesus described to his disciples in these verses the tribulations that fell upon Jerusalem and its people in the first century A.D. These prophecies were all fulfilled with the events surrounding the first Jewish revolt against Rome in A.D. 66–73, and indeed, when Jesus first spoke these words there were many Jews alive who were still alive in A.D. 73 (see v. 21).[7]

19. Desolation. A place is made desolate by being "laid waste," made a wasteland without inhabitants. A person is made desolate by being left alone without companions or comfort. The people of "this generation," that is, the Jews of the second half of the first century, would be made desolate as individuals, and their homes and cities would become desolate places. An incredibly large number of Jews would die (Josephus said it was over a million),[8] and many of the remainder would be driven out or sold as slaves into all corners of the world. Their temple would be destroyed so thoroughly that not one stone would be left standing upon another (see v. 20).

In A.D. 68, the Roman general Vespasian and his son Titus took a large Roman army into Israel to subdue rebellious Judah. When Titus surrounded Jerusalem, most who tried to escape were either chased back into the city or were caught and crucified. Within the walls of the Holy City, rival political factions, like Gadianton robber bands, stole the possessions of citizens and the food from the mouths of women and children. Pressed by the famine, mothers ate their babies; in their madness, the political gangs fought and killed each other for control of the city and even burned each other's food supplies, all while the common enemy, the Romans, waited outside the walls for the inevitable.[9]

Like the generation before the Flood, the generation of the Babylonian conquest, and the generations at the end of the Jaredite and Nephite societies, so was the generation of the first Jewish revolt. Because the people had become ripe in iniquity, the Spirit of the Lord had ceased striving with them, and Satan had full power over their hearts (compare Ether 15:19).[10] Drunk with their own sins and with anger and rage, they could not be reached, would not repent, and were sealed up to destruction.

19. Scattered among all nations. Just as the lost ten tribes had been taken into bondage and scattered eight hundred years earlier, the Jews were dispersed among every nation on earth by the time of the Restoration, but they will be gathered again through the preaching of the gospel and by the power of the priesthood. The dispersed of Israel in many cases are not even aware of their Israelite heritage, having been absorbed ethnically and culturally by the nations they dwell among. But God will reveal them and lead them back.

21. This generation of Jews shall not pass away. Once the Jews of Jesus' day became totally ripe in their iniquity, their destruction and all of the signs preceding it occurred within one generation, or one lifetime. Not all the things that have been prophesied for the future are signs of the end, but in both the dispensation of the meridian of time—the time of Jesus and his apostles—and in the dispensation of the fulness of times—our own latter days—once those special signs of the end begin to appear, their conclusion and finale are no more than one generation away (see vv. 35, 38; Joseph Smith–Matthew 1:34). That generation will be the generation that sees the end of the times of the Gentiles—the period while Israel is scattered and the gospel is taken to every nation (see v. 30; Luke 21:24–25, 32 with Joseph Smith Translation parallels).

Bear in mind that a "generation" is a notoriously difficult

measure of time to define. Is a generation twelve to sixteen years, the biological minimum; twenty years, an average for birth of a firstborn; thirty years, the average age difference between most parents and children; seventy years, the biblical human life span; or a hundred plus years, the length of the longest individual life within a generation? Better to repent now and avoid the consequences of bad assumptions or poor math skills.

24. When that day shall come. "That day" is a stock phrase in scripture, usually meaning the end of the world. In this case, however, it refers specifically to the end of the world *of the Jews* in the first century A.D.

24. Shall a remnant be scattered. The remaining Jews were in time driven out of their promised land and scattered throughout the earth. Their blood—the blood of Israel mainly through Judah, Benjamin, and Levi—has been mixing to a limited extent with that of the Gentile nations for nearly two thousand years. The blood of Israel through Ephraim, the son of Joseph (see D&C 64:36), has been mingling much more widely among the Gentiles and for centuries longer. During the times of the Gentiles, those Gentiles who belong to Israel, whether by faith and biological descent or by faith and adoption, will be restored to Zion (see Isaiah 49:14, 20–22).

25. But they shall remain. Those Jews who were scattered, or rather their descendants, will remain where they are until *after* the times of the Gentiles are fulfilled. For this reason, the creation of the state of Israel in 1948 and the return of many Jews to that land in the time since cannot be considered the *fulfillment* of the prophecies concerning the restoration of Israel, although these events are certainly a beginning (see 2 Nephi 30:7). This preliminary gathering prepares for a fulfillment that is yet to come, but that full gathering will take place only *after* the gospel has been taken to every nation, kindred, tongue, and people and all the Gentile nations have had an opportunity to accept or reject the gospel (see 3 Nephi 16:10–12).[11]

25. The times of the Gentiles. The destruction of Jerusalem and of the Jews marked the end of the dispensation of the gospel to the Jews. When the gospel was restored in the latter days, it began with the times of the Gentiles (see v. 28), a period unique in world history in which the gospel was to be taken not primarily to the Jews as before but specifically to "every nation, kindred, tongue, and people"—to all the *Gentile* nations (1 Nephi 19:17; Mosiah 3:20; 15:28; 16:1; Alma 37:4). When the Gentile nations of all the world have had their fair chance to accept or reject the gospel, it will be taken from them and will go once again to the children of Judah and all of the house of Israel (compare D&C 90:9). After the "times of the Gentiles" are over, the dispersed of Israel will finally be gathered together.[12]

26. In that day. "That day" here refers to that last day, time, or generation in which the times of the Gentiles will be fulfilled and the signs of the end will begin to occur (compare v. 30).

26. Wars and rumors of wars. As we approach the end of the times of the Gentiles and come closer to the second coming of Christ, social and political conditions on the earth will deteriorate and the earth will become a very dangerous place. People will become disheartened, or lose heart—"men's hearts shall fail them." This refers to the hopelessness and despair born of a world filled with crime and violence "as it was in the days of Noah" (Joseph Smith–Matthew 1:41; Matthew 24:37). These sickening conditions will lead many to conclude wrongly that the Savior is not coming until the whole earth has been destroyed.

27. The love of men shall wax cold. As we approach the end and Satan's influence increases over the world, natural human love and affection will decrease outside of Zion. Indications that human love is waxing cold might include the following: spouse and child abuse will increase; divorce rates will rise; many parents will no longer feel love for, or a responsibility toward, their children; and abortion will abound. Traditional families will cease to be the norm or even to be valued; the bond between men and women will diminish as traditional relations between the sexes are defined by society as adversarial, abusive, or exploitative;

neighbors will victimize neighbors; families will fight over the trinkets of the world; and friends will betray friends for baubles.

28. And when the times of the Gentiles is come in. Verse 28 marks a chronological break from verses 25–27. The times of the Gentiles "came in" in this dispensation with Joseph Smith and the restoration of the gospel to the earth. The Book of Mormon prophets understood the latter-day Church to be established by Gentiles (see 1 Nephi 13:39–40; 15:13; 3 Nephi 26:8; Mormon 7:8; Ether 12:22; see also D&C 14:8; 109:60), who would take the Book of Mormon to other Gentiles and also to the descendants of Lehi. The times of the Gentiles will be fulfilled when the latter-day Church has completed its mission to take the gospel to every nation and when the majority of Gentiles have rejected it in favor of "the precepts of men" (see vv. 29–30). The restoration of the gospel and the times of the Gentiles are the twin events heralded in John's prophecy of the last days: "And I saw another angel fly in the midst of heaven, having the everlasting gospel to preach unto them that dwell on the earth, and to every nation, and kindred, and tongue, and people" (Revelation 14:6).

31. An overflowing scourge. It is common to hear the present curse of AIDS discussed as a fulfillment of this prophecy. This scripture combined with verse 30, however, seems to place this scourge in the generation that sees the times of the Gentiles fulfilled—an event which cannot be said to have happened quite yet.[13] Certainly the recent and sudden appearance of the Ebola virus with its staggering death rates ought to warn us of the possibility of even more horrific plagues out there, as yet unknown to us, that could desolate the world when God pours out his judgments.

Elsewhere we are told that this scourge "shall continue to be poured out from time to time, if they repent not, until the earth is empty" (D&C 5:19), and that "it shall not be stayed until the Lord come" (D&C 97:23; see also D&C 84:97). Whatever the scourge is to be, the prophecy of its arrival cannot be "fulfilled" until after the gospel has been taught in every nation, kindred, tongue, and people and the Gentiles have rejected it. Nor can this prophecy be deemed fulfilled until the sickness has covered the whole land and left it "desolated," which our contemporary diseases have not yet done.[14]

On the other hand, perhaps the "scourge" spoken of could include such nonbiological plagues as the wickedness, crime, war, and utter despair that will descend upon Babylon at the end (see Zechariah 14:12, 15, 18, in which the plague is said to consume the flesh of the wicked at the last day).

32. Stand in holy places. Places become holy not necessarily by location but rather through what is or has been done there. President Ezra Taft Benson defined "holy places" as follows: "Holy men and holy women stand in holy places, and these holy places include our temples, our chapels, our homes, and the stakes of Zion, which are, as the Lord declares, 'for a defense, and for a refuge from the storm, and from wrath when it shall be poured out without mixture upon the whole earth' (D&C 115:6)."[15]

33. Earthquakes . . . and many desolations. As the end-time approaches, disasters that leave the land desolate, such as earthquakes, famines, floods, droughts, storms, and wars, will increase. The world that has rejected God's word as it comes in the scriptures or by the mouths of prophets and missionaries will hear it spoken considerably louder in the voice of disasters that leave in their wake a desolated landscape (see D&C 43:25).[16] Still, as in the days of Noah, they will not listen, but will thirst all the more for violence and blood.

35. Ye may know. The coming of all the promised curses and plagues upon the wicked, both in the first century and in our own future, will be a testimony to the faithful that the promised blessings will also come and that the end is very near.

37. Behold the fig-trees. One characteristic of a fig tree is that it does not put forth its leaves until relatively late in the season, long after most of the trees are in full leaf. The Savior used this feature in a parable concerning his second coming. Although the world will not know the day nor the hour of his coming, we should observe the signs of the times, for when the fig tree puts forth its leaves, we know that summer is nigh. In other words, when the signs of the Second Coming begin to be made manifest, we know that the Second Coming is nigh or near at hand[17] (see D&C 106:4–6).

39. Shall be looking forth. Those who "fear" God, that is, those who hold him in reverence and awe, will be looking forward to the Second Coming—they will *want* it to come! The second coming of Christ will be to them deliverance from the wickedness of the fallen world of Babylon.

40. They shall see. Perhaps some of the signs of Christ's coming will be seen only by those who are really looking for them. On the other hand, perhaps only the righteous will see that the increase in visible, natural disasters and other strange phenomena are not due simply to nature but are warning signs and a last call for repentance from the Lord, who is about to come in judgment with righteous indignation.

43. The remnant. This verse refers to the remnant of the Jewish people who have been scattered throughout the world. By the time of the coming of the "last day," they shall have been gathered together "unto this place," that is, to the place where Jesus spoke these words to his disciples—in old Jerusalem (see 2 Nephi 30:7).

44. They shall look for me. The antecedent for *they* is the remnant described in verse 43 who fear God and are looking for the coming of their Messiah but do not yet know that their longed-for Messiah is Jesus Christ. The Jews have the prophecies of the Old Testament concerning the last days and the coming of the Messiah. They will recognize some of the signs and will be looking for his coming. Then they will see him coming in the clouds of heaven, and the prophecy of Jesus to the Jews in Matthew 26:64 will be fulfilled (see also Mark 14:62).

45. The arm of the Lord shall fall. That is, fall in judgment upon the wicked. The image is of one who delivers a smiting blow. Before this mighty judgment upon the world, the archangel

Michael will sound his trumpet (see D&C 29:13, 26) and the righteous, both living and dead, will be lifted up off of the earth to meet Christ in the air (see also D&C 88:96–98; 133:56; 1 Thessalonians 4:15–17).

46. If ye have slept in peace. Those righteous dead who enjoyed the peaceful rest of paradise between death and resurrection, as opposed to suffering for their sins in hell, will be resurrected. They will be raised up to meet Christ in the air at his coming, and their redemption will be perfected, or made complete or whole.

47. Then shall the arm of the Lord fall.[18] Once the Saints in the new and everlasting covenant, both living and dead, have been raised up to meet the Lord, *then* his indignation and judgment will fall upon the wicked residue who are left behind upon the earth.

This passage, like most others dealing with the last day, leaves ambiguous the fate of those mortals who are worthy of terrestrial glory but not of celestial glory when the Savior comes. Since the millennial earth will possess a terrestrial glory, however, and since the terrestrial are referred to elsewhere as "Christ's at his coming" (D&C 88:99) and as being resurrected in the first resurrection (see v. 54), though not in the "morning," it is possible that the living who are worthy of a terrestrial glory will also be preserved and participate in the millennial kingdom: "Some members of the Church have an erroneous idea that when the millennium comes all of the people are going to be swept off the earth except righteous members of the Church. That is not so. There will be millions of people—Catholics, Protestants, agnostics, Mohammedans, people of all classes and of all beliefs—still permitted to remain upon the face of the earth, but they will be those who have lived clean lives, those who have been free from wickedness and corruption. All who belong, by virtue of their good lives, *to the terrestrial order,* as well as those who have kept the celestial law, will remain upon the face of the earth during the millennium."[19]

48. This mount. This word refers to the Mount of Olives in

Jerusalem, where Jesus was when he told these things to his disciples (see Zechariah 14:4).

49–50. These verses describe the anguish, despair, and self-reproach of the wicked just prior to their destruction at the return of the Lord. They shall then be consumed by burning, and the earth will be purified by fire to become a fit habitation for Christ and his Saints.[20] It is possible that "they that watch for iniquity" means those who keep their eyes open for the opportunity to commit sin, who watch for their chance at wickedness and take it when it comes.

51–53. These verses describe the long-awaited collective repentance and conversion of the Jews. This is not repentance for the death of Christ, for these Jews are not guilty of that. Rather, it is the same repentance that all who come to Christ must go through. Though a few individual Jews have joined the Church since its founding in 1830, the mass conversion described in scripture will not take place, nor will the gathering of Israel be completed, until after the coming of the Lord. When the Gentile nations have heard and rejected the gospel and the world is ripe in iniquity, then the times of the Gentiles will be over, the Savior will return, and the Jews will be converted and redeemed. But this great mass conversion will await the personal appearance of Christ to the Jews in Jerusalem at the last day.

54. And then shall the heathen nations be redeemed. The Saints of God, those who will inherit his celestial kingdom, will be resurrected *before* Christ descends from the heavens to the earth and *before* the wicked are punished (see vv. 45–48). Then *after* the resurrection of the celestial Saints, and *after* the Savior descends to the Mount of Olives (see v. 48), and *after* his arm has fallen upon the wicked to destroy them (see v. 47), and *after* he has conversed with and converted the Jews at Jerusalem (see vv. 51–53), then the resurrection of the terrestrial, "heathen" dead will take place (see v. 54; D&C 88:99) in what might be called the "afternoon" or "evening" of the first resurrection. But it is still the *first* resurrection during which they will be raised and not the second or last resurrection (for the wicked) at the *end* of the thousand years (see Revelation 20:5–6).[21]

Generally the scriptures divide the world into just two categories—Jews and Gentiles, or heathens (the Bible translates the same words, *goyim* in Hebrew and *ethnikoi* in Greek, variously as either "the Gentiles," "the nations," or "the heathen"). In this last dispensation, however, it is possible to further divide the Gentile nations into "Christian nations"—those Gentile nations who have some knowledge of Jesus Christ—and "heathen nations"—those Gentile nations who have no knowledge of Christ.[22] This is the distinction intended here by the use of "the heathen nations" (compare D&C 90:10). These heathen nations, who know nothing of Christ or of his commandments, are also referred to as they who "have sinned without law" (Romans 2:12), "they who died without law" (D&C 76:72), or "the spirits of men kept in prison, whom the Son visited . . . who received not the testimony of Jesus in the flesh, but afterwards received it" (D&C 76:73–74).

The common denominator for all these descriptions is the idea that as a general rule and because of their ignorance, these peoples may be judged more leniently for their transgressions than either Israel or the so-called Christian nations. Because they didn't have the Lord's commandments, the heathen will be less likely to be judged "wicked" than will members of the Church or other Christians who knew and rejected the commandments. Thus Doctrine and Covenants 45:54 holds out much greater hope for the unbaptized heathen than did the majority of Christian churches in 1831, most of whom taught that the unconverted "heathen" burned in hell forever and ever.

The heathen, then, did not become Christ's own—that is, his sons and daughters—during their mortal lives by entering the gospel covenant, nor were they initially his in the spirit prison—unlike the Saints who rested in paradise. But they will later gain a testimony of Jesus and be redeemed "at his coming" (D&C 88:99) and resurrected in the first resurrection.

The terrestrial glory of the heathen nations is not *prescriptive,* that is, it is not a fate that God imposes on them because they are heathens. Their equal chance for celestial glory has not been taken from them. Rather, this verse is *descriptive;* it merely describes the pattern that will, for whatever reasons, generally occur, and it is important to note that there will be many exceptions to the rule. On the one hand, for example, those heathens who accept the gospel, or who lived the intent of the gospel even without having a knowledge of it (see Romans 2:14–27), or who would have received the gospel if they had only been given a chance, will receive *celestial* glory as Saints of God (see D&C 137:7–9) and will be resurrected in the "morning" of the first resurrection with the other Saints (see D&C 45:54).

"There are millions of people, both among the Christian and heathen nations, that are still in darkness, and exclaiming, 'Oh, how glad we would be to have some knowledge of the Gospel of salvation!' By-and-by, when the Lord sends forth his servants and his angels to gather them, they will be brought home to Zion and be taught the peaceable things of the kingdom; and those that abide a celestial law will receive a celestial glory."[23]

On the other hand, those heathens who, regardless of their ignorance of Christ, simply loved evil, will suffer the fate of the wicked at Christ's coming and will be resurrected to telestial glory at the end of the Millennium.

54. It shall be tolerable for them. Though many heathens will inherit celestial glory, they will be the exception rather than the rule. On the other hand, the heathen nations will be redeemed from the devil through Christ and will be resurrected in the first resurrection, their glory being greater than that of those who are assigned to the telestial kingdom. Their terrestrial glory, neither the highest nor lowest degree, will thus be "tolerable" for them.

Once again, exceptions to the general pattern will include all those heathen who accept the gospel in the flesh, or who would have done so had they received the opportunity (see D&C 137:7;

Articles of Faith 1:2). Similarly, the wicked heathen, like the wicked of all nations, will receive telestial glory.

55. Satan shall be bound.[24] The binding of Satan shall be accomplished in two ways. First, all the wicked people, his willing instruments, will have been destroyed, and all those who remain upon the earth will be celestial or terrestrial in nature and will be committed to Christ. Consequently, there will be no one through whom Satan can act to accomplish his will (see 1 Nephi 22:26; D&C 101:28). Second, since Satan will be not only bound but "sealed" (Revelation 20:3), we may assume that the power of God will directly restrict his activities and neutralize his influence.[25]

56–59. The ten virgins. Usually we apply the parable of the ten virgins (see Matthew 25:1–13) to the Church itself to contrast the fates of valiant and negligent Saints. President Spencer W. Kimball indicated that the ten virgins represent the members of the Church, not the rank and file of the world (see *Faith Precedes the Miracle,* 253). When so applied the five wise virgins are those who have received the truth, are led by the Spirit, and are not deceived (see v. 57), and the foolish virgins are the wicked who are "hewn down and cast into the fire," those who are unworthy and unprepared to abide Christ's coming or his judgments.

57. Abide the day. This phrase means to survive "that day," "the last day," and to continue to live, or abide, upon the earth after the coming of Christ and the destruction of the wicked.

58. The earth shall be given unto them. Christ is speaking of those who are alive and mortal at his second coming. If they are righteous, their mortal lives shall continue into the Millennium (see v. 57) and the earth will be given to them for a temporal inheritance (see v. 58). They will continue to have mortal children in the Millennium, and those children will grow up with their agency but without sin. The mortal population of the earth will continue to grow throughout the Millennium.

Verses 58–59 also mark the end of the quotation from the Savior's teachings to his disciples in the first century (see vv.

16–59). With verses 60–75 there is a change of setting, and these verses are given directly to Joseph Smith and to the Latter-day Saints.

60. Until the New Testament be translated. Until 7 March 1831, the date Doctrine and Covenants 45 was given, Joseph and Sidney worked on the Joseph Smith Translation for the book of Genesis only. Here in verses 60–61 the Lord invites them to begin work on the New Testament. The translation of Joseph Smith–Matthew began the next day, 8 March 1831, which indicates the importance the prophet Joseph Smith placed upon the work.

60. This chapter. This phrase probably refers to Matthew 24 in the New Testament, now found in the Pearl of Great Price as Joseph Smith–Matthew.

60. In it all these things shall be made known. The antecedent of *it* is the Joseph Smith Translation of the New Testament, including prominently Joseph Smith's translation of Matthew 24. This particular chapter, Joseph Smith–Matthew, does indeed reveal details of Christ's prophecies to his disciples about the Second Coming, details that were lost between the first century and 1831. The information found there was intended specifically for the Saints of the latter days in order to prepare them for what was coming.

63. Wars in your own lands. This prophecy undoubtedly refers to the Civil War, at this time still thirty years away, and perhaps also to other wars we have not yet experienced (see D&C 38:29–32; 87:1–8).

64. Western countries. The safety of the Saints was in moving from their eastern homes in New York and Pennsylvania and gathering to the West—first west to Ohio, then west to Missouri if they could establish Zion there, and if they could not, yet further west to Deseret. Though they did not establish a Zion in Missouri, by following the prophet Brigham Young to the mountains of the West the Saints were still spared the desolating slaughter of the Civil War.

65. Purchase an inheritance. The Lord here made it clear to the Saints how they were to acquire lands in "the western countries" to establish Zion. They were to "gather up" their riches and buy the lands.

66. The New Jerusalem. Zion will be larger than just one city, but the center place will be in Jackson County, Missouri, and will be called New Jerusalem. This New Jerusalem and the old Jerusalem of David and Isaiah will both be world capitols in the Millenium. "In the scriptures four words seem closely related to the concept of Zion: *gathering, preparation, defense,* and *refuge.* The tribulations and judgments that will be poured out upon the world prior to the Second Coming will be so extensive and devastating that if the Lord did not prepare a means of preservation, his people too would perish. But he has prepared a means for his people to escape those terrible times; that means is Zion."[26] In the terrible times that precede the coming of the Savior, there will be no safety or security anywhere upon the earth except in Zion, which will be governed by the laws of God and protected by the power of God.[27]

67. Glory of the Lord . . . terror of the Lord. For the righteous Saints, Zion will be glorious, but for its enemies Zion will be terrible. The power of the Lord will terrify all Zion's enemies so that they will fear to approach her.

68–71. In the period before the coming of the Savior, there will be no peace or security anywhere or with anyone outside of Zion. The rest of the world will become an armed camp, and the whole world will be full of blood and schemes "as it was in the days of Noah" (Joseph Smith–Matthew 1:41). The inhabitants of the earth will then be as Noah's neighbors were, as the Jews of Lehi's day, as the Jews of the first revolt, and as the Jaredites and Nephites on the eve of their destruction (see Ether 15:19–22; Moroni 9:2–5, 8–23). Those who will neither commit violence nor suffer it must flee to Zion, the only refuge of safety on earth.

72. Keep these things from going abroad. It was not yet the right time to publish or preach to the world the things found in this revelation, as they could be misunderstood or distorted and could arouse the anger of the world against the Saints more quickly as they tried to establish Zion in Missouri.

74. He shall be terrible unto them. There will be some time between the resurrection of the righteous and the final destruction of the wicked. Apparently, this will be ample time for the wicked to realize what is happening and to wish the mountains would fall on them instead (see also v. 75).

1. *Early Latter-day Saint History,* 45–46.
2. 1:158.
3. See *Teachings,* 170.
4. *History of the Church,* 4:209–10.
5. See Commentary on D&C 38:4.
6. See Commentary on D&C 19:1.
7. See the description of these events by the Jewish historian in *Josephus, the Jewish War.*
8. See Josephus, *Josephus, the Jewish War,* 450.
9. See Josephus, *Josephus, the Jewish War,* 387–401, 416–17.
10. See Josephus, *Josephus, the Jewish War,* 388–90.
11. See Commentary on v. 25.
12. See Commentary on v. 9.
13. See Commentary on v. 28.
14. See Commentary on v. 19.
15. "Prepare Yourselves for the Great Day of the Lord," 68.
16. See Commentary on D&C 43:25.
17. See Melvin J. Ballard, in Conference Report, Oct. 1923, 32; Commentary on D&C 106:4–6.
18. See Commentary on v. 45.
19. Smith, *Doctrines of Salvation,* 1:86; emphasis added.
20. See Commentary on D&C 27:18.
21. See Smith, *Doctrines of Salvation,* 2:296.
22. See McConkie, Mormon Doctrine, 346–47.
23. Brigham Young, in *Journal of Discourses,* 9:138–39.
24. See Commentary on D&C 43:31.
25. See John Taylor, in *Journal of Discourses,* 25:89; McConkie, *Doctrinal New Testament Commentary,* 3:570–71.
26. *Doctrine and Covenants Student Manual,* 98.
27. See Smith, *Teachings,* 71, 161.

46

BACKGROUND

In Kirtland on 8 March 1831, one day after receiving Doctrine and Covenants 45, the Prophet Joseph Smith received two more revelations which are also now contained in the Doctrine and Covenants as sections 46 and 47. Concerning Doctrine and Covenants 46, the Prophet wrote only one line in the *History of the Church:* "The next day after [D&C 45] was received, I also received the following revelation, relative to the gifts of the Holy Ghost"[1]—Doctrine and Covenants 46.

John Whitmer, who in the second of these two revelations (Doctrine and Covenants 47) was appointed Church historian, recorded some additional background to Doctrine and Covenants 46: "In the beginning of the church, while yet in her infancy, the disciples used to exclude unbelievers, which caused some to marvel, and converse of this matter because of the things that were written in the Book of Mormon [see 3 Nephi 18:22–33]. Therefore the Lord deigned to speak on this subject [D&C 46], that his people might come to understanding and said that he had always given to his Elders to conduct all meetings as they were led by the Spirit."[2] Thus, verses 1–7 were likely given to correct what had become the practice of the Church at that time in excluding nonmembers from its services, so that Church practice would agree with the policy described in 3 Nephi 18:22–33 and perhaps also in Moroni 6:7–9.

Because Church meetings were always to be conducted according to the inspiration of the Holy Spirit, it was necessary to help the Saints recognize the influence of the Spirit and also how to distinguish it from false and counterfeit spirits. Then, as now, some Christian denominations sought and received manifestations of "the spirit" that were rather questionable and that sometimes led to bizarre or shocking behavior. Having been converted to the restored gospel from charismatic backgrounds, some Kirtland Saints had been particularly prone to the influence of these counterfeit spirits and their "gifts."[3] Here in section 46, the Lord clarifies for the Saints in Kirtland the nature and purposes of the genuine gifts of the Holy Ghost.

COMMENTARY

2. But notwithstanding those things which are written. Despite the many wonderful things found written in the scriptures, such as 3 Nephi 18:22–33, and in other sources on how to conduct Church meetings (for example, D&C 20), the prompting of the Holy Ghost is always the final authority in this matter for those who preside. The planning and conducting of meetings must not become too controlled by habit, tradition, agendas, or set procedures. The Church is, after all, a "living church" (D&C 1:30), one that receives and responds to the direct revelations of God granted through the Spirit, and the Spirit must then have the final say in how to conduct our meetings, just as it must have the final say in how to conduct our lives.

3. Ye are commanded never to cast any one out from your public meetings. Though the Spirit is the highest authority on how meetings are to be conducted, there is one principle that the Spirit observes and so also must those who preside: they must not exclude from the public meetings of the Church any who desire to attend. However the Spirit may direct a "public" meeting to be conducted, it must remain open to the public. Yet even this command must be understood to have its bounds, for individuals may be asked to leave even public meetings if they are disruptive or if they constitute a danger to others present.

On the other hand, some Church meetings are *not* public, such as bishopric and presidency meetings, council meetings, and meetings held in temples, and attendance at these meetings may be controlled.

4. Not to cast any one who belongeth to the church out. This instruction refers to those who are disfellowshipped or on probation as well as any who have offended others or who might be deemed unacceptable for any other reason. All members of the Church have a covenant obligation, and therefore a logical right, to attend sacrament meeting—even those who are "out of favor" with their brothers and sisters.

4. Let him not partake until he makes reconciliation. The right to attend sacrament meeting is, however, not necessarily a right to partake of the sacred elements of the sacrament. Elder David O. McKay stated that "to partake of the sacrament unworthily is to take a step toward spiritual death."[4] Therefore, out of love and concern for the individual as well as out of duty to maintain the high standards of the Church, presiding authorities should not allow one who is known to be involved in serious sin to partake of the sacrament. It is nothing less than mockery for a person to partake of the sacrament as though renewing sacred promises to keep covenants when that person has no intention of keeping the commandments. A leader who prevents this from happening preserves the sanctity of the ordinance and also protects the would-be partaker from a sin of hypocrisy, mockery, and defiling what is sacred. It therefore is imperative that we each examine ourselves before we partake.

5. Who are earnestly seeking the kingdom. It is altogether appropriate for investigators to attend sacrament meeting and other public Church meetings. Presumably, investigators will feel the Spirit of God more strongly at Church meetings, where the Spirit has been specifically invited and should direct what is said and done, than in most other settings.

6. Your confirmation meetings. In the early days of the Church it was common to baptize people on one day and then later to confirm them in a public meeting held specifically for that purpose. In the modern Church it is more likely that individuals who have been baptized will be confirmed in sacrament meeting or in a fast and testimony meeting that serves the same purpose as the earlier confirmation meetings.

7. But ye are commanded in all things to ask of God. It is common for members to ask of God when they lack blessings or knowledge, but verse 7 makes it clear we are to pray and to ask for God's involvement in all our affairs. To view ourselves as spiritually self-sufficient or as in some degree independent of God is not a virtue, nor is the feeling that we are doing just fine by merely touching base with him once in a while. To communicate with God regularly in all aspects of our lives is not just good advice or a sweet invitation; it is a *commandment,* clearly and expressly stated here and in many other places in the revelations as well.[5]

7. That which the Spirit testifies unto you. The whole focus of Doctrine and Covenants 46 is on following the promptings of the Spirit, whether in conducting meetings or in the temporal details of our lives.

7. Considering the end of your salvation. This phrase means keeping in mind your ultimate goal of salvation. As we prayerfully live out our lives, we should give careful consideration to how each of our daily choices will affect our salvation.

7. Doctrines of devils, or the commandments of men. Some false doctrines are satanically inspired, and others are examples of how even sincere human beings can follow their own reasoning and get things all wrong. Still, either kind of error will keep us from knowing and following the truth and will ultimately lead us away from God and our Savior.[6] There are three possible sources of revelation: God, man, and Satan. Of the three, only God is a reliable source.

8. That ye may not be deceived seek ye earnestly the best gifts. "The evil one has the power to tap into . . . channels of revelation and send conflicting signals which can mislead and confuse us."[7] This being the case, it is important that individuals in the Church be on guard against the possibility of deception, and the best defense against deception is frequent communication with God, especially through receiving and exercising the gifts of the Spirit. Because some gifts of the Spirit are more spiritually useful or contribute more directly to our salvation than others, we should seek after these *best* gifts.[8] Paul, for example, placed a higher value on the gift of prophecy than on the gift of tongues (see 1 Corinthians 14:1–4).

Not every supernatural occurrence is from God. Many apparently supernatural events are deceptions created by man; others, whether apparent or real, are of Satan. If we can learn through frequent communication in prayer and through exercising our proper gifts to recognize the voice of the true Spirit, we shall be less vulnerable to the counterfeits of men or of Satan.

9. They are given for the benefit of those who love me. The purpose of the gifts of the Spirit is to bless those who love God and to help them avoid deception. They are not given as signs to prove the gospel's truth to skeptics, nor to confer status, nor to develop faith in the Saints who possess them. They are received only *after* we have demonstrated our faith, and they are given to benefit us individually and the Church collectively. As we communicate with God through frequent prayer and as the Holy Spirit communicates with us through his gifts, we will find ourselves led away from deceptions.

9. Keep all my commandments. Since none of the Saints keep all God's commandments all of the time, note the great mercy extended to us in the next phrase: "*and* him that *seeketh* so to do."[9] If we are genuinely trying to keep the commandments of God but fail from time to time, the gifts and blessings of the Spirit are still promised us for our benefit. The gifts of the Spirit are for those who succeed in keeping all of the commandments—*and* for those who earnestly *try* to keep them but sometimes do not succeed.

9. Consume it upon their lusts. Some in the Church seek to possess the gifts of the Spirit for carnal reasons rather than for reasons of building the kingdom of God. The desire for a sign is one such "lust" of the flesh. Sign seeking is the carnal mind demanding that the Spirit prove itself on the physical or empirical level, the level of the flesh. But faith is neither a response to miracles nor the fruit of miracles, rather it is the soil from which miracles grow (see Ether 12:12).

11–29. This discourse on the gifts of the Spirit bears strong similarities to the material found in 1 Corinthians 12:3–11 and Moroni 10:8–17.

11. For all have not every gift. It is unusual for any single individual to enjoy all the gifts of the Spirit, but every faithful individual has the right to at least one gift. It should be understood that these are not primarily gifts of the priesthood, but gifts of the Spirit, and all members, whether male or female, share in these gifts of the Spirit just as they share in possessing the gift of the Holy Ghost. Of course, if we never serve God or seek after the Spirit in our lives, we may never know what our particular gifts are—for the gifts of the Spirit are discovered and improved as we serve God in building his kingdom.

12. That all may be profited thereby. The gifts of the Spirit are distributed one to Brother X, some others to Sister Y, and others still to Brother or Sister Z, so the Saints will better understand that we need each other. We are meant to join together in one body to complement each other's strengths and compensate for each other's weaknesses. Collectively, we possess all the gifts. One person may enjoy the gift of healing, and another the gift of knowledge. Sometimes our leaders ask us to do something that seems not to be one of our gifts so we can grow, and at different times we could be given different gifts. In this manner, the

Church, all of us together as brothers and sisters, possesses every necessary gift. And so it follows that we need each other, each of the members needs the whole body. By design, no single individual is intended to be spiritually self-sufficient.

13. To know that Jesus Christ is the Son of God. This describes a different, more powerful gift than being certain through our faith. This is the gift of direct, empirical *knowledge* of Christ, the kind of knowledge that Joseph took with him when he left the Sacred Grove. It is to know of oneself and not of another, just as the Three Witnesses of the Book of Mormon came to *know* by personal experience, by seeing, hearing, and touching. When the brother of Jared came to know in this sense by personally seeing God, it is said that "he had faith no longer, for he knew, nothing doubting" (Ether 3:19). Thus, in this life, some know by a direct, personal, and empirical encounter, while others believe through faith (see D&C 76:117–18).[10] Either condition is sufficient for celestial glory.

Some, who have seen the Savior, have touched him and heard him speak, *know,* as Thomas, Peter, Paul, or Joseph Smith knew (or as promised in Doctrine and Covenants 67:10; 93:1; and 3 Nephi 12:2). This knowledge is said to come *by* the Holy Ghost, whose sustaining presence alone makes gaining such knowledge possible, in the same way that sinning against such knowledge is called a sin *against* the Holy Ghost (see D&C 76:35).[11]

14. To believe on their words. Most members have not received the kind of empirical knowledge described in verse 13. For most it is given to believe, also through the witness of the Holy Ghost, the testimony of those who do know empirically. This ability to believe the testimony of others through the witness of the Spirit is no trivial gift, and we are promised eternal life if we continue faithful to the witness that confirms to us the testimony of others who have personally seen and experienced. To believe the testimony of Joseph Smith or of the Three Witnesses of the Book of Mormon is a choice gift of the Spirit.

This certainty may come through the witness of the Spirit, or it may come through one's own personal experience, the evidence of one's own senses. Both types of certainty are commonly, and rather loosely, referred to by the Saints as "knowing." But these are not the same *kind* of knowing, for one is the certainty of faith and the other is the certainty that requires "faith no longer" (Ether 3:19).

15. The differences of administration. This phrase is first used in 1 Corinthians 12:5, where the Greek means "the different kinds of ministries" or "differences in ways of serving." The full sense might be rendered something like "the differences in how God has equipped each of us to serve." Moroni seemed to use the term this way in Moroni 10:8, when he said, "And there are different ways that these gifts are administered" by God to the Saints, which captures the true sense of 1 Corinthians 12:5. Thus, to know these differences of administration is to recognize how God has endowed different individuals with different gifts and with different "styles" or ways of doing things. One prophet, bishop, or Relief Society president might have completely different gifts or a completely different style from that of his or her predecessor, yet they are equally called of God to their ministry. There is not just one correct way of serving the Lord or of magnifying a calling.

By extension, it follows that Church leaders who recognize the differences of God-given gifts and ways of using them among the individual Saints will also know how best to utilize these different individuals for the benefit of all.

16. Diversities of operations. Again, the Greek behind the parallel at 1 Corinthians 12:6 means the "differences in activities" or the "different kinds of things that go on." It is a gift of the Spirit to be able to see what is *really* going on around us, to recognize the operation or activity of an influence, movement, or trend, to know what is at work and whether it is of God. Blessed is the flock whose shepherd has this gift.

17–18. The word of wisdom . . . the word of knowledge. This word of wisdom is not related to what we usually call the

Word of Wisdom in the Church. For example, note that it is by "*the* word of wisdom" that "*a* Word of Wisdom" is later given to the Church in Doctrine and Covenants 89. The gift of the Spirit called the word of wisdom is the gift of possessing wisdom, particularly in thinking, speaking, and counseling. Wisdom is knowledge or data *plus* judgment, understanding, or common sense. Knowledge in its narrowest sense is merely accumulated facts or information, and the word of knowledge is the ability to possess and convey information. But the word of wisdom is knowing how to interpret or apply information correctly and with sound judgment for the benefit of oneself and others.

19–20. Faith to be healed/to heal. Oddly, faith to heal and faith to be healed are different gifts of the Spirit. Since healing is based on the power of faith, either the one blessed or the one giving the blessing, or both, must possess sufficient faith for a healing to take place. In the case of healing and being healed, the one gift supplements the other. In the case of healing by priesthood blessing, the power of the priesthood may magnify the faith of those involved in the blessing, but it is still faith that is the indispensable element and the operative principle, both in healing and in being healed.

23. The discerning of spirits. The Greek words behind this phrase in 1 Corinthians 12:10 mean "the ability to judge between spirits." In other words, this gift of the Spirit is the ability to tell whether a spirit is of God or not. The Prophet Joseph Smith once said that "nothing is a greater injury to the children of men than to be under the influence of a false spirit when they think they have the Spirit of God."[12] The gift of discernment of spirits protects those who enjoy it.

Note, however, that a "spirit" does not necessarily refer to a single supernatural being in the usual sense, but may also refer to more general or subtle forces at work in the Church. Thus the phrase "a spirit of rebellion" may not refer to a single evil spirit, but to a general influence upon, or a tendency manifested by, or a feeling detected in many Saints at once. This general influence of evil may also be referred to in the singular as a "spirit," though there may be many agents—both spiritual and temporal—involved. The gift of discernment allows its possessors to analyze also these more general forces at work in a family, ward, or branch, and to know whether they are or are not from God. Additional information on the discernment of spirits is given in Doctrine and Covenants 50:30–33; 129:4–8.

24–25. To speak with tongues/interpretation of tongues. The Holy Ghost is a testator and a revelator, and the gifts of the Spirit are designed to reveal and to testify, to *communicate* the mind or the powers of God to men. In the biblical world, the words for *tongue* and *language* were the same. The gift of tongues is therefore the gift of languages. This gift is designed to reveal and communicate, in this case to reveal and communicate through the Spirit where the barriers of language might otherwise hinder the work. Where the tongues of men are involved, the model of how the gift works can be found in Acts 2:4–11, where the disciples spoke in their own language, but the crowd that had gathered heard each in his own language. When the Spirit causes an individual to speak in a tongue unknown to himself or his hearers, whether it be a human language or the language of the angels, the gift of interpretation is also granted if the utterance is genuine, so that communication and revelation may take place (see 1 Corinthians 14, esp. vv. 27–28). In these cases, the valid exercise of the one gift may also require the presence of the other.

From the beginning, the gift of tongues has been one most counterfeited by false spirits. Those who are preoccupied with this gift are often spiritually out of balance or just plain deceived. Joseph Smith counseled: "Be not so curious about tongues, do not speak in tongues except there be an interpreter present; the ultimate design of tongues is to speak to foreigners, and if persons are very anxious to display their intelligence, let them speak to such in their own tongues. The gifts of God are all useful in their place, but when they are applied to that which God does not intend, they prove an injury, a snare and a curse instead of a blessing."[13]

27. And unto the bishop of the church. To those who are appointed to preside over the Church are given the keys of discernment to know by the Spirit the source of all spiritual manifestations within their stewardship. These may then declare with authority that a manifestation is or is not of God.

28. He that asketh in Spirit shall receive in Spirit. It is not inappropriate for the members of the Church to seek to possess the gifts of the Spirit, but these gifts are usually given in proportion to our service and, therefore, to our need. According to verse 29, the head of the Church possesses all the gifts of the Spirit. If we will get the Spirit of God and, *prompted by the Spirit,* ask God for additional spiritual gifts, the object of our prayers will be granted.

31. All things must be done in the name of Christ. As fallen and sinful beings, we cannot expect to command the powers of heaven in our own unworthy names. Christ alone in his perfect and infinite righteousness is worthy of the great blessings and powers of heaven. Therefore, when we act, pray, or speak in the name of Jesus, we acknowledge that we do so as those who have become one with him, and that we are his servants exercising his rights and powers with his permission. Since Christ is the only perfectly sinless, righteous, and worthy being, it is *his name* only that can command the powers of heaven, but he allows those who are his to "take his name upon them" and to use its power in his service.

---

1. 1:163.
2. *Early Latter-day Saint History,* 51.
3. See Background to D&C 41–43, 50; *History of the Church,* 1:146–47, 154; Whitmer, *Early Latter-day Saint History,* 36, 42–43, 62.
4. In Conference Report, Oct. 1929, 14–15.
5. See Commentary on D&C 32:4.
6. See Pratt, *Autobiography of Parley P. Pratt,* 48.

---

7. Boyd K. Packer, in Conference Report, Oct. 1989, 17.

8. See Smith, *Teachings*, 246.

9. Emphasis added.

10. See Commentary on D&C 76:117–18.

11. See Commentary on D&C 76:35.

12. *Teachings*, 205.

13. *History of the Church*, 5:31–32.

47

BACKGROUND

O n the same day that Joseph Smith received Doctrine and Covenants 46, he also received a revelation directed to John Whitmer now numbered as Doctrine and Covenants 47. Since the time of Adam and Eve, the Saints of the Lord have been instructed to keep records of both their spiritual and temporal affairs, their divine revelations, and their history. In our own time this commandment is found in Doctrine and Covenants 21:1 and elsewhere. Adam, Enoch, Abraham, Moses, Nephi, Mormon, Matthew, Mark, Luke, and John, among many, many others, have obeyed this commandment to record their sacred and secular activities, to the benefit of millions who came after them.

From the beginning of the restored Church, records have also been important. Martin Harris, Emma Smith, Oliver Cowdery, David Whitmer, Sidney Rigdon, and John Whitmer all served as scribes or secretaries for the Prophet in recording revelations, translations, historical data, or other information, but there seems to have been some difficulty in keeping a permanent recorder. On 8 March 1831, the day after receiving Doctrine and Covenants 45 and the same day Doctrine and Covenants 46 was received—not even a year after the organization of the Church—the Lord instructed Joseph to call John Whitmer as Church historian. Though Oliver Cowdery had already served in this capacity part-time, John Whitmer is generally credited with being the first full-time and permanent Church historian of the Restoration.

John Whitmer had actually been invited to accept this position some time earlier, but being reluctant, he asked Joseph to inquire whether it was the will of the Lord. "I was appointed by the voice of the Elders to keep the Church Record. Joseph Smith Jr. said unto me you must also keep the Church history. I would rather not do it but observed that the will of the Lord be done, and if he desires it, I desire that he would manifest it through Joseph the Seer. And thus came the word of the Lord."[1] On 9 April 1831, John was sustained in his twin callings as both Church historian and Church recorder by a special meeting of elders in Kirtland.[2]

John Whitmer's reluctance to accept this calling may explain the meager results of his labors. He began his duties by his own account on 12 June 1831 and served in this capacity, though not always with exemplary diligence, until his excommunication on 10 March 1838. In those seven years he produced only a hundred pages of text, four of which have since been torn out and lost.[3] At the time John Whitmer left the Church, he took the historical records that were in his possession with him, and they eventually became the property of the Reorganized Church of Jesus Christ of Latter Day Saints. From that source several editions of his work have been published. Doctrine and Covenants 69:2–8 also gave John additional instructions on his duties as Church historian.

COMMENTARY

1. My servant John. This revelation is directed to John Whitmer, one of the Eight Witnesses of the Book of Mormon. He had aided Joseph as a scribe in Fayette, New York, during the summer of 1829, when the Book of Mormon was being translated and also later during the Prophet's work of the Joseph Smith Translation.

1. A regular history. The historical records kept up to this time had been rather irregularly attended to. It was time for the Church to have a permanent historian (see v. 3). John Whitmer's duties were not confined to keeping the records or writing a history, however, for he is here called to transcribe anything that may come to Joseph. Certainly, the continuing need for John's service as a scribe is attested by the timing of this calling. It was received on the same day that Joseph and Sidney began work on the Joseph Smith Translation New Testament (see D&C 45:60–61). John transcribed much of the manuscript of the Joseph Smith Translation and was also a scribe for the project at times.

3. The church record and history. Besides being the Church historian, John Whitmer was also to serve as the Church recorder and keep what we would call today membership and statistical records.

3. Oliver Cowdery I have appointed to another office. This likely refers to Oliver's calling as "second elder of this church" (D&C 20:3) and as leader of the Lamanite mission (see D&C 28:8; 30:5–6), where Oliver was still serving at the time this revelation was received.

---

1. *Early Latter-day Saint History,* 56.
2. See Cannon and Cook, *Far West Record,* 5.
3. See *Early Latter-day Saint History,* 22.

48

BACKGROUND

It was now early to mid March 1831, and the Prophet Joseph had been in Kirtland, Ohio, less than two months. Beginning in the latter part of March and during April and May, hundreds of New York Saints and others from the East arrived in the Kirtland area, obedient to the commandment and promise of the Lord given to them in Doctrine and Covenants 37:3; 38:32, 37; 39:15 (see also D&C 45:64). These "eastern brethren," having sold their own homes for the gospel's sake, often at a considerable loss, would need places to live and would be expecting at least some help from Joseph and the Kirtland Saints.

The law of consecration and stewardship had not yet been implemented in Kirtland, however, mostly because there were not sufficient properties in the Kirtland area to provide for even the local Saints, let alone for the many who would shortly be gathering to Ohio from the East.[1] The question was how to provide for the newcomers.

Also, at this time no one knew where Zion was going to be built, but because Ohio was designated as a "gathering place," many Saints expected Zion to be established there. The Saints did not know if they should plan on staying in Ohio permanently or plan on moving again soon. Should the incoming Saints buy homes and farms in the Kirtland area, or should they rent them?

Should the Church invest its limited funds in Ohio to purchase inheritances for incoming Saints or conserve its money to build Zion somewhere else? Such questions prompted the Prophet to ask the Lord concerning what was to be done: "Upon inquiry how the brethren should act in regard to purchasing lands to settle upon, and where they should finally make a permanent location, I received the following"[2]—Doctrine and Covenants 48.

COMMENTARY

1. For the present time. This phrase, used three times in the first three verses, clearly implies that the stay in Ohio would not be permanent. Yet in Doctrine and Covenants 51:17 the Lord advised the Saints to act as though they would be in Ohio for years (and many were), and in Doctrine and Covenants 64:21 they were told to maintain a strong presence in Kirtland for at least five more years,—until the Kirtland Temple could be dedicated.

2. Impart to the eastern brethren. The Kirtland Saints were commanded to consecrate what property they possessed to the needs of the New York Saints who would soon be arriving. Many in Ohio obeyed this commandment for the benefit of incoming Saints who had already given up their own homes and lands to gather to Kirtland. Joseph and Emma themselves lived in shared or borrowed lodgings for much of their time in Kirtland.

3. Inasmuch as ye have not lands. After the consecrated Ohio properties were all given out as stewardships, those New York Saints who were still arriving had to find accommodations in the area as best they could and at their own expense.

4. Save all the money that ye can. Because Ohio was *not* finally to be Zion, however, the Church could not expend its precious cash resources unwisely by buying up property there. The financial resources of the Church were to be conserved as much as possible, and added to when possible, for the building of Zion in a not-yet-revealed location.

4. Land for an inheritance, even the city. The inheritance mentioned here is an individual portion in Zion, and the city is the New Jerusalem to be built in the land of Zion. Our portion in Zion is called an inheritance because the faithful children of Israel receive it by right of lineage as the children of Abraham, to whom God promised a holy land for his children to inherit along with the other blessings promised to their fathers in the Abrahamic covenant (see D&C 27:10; Abraham 2:6). "The children of Abraham" is a phrase that includes not only his righteous literal posterity but also those righteous Gentiles who have faith in Christ and become Abraham's children by adoption (see Galatians 3:7–9, 14).

Our portion in Zion might also be called an inheritance because Jesus Christ has begotten those who believe in him to become his sons and daughters (see Mosiah 5:7; 27:25; Alma 7:14; Ether 3:14). Through the death of Jesus, we, as his "born again" children, become joint-heirs with him and inherit all that the Father has promised him (see Romans 8:14–17; Hebrews 9:15–17). Our portion in the earthly Zion is a symbol and token of our portion in the coming celestial world, the ultimate "promised land."

5. The place is not yet to be revealed. No one knew at this time exactly where Zion would be built, but that information would be given after the "eastern brethren" had gathered to Ohio. Three months after Doctrine and Covenants 48 was given, and after the majority of the New York Saints had arrived, the Lord revealed to the Church in Doctrine and Covenants 52:2–3 that Missouri was the land consecrated to the Saints. He did not specify, however, that Zion would be built in Independence, Missouri, in Jackson County, until an additional month after that (see D&C 57:1–5).

5. Certain men appointed. This phrase refers to an advance party of Saints that would be sent ahead to scout the area, make the necessary arrangements, purchase the land, and lay the foundations of the New Jerusalem in order to prepare Zion for the gathering of the Saints. This commandment was obeyed, and the prophecy that the place would be revealed to these men was fulfilled three or four months later when Doctrine and Covenants 52 and 57, respectively, were received.

6. Purchase the lands. The Lord had already revealed in Doctrine and Covenants 45:65 how the land of Zion was to be acquired: it was to be purchased. The Saints would not find the lands they sought unoccupied, nor would Joseph lead the Church to take them by conquest as Joshua had done in obtaining the lands of the Canaanites. The Lord expected the Church generally and the Saints individually to purchase the lands that would be pointed out to them.

6. To be gathered with your families. The basic unit of Zion, or the Church and kingdom of God upon the earth, is the family.

6. The presidency and the bishop of the church. The First Presidency holds the keys of gathering and instructs the Saints as to who should gather where, when, and how. The bishop's duty is to apportion to each man and his family their inheritance in Zion once they arrive there (see D&C 42:30–35; 57:15; 90:30).

6. And which ye shall hereafter receive. For the Saints then, as now, the revelations of God are never finished. What we know *now* must always be understood as somewhat tentative, pending further light and knowledge the Lord might reveal on any given subject. For this reason a true systematic theology of the Latter-day Saints can never be written, for the complete "system" will never be fully revealed, at least not in this world. The Saints know that God can at any time "reveal many great and important things pertaining to the Kingdom of God" (Articles of Faith 1:9), and such new revelations could change our understanding of previous revelations. Thus, the Saints must both be obedient to what has already been received and yet remain flexible and open to the possibility of new insights or a new perspective received from additional revelation.

---

1. See Backman and Perkins, "United under the Laws of the Celestial Kingdom," 173–75.
2. *History of the Church,* 1:166.

49

BACKGROUND

In early March of 1831, perhaps as early as 7 March, fifty-year-old Leman Copley went from his farm in Thompson, Ohio, about sixteen miles northeast of Kirtland, to see the Prophet Joseph Smith. Leman had recently been baptized, but he was afraid to accept ordination to preach and wanted to know the will of the Lord on the matter. He also wanted missionaries to be sent to the members of his former church, for whom he still had great affection and respect.

Leman Copley had been a member of the United Society of Believers in Christ's Second Appearing, or the Millennial Church, more commonly known as Shaking Quakers or just Shakers. These people acquired the latter nicknames because they dressed like the Quakers, among whom they had their origins, and because of their habit of physically trembling and shaking in religious meetings. They also practiced a kind of ecstatic group dancing that could become quite frenzied and often led to shaking, twirling, shouting, and singing in tongues.

The Shakers had begun in England in the mid-eighteenth century, in some degree of proximity with the Quaker movement. By 1774, a woman named Ann Lee (married name Ann Stanley) had assumed leadership of the Shakers. Because of her great piety and her great suffering—especially in childbearing, since all four of her children died as infants, and also on account of her sufferings as a wife, because her husband eventually deserted her—many around her began to believe that Ann Lee was the Messiah whose return they were awaiting. They believed that the Messiah's first appearance was in the form of Jesus Christ and the second appearance was in the form of Ann Lee. The little group of Shakers moved to America to avoid persecution in England.

In the United States Ann Lee's movement adopted a communal form of living, with group ownership of possessions. The religion grew fairly rapidly, until by 1831 there were about eighteen Shaker communities in the U.S., all known and respected for their piety, order, and industry. "Mother Ann," as Ann Lee was known, taught that sex was the root of most evil; although Shakers did not formally forbid marriage, they believed that celibacy was the way of the Lord and would lead the faithful to a higher reward in the afterlife than would be received by those who were married. Shakers were pacifists; they looked on wealth or luxury as sins and they denied the doctrines of the trinity, vicarious atonement, and resurrection of the flesh. They also believed that the need for physical ordinances such as baptism had ceased with the ancient apostles, that the Millennium had begun with the ministry of Ann Lee, and that sickness and disease were sins. After Mother Lee's death some Shaker leaders also taught that their followers should avoid meats, especially pork.[1]

Leman Copley had once been a Shaker but, according to Shaker historical records, could not manage to live the celibate life.[2] He had moved away from the Shakers but still admired their doctrines and was anxious to have missionaries sent back to their community, about fifteen miles west of Kirtland at North Union, Ohio—now known as Shaker Heights in Cleveland.

Of the setting for Doctrine and Covenants 49, Joseph Smith wrote: "At about this time came Leman Copley, one of the sect called Shaking Quakers, and embraced the fulness of the everlasting Gospel, apparently honest-hearted, but still retaining the idea that the Shakers were right in some particulars of their faith.

In order to have more perfect understanding on the subject, I inquired of the Lord, and received the following"[3]—Doctrine and Covenants 49. John Whitmer added, "Leman Copley one of the disciples, who was formerly a shaker quaker, he was anxious that some of the elders should go to his former brethren and preach the gospel. He also feared to be ordained to preach himself, and desired that the Lord should direct in this and all matters."[4] Leman Copley subsequently accompanied Sidney Rigdon and Parley P. Pratt on a mission to the Shakers.

The mission to convert the Shakers in March 1831 proved largely unsuccessful.[5] The congregation of Shakers formally rejected the message sent to them in Doctrine and Covenants 49. Also, Leman Copley's testimony was shaken, and his loyalties returned to the Shakers once again. By June he had broken his promise given in March to allow the recently arrived New York Saints to settle on his land, and with the help of Shaker leader Ashbel Kitchell, he had the Saints evicted from his land.[6] His betrayal forced these Saints to abandon the improvements they had made to Copley's farm and move on to Missouri immediately. For this Copley was disfellowshipped, but he was back in full fellowship again by October 1832. In 1834, however, Leman bore a false testimony against Joseph Smith in a lawsuit the Prophet had filed against Philastus Hurlburt, and for this Leman Copley was excommunicated. On 1 April 1836, he apologized to the Prophet for his false testimony and was accepted back into the Church.[7] Leman Copley never gathered with the Saints in Missouri, Illinois, or Utah. He died in Ohio in 1860 and is buried in Thompson, Ohio.[8]

COMMENTARY

1. Sidney, and Parley, and Leman. Sidney Rigdon, Parley P. Pratt, and Leman Copley were commanded by the Lord to preach to Leman's former fellows in the Shaker community at North Union, Ohio.

2. They are not right before me. The missionaries were going to the Shakers to teach them and to call them to repentance. Though the Shakers have become thoroughly romanticized in modern thought, there was something distinctly "not right" about their beliefs and practices at the time of Joseph Smith. The Shaker rejection of the sacred nature of marriage, sexuality, and the family would alone account for the Lord's statement here. John Whitmer recorded later that the Shakers had been "bound up in tradition and priestcraft, and thus they are led away with foolish and vain imaginations."[9]

4. Leman shall be ordained. Leman Copley had been concerned about being ordained to the priesthood, which the Lord here commands to be done. Leman himself, in company with others, was then commanded to take the gospel to the Shakers.

4. Not according to that which he has received of them. There is always a tendency to preach to those of another faith by trying to persuade them from their own point of view that the restored gospel must be true. Such an approach avoids asking investigators to give up or change any of their original beliefs, and avoids any sense of confrontation between the old and the new. This is not how the Lord wanted this mission to be undertaken. The Shakers were to be confronted with the simple truth. The missionaries were to read the message of Doctrine and Covenants 49 and command the Shakers to repent. They would teach the doctrines of the Restoration, the Book of Mormon, and the divine calling of Joseph Smith without embarrassment or apology.

4. Otherwise he shall not prosper. The Lord asked a lot of Leman Copley. He still had a very high regard for the Shakers and for their religion, but he had to choose. He could teach the restored gospel with the courage of his testimony to his former friends, or he could lose his conviction of the truth and come under condemnation. Unfortunately, Leman temporarily lost his convictions, which caused difficulties among the Saints back in Thompson (see D&C 56).

5. Mine Only Begotten Son. Remember that it is Jesus Christ who speaks in the Doctrine and Covenants, though here as elsewhere he spoke the words of the Father, whom Christ represents as though he were the Father. Christ is in all things the agent and word of his Father.

5. Saved . . . damned. There is no salvation in this life or the next except by receiving Jesus Christ. Those who receive Christ in this life, or who would have if given the opportunity, will avoid damnation in hell, meaning the spirit world, between death and resurrection. Those who reject the gospel in mortality but receive Christ in the spirit world will receive some degree of glory and avoid ultimate damnation to hell, or outer darkness, in eternity.

6. Even as they listed. To *list* is to "desire." This sentence means that "they did to me whatever they desired."

6. Till he descends on the earth. See Doctrine and Covenants 45:48–57.[10]

6. Which time is nigh at hand. This contradicts the Shaker teaching that Christ had already come to earth a second time in the form of Ann Lee.

7. But the hour and the day no man knoweth. See Matthew 24:36; Mark 13:32. Despite all the energy and ingenuity of many Christians, both LDS and non-LDS, it still remains that *no one* on earth will know when the Son of Man is coming until it happens.[11]

8. All are under sin. As long as we remain in mortality we shall all be prone to sin and will come short of the perfection of God. From God's perspective every one of us is sinful, having at least one weakness (see Romans 3:9–10, 23). While we remain in mortality, our only hope of perfection is the perfection "in Christ" promised by the Lord's servant Moroni (Moroni 10:32–33; see also D&C 76:69).

8. Holy men that ye know not of. There are men who have been made "perfect in Christ" (Moroni 10:32–33), who have been taken by God for his own purposes and whose carnal natures have been erased or otherwise overcome. Perhaps these are trans-lated beings, about whom we know nothing, who have been given missions and assignments upon the earth or elsewhere.

9. Mine everlasting covenant. Because of the imperfection of human beings, God has revealed again the new and everlasting covenant of the gospel (see D&C 66:2) to the earth, so that our sins may be forgiven through the atonement of Christ and through our individual faithfulness.

10: That which I have promised I have so fulfilled. The promises made to the fathers—Abraham,[12] Isaac,[13] and Jacob,[14] as well as to Lehi, Nephi, Moroni, and so on—about the fulness of the gospel coming once again to their posterity have been fulfilled in the Restoration. The Gentile nations will either repent and bow before Jesus Christ, and thus become the seed of Abraham by adoption, or they will not repent and will be laid in the dust by the power of God.

11. This people. This phrase refers to the Shakers.

11. Peter. Peter is mentioned in this verse because the response in verses 11–14 was essentially Peter's message to the Jews on the day of Pentecost as recorded in Acts 2:38. Moreover, Peter's clear teaching in this New Testament passage corrected a major doctrinal error of the Shakers—baptism *is* necessary to sal-vation.

12–28. These verses are addressed directly to the Shakers by the Lord and correct many of their false doctrines.

13. Repent and be baptized. Because the Shakers did not believe in the necessity of baptism—they believed that one could live without sin—this verse was obviously meant to correct that view. The "holy commandment" mentioned here likely refers to Peter's great charge to the Jews found in Acts 2:38 to "Repent, and be baptized."

15. Whoso forbiddeth to marry. See Genesis 2:24; 1 Timothy 4:3; Hebrews 13:4. This corrected another major doc-trinal error of the Shakers. While the Shakers technically did not *forbid* marriage, the social pressure against it was enough to drive people like Leman Copley out of their communities if they could not be celibate. Because marriage, sexuality, and family are important parts of God's eternal plan and of the new and everlasting covenant, Satan will always try to destroy them or turn men's minds away from their proper uses. Throughout the history of Christianity, one may detect the workings of the adversary in those branches of the historic Christian church that forbade marriage or, like the Shakers, insisted that a higher reward awaits in heaven for the celibate. Few things so directly contradict the plan of God as do the practice of celibacy, divorce, abortion, abuse of spouse or children, or anything else that denies the sacred and eternal character of marriage and family.

16. One wife. The primary intent of the reference to one *wife* here (compare 1 Timothy 3:2, 12; Titus 1:6) was likely to establish for the Shakers that marriage is endorsed by God and is part of his plan for human beings. Some of our own people are also in need of reminding that God requires of each man "*one* wife." That is, there will be no excuses for neglecting the commandment to marry.

16. Earth might answer the end of its creation. The earth was created to be a home and testing ground for billions of mortal beings. Without marriage and procreation upon the earth to create future generations of mortals, the purpose (or end) for which the earth was created, to provide a mortal experience for all of the Father's spirit children, would be thwarted.

17. The measure of man, according to his creation before the world was made. This is the first scripture in the Doctrine and Covenants to deal with the topic of premortal existence. The "measure of man" is the number of human beings created to live upon the earth, and this number is fixed.[15] The earth was created to be filled with the measure or number of spirit children who were begotten with the intent that they should live here. And when were these spirits created? "Before the world was made." A certain number of spirits will be born into mortality during the Millennium when the earth is in its terrestrial or paradisaical state, but these persons will also be part of the "measure of man," the number of those designated to experience their mortality upon this earth.

18. Forbiddeth to abstain from meats. The exact wording here is somewhat difficult, but the meaning is clear: anyone who forbids the use of meat is not of God (compare 1 Timothy 4:3). This corrected yet another common doctrinal error among the Shakers.

19. Ordained for the use of man. Contrary to some current thinking in the world around us, animals are *meant,* "ordained," to be used by human beings for food, for leather, for fur, and so forth. These are purposes they were created for. There is no sin in killing animals for human use; the sin is in *wasting* what is killed (see v. 21). Humans do have an obligation to justify the death of an animal by using it for the benefit of humanity, which is the purpose of its creation, whether for food, clothing, or income—to "have in abundance." Abraham, the friend of God and father of the faithful, was, after all, a shepherd, and Peter was a commercial fisherman. They made their living from the use of animals (see also D&C 59:16–21, which includes pleasing the eye, gladdening the heart, and enlivening the soul as valid uses of animals and animal products).

20. It is not given. It was never intended or ordained by God that one human being should have more of the earth's bounty than another. The celestial law is equality through consecration and stewardship. Division into rich and poor upon the earth is the design and work of Satan. This unnatural division destroys the rich by the pride of their riches and by breeding the feeling that they are superior to the poor and deserve better treatment simply because they are rich. It also destroys the poor with the trials of grinding poverty, starvation, exposure, disease, and by breeding the feeling that the poor are inferior simply because they are poor. One reason why "the world lieth in sin"—that is, the whole world is to be blamed before God—is that we generally prefer and sustain Babylon's economic systems based on competition motivated by self-interest rather than Zion's economic system based on cooperation motivated by compassion.

21. That sheddeth blood or that wasteth flesh. The shed blood and the wasted flesh envisioned here is the flesh and blood of animals. The key interpretive phrase comes at the end of the verse: "and hath no need." It is all right to shed the blood of animals where there is need; that is the purpose for which they were created (see v. 19; D&C 89:12–13). It wasn't the Latter-day Saints but the Shakers who avoided eating meat. The Lord here corrected their view by revealing that he expects humans to use animals as long as they have a need—whether for food, clothing, or income (see v. 19). The sin is to kill without a proper use for what is killed or a righteous purpose for killing it.

22. In the form of a woman. Shakers believed that God was both male and female and was therefore adequately represented by both male and female forms, that Christ had already come as a male in the meridian of time, and that "she" therefore had returned at the second coming in the female form of "Mother Ann" Lee. Once again, this verse corrected the Shaker belief. The Lord added that the Son of Man would not come disguised as *any* mortal living on the earth, male or female. He will come as the scriptures explicitly describe him as coming: "in the clouds of heaven" with power and great glory (Matthew 26:64).

23. Be not deceived. The Second Coming has not already occurred; the Millennium has not already started. When it does come, we will see all the scriptural signs and events as reviewed in the remainder of verse 23.

24. Before the great day of the Lord. The Lord here listed some of the many things that must yet happen before the day of his appearance.

24. Jacob shall flourish in the wilderness. This statement, given in 1831, was a remarkable prophecy that modern Israel, the LDS Church, would be driven into the wilderness, where they would prosper and grow. Of this verse Elder Bruce R. McConkie wrote: "The physical gathering here alluded to is the assembling of the Latter-day Saints in the tops of the mountains in western America. It is there that Zion shall flourish upon the hills and rejoice upon the mountains. The wilderness referred to is the then-uninhabited areas that were colonized by Brigham Young less than a score of years later."[16]

24. The Lamanites shall blossom as the rose. Part of the gathering of Israel in the latter days is the gathering of the Lamanites and their coming to a knowledge of their ancestral heritage and of the gospel. "And as to the day when the Lamanites shall blossom as the rose, it has scarcely commenced. They are not yet, except in a beginning degree, the pure and delightsome people of whom the scriptures speak."[17] *Before* the Savior comes again, the Lamanites will have claimed their rights as children of Israel, and as a people they will have blossomed as the rose.

25. Zion shall flourish. Before the second coming of Christ the Saints will have established a flourishing Zion upon the earth.

26–28. It is difficult to know where the message to the Shakers, which began in verse 12, ends. Are verses 26–28 addressed to the Shakers or to Sidney, Parley, and Leman? Notice that "shall not be confounded" (v. 27) is a phrase from the writings of Peter (see 1 Peter 2:6), in whose style the message to the Shakers was to be delivered (see D&C 49:11). Nevertheless, the command to "go forth as I have commanded you," in verse 26, makes it likely that at least these last three verses are directed to the missionaries.

27. I will go before you and be your rearward. God would be both their scout and their rear guard.

1. See Sperry, *Doctrine and Covenants Compendium,* 204–9; Ahlstrom, *Religious History of the American People,* 492–94.
2. See Flake, "Shaker View of a Mormon Mission," 96–97.
3. *History of the Church,* 1:167.
4. *Early Latter-day Saint History,* 59–60.
5. Refer to Commentary on D&C 81:1.
6. See Porter, "Colesville Branch in Kaw Township," 282–83.
7. See Smith, *History of the Church,* 2:433.

8. See also Cook, *Revelations of the Prophet Joseph Smith*, 67.

9. *Early Latter-day Saint History*, 61.

10. See also Commentary on D&C 45:48–57.

11. See Smith, *Teachings*, 341.

12. See Genesis 17:7–21; 22:16–18; Abraham 2:6–11.

13. See Genesis 26:3–5.

14. See Genesis 28:13–15.

15. See Talmage, *Articles of Faith*, 194; Smith, *Gospel Doctrine*, 94; Brigham Young, in *Journal of Discourses*, 8:352.

16. *Millennial Messiah*, 210–11.

17. McConkie, *Millennial Messiah*, 211.

DOCTRINE AND COVENANTS

50

BACKGROUND

In the short period of time between the departure from Kirtland of the missionaries to the Lamanites in November 1830 and the arrival of the Prophet Joseph Smith in February 1831, the Kirtland Saints had been left mostly to themselves. Their natural leaders, Sidney Rigdon and Edward Partridge, had gone to New York to see the Prophet and had stayed there. The Ohio Saints were new members of the Church, and they still carried with them some false beliefs from their previous religions. Consequently, Satan sought to take advantage of their inexperience and lack of strong local leadership by sending false influences among them. Thus, the leaders of the Church in Kirtland found it necessary to rebuke some of the influences at work there. These deceiving spirits and their activities have already been mentioned in connection with Doctrine and Covenants 42–43, 45–46.

Of the events surrounding the reception of Doctrine and Covenants 50, Joseph Smith wrote simply, "In May [1831], a number of Elders being present, and not understanding the different spirits abroad in the earth, I inquired and received from the Lord the following"[1]—Doctrine and Covenants 50.

Parley P. Pratt, one of the elders present on that occasion who had just returned from his mission to the Shakers (see D&C 49), added a fuller account: "As I went forth among the different branches, some very strange spiritual operations were manifested, which were disgusting, rather than edifying. Some persons would seem to swoon away, and make unseemly gestures, and be drawn or disfigured in their countenances. Others would fall into ecstacies, and be drawn into contortions, cramp, fits, etc. Others would seem to have visions and revelations, which were not edifying, and which were not congenial to the doctrine and spirit of the gospel. In short, a false and lying spirit seemed to be creeping into the Church.

"All these things were new and strange to me, and had originated in the Church during our absence [from Kirtland], and previous to the arrival of President Joseph Smith from New York.

"Feeling our weakness and inexperience, and lest we should err in judgment concerning these spiritual phenomena, myself, John Murdock, and several other Elders, went to Joseph Smith, and asked him to inquire of the Lord concerning these spirits or manifestations.

"After we had joined in prayer in his translating room, he dictated in our presence the following revelation"[2]—Doctrine and Covenants 50.

In June 1831, after most of the Church leaders had again left Kirtland to visit Missouri, Jared Carter, another elder who had been present when section 50 was received, wrote in his journal that a false spirit troubled the Churches in Ohio while the leading Brethren were away. Brother Carter was at first appalled at the number of seemingly knowledgeable Saints who blindly accepted as manifestations from God any "spiritual phenomena" that occurred. Carter's natural humility and the pressure of the majority opinion almost led him to accept these false influences himself, but he knew something was not right and finally asserted himself to apply the counsel given in Doctrine and Covenants 50, and the deceitful spirit was quickly unmasked and dealt with.[3]

According to the edition of *The Evening and the Morning Star* in which section 50 first appeared,[4] the exact date of this revelation was 9 May 1831.

COMMENTARY

1. The living God. This phrase refers to Jesus Christ (see D&C 14:9).

1. Words of wisdom. The phrase here has nothing specifically to do with Doctrine and Covenants 89, generally referred to as *the* Word of Wisdom, but is used as a general and proper designation for any counsel from the Lord.

2. False spirits. False spirits may influence the hearts and minds of the world indirectly by spreading false ideas, doctrines, and reasoning, or they may manifest themselves directly by masquerading as divine messengers or by assaulting and attempting to overcome and possess someone physically. All of these deceptions were occurring in Kirtland.

3. Satan. Satan can and does provide so-called "spiritual" experiences even to members of the Church, and the spiritually careless or undiscerning may be fooled into believing their experiences are of God when the source is actually Satan. Joseph Smith once observed that "nothing is a greater injury to the children of men than to be under the influence of a false spirit when they think they have the spirit of God."[5] It is clear that Satan was having some influence upon the Saints in Kirtland.

5. They who are faithful and endure. In this context, the reference is to those who are *not* deceived by spiritual manifestations into accepting doctrines or practices contrary to the teachings of the Church or in violation of their covenants.

6. Deceivers and hypocrites. Even at this time, May 1831, there were already among the Saints those who made spiritual claims that were not true, or who for temporal or even carnal reasons pretended to enjoy spiritual gifts they did not actually possess. The English word *hypocrite* comes from the Greek word *hypocrites* meaning an "actor" or "one who plays a role." It is simply an unpleasant fact of life that in the Church, in 1831 as well as now, there have been spiritual pretenders and spiritual deceivers, some of whom even manage to remain undetected in this life by the Saints or their leaders (see v. 8).

Consequently, it follows that no idea, doctrine, literature, or business proposition should be accepted simply because it is promoted by a member of the Church, for it is not Church membership or association that is the test of trustworthiness but habitual and observable compliance with the "truth and righteousness" of God (v. 9). Hypocrites and role-players in the Church can do great damage when their real character is revealed, to the disillusionment of weaker members who thought they represented the Church.

7. Such shall be reclaimed. The deceived or disillusioned shall be reclaimed, but not the deceivers, for the unrepentant hypocrites and pretenders will be cut off from Christ and his Church either in this life or the next (see v. 8).

9. Don't get carried away with religious hyperbole. We are not to pretend to have gifts or to have had experiences that we haven't really had. We are not to exaggerate, embellish, or be overly dramatic—as an actor or one playing a role might do. Our religion must be what we really believe, what we really feel, and what we really are—not a role we adopt for Church occasions.

10–12. Come, . . . and let us reason together. Compare Isaiah 1:18. The Lord offers to state his case in human terms using a sort of Socratic method of reasoning by question and answer, so that we humans can clearly see his points.

13. Unto what were ye ordained? For what purpose were you ordained? The answer, of course, is to teach the gospel by the power of the Holy Ghost, which testifies of the truth in the hearts of its hearers (see v. 14). Thus, we were ordained and we preach in order to provide the Holy Ghost an opportunity to testify. It follows, then, that if we preach or teach by some other method or under some other influence than the Holy Ghost, we have turned away from our ordained purpose.

15. Spirits which ye could not understand. The major role of the Holy Ghost is to reveal, teach, testify, enlighten, clarify, communicate, and so on. Thus, the genuine influence of the Holy Ghost brings with it knowledge and understanding. For the elders to accept in place of the Holy Ghost spirits or influences they could not understand and which brought no light, knowledge or comprehension, was a betrayal of their ordained purpose and mission. To turn from the enlightening influence of the Holy Ghost to the influence of other programs, agendas, methods, or spirits is foolish and disloyal.

17–21. If we are ordained to preach the truth by the witness of the Holy Ghost, then it follows that preaching anything else or preaching the gospel under any other influence or by any other method than by the Holy Ghost is contrary to the purpose of our ordination and is not of God. For example, a missionary might be successful in convincing an audience by scholarly argument and human reasoning of the importance of the Dead Sea Scrolls, but such a transaction might not be of God. When commissioned to speak for the Lord, teachers must speak as moved upon by the Holy Ghost, and the substance of their communication should be the precepts of the restored gospel.

23. Edify. *Edify* means "to build up." If a person, doctrine, spirit, or influence does not build us up, bless us, or somehow make us better, then it is darkness and should be shunned. What edifies, however, can often be difficult or painful. Edification does not usually mean taking the easy way out.

24. That which is of God is light. This is such a simple test! If an idea or influence brings anxiety, confusion, darkness, uncertainty, disillusionment, alienation, or loss of testimony, then it does not come from God, whose influence always enlightens, edifies, and testifies. Individuals may hurt themselves by stubbornly refusing to let go of a negative idea or influence that they genuinely believe to be "spiritual" without having discerned exactly *what* spirit may actually have been its source.

26. Appointed to be the greatest. Those who possess the fulness of the gospel, the gift of the Holy Ghost, and the ordination and charge to preach or preside are to be teachers and leaders over all who do not have these gifts and callings, no matter how young, unlearned, or unblessed they may be in all the other categories by which the world chooses teachers and leaders.

Teenaged missionaries with little or no wealth or education might be called even from undeveloped areas of the world to teach or preside over the rich, the learned, the famous, or the powerful anywhere on earth. Even so, those who preach and preside are to be servants in spiritual things for those they minister to, just as Jesus Christ who presides over all things came to be the servant of all (see Mark 10:42–45).

27. Possessor of all things . . . all things are subject unto him. Ordination to the Melchizedek Priesthood and a calling to preside in Zion qualify the righteous to draw upon all the powers of eternity in magnifying their calling. To a faithful priesthood leader in the righteous pursuit of his duty, even the spirits are subject. He may ask in righteousness for anything necessary to perform his calling, and receive it (see vv. 28–30).

28–29. Purified and cleansed from all sin. This phrase does not mean that all who exercise the priesthood must first become morally perfect. The only way anyone can become pure or clean is through faith, repentance, and baptism. Those who have entered into the gospel covenant in good faith and are keeping their covenants are "purified and cleansed from all sin" on an ongoing basis by the power of the atonement of Christ through the cleansing fire of the Holy Ghost (see 2 Nephi 31:17).[6]

The power to perform miracles and literally to move mountains requires a pure character. As we progress in our individual, personal righteousness through the power of the Atonement, we may eventually receive the blessing that God will grant our every wish and prayer (see vv. 29–30). This is the power to perform miracles in the name of the Lord, as did Moses and Joshua. This was the blessing of Nephi, for example, in the Book of Mormon (see Helaman 10:5). It was a blessing enjoyed by the Prophet Joseph Smith,[7] and it is a gift that is conditional upon personal purity and trustworthiness.

31. If you behold a spirit manifested. Because faithful

leaders may call upon all the powers of heaven, and because even the spirits are subject to them in the righteous pursuit of their duties, such leaders may ask the Lord to reveal the nature and purpose of any spirit who manifests itself within their steward-ship, and the Lord will cause them to receive it. If, however, knowledge and understanding are not forthcoming, if a leader receives "not that spirit," that is, if he still cannot understand it after praying about it, then he may know that the spirit or influ-ence in question is not from God (see v. 32).

32–34. Priesthood leaders have no real power of their own, only the power granted to them by God. Thus, they must not allow themselves to lose their proper humility in being merely the servants or instruments of God. Priesthood power is not magic, nor are priesthood holders like wizards who can use the power of God independently of God for their own purposes. Rather, priest-hood holders are faithful servants whom *God* uses for *his* pur-poses, and this knowledge brings with it a certain humility. A loss of perspective or of humility in this matter can lead to an individ-ual loss of priesthood power and consequently to being overcome by the evil that one seeks to rebuke.

35. Which ye shall hereafter receive. In Doctrine and Covenants 129 further information was given to the Saints about dealing with angels and spirits and the ordinances of the temple.

35. The kingdom is given you. What a wonderful situation the faithful Saints enjoy. On the one hand the Father gives them the kingdom, and on the other hand they are given power through Christ to overcome everything outside the kingdom. Truly the righteous and obedient possess all things! (see vv. 27–30).

37. Joseph Wakefield. Joseph Wakefield, from Watertown, New York, was apparently a convert in the New York period. In this verse he was called to be a companion to Parley P. Pratt in vis-iting the branches of the Saints "rebuking the wrong spirits" and "setting in order things that were wanting."[8] Joseph Wakefield was excommunicated in 1834. Among other things, he was offended that Joseph Smith once came out of his translating room in Kirtland and immediately began playing with children, a practice he thought incompatible with the dignity and high office of a prophet.[9]

38. John Corrill. Baptized four months earlier in January of 1831, John Corrill was also called on a mission. Like Joseph Wakefield, John was among the first group of men to be ordained to the office of high priest on 3 June 1831, a month following receipt of this revelation.[10] John Corrill became disaffected in Missouri and was excommunicated from the Church on 17 March 1839.

39. Edward Partridge. It seems that Bishop Partridge had attempted for some reason unknown to us to interfere with the missionary callings confirmed by the Lord in verses 37–38. His mistake may have been due to inexperience: he had been in the Church less than six months at the time. Here he was assured that he would be forgiven if he repented of his error.

40. Ye are little children. The Church had been organized at this time for only about thirteen months. All of the members, including Bishop Partridge, were yet immature in their under-standing of the gospel, but those who remained faithful would grow in grace and truth.

41. Fear not, little children, for you are mine. This term of endearment indicates to those Saints who honor their covenants, though they may be immature and childlike, that they may take heart in being *Christ's* children through the second birth of the gospel. Faithful Saints then and now should be comforted in knowing that they belong to Christ and that Christ has overcome all things. He will not lose any of them, and nothing can take them out of his hand (see v. 42). Further, if the Father and the Son are one, and the faithful Saints are one with the Son, then they are also one with the Father (see v. 43). There is nothing the faithful Saints need fear in this life or the next—so long as they remain faithful.

44. The good shepherd, and the stone of Israel. See

Genesis 49:24; Isaiah 8:14; 28:16; Psalm 118:22 in the Old Testament; Matthew 7:24; 21:42; John 10:11 in the New Testament; and Alma 5:38–39; 3 Nephi 11:39–40 in the Book of Mormon.

45. You shall hear my voice and see me. The obvious reference is to the last day, when the faithful will actually see and hear the Lord at his second coming (see John 14:16; D&C 88:3–6).

1. *History of the Church,* 1:170.
2. *Autobiography of Parley P. Pratt,* 48.
3. Journal of Jared Carter, in Harold B. Lee Library Special Collections, MSS SC 547, 4.
4. See Phelps, "Commandment, Given May 9, 1831," 1.
5. *History of the Church,* 4:573.
6. See Commentary on D&C 20:30.
7. See *Teachings,* 340.
8. Pratt, *Autobiography of Parley P. Pratt,* 51.
9. See Cook, *Revelations of the Prophet Joseph Smith,* 69, 134.
10. See Cannon and Cook, *Far West Record,* 6–7.

51

BACKGROUND

Doctrine and Covenants 51 was received in May 1831. Five months earlier the Saints in New York, Pennsylvania, and elsewhere had been commanded to gather in Ohio (see D&C 37:3). Around that same time they had also been promised that they would receive the law of the Lord in Ohio and would be endowed there with power from on high (see D&C 38:32). Since that time, the Lord had commanded that the Kirtland area should be heavily proselytized in order to provide the Church there with additional strength and resources for the incoming Saints (see D&C 44:3–4). The Lord also directed the Kirtland Saints to prepare to share their own lands with the newcomers as far as possible (se D&C 48:2–3).

In May of 1831, as the obedient eastern Saints actually began to arrive in Ohio, it became necessary to organize and to provide for them. This responsibility fell mainly on Edward Partridge, at that time the Church's only bishop. At the request of Bishop Partridge, Joseph Smith traveled to Thompson, Ohio, about sixteen miles east of Kirtland, where most of the Colesville, New York, branch had gathered. This branch consisted largely of the extended family of Joseph Knight Sr., including Joseph's son, Newel, and their friends and acquaintances. The Colesville Saints had been particularly persecuted in New York and had given up much to gather to Ohio, and Joseph Smith and Bishop Partridge were anxious to know how to provide for them. On a large farm in Thompson, which Leman Copley had offered to share with his fellow Saints (see D&C 49), Bishop Partridge received Doctrine and Covenants 51 through the Prophet Joseph Smith. The probable date of this revelation is May 1831.

Section 51 applies that part of the law of the Lord generally referred to as the law of consecration (see D&C 42:30–39) to the specific circumstances of the Saints between 1831 and 1833, first in the Kirtland area—that is, at Thompson, Ohio—and later in Missouri. As originally received, Doctrine and Covenants 51 directed the Saints to legally deed over all their property and possessions to the bishop as agent for the Church. Stewardships would then be appointed back to them, but legal title to their stewardship remained with the bishop. Should a steward over consecrated property leave the Church, he could therefore take nothing of his original property with him. This was all in accordance with the law of the Lord given earlier (see D&C 42:30–32).

In March 1833, however, a Missouri court held that irrevocably deeding all of one's property to the Church was not a practice that should be allowed, since it conflicted with the court's views of fairness and its understanding of the intent of British common law. The Missouri court ordered that property formerly consecrated to the Church be returned to its original owner, in this specific case an apostate member named Bates. Since the intent of section 51 was that all aspects of consecration should be strictly legal, Joseph revised the wording of the revelation to accommodate the court's decision by deleting the verse between the present verses 2–3 that instructed Edward Partridge to retain legal title to consecrated properties. Joseph also added verse 5, which clarifies that stewardships are the private property of their stewards.[2]

While the specific forms of consecration observed in Ohio and Missouri are no longer practiced today, the law of consecration itself has never been rescinded. The obligations of consecration laid upon the Church by the law of the Lord (see

D&C 42:30–39) are still binding and are observed today largely by the payment of tithes and offerings, by accepting Church callings, by sacrificing the time and other resources sometimes necessary to magnify those callings, and by covenanting to make whatever further temporal sacrifices the Lord may ask of us.

COMMENTARY

1. How to organize this people. As the only bishop in the Church, the responsibility for the organization and temporal welfare of the incoming Saints fell to Edward Partridge.

2. According to my laws. Zion can be created only upon the principles of heaven. Barely three months before this revelation was given, on 9 February 1831, the Lord had given the Church his law, including the law of consecration (see D&C 42:30–39). Doctrine and Covenants 51 taught Bishop Partridge and the Saints how to apply the law of consecration to their circumstances in Ohio.

Technically, the united order, also called the united firm, was a specific business partnership of between nine and twelve Church leaders in Ohio who covenanted to hold property and assets as an "order" and to conduct their business according to the principles of consecration. This order was created by revelation in Doctrine and Covenants 78 and was discontinued in Doctrine and Covenants 104, after about two years. This "united order" was a different system of consecration from that practiced in Missouri or any practiced later in Utah. Although the terms "law of consecration" and "united order" have historically been used interchangeably, technically they have two different meanings. The law of consecration is the general phrase for that system of which the united order was but one specific example.

It should also be noted that the law of consecration has been applied to Saints differently in many different times and circumstances, and that while the principles of consecration will always remain the same, we should not assume this law will be applied to a future Zion in the exact form described here.[3]

3. Every man equal. Equality here does not refer to equality of *result*, so that everyone receives exactly the same stewardship. Rather, the equality here is an equality of *process*, so that everyone receives their stewardship upon common principles. The criteria to be considered in assigning stewardships are specified here as family, circumstances, wants, and needs. Thus, one family might have a larger home than another if they had more children, or another family might have a customized van if someone in the family were disabled. One family might have skis and golf clubs in its closet and another might have basketballs and fishing rods. Some stewards might farm; others might teach school or manufacture computer chips. The principles of consecration will not force us all to be identical, but will treat each of us with equal consideration for our particular families, circumstances, wants, and needs. Note particularly the generous consideration given to personal preferences, or "wants," in establishing these stewardships (see D&C 82:17).

4–5. Give unto him a writing . . . deeded unto him. Under the form of consecration directed in the present wording of Doctrine and Covenants 51, persons entering into this covenant were still to donate all they possessed to the Church for the care of the poor and the needy, but they then received back by written deed that portion of their property or possessions that the bishop designated as their stewardship. After 1833 individual stewardships remained personal, with private property legally owned by the stewards themselves.

Under this system, if a steward lost his membership in the Church, his assigned stewardship remained his own private property. When an individual left the Church, he was free to take his private stewardship with him. Any additional assets, however, which an excommunicated member may once have consecrated to the bishop and which had not been deeded back to him, constituted a gift to the poor and the needy. These remained with the Church and could never be reclaimed.

7. This people. This phrase refers to the members of the Church who had entered the covenant of consecration. Assets consecrated to the bishop were to be used for the welfare of Church members who were themselves living the law of consecration.

7. Appointed unto. That is, provided for the use of.

8. An agent. The agent, of course, could be Bishop Partridge or someone appointed by and answerable to him.

9. Be alike . . . receive alike. The Saints have no rich or poor among them (see Moses 7:18). To truly become one, the Saints must be willing to share their temporal blessings freely with other Saints. The personal need to be rich, to have more than one's brothers and sisters, is incompatible with the establishment of Zion.

10. Another church. This phrase refers to another *branch* of the Church, such as the Church in Missouri as opposed to the Church in Thompson. Contemporary terms might be other stakes, districts, or missions. At this time, apparently, the Lord wished the different areas of the Church to remain financially separate from each other, and the consecration of properties within the different units were to be handled separately.

13. A storehouse. Consecrated resources beyond what was needed to provide stewardships or to support the poor and needy were to be deposited with the bishop, who would then administer those resources as needed in the future. As diligent stewards produced more than they needed for their own support, these surpluses were also conveyed to the bishops' storehouse. Though bishops' storehouses may have changed configuration in different times and places, they continue to operate in the Church today on the same general principles as stated in sections 42 and 51.

14. He shall be employed. In most cases, those who are asked to serve the Church full time also have a right to temporal support through the resources of the Church (compare D&C

31:5; Luke 10:7). In Kirtland, Bishop Partridge was to be employed full time in managing the consecrations of the Saints and administering those resources to the poor and the needy. These duties made it difficult for him to pursue his trade as a hatmaker at his home in Painesville, Ohio. In consideration of his circumstances, the bishop was allowed appropriate compensation from the storehouse.

16. This land. For the Saints generally, "this land" referred to the area around Kirtland, Ohio, but for the Colesville Saints, to whom Doctrine and Covenants 51 was specifically given, it referred to the Leman Copley farm in Thompson.

16. For a little season. The Lord informed the Saints that for them Kirtland was just a stopover. In fact, the "little season" for the Colesville Saints lasted only about six weeks. Leman Copley, who had offered to share his farm with the incoming Saints, withdrew his offer when Bishop Partridge began organizing things according to the law of consecration as directed in this revelation (see D&C 54). On 3 July, at the Lord's direction, the Colesville Saints left Thompson, Ohio, for Jackson County, Missouri (see D&C 54:8).

17. As for years. Though Kirtland was home to the Ohio branch of the Church for years (see D&C 64:21–22), it was only a brief stop for the Colesville Saints. Yet no place is so "temporary" that it allows us a time-out from living the principles of the gospel. Wherever we find ourselves, we must be Saints. The same labors of love, diligence, industry, and service, the same spiritual obligations to build Zion as best we can, are required of us in short-term habitations as in permanent ones. Thus, students and others who are just "passing through" some unit of the Church are expected to make the same investments of time, money, service, and emotional support to their "temporary" wards and stakes as to those in which they expect to live permanently.

18. This shall be an example. Bishop Partridge received a clear indication that the Lord would be implementing the law of consecration in other places besides the Kirtland area. When he did, it would be according to the pattern given in Doctrine and Covenants 51. Edward Partridge was called to Missouri less than one month later (see D&C 52:3, 24).

19. The joy of his Lord. See Matthew 24:45; 25:21. The joy described here is possibly both objective and subjective. That is, those who are judged worthy to enter into the presence of the Lord not only feel his joy at their return, but also receive for themselves the kind of celestial joy he has.

1. See Commentary on D&C 68:13.
2. A good review of the historical development of the law of consecration and the United Firm may be found in Cook, *Joseph Smith and the Law of Consecration,* 5–39.
3. See Commentary on D&C 42:30.

DOCTRINE AND COVENANTS

5 2

BACKGROUND

By June 1831, most of the eastern Saints had arrived in the Kirtland area, and many had, for the moment at least, been settled on land belonging to Leman Copley in Thompson, Ohio. In obedience to the command of the Lord given the preceding February (see D&C 44:1), the Church then held its fourth conference, a priesthood conference, in Kirtland on 3–6 June.

Brief minutes of this conference were taken by John Whitmer, and his minutes tell us that forty-four elders attended. It was also at this conference, the first held in Ohio, that Joseph Smith ordained five brethren to the "high priesthood." They were the first ordained high priests in the restored Church. Then Lyman Wight, one of the high priests ordained by Joseph, was instructed to ordain Joseph Smith and seventeen other men to the high priesthood also.[1]

It should be remembered that Peter, James, and John had bestowed apostolic authority upon Joseph Smith and Oliver Cowdery in 1829—including the authority to ordain high priests—and it was by this apostolic authority and by his office as first elder in the Church that Joseph ordained Lyman Wight and the others as high priests. Lyman was instructed to ordain Joseph to the office of high priest *within the Church*, which had not been done by Peter, James, and John, because the Church had not yet been restored when they ordained Joseph in 1829. It must be noted that in this ordination, Lyman Wight did not bestow upon Joseph Smith any priesthood authority that Joseph didn't already hold. This same pattern of "double" ordination was also followed on 6 April 1830, when the Church was organized. On that date Joseph Smith and Oliver Cowdery ordained each other as elders in the Church, even though they already held apostolic authority from Peter, James, and John. As particular priesthood offices were created in the Church, it was necessary even for Joseph Smith to be installed therein according to the revealed pattern. Though Joseph had been an apostle of the Lord Jesus Christ since May of 1829, he became first an elder and then a high priest in the Church only as those offices came into existence, and he did it in the revealed manner.

The Prophet Joseph Smith wrote that during this conference "the Lord displayed His power to the most perfect satisfaction of the Saints. The man of sin was revealed, and the authority of the Melchizedek Priesthood [the office of high priest] was manifested and conferred for the first time upon several of the Elders. It was clearly evident that the Lord gave us power in proportion to the work to be done, and strength according to the race set before us, and grace and help as our needs required. . . . Faith was strengthened; and humility, so necessary for the blessing of God to follow prayer, characterized the Saints.

"The next day, as a kind continuation of this great work of the last days, I received the following"[2]—Doctrine and Covenants 52.

It appears that the date recorded for this revelation in the heading of the Doctrine and Covenants, 7 June 1831, is incorrect. As Joseph indicated in *History of the Church*,[3] this revelation was given the day after the conference closed. Since it was a three-day conference, beginning on Friday, 3 June, and ending on Sunday, 5 June, the revelation had to have been received on Monday, 6 June—a date supported by contemporary accounts.[4]

COMMENTARY

2, 5. Missouri, . . . the land of your inheritance. The Lord directed that the next conference of the Church was to be held in Missouri, which was identified as the land to be consecrated as an inheritance to the Saints. The exact location of Zion, however, was not yet revealed.

3. Joseph Smith, Jun., and Sidney Rigdon . . . to leave their homes. This was a special hardship for Joseph and his wife Emma. Emma had arrived in Kirtland six months pregnant. The Smiths had first boarded with the Whitneys, and had been in their own quarters on the Morley farm less than three months. Barely a month before this call was received, Emma had given birth to twins who both died within a few hours—her second and third babies to die at birth. Soon afterward the Smiths had adopted the Murdock twins, and now Joseph was called to leave Emma in Kirtland to the care of friends and travel to Missouri for the sake of Zion. The sacrifices required by the Lord in these early days were no less difficult for Joseph and Emma than they were for the other Saints.

7–33. Twenty-eight elders besides Joseph and Sidney were issued calls to travel as missionaries to Missouri by different routes, preaching the gospel as they went. Excellent biographical summaries for these and all other individuals mentioned in the Doctrine and Covenants may be found in Dean Jessee's *Papers of Joseph Smith.*[5]

9. Saying none other things. The missionaries to Missouri were reminded not to teach the learning of men or their own ideas but to say only those things taught in the scriptures or revealed to them by the Holy Ghost.

10. Let them go two by two. This is one modern scriptural base for the practice in the Church of sending out missionaries in pairs.

11. Cut my work short in righteousness. The Lord will make "short work" of the world when he moves suddenly and in total righteousness to end it and to establish his millennial kingdom of righteousness. Missionaries, like these called to Missouri, are sent out to warn and prepare the world for the sudden and righteous judgments of God that are soon to come.

14–19. A pattern . . . for Satan is abroad. It is not enough that one pray, or even that one pray with a contrite spirit; neither is it enough merely to preach the true gospel to be counted the Lord's representative. Since deceivers, hypocrites, imposters, and the influence of Satan are part of this world even in the Church (see D&C 50:7–8), alongside genuinely godly individuals and influences, the Lord explained one way to distinguish who or what is of God from who or what is not of God (see vv. 15–19).

To be "of God," one must obey his ordinances and bear the fruits of that obedience. On the other hand, those who are overcome by the world, who do not obey his ordinances or bear the fruits of righteousness, are not of him, even if they were properly called at one time. Those who genuinely represent God obey him. Influences or spirits genuinely of God motivate humans to obey him. This is the pattern by which the godly or satanic character of all people and of all influences may be surely discerned.

Moreover, this pattern may be applied in two ways: it was the manner in which the missionaries to Missouri could judge the people and influences they encountered on their way, but it is also the way in which true missionaries may be discerned from those who are hypocrites or imposters giving only lip service to their callings.

15. Obey mine ordinances. Ordinances here may refer both to priesthood ordinances specifically and to God's commandments generally.[6]

20. And the days have come. This expression refers to the last days prophesied of in the scriptures, when the fulness of the gospel would be preached and when it would be done unto men as unto the centurion anciently (see Matthew 8:13), according to their faith.

22. Ezra Thayre. This commandment for Ezra Thayre to travel to Missouri as a companion to Thomas B. Marsh was revoked less than two weeks later (see D&C 56:5) due to Ezra's lack of preparation. He was called again seven months later (see D&C 75:31).

22. Unto this same land. That is, to Missouri.

32. Newel Knight and Selah J. Griffin. The commandment given these two brethren was also changed through no fault on their part (see D&C 56:6–7).

33. Unto one place, in their several courses. All the missionaries called or sent to Missouri were to travel to the same destination but by different routes in order to preach to as many different people as possible on the way.

37. Heman Basset. One of the Kirtland Saints involved in "the family" before the arrival of Joseph Smith,[7] Heman was one of those most caught up in the false spiritual manifestations discussed in Doctrine and Covenants 46, 49–50. He had left the Church by May 1831, a month before this revelation was received. "That which was bestowed upon" him was the office of an elder in the Church and a call to preach the gospel in the Kirtland area.

37. Simonds Ryder. Simonds Ryder also became dissatisfied with the Church and apostatized before the end of 1831. He later reported that in a letter from Joseph and Sidney Rigdon calling him to preach, and in his license to preach, his last name had been spelled with an *i* instead of a *y*, thus indicating to Simonds that Joseph was not an inspired prophet of God because he could not spell Simonds's name correctly.

39. The residue of the elders. Verses 39–40 were directed to those elders who were not called to Missouri but were to remain in Ohio and build up the Church there.

39. Let them labor with their own hands. This phrase is a reminder that the law of consecration as practiced in Kirtland was not going to mean a free ride for anyone but was an opportunity and an obligation to work as faithful stewards for the benefit of all. Those who were more interested in what they could get from the labor of others than they were in what they could contribute to the building of Zion valued material possessions above their covenant obligations and therefore could be accused of "idolatry" as well as wickedness. Practicing even the true religion for purposes of financial benefit rather than to serve and worship God is a form of idolatry—worshiping the blessings more than the Lord who gives them.

40. The poor and the needy. Caring for the poor and the needy is part of the law of the gospel (see D&C 104:18) and is a nonnegotiable requirement of the Saints or of a celestial individual.

41. A recommend. The Lord had commanded that those moving from branch to branch carry a recommend (see D&C 20:64, 84), a written document certifying the holder's worthiness and good standing in the Church. Even the leaders of the Church were required to observe the policy (see also D&C 72:17–19). In our own time this requirement is observed by forwarding individual membership records from one Church unit to another. Also, with modern means of communication, a bishop can contact a new member's previous bishop for confirmation of good standing even before receiving printed membership records.

42. The land of your enemies. This phrase is a clear foreshadowing of the difficulties to come. When the Saints began to gather in Jackson County, Missouri, the local non-LDS inhabitants quickly became antagonistic. Perhaps the language here also suggests the typology or symbolism of the Exodus. Just as the land promised to the children of Israel was already held by hostile Canaanites, so Missouri was already in the hands of "Gentiles" who either were or would soon be antagonistic to the Church.

43. The city. The city of New Jerusalem, the latter-day Zion.[8]

44. Lift them up. See Commentary on Doctrine and Covenants 17:8.

---

1. See Cannon and Cook, *Far West Record,* 6–8.
2. *History of the Church,* 1:175–77.
3. See above citation.
4. See Cook, *Revelations of the Prophet Joseph Smith,* 71.

5. See also Black, *Who's Who in the Doctrine and Covenants.*

6. See Commentary on D&C 1:15.

7. See Background to D&C 41.

8. See Commentary on D&C 42:9.

53

BACKGROUND

Algernon Sidney Gilbert was one of the original converts of the missionaries to the Lamanites (see D&C 28:8; 30:5; 32:1–3) during their stay in Kirtland, Ohio, during the late fall of 1830. Sidney, then just short of his forty-first birthday, was a partner to Newel K. Whitney in N. K. Whitney & Co., a successful general merchandise store in Kirtland.

Since Sidney Gilbert had not been given any calling or assignment by the Lord during the conference of June 1831 (see D&C 52), he approached Joseph Smith after the close of the conference and asked what the Lord would have him do. Joseph wrote that Doctrine and Covenants 53 was received in answer to Sidney's inquiry.[1] According to the *Far West Record*,[2] Sidney Gilbert was ordained an elder by Joseph Smith on 6 June 1831, along with W. W. Phelps (see D&C 55) and others. Doctrine and Covenants 53 and 55 must therefore be dated together on or before 6 June 1831.

In obedience to his call, Sidney Gilbert departed for Missouri with the Prophet Joseph and others on 19 June, less than two weeks later. There he served as an agent for the Church in buying land and opening another small store (see D&C 57:6–8), to be named Gilbert and Whitney, which also served as a bishops' storehouse. "He was devoted and faithful and sacrificed all of his goods during the persecutions in Missouri. He lacked confidence in his ability to preach, however, and, according to some reports, he said he 'would rather die than go forth to preach the Gospel to the Gentiles' (*History of the Church,* 2:118). Ironically, he later contracted cholera and died [29 June 1834]. Heber C. Kimball recorded in his journal that 'the Lord took him at his word.' Elder B. H. Roberts wrote of Brother Gilbert, 'The remarks in the body of the history, and this expression from Elder Kimball's journal are liable to create a misunderstanding concerning Brother Algernon Sidney Gilbert, *than whom the Lord has had few more devoted servants in this dispensation*' (*History of the Church,* 2:118n)."[3]

COMMENTARY

1. Your calling and election. This is the only occurrence of the phrase "calling and election" in the Doctrine and Covenants. Here it refers to Brother Gilbert's *church* calling—what the Lord called and chose him to do.

2. You shall forsake the world. To forsake the world is to abandon it and its secular concerns and values. For Sidney Gilbert this meant leaving his business in Kirtland to attend to the Lord's business in Missouri. Sidney was to become an elder, preach the gospel, and labor as an agent for the Church and as an assistant to Bishop Partridge.

3. Take upon you mine ordination. Sidney Gilbert was ordained an elder on 6 June 1831, indicating that the date of this section is on or before 6 June.

3. Remission of sins. The phrase is evidently used here as a synonym for baptism.

4. An agent unto this church. Sidney Gilbert's assignment as an agent unto the Church included his becoming a real estate buyer in Missouri to acquire land for stewardships and for Church buildings.

4. Appointed by the bishop. Since Bishop Partridge had just been called to Missouri (see D&C 52:24), it was clear that if Sidney Gilbert was to assist the bishop and work under his direction he must go to Missouri with him.

6. First ordinances which you shall receive. If ordinances are understood here to mean commandments, as seems likely,[5] then this reference was to further instructions that Sidney Gilbert would receive pertaining to his duty as agent for the Church.

7. He only is saved who endureth unto the end. To endure to the end is to remain faithful to one's covenants until death—as did A. Sidney Gilbert. No amount of righteous living early in their lives will save those who abandon their commitments to God later on. To receive all our promised blessings, we must still be faithful and obedient at the end of our lives. One cannot "retire" from gospel covenants, nor can any amount of youthful righteousness justify disobedience as we grow older. Time and circumstance may reduce our abilities, but they must not reduce our commitment.

1. See *History of the Church,* 1:179–80.
2. See Cannon and Cook, 9.
3. *Doctrine and Covenants Student Manual,* 113; emphasis added.
4. See Commentary on D&C 68:12.
5. See Commentary on D&C 1:15.

54

BACKGROUND

Leman Copley[1] owned 759 acres of land in Thompson, Ohio. When Leman joined the Church, he agreed at first to share his land in Thompson with the Saints who were arriving from the East. The agreement apparently was that Leman would consecrate half of his farm and sell the other half to the Church at fair terms.[2] When Leman returned, however, from the Shaker mission that he himself had enthusiastically proposed but which was unsuccessful, he appeared to have been somewhat "shaken" himself, and he began to wonder if his former church was not right after all and the restored Church wrong.

To make matters worse, when Leman returned to Thompson many of the members there, people who were living on his land through his generosity, blamed him for deceiving them with the hope of converting the Shakers and would not "own him for one of them."[3]

When Bishop Edward Partridge began to divide up Leman's farm on the principles of consecration (see D&C 42, 51) according to the earlier agreement, Leman, who had not yet legally conveyed his property to the Church, withdrew his offer. In the bitter exchanges that followed, Leman ordered the Colesville Saints off his land. He also charged them rent for the time they had lived there, despite the fact that they had planted his fields, built fences, and made other major improvements to the property.[4]

These events put the Colesville Branch in a difficult spot. Therefore, as Joseph Smith recorded, "They sent in Newel Knight and other Elders, to ask me to inquire of the Lord for them; which I did, and received the following"[5]—Doctrine and Covenants 54. While the date recorded for Doctrine and Covenants 54, June 1831, is correct, there is some evidence that it may have been received after Doctrine and Covenants 55, which is also dated in June 1831. Sections 53 and 55 both deal with ordinances that were performed on 6 June, and therefore these revelations must be dated on or before that date. Doctrine and Covenants 52 was also received on 6 June, while Doctrine and Covenants 54 refers to events after that date; for example, the change in Newel Knight's call mentioned in Doctrine and Covenants 54:2. Thus, Doctrine and Covenants 52 was received on 6 June 1831. Sections 53 and 55 were also likely received together on 6 June, but section 54 was received after 6 June and is presently out of chronological order.[6]

COMMENTARY

2. Newel Knight. Newel Knight was called as a missionary to Missouri a few days before this revelation was received (see D&C 52:32). In view of the difficulties that had developed with the Colesville Branch, there was a question of whether or not Newel should go on his mission or remain with the branch. The Lord's answer would be yes to *both* options. Newel Knight would still go to Missouri, but as president and leader of the branch at Thompson (see D&C 56:7), which would also go there.

2. Stand fast in the office. Newel Knight's office was that of presiding elder in the Thompson, Ohio, branch, which in turn was made up almost entirely of the Saints from Colesville, New York. His commandment to stand fast in this office would seem to imply a release from the command in Doctrine and Covenants 52:32 that Newel travel to Missouri with Selah Griffin, though that command was not explicitly revoked until a little later (see D&C 56:6–7).

3. Let them repent. The members of the branch at Thompson had been narrow and unkind to Leman Copley in reaction to the failure of the Shaker mission. Some had also shown selfishness rather than humility or gratitude over the prospects of receiving stewardships from the Copley farm in Thompson. Their own attitudes and behavior—for example, their short-sighted treatment of Leman Copley—had contributed in some degree to the loss of the Thompson properties and made them as homeless persons extremely vulnerable to the enemies of the Church in Ohio.

4. The covenant which they made unto me. These words are addressed not just to Leman Copley but to the entire Thompson branch, some of whom shared blame with Leman for the failure of this attempt at consecration.

5. Him by whom this offense cometh. While there was apparently enough preliminary blame to go around, the actual breach of the covenant was effected by Leman Copley, who took back his consecration.

5. Better . . . that he had been drowned. The fate of the faithful who may drown or die any other way, for that matter, is preferable to the fate of the unfaithful who may live long lives and die in their beds (compare Matthew 18:6–7).

7–8. Go to now and flee . . . unto the land of Missouri. The branch at Thompson, made up mainly of people from Colesville, New York, was commanded, with very little notice, to leave Ohio and move on to Missouri. About sixty faithful members obeyed this commandment, leaving Ohio on 3 July and arriving in Independence, Missouri, on 25 July. The Colesville Saints stuck together in Ohio and throughout their lives in the Church, partially through family ties and other natural bonds of affection but perhaps also in obedience to those verses of the law of the Lord that instructed the New York Saints "to be together as much as can be."

7. Appoint whom you will. Not surprisingly, Newel Knight was chosen to lead the members of the Thompson branch to Missouri.

9. Seek ye a living like unto men. Though the Colesville Saints had already entered into the covenant of consecration in Ohio, because of their circumstances the Lord instructed them to earn their living in Missouri as best they could by normal secular means until another inheritance could be prepared for them. This was an exception to the rule, for normally only those Saints who agreed to live by the law of consecration in Missouri were supposed to emigrate there from the East.

10. Find rest to their souls. See Commentary on Doctrine and Covenants 15:6.

1. See Background to D&C 49.
2. See Cook, *Joseph Smith and the Law of Consecration,* 15.
3. Flake, "Shaker View of a Mormon Mission," 98.
4. See Perkins, "Ministry to the Shakers," 211–24.
5. *History of the Church,* 1:180.
6. See also Cook, *Revelations of the Prophet Joseph Smith,* 71.

DOCTRINE AND COVENANTS

55

BACKGROUND

Sometime during or slightly before the end of the conference on 6 June 1831, a nonmember named William Wines Phelps arrived in Kirtland with his family from Canandaigua, New York, and presented himself to the Prophet Joseph "to do the will of the Lord."[1] W. W. Phelps had earlier purchased a copy of the Book of Mormon from Parley P. Pratt and had in the meantime become convinced of the truth of the Restoration. Before moving to Kirtland, William Phelps had been a newspaper editor and publisher. When Joseph inquired the will of the Lord concerning Brother Phelps, he received the answer now recorded as Doctrine and Covenants 55.

W. W. Phelps brought great talent to the early Saints. His experience as a writer, editor, and publisher qualified him for the call issued here and helped him in his subsequent calling as publisher of the Church's first newspaper, *The Evening and the Morning Star,* in Missouri. Brother Phelps also wrote the lyrics to many favorite LDS hymns, including "Gently Raise the Sacred Strain," "Praise to the Man," and "The Spirit of God."

According to the *Far West Record,*[2] W. W. Phelps (see D&C 55:2) and A. Sidney Gilbert (see D&C 53:3) were ordained elders by Joseph Smith on 6 June 1831, together with several others. It follows that sections 53 and 55, which accompanied those ordinations, ought to be dated together sometime on or before 6 June. Since Doctrine and Covenants 54 deals with events that probably took place *after* 6 June, it is likely that Doctrine and Covenants 55 is out of its correct chronological order, belonging properly with section 53 and prior to section 54.

COMMENTARY

1. William. William Wines Phelps.

1. With an eye single. See Commentary on Doctrine and Covenants 4:5.

2. Thou shalt be ordained. The *Far West Record* recorded that W. W. Phelps was ordained an elder by Joseph Smith Jr. on 6 June 1831.[3]

4. To assist my servant Oliver. Oliver Cowdery, the second elder of the Church (see D&C 20:3), had remained in Missouri since arriving there six months earlier as head of the Lamanite mission. As the second elder, Oliver was also the effective head of the Church in Missouri, and W. W. Phelps was called to assist Oliver there by doing the work of writing, editing, and publishing. William's calling was so important to the Church, however, that a short time later the Lord instructed Oliver to assist William (see D&C 57:13)—to make sure he had the resources necessary to complete his calling.

4. To do the work of printing. As a former newspaperman and publisher, W. W. Phelps was uniquely qualified to set up and oversee the Church's printing endeavors. A Zion people would need books: textbooks for their schools, scriptures for the members, pamphlets and tracts for their missionaries, and newspapers to communicate the news of the Church and the teachings of its leaders. Brother Phelps arranged for the Church's first printing press to be set up in Independence, Missouri, and published *The Evening and the Morning Star* there between June 1832 and July 1833. He was in the process of publishing the Book of

Commandments when interrupted by a mob that destroyed the press in July 1833.

4. Books for schools. Zion people are educated people, and very early in the organization of the Church, the Lord informed the Saints of his desire that education be a high priority. W. W. Phelps was largely unsuccessful in completing this part of his calling, however. A year later, in June 1832, Brother Phelps wrote in the first edition of *The Evening and the Morning Star,* "Those appointed to select and prepare books for the use of schools, will attend to that subject, as soon as more weighty matters are finished."[4]

5. Take your journey. Having just arrived in Kirtland, and not yet even a member of the Church, W. W. Phelps was called to continue on to Missouri as a missionary with the Prophet Joseph and his party. Joseph Smith, Sidney Rigdon, William Phelps, and others left Kirtland about two weeks later, on 19 June 1831.

6. Joseph Coe. Joseph Coe had recently been baptized and ordained. He made the trip to Missouri as commanded and returned to Kirtland. He served in various callings there, worked to build the Kirtland Temple, and participated in the laying of its cornerstone. Joseph helped in the securing of the Egyptian mummies and their papyri in 1835. He became dissatisfied with the Church in 1837, however, and was excommunicated in December 1838. When the Church moved on to Missouri and Illinois, Joseph Coe remained behind in Kirtland.[5]

6. The residue. The rest of the Lord's instructions would be made known later (compare with D&C 57:16).

---

1. Cook, *Revelations of the Prophet Joseph Smith,* 86–88.
2. See Cannon and Cook, 9.
3. See Cannon and Cook, 9.
4. "Common Schools," 6.
5. See Cook, *Revelations of the Prophet Joseph Smith,* 86–87.

56

BACKGROUND

When Frederick G. Williams joined the Church and went to Missouri with the missionaries to the Lamanites in November 1830, seven months before Doctrine and Covenants 56 was received, he left both his family and his 144-acre farm behind in Kirtland. The following spring, sometime before May 1831, the Williams family, the Prophet's father, Joseph Smith Sr., and Ezra Thayre, one of the incoming New York Saints (see D&C 33:1), had reached some kind of agreement concerning the use of the Williams farm. By the time Ezra Thayre received his mission call to Missouri in June (see D&C 52:22), at least these three families, and maybe more, had been sharing the Williams farm and its facilities for some weeks.

In May 1831 Joseph Smith Jr. received a revelation concerning the Williams farm and the families living there.[1] This revelation was not included in the Doctrine and Covenants, but it does give some background to sections 54 and 56. According to this revelation, Joseph Smith Sr. was to manage the Williams farm and all three families were to live there together until the Church could build another house for the Thayres on the same property. Also, a share of the property was to be deeded in stewardship to Frederick G. Williams—who still legally owned it all but had left it at the disposal of the Church when he went to Missouri.

Ezra Thayre was one of the New York Saints who went to Kirtland with a fair amount of cash, presumably from selling his New York property. It appears that he had agreed to consecrate his holdings to the Lord and had received in return a promised interest in the Williams farm. But when Ezra was called to Missouri, he wanted to secure his financial interest in Kirtland by receiving some kind of consideration: either by getting his money back or by receiving legal title to a portion of the Williams farm (see vv. 9–10). Essentially, Thayre wanted to *own* his stewardship at a time when this was not the practice of the Church.[2] Though called as a missionary to Missouri, Ezra would not go until his personal interests were secured. His stubbornness in the matter made it necessary for another companion to be provided for Thomas B. Marsh, who was ready to go as commanded. Four months later, on 10 October 1831, a conference of elders in Kirtland rebuked Ezra for his pride and stubbornness, but no other action was taken against him at that time.[3]

It is possible to assign Ezra Thayre too much blame for the failure of the Saints in Ohio to live the law of consecration. He was clearly reluctant to go to Missouri with his financial interests unsecured, but he did *not* put the Saints off his land, as did Leman Copley, nor did he cease to associate with the Church. There is no evidence that Ezra Thayre, who lived in Kirtland, was in any way involved in the troubles at Thompson, Ohio, between Leman Copley and the Colesville Saints (see D&C 54). Further, Ezra Thayre must have repented of his errors, whatever they were, for another call as a missionary to Missouri was made to him seven months later on 25 January 1832. Ezra accepted that mission call and fulfilled two other missions for the Church after that. Later in Kirtland, he participated in the School of the Prophets and served as a land buyer for the Church. He was a member of Zion's Camp in 1834, and though briefly disfellowshipped in 1835, he moved to Missouri with the Saints in 1838 and fled with them to Illinois the following year. He was a prominent Church member in Nauvoo and a member of the council of fifty there. After the death of Joseph Smith, however, Ezra Thayre did not support the leadership of Brigham Young, but stayed in the East, eventually joining the Reorganized Church.

Joseph Smith recorded the events leading to section 56 as follows: "Elder Thomas B. Marsh came to inquire what he should do; as Elder Ezra Thayre, his yoke-fellow in the ministry, could not get ready to start on his mission as soon as he (Marsh) would; and I inquired of the Lord, and received the following"[4]—Doctrine and Covenants 56.

COMMENTARY

1. Who profess my name. Talk is easy; commitment is more difficult. "Not every one that saith unto me, Lord, Lord, shall enter into the kingdom of heaven; but he that doeth the will of my Father which is in heaven" (Matthew 7:21). Those who merely profess Jesus' name while rejecting the obligations of taking his name (for example, D&C 20:77) will not receive the blessings of ordinances performed "in his name"—including baptism, confirmation, and sealing.

1. The day of visitation and of wrath. The judgments associated with the second coming of Christ.

2. Take up his cross and follow me. This phrase is an injunction to make whatever sacrifice is necessary to obey the Lord, just as the Lord made every sacrifice necessary to obey his Father. According to the Joseph Smith Translation, "For a man to take up his cross, is to deny himself all ungodliness, and every worldly lust, and keep my commandments" (Joseph Smith Translation–Matthew 16:26).

2. Shall not be saved. *Saved* is used here to mean "inherit the celestial kingdom." It should be noted, however, that in other scriptures, *saved* is sometimes used to mean inheriting any degree of glory (for example, D&C 76:42–44). It is one thing to be saved from hell—Satan's portion of the spirit world—when one dies and to enjoy paradise instead; it is another thing to suffer the domin-ion of Satan after death and to finally be "saved" from him only at the last resurrection. The righteous are saved from Satan and from hell in both senses; the wicked are saved only in the latter sense (see D&C 76:44). Only sons of perdition are not saved in either sense (see D&C 76:37).

3. Cut off. Temporally, this is being excommunicated; spiri-tually, it is being cut off from the Lord's presence.

4. I, the Lord, command and revoke. Commandments, even commandments dealing with the future, are not prophecies; they are not even implied prophecies. The Lord sometimes gives com-mandments he knows will not be obeyed, because we must be allowed to exercise our agency, both individually and collectively as a Church. "Thou shalt" or "thou shalt not" are not statements of future facts, but commandments whose blessings are condi-tioned upon our obedience (see D&C 58:30–33). Whenever the disobedience of some renders the obedience of others impossible or impractical, God is prepared with alternate instructions to reach his intended goals (see D&C 124:49–50).

5. Thomas B. Marsh. Thomas Marsh and Ezra Thayre were called to be companions on a mission to Missouri (see D&C 52:22). Obediently, Thomas was ready to go by mid-June. Disobediently, Ezra was not.

5. Selah J. Griffin. Since Newel Knight was also about to have his instructions changed (see v. 7), his intended companion, Selah J. Griffin, would be available as a substitute companion for Thomas Marsh. Thomas and Selah left together and on time.

7. Remain with them. The difficult circumstances of the Saints at Thompson, who had been evicted from Leman Copley's farm and had nowhere to go, made it necessary that Newel Knight stay with them and lead them to Missouri instead of traveling as a missionary with Selah Griffin.

8. Selfishness. It seems Brother Thayre put concern for his own financial future above the success of the Missouri mission, above his obligation under the covenant of consecration, and above obedience to the direct commandment of God.

8. The former commandment. This phrase refers perhaps to Doctrine and Covenants 51:3–15, but more likely to private instructions given to Ezra Thayre that have not been preserved.

9. No divisions made upon the land. That is, no subdividing of the Williams farm where Ezra Thayre was living in Kirtland. Ezra had proposed dividing up the farm as a way of satisfying everyone's needs and interests.

9. He shall be appointed still. Apparently, Ezra Thayre did repent, because the land was not divided, he was not paid back and excommunicated (see v. 10), and he was again called to Missouri seven months later, on 25 January 1832.

10. Otherwise he shall receive the money. Ezra Thayre could not have legal title to part of the Williams farm. If he insisted, he could have his money back and lose his membership in the Church at the same time.

12. Joseph Smith, Jun., must needs pay. If Ezra demanded his money back and Joseph had to pay him out of Church funds, then the expense "would be repaid to him by the Lord, in order that those persons who made the contributions to him (Joseph) may have their money refunded proportionately in the form of land in Missouri."[5] Those who consecrated their resources to the Lord in Kirtland would receive land for inheritances in Missouri.

14. Saith the Lord unto my people. This commandment was to all the Saints, but perhaps particularly to those in Ohio who were struggling with pride and with obeying the revealed principles of consecration.

14. You seek to counsel in your own ways. They sought to explain to God why *he* must do things the way *they* think he should. Seeking to correct God—to lead, guide, counsel, advise, or instruct him—continues to be a major stumbling block for some people in the Church today. Many who disagree with the Lord's commandments seek to explain why his ways are wrong while their own ways are correct.

15. Your hearts are not satisfied. In other words, you don't think you have enough.

15. Ye obey not the truth. Note that truth is not something primarily to be *believed*, but something to be *done*. Merely believing the truth has no saving force, but obeying or doing the truth does (see Romans 2:8; Galatians 3:1; 5:7; James 2:19; 1 Peter 1:22; 1 John 1:6).

15. Pleasure in unrighteousness. Note that pleasure in itself is not evil but that taking pleasure in unrighteousness is.

16. Rich men. This phrase refers to those who would get less back temporally from living the law of consecration than they would put in. The sin is not in being rich; the sin is in being unwilling to live the law of consecration and to give up the pleasure of having more than your fellow Saints. No matter what else such members may do, no matter what their other strengths and accomplishments in the Church may be, no matter what positions they have held, if they are unwilling to stop being rich so that their brothers and sisters can stop being poor, then they can neither establish Zion nor inherit the celestial kingdom.

17. Poor men. This phrase refers to those who would get more back temporally from living the law of consecration than they would put in. Those poor who receive increased assets through the law of consecration must do it with a spirit of humility and gratitude rather than with a "welfare rights" mentality, demanding the assets of working people. Greed is a sin that plagues both the rich and the poor! Just as the unredeemed and greedy rich often despise the poor and withhold from them what is necessary to live, so the unredeemed and greedy poor often hate the rich and lust after their wealth. Those poor who seek to live the law of consecration out of greed or out of the desire to avoid working for a living can neither establish Zion nor inherit the celestial kingdom.

18. The poor who are pure in heart. They will enjoy the temporal blessings of the earth whenever Zion is truly established, whether by the Saints in this dispensation or by the Lord at his coming.

18. The fatness of the earth. *Fatness* in this context means abundance, having more than is needed. The poor who are pure and contrite in heart will have all they need, all they can use, of the bounties of this earth—and more besides. When the law of consecration is implemented to its fullest extent by a Zion people, all those who live under it will have enough and to spare—not just of their needs, but of their wants as well (see D&C 51:3; 82:17).

19. The Lord shall come. The One who will finally come in power and glory to right every wrong, who will remove both iniquities and inequities from the Church and from the earth, and who shall justly adjudicate the proper inheritances of all the Saints, is the Lord Jesus Christ himself and none other (see D&C 85:7).

20. Forever and ever. This earth will become the celestial kingdom for all those who have lived upon it and are worthy of that degree of glory. Thus, an inheritance upon the earth "forever and ever" is an eternal inheritance in the celestial kingdom of God. Taken literally, the imagery indicates that the real estate of the glorified earth will be divided up among the Saints "according to that which they do" (v. 13).

1. See Smith, *Kirtland Revelation Book,* 91–92.
2. See Background to D&C 51.
3. See Cannon and Cook, *Far West Record,* 15–16.
4. *History of the Church,* 1:186.
5. Sperry, *Doctrine and Covenants Compendium,* 229.

57

BACKGROUND

When Joseph Smith left for Missouri according to the commandment received in Doctrine and Covenants 52, he had been living in Kirtland for a little less than five months. He and his wife, Emma, had been living in their own quarters for less than three months. In such a short time, organization of the Church in Kirtland was not anywhere near completed, but already the Lord had made it clear that establishing the Church in Kirtland was not the long-term goal of the Church. Kirtland was merely a staging area or preliminary gathering point for the establishment of Zion in far-off Missouri. Therefore, Joseph Smith and other worthy Saints, including the Colesville Saints from New York, were commanded to continue on to Missouri to prepare for Zion in that place. On 19 June 1831, within two weeks of receiving Doctrine and Covenants 52, Joseph and the other elders addressed therein, with the exception of Ezra Thayre (see D&C 56:5), left Kirtland for Missouri. The Church was then only fourteen months old.

At this time no one, including the Prophet, knew exactly where Zion was to be built. Previous revelations had suggested that it would be "on the borders by the Lamanites" (see D&C 28:9), "into the western countries" (see D&C 45:64), and "into the regions westward, unto the land of Missouri" (see D&C 54:8). Oliver Cowdery and the missionaries to the Lamanites, however, still faithful to their call (see D&C 28:8), were laboring in the vicinity of Independence in Jackson County, Missouri, so it was there that the Prophet and his company first headed. The Prophet and his companions—Sidney Rigdon, Martin Harris, Edward Partridge, W. W. Phelps, Joseph Coe, and Sidney and Elizabeth Gilbert—traveled about one thousand miles in less than a month by wagon, canal boat, stagecoach, river boat, and by foot, arriving in Independence by 17 July 1831.[1] Doctrine and Covenants 57 was received on 20 July.

Joseph Smith recorded his reunion with Oliver and the missionaries to the Lamanites as follows: "The meeting of our brethren, who had long awaited our arrival, was a glorious one, and moistened with many tears. It seemed good and pleasant for brethren to meet together in unity. But our reflections were many, coming as we had from a highly cultivated state of society in the east, and standing now upon the confines or western limits of the United States, and looking into the vast wilderness of those that sat in darkness; how natural it was to observe the degradation, leanness of intellect, ferocity, and jealousy of a people that were nearly a century behind the times, and to feel for those who roamed about without the benefit of civilization, refinement, or religion; yea, and exclaim in the language of the Prophets: 'When will the wilderness blossom as the rose? When will Zion be built up in her glory, and where will Thy temple stand, unto which all nations shall come in the last days?' Our anxiety was soon relieved by receiving the following"[2]—Doctrine and Covenants 57.

The Saints from Colesville, who had settled temporarily at Thompson, Ohio, arrived in Independence, under the leadership of Newel Knight, five days after this revelation was received, on 25 July 1831.

COMMENTARY

2. This is the land of promise. In Doctrine and Covenants

42:35–36 the Lord had promised the Saints that the location of the New Jerusalem (see Ether 13:1–12) would be revealed to them in the future. In Doctrine and Covenants 52:1–5 Joseph Smith and Sidney Rigdon were commanded to go to Missouri to hold a conference and were promised that if they were faithful the Lord would reveal to them the land of their inheritance. Doctrine and Covenants 57:1–3 fulfills those two promises.

2. City of Zion. See Commentary on Doctrine and Covenants 38:4.

3. Independence is the center place. Since Zion will eventually grow to encompass all the Saints of God in all their many stakes, *Zion* is not always a very specific term geographically. The location of the center place of Zion, however, and the place of Zion's temple are very specific indeed. The temple site was dedicated on 3 August 1831 by Joseph Smith.

4. The land should be purchased. A parcel of land containing the temple site—63-¼ acres—was purchased by the Church on 19 December 1831 from Jones H. Flournoy for $130.[3]

4. And also every tract lying westward. The Saints were instructed to buy all the land between Independence and the so-called permanent Indian frontier—95 degrees longitude. In 1831 the territory west of that line, roughly the Missouri state line but extending into Kansas, was federal Indian territory. The revelation here refers to the Lamanites—members of the house of Israel—as "Jews" and the non-Indian inhabitants of Missouri as "Gentiles." Lamanites can rightly be called Jews since some of their ancestors were Mulekites, who were actually from the tribe of Judah, and because Lehi's family understood the nation of Judah to be their political and cultural homeland.

5. Every tract bordering by the prairies. The Lord instructed the Saints to buy, as they were able, all the land between Independence and the border of the Indian territories to the west.

6. Sidney Gilbert. Sidney Gilbert had been called to be an agent for the Church under Bishop Partridge (see D&C 53:4).

Sidney would receive consecrations, stewardship surpluses, and funds through Bishop Partridge, and other funds from Church members in the East, and he would use those funds to, among other things, purchase property for more stewardships in Zion, within the area designated by the Lord in verses 3–5.

7. Edward Partridge. Bishop Partridge was to continue in his calling (see D&C 41:9; 42:10), receiving consecrations and assigning stewardships to the Saints just as he had been instructed in Doctrine and Covenants 51.

8. Establish a store. Sidney Gilbert was to open a retail store in Independence, the profits of which could be used to buy land for stewardships and to meet other Church financial needs. At the same time the store provided goods needed by the Saints and others in the area and eventually also served as a bishops' storehouse for the benefit of the poor and needy in Zion. Managing this store was Sidney Gilbert's personal stewardship in Missouri.

9. Obtain a license. The Saints were settling right on the line between the United States and the Indian territory (today approximately the Missouri-Kansas border) and apparently intended to operate on both sides of this border. On the first Sunday in Zion, W. W. Phelps preached to a mixed audience of Native Americans and settlers on the western side of the border,[4] and as an agent for the Church in Independence, Sidney Gilbert would undoubtedly need to send goods across the border, which was only a few miles away (see v. 10). Any trade across the state line into Indian territory, however, was closely controlled by the federal government. Therefore, it was necessary for Sidney to get a permit to send goods across the border to the Lamanites,[5] to the missionaries, and to other Saints operating there.

10. Those who sit in darkness. The phrase is used here particularly in reference to the Lamanites in the Indian territory, among whom the Saints would attempt to labor: "Looking into the vast wilderness [Indian territory] of those that sat in darkness."[6] The missionaries to the Lamanites had already preached to the Shawnees and Delawares west of the border, and the Saints at this time still intended to further evangelize the Lamanites there.[7] Oliver had already notified the Prophet of the great tribe known as Navajos "three hundred miles west of Sante Fe," and it was envisioned that the Latter-day Saints and the Lamanites would one day mingle together.[8] Also, the two earliest manuscript copies of Doctrine and Covenants 57 read in verse 9: "That he may send goods also unto the Lamanites even by whom I will as clerks employed in his service and then the gospel may be proclaimed unto them."[9]

11–12. William W. Phelps. Consistent with the commandments given to him earlier, Brother Phelps was instructed to carry on his assignment of printing, selecting, and writing (see D&C 55:4) in Independence, Missouri. His stewardship was to be a printer and to make whatever money he could at that trade "in righteousness" (v. 12), while also meeting the printing needs of the Church. Whatever surplus William acquired in his occupation would, of course, be subject to the law of consecration.

13. Let my servant Oliver Cowdery assist him. Oliver Cowdery was a literate man, and it may be that some of his literary skills would be needed to help W. W. Phelps complete his assignment. Oliver was not being demoted, however, to a printer's helper. Rather, as Oliver presided over the Church in Zion, he was to see that W. W. Phelps had whatever he needed—including Oliver's personal help—to perform his assigned role. He would "assist" Brother Phelps in the same way that a good bishop "assists" some members of his ward to magnify their callings.

As a result of this commandment, W. W. Phelps and Oliver Cowdery began the process of buying and moving a printing press all the way from Cincinnati, opening a printing office, and publishing a monthly newspaper, *The Evening and the Morning Star,* as well as printing other tracts for the Church. Eventually, they were instructed to publish the Book of Commandments (see D&C 70:1–3; 72:20–21), which task was underway when a mob destroyed the printing office and press on 20 July 1833.

13. Proved by the Spirit. That is, "approved" by the Spirit.

14. With their families. Originally, the calls issued to the Missouri missionaries were for themselves alone (see D&C 52:3–8, 22–44). Here those who are instructed to stay in Missouri are commanded to move their families to Independence as well.

15. Let the bishop and the agent make preparations. These preparations were for the Colesville Saints who had been commanded to "flee the land" of Ohio and proceed to Missouri (see D&C 54:7–8). These families were well on their way at the time this revelation was received, and they arrived in Zion five days later, on 25 July, needing the Church's support.

1. See Cook, *Revelations of the Prophet Joseph Smith,* 91.
2. *History of the Church,* 1:189.
3. See Cook, *Revelations of the Prophet Joseph Smith,* 91–92.
4. See Smith, *History of the Church,* 1:190–91.
5. See Commentary on v. 10.
6. Compare Smith, *History of the Church,* 1:189.
7. See Smith, *History of the Church,* 1:183–85.
8. Gentry, "Light on the 'Mission to the Lamanites,'" 230.
9. Smith, *Kirtland Revelation Book,* 90; see also Woodford, Historical Development, 1:728–31.

58

BACKGROUND

J oseph Smith and several of the missionaries to Missouri had arrived in Jackson County around 17 July 1831, and Doctrine and Covenants 57, which designated the location of the temple and of the center place of Zion, was received on 20 July. The Colesville Saints, consisting of about sixty persons under the leadership of Newel Knight, arrived on 25 July.

Joseph recorded the events of that first week in Zion as follows: "The first Sabbath after our arrival in Jackson county [coincidentally, the 24th of July], Brother W. W. Phelps preached to a western audience over the boundary of the United States, wherein were present specimens of all the families of the earth; Shem, Ham and Japheth; several of the Lamanites or Indians—representative of Shem; quite a respectable number of negroes—descendants of Ham; and the balance was made up of citizens of the surrounding country, and fully represented themselves as pioneers of the West. At this meeting two were baptized, who had previously believed in the fulness of the Gospel.

"During this week the Colesville branch, referred to in the latter part of the last revelation [57:15], and Sidney Rigdon, Sidney Gilbert and wife [Elizabeth] and Elders Morley and Booth, arrived. I received the following"[1]—Doctrine and Covenants 58.

On 2 August 1831, the day following the reception of

Doctrine and Covenants 58, Joseph and Sidney helped members of the Colesville Branch "lay the first log, for a house, as a foundation of Zion," a combination church and school in Kaw Township, twelve miles west of Independence.[2] Following the Lord's instructions (see v. 57), Sidney Rigdon also consecrated and dedicated Jackson County, Missouri, specifically as the land of Zion and for the gathering of the Saints. According to Oliver Cowdery, "Brother Sidney Rigdon stood up and asked saying: Do you receive this land for the land of your inheritance with thankful hearts from the Lord? answer from all we do. Do you pledge yourselves to keep the laws of God on this land, which you never have kept in your own lands? we do. Do you pledge yourselves to see that others of your brethren who shall come hither do keep the laws of God? we do. After prayer he arose and said, I now pronounce this land consecrated and dedicated to the Lord for a possession and inheritance for the Saints (in the name of Jesus Christ having authority from him.) And for all the faithful Servants of the Lord to the remotest ages of time. Amen."[3]

On the next day, 3 August 1831, two days after Doctrine and Covenants 58 had been received, Joseph Smith laid the cornerstone of the temple in Independence a mile and a half west of the new brick courthouse. According to the commandment in verse 57, Sidney Rigdon consecrated the ground and pronounced the land dedicated to the Lord.[4] On the following day, the Prophet Joseph Smith dedicated the temple site.

COMMENTARY

1. Concerning you, and also concerning this land. The Saints in Missouri knew what the basic principles were for establishing Zion (see D&C 42, 51), they knew where Zion was to be established (see D&C 57), and they knew who among the Saints were to begin establishing it (see D&C 52–57). What they did not know was *how* to proceed and exactly what to expect in the future. It is natural that they would want the Lord to issue them detailed instructions for every step of the way. Doctrine and Covenants 58 was given largely to answer their concerns, both individually and collectively, and to remind them that true Saints should not expect to be led or commanded in everything but should employ their own initiative in working for good causes (see vv. 26–29).

2. Whether in life or in death. The Lord here began to prepare the Saints for the truth that while the rewards of obedience are sure and certain, for some those rewards would come only after further tribulation and perhaps even death. Zion would not be established easily or all at once, and the Saints might not enjoy its blessings in their lifetime.

3–4. Ye cannot behold . . . ; the hour is not yet. Despite the revelations they had received, the Saints could not see what was about to happen to them and to Zion in the larger plan of God. The faithful Saints would indeed receive their promised inheritance and glory—of this there was no doubt—but only after many more trials and sacrifices. This was something the members were largely not expecting.

5. Remember this. In their first two weeks in Missouri, in the first blush of the Saints' enthusiasm, the Lord foreshadowed for them the tragedies that were yet to come. The Saints needed to remember when things got bad in the years ahead that in the very beginning of their attempt to establish Zion, the Lord had warned them of the coming tribulations. He warned them of the trials to come when no one could see even a troubling cloud on the horizon. How were the Saints at that time to know that Jackson County, like Kirtland, would not be a permanent place for them, even though it had been dedicated and consecrated for that purpose?

6. For this cause . . . that you might be obedient. An important purpose for the commandment to establish Zion was not so much to establish Zion physically but to establish a *spiritual* Zion—a faithful, obedient, and consecrated people. The

Saints are still establishing spiritual Zion in this way today in all the stakes of Zion throughout the world. The physical Zion will yet be built in this dispensation, and on the very ground dedicated for that purpose in 1831. But in the meantime, each of us can establish spiritual Zion in our own homes and in our own hearts by obedience and faithfulness to the Lord. When the Lord's people have at last become a righteous people, the Lord will direct them to the appropriate place.

6. The things which are to come. This phrase refers to the events associated with the end of the world and the second coming of Christ, including the inevitable establishment of a physical Zion in Jackson County, Missouri. The Church's investment in Zion, the beginning made by these pioneers, testifies that Zion will be built as the prophets have spoken, while the pioneers' consecration and sacrifice is a testimony to later Saints of what will be required of us to build it.

7. That you might be honored. What praise from the Lord for these obedient Saints of Zion! Even though Zion was not fully established, those who obeyed God and consecrated all they had to the beginning of it were held in honor by the Lord himself in being allowed to initiate that great work.

7. Laying the foundation. Here the Lord revealed his intent in sending consecrated Saints to Jackson County. They were to establish the location and lay the foundations of Zion. They did not yet understand that a later generation would actually build the holy city.

8. A feast of fat things. The Saints' attempt to establish Zion would also bear record of the social conditions that will one day be established upon the earth (see also vv. 9–13). The fulness of the gospel brings both spiritual and temporal plenty. "One great purpose of God in establishing Zion is to save the world, through its laws and institutions, from the curse of poverty and destitution. The object is to give to the world an entirely new social order, to establish a community in which even the poor would share the 'fat things' with 'the rich and the learned, the wise and the noble.'"[6] Before the second coming of the Lord the gospel will be preached in all the world, and all the nations of the earth will be invited to enjoy both its spiritual and temporal blessings.

8. Wine on the lees well refined. The phrase "wine on the lees" is used in the King James Version of the Bible as the translation of the Hebrew *shmarim,* which literally means "dregs." When drinking wine from a cup is given a positive connotation, as it is here, the dregs mean the strongest, sweetest and most concentrated portion of the fermented product—the "fat part" (see Isaiah 25:6). These concentrated dregs, which contained the most flavor, were similar to a jelly or preserve and were considered a great delicacy.

On the other hand, when drinking is given a negative connotation—for example, if the cup were bitter like gall or vinegar—then the dregs are the bitterest and most difficult portion to drink (as in Psalm 75:8; Alma 40:26). The lees or the dregs represent the most concentrated part of a substance or, metaphorically, of an experience. If a drink is sweet like wine, then the dregs are the sweetest part, but if the drink is bitter like vinegar, then the dregs are the most bitter part.

9. A supper of the house of the Lord. The terminology here reveals that this supper is in part figurative, for its blessings will be received in temples. This is the same supper that is referred to in other places as the marriage feast of the Lamb, when Jesus as the bridegroom comes to the earth to receive his bride—the Church—unto himself with joy and rejoicing (see Revelation 19:7–9, 17).[7]

10–11. First, the rich and . . . then . . . the poor. Before the Second Coming, the gospel will be preached in a world still steeped in sin. It is inevitable that the wealthy and the educated will have some advantage in learning the gospel under these conditions, just as they have advantage under Satan's system in most other things. But when the Lord makes his move to overthrow the kingdoms of this world, and replaces their governments and social orders with his own in the day of his power, then all injustices and all worldly advantages will be done away, and the righteous poor will receive full measure of the blessings of the gospel. The injustices of ignorance and poverty and the disadvantages these impose will not be done away until the Savior comes in the day of his power, but when he comes, these evils will cease.

13. That the testimony might go forth. The testimony is that of future events associated with the end of the world and the second coming of Christ and the changes these events will bring to the earth and its people (see vv. 7–11).

14. Edward Partridge, and . . . his mission in this land. Edward Partridge had previously been called as bishop of the Church (see D&C 41:9). As such, his proper functions included assigning stewardships and judging the hearts and behavior of the Saints relative to the law of the Lord. This would continue to be his particular function when called to stay in Missouri (see v. 24). There can be no doubt that Bishop Edward Partridge was the individual called of God and appointed to "divide unto the saints their inheritance" in Zion (D&C 57:7).

15. Unbelief and blindness. Compare Doctrine and Covenants 84:55–57; 85:8. During their weeks in Missouri together, "Bishop Partridge several times strenuously opposed the measures of the Prophet, and was sharply reproved by the latter for his unbelief and hardness of heart."[8] Despite his high calling as the bishop in Zion, if Edward had not repented of this attitude he would have fallen. Bishop Partridge was a good man with a firm testimony of the gospel, and he eventually sacrificed all he had for the kingdom. But he also had some very firm opinions about *how* Zion was to be built, opinions which were at odds with the instructions he received from Joseph Smith. These differences with the Prophet continued for some time and would eventually contribute to the loss of Zion in Jackson County, Missouri.[9] Edward Partridge would not be the last Saint to doubt the word or plans of the prophets.

16. His mission. Edward Partridge was the bishop in Zion. Newel K. Whitney would preside as the bishop in Kirtland (see

D&C 72:2–8). Neither presided over the other, and neither was a Presiding Bishop in the modern sense, which office was not created until later (see D&C 124:41).[10] Bishop Partridge was also the acknowledged leader of the Church in Missouri until 1834, when a presidency of local high priests was appointed.

17. A judge in Israel. It must be remembered that bishops judge only for one's standing or one's stewardship in the Church (see D&C 64:40; 107:72–74) and are not to be thought of as empowered to judge infractions of civil law or to impose punishments for crimes (see D&C 42:79–86).

20. Let God rule him that judgeth. Judges in Israel have no right to rule according to their own ideas but only as they are themselves ruled by the will of God.

21. Let no man break the laws of the land. It can be a temptation for religious groups to think that since they obey a higher law, they are no longer bound to observe the secular laws of the land. The Lord here prohibits such thinking among the Saints. Unless specifically commanded otherwise, the Saints are to observe the constitutionally valid law of the land. This includes observing legalities in business, obeying speed limits, paying taxes, and so on.

22. Be subject to the powers that be. See Romans 13:1–7. In other words, the Saints, even those living the law of consecration, are to be good citizens and obedient to civil authorities—but only until the Savior comes. After his coming there will be no laws but his laws, and the Saints will be subject to no other power but his (see D&C 38:22).

22. Whose right it is to reign. This refers to Jesus Christ.

23. The laws of the church. The Lord wants the Saints to distinguish between the laws of the Church, by which fellowship and the right to an inheritance are decided within the Church, and the laws of the land, by which the Saints are to be governed in civil matters. There is also an implied caution here against attempting to turn the law of the Church into the law of the land.

26. It is not meet that I should command in all things. It is natural that the Saints should want specific, detailed directions from God in all their undertakings, but it is not good that this should be so. The Lord wants self-starters. He wants aggressive Saints who can see what needs to be done and do it without always being told. He wants sons and daughters who can learn the principles of the gospel and then apply them in their own lives to solve their own problems (see v. 27). This is how we grow.

Those Saints who cannot act without divine instructions are spiritually lazy. We are not here to have our every thought and action dictated to us by God as though we were robots receiving programming. We are here to learn how to make right choices using our own hearts and minds and our own agency. Modern Saints should be exploring, testing, probing, and trying to find ways to apply gospel principles to bring about good every day. As it is the nature of God to bring order out of chaos and light out of darkness, so it must be the nature of his children to make things better wherever they go—even without being specifically commanded in every detail.

Is your neighbor sick? Is your yard a mess? Is the graduation rate low at your local high school? Does your area lack clean water? Is there no health care available in your community? Is there a famine somewhere? Does anyone you know need to hear the gospel? Does a child need more of your time? Surely the principles we learn in church ought to imply or suggest some course of personal action to our consciences in these circumstances or in thousands of others like them. We should reread verses 26–29. God's true sons and daughters set about to do good in this world, without selfish intent and without necessarily being commanded to do so.

29. Receiveth a commandment. Remember that *commandment* is often used as a synonym for "revelation" in the Doctrine and Covenants. Thus, the condemnation spoken of here cannot be limited to violations of specific "thou shalts" or "thou shalt nots" but also applies to resisting the general information and programs revealed to the Saints by the Lord.

29. The same is damned. The verb *to damn* comes from a Latin root meaning "to condemn," or "to pronounce guilty." It is unrelated to the similar verb *to dam,* meaning to stop or to block one's progress. Despite common confusion of these two verbs, and though the effect of being damned might also be to be dammed (as several writers have pointed out), "to be damned" does not *merely* mean having one's progress stopped. It means to be condemned, to be judged guilty or worthy of punishment. In a spiritual sense it means being declared guilty of sin, the exact opposite of being "justified" or declared innocent of sin.

Thus, according to this verse, refusing to do what good we can when we have the opportunity simply because "we don't *have* to" is an attitude with serious spiritual consequences. To resist the revelations, or to accept them only grudgingly, or to do good only when specifically commanded, is to find ourselves condemned, "damned," and consigned, if we don't repent, into the power of Satan to suffer for our sloth and hard-heartedness.

31. Who am I. This is a rhetorical question equivalent to "Do you think I'll declare the guilty innocent?" or "Do you think I won't keep my promises?" It anticipates a negative response.

32–33. Many of God's blessings are promised contingent upon living certain principles or keeping certain commandments. When we obey the commandments or live the principles, we receive the promised blessings. But some people expect God to give them these conditional blessings anyway, even without their obedience. When this does not happen, they unjustly condemn God, his prophets, or his programs as false and his promises as unkept.

33. Lurketh beneath. The payoff for their disobedience and unjust criticism will come from Satan, as the wages of sin, rather than from God.

34. This land. The land referred to is Jackson County, Missouri, or Zion.

35. Martin Harris should be an example unto the church. Martin Harris had previously been commanded to offer up his possessions to publish the Book of Mormon (see D&C 19:26, 34–35). He then moved with the Saints to Ohio and traveled with the Prophet to Missouri. Orson Pratt observed that "Martin Harris was the first man that the Lord called by name to consecrate his money, and lay the same at the feet of the Bishop in Jackson County, Mo., according to the order of consecration. He willingly did it; he knew the work to be true; he knew that the word of the Lord through the Prophet Joseph was just as sacred as any word that ever came from the mouth of any Prophet from the foundation of the world. He consecrated his money and his substance, according to the word of the Lord. What for? As the revelation states, as an example to the rest of the Church."[11]

36. A law unto every man. Kirtland was to be a collection point and a staging area to organize the Saints in the East and prepare them for Zion. The Lord here commanded that only those Saints who had agreed to consecrate all their possessions, as Martin Harris had (see v. 35), were to emigrate to Zion (compare vv. 44, 46). Unfortunately, many of the Ohio Saints disregarded this commandment and moved to Jackson County, Missouri, before being called to do so and without having entered into the covenant of consecration. Spiritually unprepared, disobedient to counsel, and unwilling to live the law of consecration, they eventually caused economic, social, and spiritual problems in Missouri that contributed to the loss of Zion there.

41. He *seeketh* to excel.[12] W. W. Phelps's attitude toward other Saints was *competitive* rather than *cooperative*. He wanted to get ahead of them rather than become one with them. It is not evil to pursue excellence; indeed, Jesus was the most excellent of all men. But Jesus also sought to share his merits with us to make us as he is, rather than simply wanting to outperform us. The pursuit of personal excellence for the glory of God and the benefit of our fellows is a positive virtue, but the competitive urge that simply compels us to win for our ego's sake is not. Evidently, it is in this latter sense that Brother Phelps "[sought] to excel" and was condemned for it. The compulsive need always to beat our brothers and sisters, to establish our superiority over them by always winning, is as incompatible with establishing Zion as is the need to have more money, a newer car, or a larger house than they do.

42. I, the Lord, remember them no more. This is, of course, a restatement of the gospel covenant. If we have faith in Christ, repent, and submit to baptism, then our sins will be remitted and we will be sanctified by receiving the gift of the Holy Ghost (see 3 Nephi 27:16, 20). Should we sin after baptism we can repent again and partake of the sacrament to renew our baptismal covenant on these same terms.

Note that this scripture does not promise that repentant sinners will forget their sins; neither does any other scripture. Alma 36:19, for example, says only that Alma remembered his *pains* no more, and that the memory of his sins didn't tear him up anymore. Rather, we are promised that the Lord will remember them no more.

43. Confess them. True repentance requires an honest admission of wrongdoing and usually to the injured parties. This may mean admitting our sins to ourselves, to our spouse or family, to other individuals, to larger groups, and to the Lord. Where we may have sinned against our covenants with God and our membership in his Church, a bishop or stake president, as the Lord's agent and agent of the Church, must listen to our confession and determine our standing in the Church. Unwillingness to admit our sins to the injured parties by confession indicates that true repentance has not yet taken place, for our desire to be cleansed of sin is weaker than our desire to hide our faults and protect our egos.

43. Forsake them. To *forsake* means to abandon. To forsake our sins is to leave them behind and to leave them alone. It sometimes also means leaving people, places, or things associated with those sins or tying us to those sins, however painful that may be (see Joseph Smith Translation–Mark 9:40–44). Ultimately, it means to forsake even *wanting* to sin, as occurs when our hearts are finally changed and our desires are purified (see Mosiah 5:2).

44. The residue of the elders. The Lord addressed those Missouri missionaries who had not been specifically called to remain in Independence and instructed them on his will for them (see vv. 44–65).

44. The time has not yet come, for many years. The Lord was not willing for most members of the Church to go to Zion yet, nor for many years to come (compare D&C 51:17, "as for years"; D&C 64:21, "space of five years"). It would actually not be until seven years later, in 1838, that most of the Ohio Saints were called to Missouri. The Lord desired that Zion be built up slowly (see v. 56), that the land be purchased by contributions from the Ohio Saints (see v. 49), that missionary work be done in Missouri (see v. 48) and in all the world (see v. 64), that the Prophet remain in Kirtland (see v. 58), and that other preparations be made over a period of years.

Unfortunately, overeager and disobedient Saints refused to follow the Lord's plan for gradual, economically sensible, and spiritually consecrated settlement in Missouri but went there on their own, unbidden and unprepared, and expecting the bishop in Zion to provide them with an inheritance. The financial and logistical strain on the resources of the Saints in Independence eventually proved too great, while too many of these incoming Saints were too greedy, too inexperienced, too self-willed, or too disobedient to help in establishing Zion.[13] Since they did not live according to the covenant that was made when the land was dedicated,[14] in barely more than two years the Lord allowed the Saints to be driven off the land (additional reasons are given in D&C 101:7–8; 103:3–4; 105:11, 17).

45. Push the people together from the ends of the earth. According to the blessing of Moses upon the tribe of Ephraim, this specific task would be Ephraim's in the latter days (see Deuteronomy 33:17). Therefore, most of the elders of the Church, the modern tribe of Ephraim, were to continue laboring in the world, making converts from every nation instead of coming immediately to build Zion (see D&C 64:36).

46. Return to their homes. The Saints were to go back to Ohio.

49. Let there be an agent appointed. Because Bishop Partridge had been called to remain in Missouri, it would be necessary for someone else to be appointed to take over his function of receiving funds from the Saints in Ohio for the purchase of lands in Missouri. This calling would go to Newel K. Whitney (see D&C 72:8).

50. Sidney Rigdon . . . shall write a description of the land. In order to encourage the Saints in Ohio and elsewhere to contribute toward the purchase of land in Missouri, Sidney Rigdon was commanded to write a description of that choice region together with an indication of the Lord's designs concerning its future. Sidney's first efforts, presented later that month after he and Joseph had returned to Kirtland, were not acceptable to the Lord, and he was instructed to try again (see D&C 63:55–56).[15] The glowing description of Jackson County found in *History of the Church*[16] is a revised version of Sidney's second, more acceptable attempt to describe Zion.[17]

51. An epistle and subscription. The description of Zion commanded in verse 50 was to be accompanied by a cover letter to local leaders that included a sign-up sheet for the members to indicate their interest in contributing. Funds would then be received by local authorities, to be forwarded to Bishop Partridge or his agents in Missouri. In this period before photography, the description of Zion by Sidney Rigdon was intended to have an effect upon the Saints similar to a promotional brochure. The subscription, or sign-up sheet, would provide Church leaders with a list of those willing to contribute or invest in the land described in the brochure.

52. To purchase this whole region. The only method approved by the Lord for acquiring land in Missouri was to legally buy it and obtain clear title.

53. Save it be by the shedding of blood. Without buying the land and obtaining clear title, arguments over ownership would inevitably lead to bloodshed—an unacceptable means of acquiring possession. Some people have incorrectly concluded that this verse implies that the Saints were authorized by the Lord to take land in Missouri by force if necessary. While it is true that property *can* sometimes be obtained in this manner, theft and murder could never be acceptable means of establishing Zion.[18] Essentially the Lord was saying, "If you don't buy the land, you'll have to kill for it, and that is unacceptable" (compare D&C 57:4–5; 63:29–31). Ironically, when blood later was shed over this land, it was mostly the blood of the Saints who held legal title to it but were driven out anyway.

54. Let there be workmen sent forth. Those Saints in the East with necessary skills for building Zion were to be called and sent there as needed.

55. Let all these things be done in order. This was a further commandment by the Lord that Zion should be built up slowly, sensibly, and according to the principles of consecration and the law of the Lord (see v. 56). Only those who were prepared and appointed to go to Missouri were to go—according to the procedures revealed to the Church. But sometimes self-willed Saints want to get ahead of the Lord and do things according to their own timetable. The violation of these instructions and procedures by Saints who would not wait to be called to Missouri contributed to the eventual downfall of the Saints there.

55. Privileges of the lands. This phrase is a report on the availability of the land and opportunities presented.

57. Consecrate and dedicate this land. On 2 August 1831, the day following this revelation, Sidney Rigdon dedicated the land of Zion to the Lord as directed here.[19]

58. Let a conference meeting be called. The Lord had also previously indicated that a conference was to be held in Missouri (see D&C 52:2). Thirty-one members attended this conference, which was held on 4 August 1831 in Kaw Township at the home of Joshua Lewis, a local convert of the missionaries to the Lamanites.[20]

60. Ziba Peterson. Ziba was one of the missionaries to the Lamanites who set out from Fayette, New York, with Oliver Cowdery ten months earlier, in October 1830 (see D&C 32:3). In April 1831, he and Oliver Cowdery traveled to Lafayette County, Missouri, and preached to the people of Lexington, baptizing forty to fifty persons.

Following this rebuke issued to him on 1 August, Ziba confessed his sins at the conference held 4 August and received forgiveness. One week later, on 11 August, he married Rebecca Hooper, one of the Lafayette County converts. Ziba Peterson later became disaffected, however, and when the Saints fled Jackson County in 1833 he and his family remained behind.

61. Also hold a conference. This conference was held 24 August 1831 in Kaw Township.[21] Several elders who had not reached Jackson County by the previous conference on 4 August attended on 24 August, with Bishop Partridge presiding (see vv. 62–63). After this second conference in Missouri, the late-arriving elders were also to return to Ohio.

64. From this place. Even though most of the Church still lived in Ohio, and would for some years to come, the perspective of the Church was changed. Independence was the "center place" from which the gospel was to go forth (D&C 57:3).

---

1. *History of the Church,* 1:191.
2. Smith, *History of the Church,* 1:196.
3. Cited in Whitmer, *Early Latter Day Saint History,* 79.
4. See Whitmer, *Early Latter Day Saint History,* 80; Smith, *History of the Church,* 1:196.
5. See Ludlow, *Encyclopedia of Mormonism,* 2:534.
6. Smith and Sjodahl, *Doctrine and Covenants Commentary,* 336.
7. See Commentary on D&C 27:5.
8. Clark, *Messages of the First Presidency,* 4:113.
9. See Background to D&C 85; Commentary on D&C 82:1; 84:56–58, 76; 85:7–8; 90:35; 101:6–8.
10. See Commentary on D&C 68:14.
11. In *Journal of Discourses,* 18:160–61.
12. Emphasis added.

---

13. See Commentary on v. 36.
14. See Background.
15. For Sidney's unsuccessful attempt, see Whitmer, *Early Latter Day Saint History*, 81–83.
16. See 1:197–98.
17. See Van Wagoner, *Sidney Rigdon*, 101–5.
18. See Commentary on D&C 63:31.
19. See Whitmer, *Early Latter Day Saint History*, 79.
20. See Cannon and Cook, *Far West Record*, 9–10.
21. See Cannon and Cook, *Far West Record*, 13–14.

59

BACKGROUND

The Saints from Colesville, New York, arrived in Jackson County on 25 July 1831, having been evicted from Leman Copley's farm in Thompson, Ohio, the preceding month. A senior member of that valiant company, Polly Knight, the wife of Joseph Knight Sr. and mother of Newel Knight, left Kirtland with a determination to see Zion even though she was at that time already in very poor health. On the journey Sister Knight became gravely ill, "'yet,' says her son, 'she would not consent to stop traveling; her only, or her greatest desire was to set her feet upon the land of Zion, and to have her body interred in that land. I went on shore and bought lumber to make a coffin in case she should die before we arrived at our place of destination—so fast did she fail. But the Lord gave her the desire of her heart, and she lived to stand upon that land.'"[1]

Polly Knight died on 6 August 1831, the first Latter-day Saint to die in Jackson County. Her funeral was held the next day, which was also a Sabbath day. Joseph Smith attended Sister Knight's funeral and afterward received this revelation on what was expected of Saints in Zion, including their enlightened observance of the Sabbath day.

COMMENTARY

1–3. These verses likely refer initially to Polly Knight, whose funeral service had just concluded, as the first of "those that die" (v. 2), "whose feet stand upon the land of Zion" (v. 3), and who had "obeyed my gospel" (v. 3). These blessings and promises also belong to all faithful Saints in Zion.

4. With commandments not a few. Note that commandments, far from being considered limitations or burdens, are here classed with revelations as examples of the blessings of God.

5–14. While some of these commandments may sound like certain parts of the law of Moses, they are, with the exception of the first part of verse 6, either New Testament commandments or parts of the old law that are here given a new gospel context. Verse 5, "and in the name of Jesus Christ thou shalt serve him," adds to the previously known commandment from Deuteronomy 11:1. The second part of verse 6, "nor do anything like unto it," expands the scope of the Mosaic prohibitions in Exodus and Leviticus to include the *spirit* of the law. Verse 7 imposes what was a specific commandment only for Levites in the Old Testament to all the Saints in this dispensation (see 1 Chronicles 23:30). Verse 8 requires sacrifice just as the law of Moses did, but this is a sacrifice of ourselves, of our own hearts and spirits, rather than of sheep or cattle. Verses 9 and 12 command us to observe the Sabbath day *specifically* by prayer and by attending our sacrament meetings. The renewal of our baptismal covenants by partaking of the sacrament is one of the most sacred acts we perform as Latter-day Saints (see D&C 27:1–14).

6. Nor do anything like unto it. President Ezra Taft Benson taught: "This means fornication, homosexual behavior, self-abuse, child molestation, or any other sexual perversion."[2] The only proper setting for sex, any kind of sex, is in consensual relations between legally married husbands and wives. Any sexual act or activity outside those bounds is forbidden by the Lord. President Spencer W. Kimball also applied this passage of scripture to abortion.[3]

9–13. These verses offer specific ways the Saints must observe the Sabbath law.

9. Go . . . and offer up thy sacraments. The Lord here makes attendance at our organized Sunday meetings, particularly sacrament meeting, a specific commandment to the modern Saints. *Sacraments* is plural here because it refers not only to the sacrament of the Lord's Supper but to all our sacred Sabbath performances—prayers, blessings, confirmations, testimonies, lessons, or anything else we may do in Jesus' name. A "sacrament" is anything said or done in the sacred name of Jesus Christ.

11. On all days. No one should get the idea that just because there is a designated Sabbath, all religious exercises, devotions, keeping the commandments, or being concerned with the things of God should be limited to Sunday only. Every member of the Church has covenant obligations to the Lord that are valid and must be observed seven days a week.

12. Thine oblations. An oblation is an offering to God. It might be an offering of money, time, talent, or anything else consecrated to God as an act of obedience or worship.

13–14. Fasting. Fasting in the religious sense cannot be equated with just missing some meals. True fasting is the attitude in which we miss those meals, an attitude of conscious sacrifice for the sake of others and for the sake of drawing away from our carnal natures while drawing closer to God. And as we draw closer to God through proper fasting, should we not rejoice? Even the food we prepare to end our religious fasts can be prepared in the spirit of fasting, the spirit of rejoicing—rejoicing not that our fast is over but that through our fast we have blessed our fellow Saints and more effectively communed with God.

In a figurative sense, the Sabbath day itself, when properly observed, may be understood as a fast; not a fast from food and water, but from the worldly concerns of the rest of the week. If we truly fast from our weekday concerns on the Sabbath, we can enter into the full joy of the Lord's day.

15. Not with much laughter, for this is sin. The Lord

doesn't have anything against happiness, gladness, or cheerfulness, as demonstrated by the last half of this verse. The prohibition against "much laughter" here should be understood as meaning prohibition against that state of silliness, giddiness, loss of dignity, and loss of control in which people are more prone to cross the line of propriety, to make light of sacred things, to mock that which is good, or to make fun of others. This prohibition should not be understood as a total ban on all humor or on any degree of laughter, since a large number of General Authorities use an appropriate degree of humor—and the Saints respond with appropriate laughter—when they address the Church in conference or on other important occasions.

In the Doctrine and Covenants the Lord commands the Saints three times concerning laughter. We are commanded to cast away "excess of laughter" (D&C 88:69), avoid "much laughter" (D&C 59:15), and cease from "all laughter" (D&C 88:121). The context of each passage is crucial and explains the variation in the three commandments. Doctrine and Covenants 88:69 is apparently describing our everyday activity as we attempt to live lives that are more and more Christlike. Thus, laughter is permitted, but not to excess. In Doctrine and Covenants 59:15 the setting is fasting, prayer, and Sabbath observance, in which there should not be "much" laughter, and in Doctrine and Covenants 88:121 the setting is the Lord's house, the temple (compare D&C 88:117, 119–20), in which there should be no laughter at all.

16. The fulness of the earth is yours. The earth and all it produces, both animal life (see v. 16) and plant life (see v. 17), are allowed for the use of the Saints. There are no kosher laws for the modern Church as there were for ancient Israel. Modern Israel, the Church of Jesus Christ, may drink milk with their meat or wear linen with wool. We can eat shellfish, escargot, rabbit, or pork. The Mosaic law's prohibitions against using certain of nature's resources do not apply to the Saints. Even the Word of Wisdom, which was not given to the Church until 1833, a year and a half later, is not so much a prohibition against *use* as it is a prohibition against *misuse* (see D&C 89). The Lord expects the Saints to use all the bounty the earth produces intelligently and appropriately (see v. 20).

19. Enliven the soul. The soul is defined in Doctrine and Covenants 88:15 as the spirit *and* the body. The things of this earth are given not just for the nourishment of the body but for the joy of the spirit as well. "To enliven" means to stimulate or to rejuvenate. Thus, the products of nature are meant to rejuvenate or renew our spirits with their aesthetic qualities as well as our bodies with their physical properties.

20. With judgment, not to excess, neither by extortion. There is a difference between *use* and *exploitation*. Humans did not "use" the passenger pigeon very wisely; they are now extinct. The resources of nature are given to man to manage, not to pillage. Wholesale destruction of natural resources violates God's command that they be used "with judgment, not to excess, neither by extortion." Perhaps *extortion,* which literally means to "twist out," here refers to forcing more from a resource than it can bear.

21. In nothing doth man offend God . . . save . . . . In using the products of nature for our own wants and needs, we need not fear that we might somehow offend God, for they are all given to us. God will, however, be offended by foolish persons who use what he has provided for them but will not acknowledge his hand in providing it—who "remove" God from their conceptual world and will not thank him (see v. 7) or keep his commandments.

22. According to the law and the prophets. The Lord points out that his word on these matters is already found in the scriptures. The Lord does not seem to appreciate being petitioned for answers he has already given. Many of the Saints would benefit from searching the scriptures and the revelations to modern prophets before asking God to solve their problems through personal revelation or divine intervention. God may already have answered their questions or solved their problems—if only they would consult the scriptures and other resources the Lord has provided.

23. Peace in this world. "Peace is the gift of God. Do you want peace? Go to God. Do you want peace in your families? Go to God. Do you want peace to brood over your families? If you do, live your religion, and the very peace of God will dwell and abide with you, for that is where peace comes from, and it don't dwell anywhere else."[4]

1. Smith, *History of the Church,* 1:199.
2. Benson, in *Ensign,* Nov. 1986, 46.
3. Kimball, in Conference Report, Apr. 1975, 8.
4. John Taylor, in *Journal of Discourses,* 10:56.

60

BACKGROUND

After three weeks in Jackson County it was time for the Missouri missionaries to return to Ohio in accordance with the instructions given them in Doctrine and Covenants 58:46. Under the Prophet's direction, missionaries had preached the gospel to those living between Kirtland and Independence and to the border settlers. The Prophet and his party had located and dedicated the land of Zion and the site of its temple during their time in Missouri. They had established a bishopric, a mercantile store, and a bishops' storehouse in Zion, and they had made plans for a publishing house. They had begun to buy land and build upon it, and they had familiarized more than two dozen Kirtland Saints with the land of Zion and how to get there.

On Monday, 8 August 1831, the day after Polly Knight's funeral and the reception of Doctrine and Covenants 59, the elders asked the Prophet Joseph Smith just how they should return to Ohio and by what routes, whether they should do missionary work along the way, and if there were any other special instructions for them. In response to their inquiries, Joseph received Doctrine and Covenants 60. Sections 60–62 constitute a unit dealing with the return from Zion, and they should be studied together.

COMMENTARY

2. They will not open their mouths. Some of the elders called as missionaries to Missouri refused to preach or bear testimony of the restored gospel while on this mission. A few expected the Lord to give them greater powers of public speaking before they would even attempt to preach. The Lord warned them that his anger was kindled against them, this being one of the more severe warnings he had given them. Note that the immediate concern here is for how the elders would behave and whether they would preach as commanded on the way back to Kirtland, a journey that commenced the next day (see D&C 61:3, 33–34).

2. Hide the talent. The elders' talents were not necessarily public speaking or preaching; they were not, in fact, all talented in this area. Their collective talent lay in their knowledge and testimony of the restoration of the gospel. This great gift brings with it the obligation that one's knowledge and testimony be shared with others who lack it (see Matthew 25:14–30).

2. Fear of man. This phrase may be understood two ways: as embarrassment, or the social fear of looking foolish to other people, or as literal fear that preaching unpopular views might put one in physical danger. Both may apply here, and either way, we must be more concerned with God's opinion of us than the opinions of mere humans.

3. It shall be taken away, even that which they have. The principle is to "use it or lose it." The consequence of refusing to bear one's testimony is losing one's testimony. Those who would rather lose their testimony than share it and bless others with it will eventually get their preference.

4. My jewels. The imagery employed here represents God as the emperor of the universe taking the finest treasures from all his vast domains to make up his "crown jewels." When this earth has fulfilled its present purpose, God will take the most precious and valuable things upon it, his obedient sons and daughters—his "jewels"—and place them in their proper settings among his treasures (compare Isaiah 62:3; Zechariah 9:16).

4. What . . . bespeaketh the power of God. *Bespeaketh* means to give evidence, to testify, or to signify. On that day when the Lord makes up his "jewels," everyone will see the shining glory and favored status of those obedient Saints who did not fear men. Their glorious exaltation before all the world, even though they may have personally been the meek, lowly, or uneducated during their mortal lives, will be God's final witness of his own infinite power.

5. A craft made, or bought. The elders ended up buying large canoes, capable of holding several men.[1]

5. It mattereth not unto me. The significance of this statement could be easily missed, but is of extreme importance. Not everything we do is a vital part of God's plan. Not every tiny detail of our lives has eternal significance. Some things just don't matter. The Lord said that as long as they "fill their mission" (D&C 61:22), it didn't matter to him whether the elders "made, or bought" a craft (D&C 60:5), whether they traveled "by water or by land" (D&C 61:22), or whether they rode on horses, mules, or in wagons (see D&C 62:7–8).

Some Saints today agonize over whether God wants them to drive a Ford or a Chevy, to buy a house or rent an apartment, to study sociology in college or dental hygiene in trade school, when God *might* not care one way or the other. Often, God does care about such things, and it is important for us to be prayerful and to follow the promptings of the Spirit. But sometimes, when we get no promptings concerning the details of our lives or the many choices we face, it may be because any of the available options is equally acceptable to the Lord, or because there may be no spiritual advantage or disadvantage of any one option over any other (compare D&C 80:3). If the Lord does not prompt us one way or the other, we should not become paralyzed and unable to proceed. We should just make the best choice we can and get on with our lives. After all, our goal is not for God to make every decision for us, but to become *like* God, with the power of independent decision and action within ourselves (see D&C 58:26–29).

5. Take your journey speedily. It may be, given the information in Doctrine and Covenants 61:3, that this means "hurry and go" rather than "go in a hurry." The elders were to *leave* Missouri quickly—they left the next morning—rather than to *travel* swiftly once they were on their way. Compare this with verse 14, where the elders are to "speedily return" but "not in haste," that is, they were to start as speedily as possible, but they were not to travel in great haste once they left.

6. Oliver Cowdery. When Oliver left on his mission to the Lamanites, the Church was located in New York, but he returned to it in Kirtland, a branch he had helped to found. For the entire ten months in between, Oliver was laboring in Missouri, and had been away from Joseph and the main body of the Saints.

6. Cincinnati. Even though Oliver and the missionaries to the Lamanites had already preached in Cincinnati without success, the leadership was still directed to go there again. A short time later, the printing press for W. W. Phelps in Zion was purchased in Cincinnati.

7. I am able to make you holy. Though all human beings are imperfect, Jesus Christ has, through his atonement, the power to sanctify, or "make holy," those who enter with him into the covenant of baptism. Through the atonement of Christ, and through their baptism, Oliver's, Sidney's, and Joseph's sins were forgiven them—just as the sins of all the Saints are forgiven them if they are faithful to their baptismal covenants.

8. Congregations of the wicked. *Congregations* are gatherings. In 1831 this word did not necessarily mean only church congregations but wherever people congregated. The term *wicked* is likely used here in the general sense of unredeemed by receiving the ordinances of the gospel. Such individuals, while not necessarily worse than the average human being, would still be "natural" men and women and therefore "enemies of God" until they had faith, repented, and were baptized.[2] What seems clear is that "congregations of the wicked" refers to groups of non-Church members as distinct from groups of Saints, which the Lord refers to as "congregations of their brethren" (D&C 61:32).

10. The money which I have given him. This phrase refers to the assets Bishop Partridge received as bishop and agent for the Church. He was to use some of those Church funds to help the elders get home to Kirtland. Those elders who could were to pay the money back in Kirtland, but those who were financially unable to pay it back were not required to do so.

12. The residue who are to come. These instructions were not for everyone who would come to Zion in the future but were specifically for those Missouri missionaries who were delayed in arriving at Jackson County until after the conference on 4 August. Among them were Hyrum Smith and John Murdock, who had come by way of Detroit (see D&C 52:8), David Whitmer, Harvey Whitlock, Levi Hancock, and Zebedee Coltrin (see D&C 60:14).

13. Thou shalt not idle away thy time. Missionaries were, and still are, called to testify of the restoration of the gospel and not to waste their time doing something else or attempting to bury their talent (see vv. 2–3) by avoiding their obligation to testify. Remember that these instructions (see vv. 12–17) were specifically addressed to the group of missionaries who were returning home.

14. Thou shalt speedily return. When the late party of missionaries to Missouri held a conference (see D&C 58:61), just as the first group did, they were given instructions to return to Kirtland in the same way and with essentially the same charge as given the earlier group (see D&C 60:5, 8).

15. Shake off the dust of thy feet. See Commentary on Doctrine and Covenants 24:15.

17. The residue hereafter. The rest of the Lord's instructions will be given later.

---

1. See Smith, *History of the Church,* 1:202; Smith, "History of Joseph Smith," 464.
2. See Smith, *Church History and Modern Revelation,* 1:258.

61

BACKGROUND

Joseph and ten other elders left Independence, Missouri, in canoes on 9 August, headed back down the Missouri River for St. Louis. A couple of the elders returning to Ohio with the Prophet had been expecting great miracles to occur in Missouri and, despite the clear statement of Doctrine and Covenants 58:3–7 that these things would take place only over time and after much trial, they were unhappy that they had not seen a more immediate fulfillment of God's promises. As a result of their false expectations being disappointed, there was some murmuring and arguing among the party as the missionaries made their way downriver (see D&C 61:20).

On 11 August, the third day of the journey, the canoe in which Joseph and Sidney were riding actually hit a "sawyer," or partially submerged tree, and was nearly overturned. The accident could easily have been fatal, for at that time the Missouri was a truly wild river without dams, locks, or levies. According to Joseph Smith, there had been other mishaps earlier that same day,[1] so the travelers stopped and made camp earlier than usual at what was then called McIlwaine's Bend, presently known as Miami Bend, about forty miles above Chariton, Missouri. After the party had left the river, William W. Phelps saw, in broad daylight, a vision of Satan riding upon the waters of the river. The rest of that day and much of the evening were spent in camp sorting out hard feelings and attempting a reconciliation between angry or offended parties. By late that evening, most of those involved had repented, apologized, and been reconciled to one another.

The following morning after prayers, on 12 August, Joseph received Doctrine and Covenants 61, which explained in part the previous day's events and the related vision given to Elder Phelps. The Prophet's own account reads as follows: "On the 9th [August 1831], in company with ten Elders, I left Independence landing for Kirtland. We started down the river in canoes, and went the first day as far as Fort Osage, where we had an excellent wild turkey for supper. Nothing very important occurred till the third day, when many of the dangers so common upon the western waters, manifested themselves; and after we had encamped upon the bank of the river, at McIlwaine's Bend, Brother Phelps, in open vision by daylight, saw the destroyer in his most horrible power, ride upon the face of the waters; others heard the noise, but saw not the vision. The next morning after prayer, I received the following"[2]—Doctrine and Covenants 61.

The first known text of section 61 appeared in *The Evening and the Morning Star* for December 1832, about sixteen months after the revelation had first been received. This was published in Missouri by W. W. Phelps, editor of the *Star,* who had himself received the vision that preceded Doctrine and Covenants 61.

COMMENTARY

1. Alpha and Omega. See Commentary on Doctrine and Covenants 19:1.

2. Whose sins are now forgiven. This phrase could refer either to their life's sins generally being forgiven through the gospel covenant or, more likely, specifically to their sins of attitude and murmuring on the previous day, which were also forgiven them through their repentance and mutual reconciliation that evening.

3. It is not needful. The Lord revealed that he did not want the *entire* group to travel quickly back to Kirtland, but that most of them should take the time to proselytize along the way, as had previously been commanded in Doctrine and Covenants 58:59 and 60:14. This may seem at first contradictory to Doctrine and Covenants 60:1, 5,[3] but the Lord explained that they were to hurry up and do missionary work rather than to hurry up and go home (see v. 4).

4. That ye might bear record. The purpose of having the elders travel together by boat up to this point was that they might testify to other Saints who might be bound for Missouri concerning the future of their experiences on the Missouri River and their vision of Satan's power over those waters (see v. 18). Almost 90 percent of the journey from Kirtland to Independence could be made by boat traveling westward upon the Ohio, Mississippi, and Missouri Rivers. A journey to Zion by water might therefore have seemed the quickest and easiest way to get there, but the Lord revealed dangers involved in traveling by water that the Saints had not understood—dangers that will increase as the end of this world approaches. Equally important was the fact that traveling to and from Zion by boat prevented the Saints from effectively preaching the gospel along their way.

Once the elders had experienced the dangers of river travel and had seen firsthand the power of the destroyer associated with it, they could bear testimony to all who followed. They had also learned by experience that those who travel upon the waters would be particularly vulnerable to Satan's power if they were not faithful. Once they had been taught these lessons and could serve as witnesses to them, the elders were no longer to seek the quickest way home but rather were to do as originally commanded (see D&C 58:59; 60:14) and preach the gospel as they went.

4. More especially hereafter. Whatever dangers were inherent in traveling upon the waters of the Missouri River would be more readily apparent in the future than in Joseph's day. It is likely that the destructive power of the waters described here will be part of the woes and destructions prophesied for the very last days (compare Moses 7:66, where Enoch described the sea in the last days as becoming "troubled"). While there was some danger in river travel in Joseph's day, especially to those whose faith was weak, the real evidence of a curse upon the waters and of their destructive power will be seen in a future time, immediately preceding the second coming of Christ.

5. Have decreed in my anger. The Lord is not angry with water as an element in itself any more than he was angry with the ground when he cursed it for Adam's sake (see Genesis 3:17–19). While the curse is upon all the waters, the Missouri River in particular will prove to be a destructive force in the last days.

6. He that is faithful. Despite some popular belief to the contrary, Doctrine and Covenants 61 does *not* prohibit travel by water, or even swimming, for missionaries,[4] for God is more powerful than Satan, and those who are faithful need not fear to ride even upon the wild Missouri. Even in those future times when the curse upon the waters will become more evident than it is now, the "upright in heart" will still be able to travel to Zion safely by water (vv. 16, 22). It is the unfaithful and the rebellious, like the rebellious elders on the previous day, who need to fear the power of Satan over the waters, for by their unfaithfulness, they render themselves susceptible to that power. Notice that when the elders at McIlwaine's Bend repented, they were allowed to continue their journey even *upon the waters* of the Missouri river (see v. 22).

7–12. Sidney Gilbert and . . . W. W. Phelps. These two brethren, who had to move their families from Kirtland to Independence (see D&C 55:5), were still to hurry home and complete those arrangements as quickly as possible. As business agent and printer, respectively, they also had to arrange for the purchase of a printing press in Cincinnati and its transport to Independence. The rest of the elders were to take only what they needed for clothing, while Sidney Gilbert, as the Lord's agent (see D&C

57:6), was to take the rest of their combined temporal resources directly to Kirtland.

13. I gave unto you a commandment. The commandment spoken of was given in section 60, especially Doctrine and Covenants 60:5.

13. I . . . will reason with you. In other words, "I will explain to you." The Lord explained the reason for the accidents and the vision of the previous day and their relationship to each other.

14. Blessed the waters. When God first created the world, both the land and the waters were blessed (see Genesis 1:10–12, 20–22). Then when Adam and Eve transgressed in the Garden of Eden, the *land* was cursed for their sakes, but the *waters* were not: "In the beginning God cursed the earth; but did he curse all things pertaining to it? No, he did not curse the water, but he blessed it."[5] From the beginning, water was ordained to be a cleansing and a purifying element. When the earth became corrupted in the days of Noah, God purified it by bringing the waters upon it. Likewise, today sinful men and women may also be purified through baptism by immersion in water. One of Christ's most important symbolic names is the Living Water or the Water of Life.

14. In the last days. This phrase is probably meant to tell us when the curse would take effect rather than when John would have pronounced it. In other words, John, either in the meridian of time or sometime since, pronounced a curse that would come upon the waters sometime in the last days. The full realization of that curse was still future in Joseph's day (compare v. 15), as it is likewise in ours. The pronouncement of the curse is past; the full effect of the curse, it seems, is in the future.

14. I cursed the waters. The reference here may be to passages in the book of Revelation written by the apostle John (see Revelation 8:8–11; 16:2–6), or perhaps to an event in the ministry of John not otherwise recorded in scripture.

15–16. The days will come/in days to come. The phrase "the last days" can be ambiguous, referring to events anytime between the Restoration in 1830 and the last, few, literal days before the second coming of Christ. This language in verses 15–16 makes it clear that "the last days" as used in verse 14 refers to a time still in the future.

17. Cursed the land, . . . blessed it. When Adam fell, the ground or the earth was cursed for his sake (see Genesis 3:17). This curse will be removed from the whole earth only when the Savior comes to establish his millennial reign upon it and renew it to "paradisiacal glory" (Articles of Faith 1:10). According to this verse, however, God has *already* removed the curse upon the land and blessed it in order that the Saints might establish Zion and enjoy its fruits. The land is no longer cursed and there is no more impediment for those Saints who will establish Zion, whether in their own hearts, in their own homes, wards, stakes, or eventually in Jackson County, Missouri.

18. Forewarn your brethren . . . lest their faith fail. Apparently, the power of Satan over those traveling upon the waters is proportionate to their lack of faith. Since some of the Missouri elders had murmured and been rebellious the day before, the power of Satan over them had increased, and they had experienced increased difficulties on their journey. W. W. Phelps was allowed to see the source of their troubles and the power Satan had been given to destroy the wicked or faithless who travel upon the waters. Future Saints traveling to Zion needed to know that should they prove unfaithful, particularly as they traveled upon untamed waters, they would find themselves vulnerable to the power of the destroyer.

19. I, the Lord, have decreed . . . , and I revoke not. The curse pronounced by the mouth of John is still in effect and will be more fully realized at a future time. Satan has been given power over the waters, and that curse will not be revoked until the Savior comes.

20. I, the Lord, was angry with you yesterday. "During the three days upon the river some disagreements and ill feelings had developed among the brethren and explanations and reconciliations had become necessary. . . . The greater part of the night at McIlwaine's Bend was devoted to these matters. The brethren became reconciled to each other, and those whose affairs more especially cried haste started overland the next morning for St. Louis, and the rest of the company continued the journey *via* the river."[6] With the repentance of the elders and their reconciliation to one another, the danger for them in traveling upon the waters was greatly lessened, so that they might, with continued faithfulness, resume their travels, even by water (see v. 6).

21. This verse is directed to Joseph Smith, Sidney Rigdon, Oliver Cowdery, Sidney Gilbert, and W. W. Phelps, who were to hurry to Cincinnati and then to Kirtland on the Lord's errand. Samuel Smith, Reynolds Cahoon, Ezra Booth, Frederick G. Williams, Peter Whitmer Jr., and Joseph Coe, the other elders present, were to take their time and preach the gospel as they returned to Kirtland by the river route.

22. It mattereth not. See Commentary on Doctrine and Covenants 60:5.

22. By water or by land. As the language here clearly illustrates, Doctrine and Covenants 61 must not be understood as a strict prohibition against travel by water. The elders had become vulnerable to Satan's power over the waters only because of their murmuring, hard feelings, and lack of faith. Now that they had repented they were no longer vulnerable and could travel by water if necessary, as long as their missionary responsibilities were not neglected (see v. 6).

23. The canal. The Ohio canal, running north and south about thirty miles west of Kirtland, connected Lake Erie with Columbus, Ohio, and the Ohio River. Since canals are manmade and do not represent waters in their natural state, it is possible that the curse upon the waters (see vv. 4–5, 14–15) does not apply. Certainly the dangers are not the same.

24–26. There is little indication in the historical record that the Saints understood Doctrine and Covenants 61 as a blanket prohibition against water travel, though they were clearly advised to travel up to Zion by land.[7] For example, Parley P. Pratt and his wife traveled to Missouri by water in the summer of 1832.[8] Rather, section 61 was seen as an expression of the Lord's preference that those called to settle permanently in Zion travel by land, perhaps because of the physical dangers of going by boat, but also because of the missionary opportunities that would otherwise be lost.

27. Unto whom is given power to command the waters. This phrase probably refers specifically to Joseph Smith, who holds all the keys and powers of the priesthood (compare Moses 1:25).

32. The congregations of their brethren. That is, the Saints in Kirtland, where the leadership of Joseph and Sidney was both missed and needed. John Whitmer recorded that while Joseph and the other leaders were in Missouri, a number of the Saints had apostatized in Kirtland, though of these many were reclaimed when their leaders returned.[9]

34. Rid their garments. This phrase means to rid them of blame for the sins of people they could have warned and converted, but did not. Notice that whenever someone *would* have been converted if only some missionary had been obedient, responsibility for their subsequent sins and ignorance is not charged to themselves alone but is shared with the disobedient missionary!

39. Whether in life or in death. Whether we are alive at the Savior's coming or have died prior to that event, we will still want to be able to "abide the day of his coming." For the living this means being allowed to stay upon the earth after his coming and to participate in his millennial kingdom. For the dead it means being resurrected with the other righteous dead on that day, in the morning of the first resurrection, also to participate in his millennial kingdom.

1. See *History of the Church,* 1:203.
2. *History of the Church,* 1:202–3.
3. See Commentary on D&C 60:5.
4. See Commentary on vv. 24–26.

5. Brigham Young, in *Journal of Discourses*, 7:162.
6. Roberts, *Comprehensive History of the Church*, 1:262–63.
7. See Phelps, "Way of Journeying for the Saints," *Evening and the Morning Star*, Dec. 1832, 5.
8. See Pratt, *Autobiography of Parley P. Pratt*, 64–65.
9. *Early Latter Day Saint History*, 80.

DOCTRINE AND COVENANTS

62

BACKGROUND

After Joseph Smith and his party of missionaries to Missouri received Doctrine and Covenants 61 on 12 August 1831, they split up, with Joseph, Oliver Cowdery, Sidney Rigdon, William W. Phelps, and Sidney Gilbert traveling rapidly overland while the rest of the elders continued downriver toward St. Louis. The next day, Joseph and his party crossed the Missouri River at Chariton, Missouri, and found there the later party of missionaries to Missouri—Hyrum Smith, John Murdock, Harvey Whitlock, and David Whitmer—who were still on their way to Zion.

Joseph Smith recorded their meeting as follows: "On the 13th [August] I met several of the Elders on their way to the land of Zion, and after the joyful salutations with which brethren meet each other, who are actually 'contending for the faith once delivered to the Saints,' I received the following"[1]—Doctrine and Covenants 62. Thus, Doctrine and Covenants 62 was received in Chariton, Missouri, on 13 August 1831.

It should be remembered that Hyrum Smith and John Murdock had been instructed to travel to Missouri by way of Detroit, so they naturally would be expected to arrive later than Joseph and his party. Brother Murdock later provided an additional reason why his group may have been late: "We Preached next day, but I was sick and went to bed, and we continued there near one week and I gave my watch in pay to Wm. Ivy to carry me in a wagon to Chariton 70 miles. We stayed there two days. Met Bro. J. Smith Jr., S. Rigdon and others, and received the Revelation recorded in the book of Covenants on page 202"[2]—Doctrine and Covenants 62.

COMMENTARY

1. Succor. See Hebrews 2:18; Mosiah 4:16. To *succor* means to give aid or help. Because Christ has personally experienced mortality and all its weaknesses and temptations, he knows how to help those in mortality who are weak and who suffer temptations.

2. Those who have not as yet gone up. Of the thirty-one men who had been called to go to Missouri (see D&C 52:3–7, 22–32; 55:1, 4, 6), only nine were in the Prophet's returning party—Frederick G. Williams and Peter Whitmer Jr. were returning *Lamanite* missionaries; Edward Partridge, Isaac Morley, and John Corrill had remained in Missouri. Doctrine and Covenants 62 was directed specifically to the missionaries who arrived in Zion after the Prophet had left. In historical context, the revelation was given specifically to Hyrum Smith, John Murdock, Harvey Whitlock, and David Whitmer, who had met the Prophet in Chariton, Missouri.[3]

3. The testimony which ye have borne. Unlike the earlier group of missionaries who were traveling with the Prophet and were chastened for not preaching along the way as they had been commanded (see D&C 60:2–3), this later group of missionaries had, by and large, successfully preached the gospel along the way and had built up the Church as they did so. Levi Hancock, Zebedee Coltrin, Solomon Hancock and Simeon Carter, for example, baptized over 120 persons between them on the way to

Zion,[4] and Parley P. Pratt recorded having established branches of the Church in Ohio, Illinois, and Indiana.[5]

3. Is recorded in heaven. A heavenly record truly is kept of all we say and do. Our faithfulness is recorded there, and the angels of heaven rejoice over our individual triumphs. Even our most private deeds have an audience who rejoices at our righteousness or grieves at our sins. One day the books will be opened—perhaps more contemporary imagery would read "the tapes will be replayed"[6]—and the deeds recorded there will speak for or against us (see 3 Nephi 27:26).

3. Your sins are forgiven you. Even though we are not yet perfect, our honest but imperfect attempts to live the gospel and teach it to others are acceptable to God. Our ultimate innocence, worthiness, and perfection are in the end his work rather than ours and constitute the highest blessings of his atonement (see D&C 76:69). Through Christ, the official tapes of our lives may be edited, so to speak, and every sin and unworthiness removed. And if through Christ all our mistakes are removed from the records, then we are left with perfect records!

4–5. See Doctrine and Covenants 58:61–63.

6. Have brought you together. That is, brought Joseph's party of eleven together with four late-arriving elders.

6. The promise. See Doctrine and Covenants 52:42–43.

6. The faithful among you. Not all the elders present on this occasion remained faithful. Ezra Booth lost his testimony on this very journey and later went public with complaints against Joseph Smith (see D&C 64:15–16).[7] Joseph Coe was excommunicated in 1838.

One reason some of the men in Joseph's party had become critical of the Prophet was that they had expected to make many converts, whereas—mostly because of their own unwillingness to preach—they actually had little missionary success. The murmurers in Joseph's party should have waited until *all* the elders had reported before complaining, for the missionaries who arrived in Zion after them had tremendous proselyting success.

7. Horses . . . or in chariots. The more contemporary term for the archaic word *chariot* would be *wagon*. Hyrum's group of "late" missionaries was delayed in part by preaching along the way and in part by John Murdock's illness, which made it difficult for him to continue toward Independence. After Doctrine and Covenants 62 was received, the missionaries traveling with John Murdock combined their money and bought a horse, thus enabling John to continue his journey with them more easily. The Lord here made it clear that he had no objection to such an expenditure if it moved the work forward.

7. This blessing. This phrase refers to the blessing of riding a horse or riding in a wagon instead of walking.

8. These things remain with you. It was up to the missionaries to decide how to administer their resources to best magnify their callings. Some people might have objected to the purchase of a horse for John Murdock as an unnecessary extravagance. After all, the elders probably would have made it to Independence eventually even without such a purchase. But it is up to individual stewards to manage their stewardships wisely for the long-term good of the kingdom. As long as our primary goal is to build the kingdom of God, we are justified in our expenditure of the Lord's resources to that end, even though we may also benefit indirectly from such a decision. Should Church leaders today spend sacred tithing funds for airplane tickets, renting vehicles, staying in hotels, and eating in restaurants when they travel on the Lord's errand? If these measures make them more effective in building up the kingdom of God, then *yes,* of course they should.

1. *History of the Church,* 1:205.
2. John *Murdock Autobiography,* 10.
3. See Commentary on D&C 58:61.
4. See Levi Hancock Journal, cited in Woodford, Historical Development, 1:784.
5. See Pratt, *Autobiography of Parley P. Pratt,* 54.
6. See Commentary on v. 3.
7. See Background to D&C 71.

DOCTRINE AND COVENANTS

63

BACKGROUND

J oseph Smith, Oliver Cowdery, and Sidney Rigdon returned to Kirtland from their mission to Missouri on 27 August 1831. The rest of their party of eleven made their way back during the next few days or weeks. Since the revelations contained in Doctrine and Covenants 57–62 had been received by the Prophet while he was in Missouri, the Kirtland Saints were not yet aware of them. Consequently, Joseph and Sidney's report of these revelations and of the events surrounding their reception caused great excitement among the Ohio Saints, who rejoiced to know that the center place of Zion had been located, that a temple site had been designated there, and that the land of Zion had been dedicated for their future inheritance. Understandably, the homecoming of the Missouri missionaries greatly increased the Saints' interest in Zion, and on 30 August 1831, three days after his return to Kirtland, Joseph Smith received this additional revelation, Doctrine and Covenants 63, on the subject of Zion and how it was to be established.

Joseph's leadership had been sorely missed in Ohio during the two and a half months he and the other leading brethren had been gone from Kirtland, for some of the Saints there had wandered. After Joseph's return an increased number of disciplinary councils were held in Kirtland, and Simeon Carter is recorded to have mourned over what he called the "falling away" that had taken place in Kirtland while they were absent[1] (compare vv. 22, 53). In addition, Ezra Booth and a few others who shared his disillusionment with the work had begun to criticize Church leaders and to question the whole idea of establishing Zion. It is not surprising, therefore, that Doctrine and Covenants 63 should also warn the Saints in Kirtland of their need to repent and to eliminate evil from among them, explaining yet *again* that they could not be God's people and could not establish Zion unless they did so (see vv. 13, 19, 63).

In his introduction to Doctrine and Covenants 63, Joseph chose to pass over the warning to the cynical and sinful, and focused instead on the new information given the Saints concerning Zion: "In these infant days of the Church, there was a great anxiety to obtain the word of the Lord upon every subject that in any way concerned our salvation; and as the land of Zion was now the most important temporal object in view, I enquired of the Lord for further information upon the gathering of the Saints, and the purchase of the land, and other matters, and received the following"[2]—Doctrine and Covenants 63.

COMMENTARY

1–19. The rebuke contained in these verses is for the Saints collectively. Not everyone is a Saint who declares himself or herself to be (see v. 1), and our worst enemies can be our own carnal natures. There is a strong reproof here for those Saints who were drawing away from the Church because they had expected to witness miracles or to experience supernatural blessings but did not do so.

1. That call yourselves the people of the Lord. Just about anyone can join the Church and become nominally a Latter-day Saint, yet among the members there are those who merely take the name or the calling and not the covenant obligations assumed by the elect. Doctrine and Covenants 63 is for all who are called Saints, both the obedient and the rebellious, though verses 1–19 apply more particularly to the latter.

3. Who willeth to take even them whom he will take. The power of life and death rests with God alone. No one dies contrary to the will of the Lord. This does not mean, however, that God arbitrarily "kills" people. Though he takes or leaves whom he will, we must remember that his work and his glory is "to bring to pass the immortality and eternal life" of his children (Moses 1:39). This is God's ruling motive in *all* that he does. Thus, God's purpose in taking or leaving this or that individual is always to maximize eternal prospects.

In speaking of the tragic death of children, Joseph Smith taught that "the Lord takes many away, even in infancy, that they may escape the envy of man, and the sorrows and evils of this present world; they were too pure, too lovely, to live on earth; therefore, if rightly considered, instead of mourning we have reason to rejoice as they are delivered from evil, and we shall soon have them again."[3] When Joseph wrote these words, he and Emma had already experienced the deaths of six of their own children, and it is unlikely that this sweet doctrine was merely a platitude for them. True, there may be many reasons why children die, but this is clearly one of them, and whatever the reason for the temporary loss, faithful parents *will* soon have their little ones again, forever and ever.

7–9. Signs. Signs are miracles, events that indicate supernatural intervention into the natural world. A *sign,* as the term is used here, means temporal evidence or proof, something sensory, tangible, or empirical, for spiritual realities. Those persons whose interest in such proofs, the lust for signs, exceeds their faith in and faithfulness to Christ, will get what they seek. In other words, they will see signs. But what they see will not bring about their salvation, for salvation comes only through faith in Christ. It is a great sin to seek more diligently or to value more highly the by-products of faith, such as signs or miracles, than we value the saving faith itself.

"Show me Latter-day Saints who have to feed upon miracles, signs and visions in order to keep them steadfast in the Church, and I will show you members of the Church who are not in good standing before God, and who are walking in slippery paths."[4]

8. Those among you who seek signs. Ezra Booth and a few others like him turned away from the Church at this time because they could not maintain their faith without frequent miracles to sustain it. Ezra Booth, a former Methodist minister, had joined the Church because he had witnessed the miraculous healing of Alice Johnson's arm by the Prophet Joseph Smith. About a month later, at a conference in June 1831, Ezra himself was overcome by an evil influence, which the Prophet quickly rebuked. Ezra expected to experience even greater miracles than these in Missouri, but when Joseph didn't meet his expectations, the sign seeker lost his faith. Actually, he had no real faith to lose, for what little belief he did have was dependent upon physical rather than spiritual evidence. The basis for his temporary and shallow belief was the miracles or signs he had experienced rather than the confirming witness of the Holy Spirit.

9. Faith cometh not by signs. Signs can neither create nor strengthen faith, for *faith* is by definition the belief in things that cannot be proven physically or empirically (see Hebrews 11:1). When someone says, "Well, if you can just prove this or give me a little more evidence for it, then I'll believe it," this is the opposite of faith, for it is a demand that spiritual realities be proven empirically before accepting that they are so; faith, on the other hand, is having confidence that something is so, even though one cannot prove it. Faith does have its own kind of evidence and proofs, but these are spiritual in nature and will not satisfy the natural mind's demand for measurable, empirical demonstration. This is why intellect or a high I.Q. are not necessary for faith and, in fact, cannot increase faith, for true faith is the ability to believe and follow what the Spirit says to us even when natural evidence or other intellectual justification for our course of action may be absent.

9. But signs follow. Nevertheless, when we have committed to live by faith without needing or seeking signs, then signs will occur. In this way faith brings miracles in its wake, where they may serve as superfluous confirmation of what we *already* knew. Miracles can never bring faith in their wake, however, for faith is believing without such proofs—"the evidence of things *not* seen" (Hebrews 11:1; emphasis added; see also Ether 12:6)—and, it might be added, not touched, tasted, smelled, or heard. In the gospel plan, signs are not designed to produce faith but rather to bless and comfort those who already live by faith. Only *after* we have exercised faith are we entitled to the confirmation of signs and miracles.

11. Only in wrath unto their condemnation. God sometimes does show signs to the wicked, as he did to Laman and Lemuel, for example, but these signs only serve as testimonies against them, that even when they know the will of God by empirical evidence, they still resist it. Those who sin against what they *know*, against what they have seen, or heard, or touched, are more guilty than those who, without empirical knowledge, simply lose their faith and sin against subjective feelings.

12. Signs and wonders for faith. It is wrong, and logically contradictory, to seek miracles or signs for the purpose of creating or strengthening faith, since faith is believing even when there is no physical evidence or logical justification. Moreover, asking God to prove himself with signs before we will believe him constitutes the sin of "tempting God" (see Deuteronomy 6:16; Jacob 7:14). Tempting God is demanding that he meet our tests, that he submit himself to be judged and evaluated by our human reasoning.

14. Adulterers and adulteresses. The Prophet established a certain link between sign seeking and adultery with the following illustration: "When I was preaching in Philadelphia, a Quaker called out for a sign. I told him to be still. After the sermon, he again asked for a sign. I told the congregation the man was an adulterer; that a wicked and adulterous generation *seeketh* after a sign; and that the Lord had said to me in a revelation, that any man who wanted a sign was an adulterous person. 'It is true,' cried one, 'for I caught him in the very act,' which the man afterwards confessed, when he was baptized."[5] This statement needs to be tempered with the understanding that while all sign seekers are adulterous persons,[6] not all adulterers necessarily seek signs. Also, those who seek a *spiritual* witness of the truth, rather than physical proof, are not sign seekers. God does not expect us to believe for no reason at all, but he does expect us to believe for spiritual reasons rather than because of temporal proofs.

Those who are guilty of adultery in the Church and who yet remain unrepentant and undiscovered are faced with three possible alternatives: (1) they will confess and repent, (2) they will eventually be discovered and their sin will be revealed anyway, or (3) they will lose the Spirit of God and will apostatize, denying what they once knew to be true (see v. 16).

16. Commit adultery in their hearts. See Doctrine and Covenants 42:24.[7]

16. Shall deny the faith. Because the Holy Spirit will not dwell in unclean hearts, those in the Church who have committed adultery and have not repented cannot have the companionship of the Holy Spirit. For them the Comforter offers no comfort, and partaking of the sacrament is hypocrisy. Left to themselves, their carnal minds can no longer discern the truth of the gospel, for spiritual things are *spiritually* discerned (see 1 Corinthians 2:14), and adulterers no longer enjoy the blessings of the Spirit. The unrepentant then usually adopt the values and perspective of the world to fill the void left in their minds and hearts by the loss of the Spirit. Such individuals will generally then kick against the Church, with its restrictions and its reminders, until they are entirely free of it.

Repentance, of course, would reverse the process, but repentance requires us to humble ourselves, to suffer some degree of shame, and to give up both the sin and those involved in it with us.

16. And shall fear. Fear before the Lord is the result of sin or lack of faith. As we approach the end of the world, the second coming of the Savior, and the judgments of God upon the world, the faithful Saints, through the atonement of Christ and the assurance of the Comforter, will not fear what comes. Faith in Christ and a testimony of his gospel turn natural fear into peace, love, joy, and confidence (see Romans 8:15; Moroni 8:16). If we really believe the promises of the Savior, we do not fear the future. In contrast, as the Second Coming and its events draw closer, the wicked and those who do not believe the words of Christ will be overcome with paralyzing fear, knowing their own filthiness and rejecting or denying the possibility of becoming clean (see Luke 21:26; 1 Nephi 22:22–23).

Even before the events of the end-time begin to play out, however, those who commit sexual sin and will not repent live in fear of discovery. They fear the loss of all things that awaits them if they do not repent, and yet they also fear repentance. They fear light, for light reveals their sins. They fear truth, for the truth about themselves is ugly. They fear death and hell, for they know Satan has gained power over them and will rule over them after their death.

17. I, the Lord, have said. See Revelation 21:8; 22:15.

17. Loveth and maketh a lie: The phrase likely refers to those who do not merely lie to achieve their ends but who actually love the process of invention and deception, and who lie for the love of lying.

17. Whoremonger, and the sorcerer. The English word *whoremonger* means "one who deals or trades in sex." In the King James Version of the New Testament, however, *whoremonger* always translates to the Greek *pornos*, which has the much broader meaning of "a sexually immoral person." Thus, *any* sexual relationship outside of heterosexual marriage renders one a "whoremonger."

The English word *sorcerer* refers to anyone who pretends to have or to control supernatural powers—for example, palm readers, psychics, mediums, astrologers, and channelers. A magician who claims to actually possess magical powers would therefore be a "sorcerer" in the scriptural sense, while a magician who claims only to be an entertainer would not be so labeled. In addition, the Greek word used for *sorcerer* in Revelation 21:8 and 22:15 (*pharmakos*) also includes those who practice quack medicine, that is, any so-called healer who claims special powers and victimizes the sick by selling phony "cures."

17. Fire and brimstone. The imagery is figurative but effective. *Brimstone* is sulphur, a hard, brittle, and flammable substance. It is called brimstone because in antiquity it was found mainly around the rims of volcanoes. It is possible that the lake of fire and brimstone is meant to evoke an image of molten lava bubbling in the crater of an active volcano.

17. The second death. The *first* death, which began immediately following the transgression of Adam and Eve in the Garden, consists of the spiritual separation from God brought about by the Fall and by our own sins. The physical, or temporal, aspects of the first death came later, though still in the thousand-year "day" of their transgression, and consisted of the separation of our spirits from our bodies in physical death (see D&C 29:41–42; Genesis 2:17).

Spiritual redemption from this first death comes by being "born again," or begotten spiritually through the atonement of Christ (see D&C 76:24). When we enter into the gospel covenant, we are reunited spiritually with God by receiving the gift of the Holy Ghost. Physical redemption from the first death—the reuniting of our spirits and bodies and a reunion with God—comes only with the resurrection (see Helaman 14:16–17). Thus it follows that the time frame of the first death extends from our mortal birth until our resurrection, *including* whatever time we may spend in the spirit world.[8]

The moment of resurrection, the reunion of spirit and body

and the reunion of mortal humans with their God, marks our final and complete redemption from the first death. This redemption comes to all through the grace of God. There is a *second* death, however, an event that takes place after the resurrection and the final judgment, when those mortals who have refused salvation are separated a second time from the presence and glory of God and are cast out of his kingdom into outer darkness.

There will be some people who continue to reject Christ and refuse to repent right down to the resurrection. Without the cleansing and atonement found in Christ, these persons will be "filthy still" at the end (D&C 88:35, 102; Revelation 22:11; Mormon 9:13–14), and must therefore be resurrected in their filthiness without any glory at all. In their case, the resurrection is a "resurrection of damnation" (John 5:29; Mosiah 16:11–12). These are the sons of perdition, who alone will be separated from God and cast out of his presence a second time to dwell in outer darkness with the devil and his angels forever and ever (see D&C 76:32–49). Hence, their fate is called the *second* death.

Sometimes in the contemporary Church, the period between death and resurrection when the wicked are cast into hell is also called a second death, but this is technically incorrect. For even the wicked will be redeemed from this hell and will eventually be saved in a kingdom of glory. The real second death will occur only after the resurrection, and the only ones who will suffer it are the sons of perdition (see D&C 76:37–43).

18. The first resurrection. That period of time in which the just and faithful Saints are resurrected is often called the "morning" of the first resurrection. This period began with the Resurrection of the Savior himself. It continues until the resurrection of the just at his second coming (see 1 Thessalonians 4:16; Revelation 20:4–6) and further includes those mortals on the earth who will be changed in a twinkling (see v. 51), even until the end of the Millennium. It also includes all those who have already been resurrected, whether in the meridian of time (see

Matthew 27:53) or sometime between the first and second comings of the Lord (such as the angel Moroni, for example).

It should be apparent, then, that the morning of the first resurrection refers not so much to a *time* as to a *quality* of resurrection. In other words, those who inherit the celestial kingdom rise in the morning of the first resurrection, whether they are resurrected at the time of Christ, at his second coming, during the Millennium, or sometime in between these events.

The "heathen nations" and others who will receive a terrestrial glory are also resurrected in the first resurrection, but not in the "morning" of that resurrection with the celestials.[9] Finally, the wicked described here in verse 17 will remain, their bodies in their graves and their spirits in hell, until after the first resurrection is over, to be raised in the *last* resurrection at the end of the Millennium (see D&C 76:85; Revelation 20:5–7, 12–15).

19–20. Ye are not justified . . . shall overcome. *Collectively* the Saints cannot be accepted as righteous, cannot be considered acquitted of all their sins, as long as so many among them remain guilty of the wickedness described in verses 12–17; remember, *ye* is always plural or collective. This weakness on the part of some people presents a problem for even the most righteous individual Saint, because only a collectively "justified" people can establish Zion.

Nevertheless, the promises of God to the individual remain, and even where the Church collectively fails to achieve its goals, individual members who keep their covenants shall overcome and receive all their promised blessings—no matter what else may or may not occur. The Saints are obligated by covenant to work together to establish Zion, but no other person's disobedience can rob a faithful Saint of his or her full, individual blessings.

20. The day of transfiguration. This earth is a living being whose cosmic history parallels that of the humans who live upon it. Before the Fall this earth existed as a *terrestrial* paradise. After the Fall, the earth, like Adam and Eve, also lost its paradisiacal glory and began its present *telestial* existence. The earth mourned the wickedness and filthiness that came out of itself and pleaded with God for cleansing (see Moses 7:48–49). Consequently, the earth was baptized by immersion and cleansed of all wickedness at the time of Noah, and it will be baptized again with fire at the second coming of the Lord. Just as baptism and receiving the gift of the Holy Ghost justify and sanctify human beings, thus transforming them into Saints, so the fallen or telestial earth will be sanctified and transfigured when it is baptized with fire at the Second Coming, and it will receive again the terrestrial or paradisiacal glory that it enjoyed before the Fall (see Articles of Faith 1:10). The actual day of the earth's transfiguration to a paradisiacal state will be the last day of its telestial existence, the day of the Savior's second coming to the earth.

21. The pattern which was shown . . . upon the mount. The reference is probably to the Mount of Transfiguration and the events that occurred there, as described in Matthew 17:1–13 and its parallels in Mark 9:2–13 and Luke 9:28–36 (see John 1:14; 2 Peter 1:16–19). Much more took place upon the mountain, however, than is recorded in the four Gospels. Like Moses on the mount in Moses 1, the apostles received a view of the heavenly patterns governing earthly events. Perhaps the use of the verb *transfigure* for both Jesus on the mount (see Matthew 17:2) and for the earth in the Millennium hints at the nature of the change Jesus experienced upon the mount.[10] God has not yet revealed to the Church all of what happened upon the Mount of Transfiguration nor even the full significance of those events that are recorded.

22. Not by the way of commandment. The Lord often expresses his will to the Church in a form other than as a commandment in order to extend mercy in long-suffering to the spiritually weak, while at the same time offering an opportunity for individual discernment and progress to the spiritually strong. Those who *know* the will of God but disregard it unless specifically commanded to obey fail to grasp the disturbing implications of their attitude.

23. Mysteries of my kingdom.[11] Those who keep the commandments of God will learn things that can only be known through personal revelation (see John 4:10).

24. Not in haste. It was the will of God that the Saints should gather to Zion but that they should gather slowly. The transfer from Kirtland to Independence had to be gradual. Perhaps one reason was that the Lord knew that a rapid influx of Saints into Jackson County could not be sustained by the resources then available. If too many people went to Zion at once, some would be left unprovided for. A rapid influx of Saints to Zion would also cause concern among the earlier settlers and would eventually create opposition and conflict. When the Saints collectively ignored the will of God that Zion be settled slowly, they were soon impoverished and persecuted just as the Lord had warned.

27. Purchase the lands. The earth, including all the property needed for Zion, already belongs to God. Nevertheless, God recognizes the stewardship of civil government, here referred to symbolically as Caesar, and generally works within the systems established by Caesar (see vv. 25–28). As long as government contents itself with its proper stewardship—the things that are Caesar's—then God is willing to operate by Caesar's rules and pay with Caesar's coin.

In Independence, Missouri, this meant that the land, which was to be a Zion for the Saints, had to be legally and lawfully purchased. Purchasing the land would theoretically put government and the law on the side of the Saints. The Lord by this time had repeatedly instructed the Church that any lands to be acquired in Zion must be purchased. No other means of acquisition would be acceptable (see D&C 42:35; 45:65; 48:4, 6; 57:4; 58:37, 49, 52).

Still, some of the Saints would not listen to the repeated word of the Lord but entertained the view that they might take the land of Zion by force of arms just like the children of Israel had taken their promised land from the Canaanites. According to the Doctrine and Covenants, this was never the plan, but the perception among non-Latter-day Saint settlers that this was the aim of the Saints, a perception given credibility by foolish talk among some Mormons, played into Satan's hands in arousing the fear and anger of the mobs.

31. If by blood. The only two ways to get the land were to buy it or to take it. Because the Saints were forbidden to take the land by the shedding of blood, if they didn't purchase the property they could not obtain it and Zion would be lost. Neither this verse nor the similar passage in Doctrine and Covenants 58:53 should be understood as allowing the Saints to consider force as a means of obtaining property in Zion. Though acquisition by force was a theoretical possibility, that course of action had been clearly and repeatedly forbidden.

31. Your enemies are upon you. If events came to the shedding of blood, then the Saints would lose Zion, for they were forbidden to acquire the land by bloodshed. "This remarkable prophecy . . . was given, as we have already remarked, at a time when no human sagacity could have foreseen such events. No man, unless he were a prophet, could have so clearly portrayed the subsequent history of the church. Had it not been for these and other predictions of a like nature, no one would for a moment have supposed, that the people of that boasted land of freedom, would shed the blood of the Saints, and drive them from the lands which they had purchased, and persecute them from city to city, and from synagogue to synagogue."[12]

31. Synagogue. The use of the term *synagogue* instead of *church* or *congregation* creates a parallel between the experiences of the early Saints and those of the disciples in New Testament times. Both groups were called upon to go to the meetinghouses of those who had much of the truth, but not all of it, and who were hostile to the disciples' claims to possess the fulness.

32. I am holding my Spirit. "Do not let this thought become confused in your minds. The Spirit He has withdrawn from the world is not the Holy Ghost (for they never had that!), but it is the light of truth, spoken of in our scriptures as the Spirit of

Christ, which is given to every man that cometh into the world. . . .

" . . . The Spirit of the Lord has been withdrawn. Not because the Lord desires to withdraw that Spirit, but because of the wickedness of mankind."[13]

At some times in history, the wickedness of humanity has made it necessary for the Spirit of God to cease its striving with the stubbornly wicked and to withdraw from them (see Genesis 6:3; D&C 1:33). Whenever this happens, destruction follows, either individually or collectively (see 2 Nephi 26:11).

33. Decreed wars. In the early days of the Church, the Saints were persecuted and driven out; causing God in turn to withhold his Spirit from the guilty. These persecutions of the Saints and the withholding of God's spirit from the wicked were followed soon after by the destruction and carnage of the American Civil War (see D&C 87).

34. The saints also shall hardly escape. *Hardly* means "with difficulty." According to Joseph Smith, "It is a false idea that the Saints will escape all the judgments, whilst the wicked suffer."[14] The experience of the early Saints shows that it will not be easy to establish Zion, but only Zion can offer us safety when the desolations and judgments of God fall upon the rest of the earth. With difficulty—through individual righteousness and through collectively establishing Zion—many of the Saints *will* escape.

35. This is not yet. Once again the Lord clearly indicated that the events being described were not going to happen any time soon but were associated with a later time in this dispensation.

36. These things. This phrase refers to the trials and destructions prior to the Second Coming.

37. Righteousness . . . and faithfulness. Taking "righteousness in his hands" would appear to indicate righteous deeds or actions, while taking "faithfulness upon his loins" may indicate sexual morality.

37. A warning voice. See Doctrine and Covenants 1:4, 18.

37. By word and by flight. The Saints were to demonstrate their own convictions concerning the coming destructions, first by preaching about them and then by fleeing to Zion to avoid them.

38. This farm. This probably refers to the Isaac Morley farm in Kirtland (compare D&C 64:20). Before 1832, most of the Saints gathering to Kirtland settled on the Morley farm, including at the time of this revelation Joseph and Emma Smith.[15] Brother Morley had consecrated his farm to the Lord and was then called to Missouri (see D&C 52:23). While he was gone, the farm was managed by Titus Billings, and at the time of this revelation Brother Morley was still in Missouri serving as a counselor to Bishop Partridge.[16]

39. Titus Billings. Titus Billings was, like Isaac Morley, a native of Kirtland, and the Morley farm had been left in his hands when Morley went to Missouri. Titus was instructed to sell the land so that the proceeds could be used to purchase land in Independence (see v. 40) and so that the members who were then living on the Morley farm would have to prepare for their move to Zion. By 12 September, less than two weeks after Doctrine and Covenants 63 was received, the Prophet and his family moved out of their little house on the Morley farm and moved in with the John Johnson family in Hiram, Ohio, about thirty miles southeast of Kirtland.

40. Them whom I have appointed. This phrase refers to Bishop Partridge, his counselors, and his agents.

41. Those who shall go up. Emigration to Zion was not supposed to be self-appointed. The Saints were to stay in Kirtland and use it as a base of operations for gathering converts from the East and for generating revenue for Zion. Many of the Ohio Saints, however, disobeyed the Lord's will and went to Zion uncalled, unprepared, and unconsecrated, thus straining the spiritual and financial resources of the Church there.

42. The store. Newel K. Whitney owned a mercantile store in Kirtland, and it was one of the largest stores in northeastern Ohio. Because the store produced revenue for the Church, Brother

Whitney was instructed to continue operating it upon the principles of consecration for the good of the Saints.

44. These things are in his own hands. The Lord trusted Brother Whitney to manage the store and consecrate the proceeds without more detailed instructions or commandments.

45. Ordained unto this power. Newel Whitney was not to be ordained the bishop in Kirtland yet (see D&C 72:8) but rather to act as an agent under and for Bishop Partridge, who remained in Missouri.

46. Speedily visit the churches. Joseph had been commanded while still in Missouri to raise money among the Ohio Saints for the purchase of more land in Zion. This fund-raising effort was to employ Sidney Rigdon's written description of the property in Jackson County together with a letter and subscription to be sent out to the churches (see D&C 58:50–51). In this verse Joseph and Oliver were commanded to visit the branches of the Church personally in order to further aid in the fund-raising effort.

47. He that is faithful. In the context of the Kirtland Church in 1831, being faithful meant at the very least being willing to consecrate one's possessions to establish and build up Zion. Faithful acts of consecration not only bring the blessings of God upon us in this life but will "follow" us into the next life (see v. 48). In other words, a record of faithfulness in this life will be accepted in the next life as sufficient indication of our character and worthiness (see Revelation 21:7).

49. The dead that die in the Lord. See Doctrine and Covenants 42:44, 46.

49. All things become new. See 2 Corinthians 5:17; Revelation 21:5. When the Savior comes a second time to establish his millennial kingdom, the earth will be raised from a fallen, telestial state to a paradisiacal, terrestrial state. This change will transform the earth and everything on it. All evil and wickedness will be removed; nothing telestial will remain.

50. He that liveth when the Lord shall come. When Christ comes the second time there will be righteous mortals, both children and adults, then living upon the earth who will be lifted up while the earth is changed and who will then continue to live out their mortal lives in the paradisiacal environment of the millennial kingdom. Adult mortals will continue to marry and bear mortal children during the Millennium, so that mortals will continue to be upon the earth during the entire thousand-year period. When these persons have lived their allotted mortal time, they will pass through the changes of death and resurrection in the "twinkling" of an eye. Old and frail mortals will be changed into glorified, resurrected beings very quickly (see v. 51).

50. The age of man. The prophet Isaiah declared that during the Millennium a child will live to be a hundred years of age (see Isaiah 65:20). Psalm 90:10, in speaking of conditions *before* the Millennium, gives "the days of our years" as "threescore years and ten," or seventy years. So a natural, mortal life span might be shorter before the Millennium than it will be during the Millennium. The important point here is that there will be no premature deaths in the Millennium, neither through disease, nor accident, nor war, nor any other telestial element. None of the mortal population of the millennial earth will die or be changed in a twinkling before their full human life span has been lived.

53. Speaking after the manner of the Lord. It has now been more than a century and a half since the Lord described these events as "nigh at hand." Because "nigh at hand" means "nearly here," why haven't these things happened yet? Because, as the Lord points out, he is speaking from his own perspective of time, a perspective that takes in all eternity. And compared with the entire telestial history of this earth, the time remaining is, indeed, relatively short.

54. Foolish virgins . . . send mine angels to pluck. The references are to the parable of the ten virgins (see Matthew 25:1–13) and the parable of the wheat and the tares (see Matthew 13:24–30, 36–43).

54. An entire separation of the righteous and the wicked.

Nothing telestial will continue into the Millennium. Doctrine and Covenants 86 teaches that the wicked will be separated from the righteous because God allows his children to demonstrate by their mortal choices what they are and what they like. Then he will segregate them according to their own free choices, so that they spend eternity with people pretty much like themselves. This segregation into wheat and tares, chaff and grain, righteous and wicked cannot take place yet, but at the last day and for all eternity thereafter, the wicked will have no influence or impact upon the righteous and will go away into their own place.

56. His writing is not acceptable unto the Lord. The writing referred to is the description of the land of Zion that the Lord commanded to be written in Doctrine and Covenants 58:50–51 (see also D&C 63:55). In his first attempt, Sidney Rigdon would not be advised by Joseph, but insisted on writing the letter his own way. It seems from the text that Sidney was trying to write theology or scripture rather than an inducement for the Saints to purchase land. In his first attempt, he clearly did not address the intended purpose of the letter in describing the land of Zion in the most attractive terms possible.[17] The glowing description of Jackson County found in *History of the Church*[18] is a revised version of Sidney's second, more acceptable attempt to write a description of Zion.

56. He standeth no longer. Sidney was threatened here with a rather severe penalty—not because of his literary failure, but because of his pride and his stubborn refusal to accept counsel or to follow the promptings of the Spirit in completing the Lord's assignment.

58. This is a day of warning. See Doctrine and Covenants 1.

59. My power lieth beneath. Though Jesus' point of origin is "from above," his power and influence, the light of Christ, "lieth beneath." As the creator of all things before the Fall, his power is the basis for all existence, the means by which things came to be and the reason why they do not fly apart (see D&C 88:6–13, 41–42; Colossians 1:16–17). Therefore, his power supports or "lieth beneath" all things. The light of Christ is the foundation that undergirds all present existence.

59. The day cometh . . . subject unto me. When the Savior comes to establish his kingdom upon the earth, nothing that will not obey him will be allowed to remain upon the earth. Beyond this, at the last judgment all those who receive any degree of glory and have any place in the mansions of the Father will be subject to Jesus Christ as their creator and redeemer and, like the elements themselves, they will obey him in their respective spheres.

61. Let all men beware how they take my name in their lips. If only we could comprehend the full majesty of Jesus Christ, we would realize what a wonderful and sacred thing it is even to speak his name. It is an even more glorious privilege to be able to speak *in* his name.

The word *vain* means "empty," "useless," or "pointless." One meaning of taking Christ's name in vain is, therefore, to use it in a manner that is empty and without effect, as do those who claim to speak or act in his name when they do not. This is not merely a question of priesthood authority, nor is this sin limited to the unordained, for even priesthood holders may invoke the name of Jesus Christ in attempting to present their own words or desires as his. Whenever we speak or act in the sacred name of Jesus Christ, we had better be sure that he really approves of what we are doing, lest we invoke his name in vain or for nothing.

Another way of taking Christ's name in vain is to speak it without purpose or merely for rhetorical effect, as does the casual blasphemer. It might even be possible to take his name in vain when we pray publicly, if the phrase "in the name of Jesus Christ, amen" is merely a formula signaling that we are finished praying and the congregation may open their eyes.

Perhaps the worst form of using Christ's name in vain is to invoke it when making promises, oaths, or covenants, and then to break them. Finally, members of the Church may take his name in vain when they take his name upon themselves in baptism and then fail to remember him and keep his commandments as they have promised to do (see D&C 20:77, 79).

63. I, the Lord, will own them. To *own* means both to "possess" and to "acknowledge." If we repent, Jesus will acknowledge us before the Father as his very own possessions (see D&C 29:27; Matthew 10:32; 1 Corinthians 6:20).

64. That which cometh from above is sacred. This phrase directs our attention back to verse 59, referring again to Jesus Christ and all that pertains to him, as, for example, his atonement, his redemption, his mercy, his love, and his grace.

64. By constraint of the Spirit. The Holy Spirit will let us know when we may rightly use the name of Christ and speak of sacred things. Whatever the Spirit directs in this regard will be correct and justified. But because the Spirit is gained through prayer, without frequent prayer we risk loss of the Spirit; and without the guidance of the Spirit, we risk taking Jesus' name in vain and otherwise speaking inappropriately of sacred things.

65. Seek them a home. Sidney Rigdon had lost his home in Mentor, Ohio, when he joined the Church the year before. At this time, the Smith family was living on the Morley farm, which the Lord had just commanded be sold (see v. 39). Thus, both Sidney and Joseph needed to find new lodgings for themselves and their families. Through this revelation the Lord could have told Joseph where to move, but, perhaps to illustrate the importance of verse 64, Joseph was instructed to find this out on his own through prayer. Within two weeks of receiving this commandment, Joseph and his family moved in with the John Johnson family, and Sidney Rigdon and his family moved into a cabin on the Johnson property.

66. These things. This phrase refers to the common, human problems of how to live, where to live, how to support one's family, and so on. These everyday challenges were a continual weight on the shoulders of the Prophet Joseph Smith and his family. The Lord did not magically resolve for them these common problems of life and mortality. They struggled to find their way and make ends meet as much as any of us, and more than most. That the Smiths accomplished what they did for the Lord, while at the same time dealing with trying domestic difficulties, bestows upon them the greater glory, as it does also for other faithful Saints in similar circumstances.

1. See Cannon and Cook, *Far West Record,* 22.
2. *History of the Church,* 1:207.
3. *History of the Church,* 4:553; compare also *History of the Church,* 6:316.
4. Smith, *Gospel Doctrine,* 7.
5. *History of the Church,* 5:268; emphasis added; see also *History of the Church,* 3:385.
6. See Smith, *Teachings,* 157.
7. See Commentary on D&C 42:24.
8. See Commentary on v. 18.
9. See Commentary on D&C 45:54.
10. See Commentary on v. 20.
11. See Commentary on D&C 6:7, 11; 8:11.
12. Lundwall, *Masterful Discourses and Writings of Orson Pratt,* 98.
13. Smith, "Predicted Judgments," 5–6.
14. *History of the Church,* 4:11.
15. See Anderson, *Joseph Smith's Kirtland,* 14, 152.
16. See Cannon and Cook, *Far West Record,* 13–14.
17. For the text of both letters, see Sidney Rigdon Papers, LDS Church Archives.
18. See Smith, *History of the Church,* 1:197–98.

64

BACKGROUND

Septermber of 1831 was a busy month for the Kirtland Saints. Joseph and Oliver had just returned from Missouri and were deeply involved in raising funds for land purchases in Zion through the subscription of members and through the consecration of some Kirtland properties and the sale of others. Because the Morley farm was to be sold as part of this effort, the large number of Saints then living there had to find new housing. Many of these members had been directed to emigrate to Zion before winter, and preparations for their long journey on such short notice consumed both time and resources.

Sidney Rigdon and Joseph Smith, who had also been living on the Morley farm, were similarly faced with finding new homes. On 12 September 1831, the day after Doctrine and Covenants 64 was received, Joseph, Emma, and their four-month-old adopted twins moved into the home of John and Alice Johnson in Hiram, Ohio, occupying a single room in the two-story Johnson farmhouse. The Johnsons were friends of Sidney Rigdon and had been converted to the Church when the Prophet healed Alice of a chronic and painful rheumatism. Sidney and Phoebe Rigdon, with their six children, moved into an old log cabin on the 304–acre Johnson farm. For the next several months, the Johnson farmhouse served as the headquarters of the Church and was the site of about eight Church conferences and more than a dozen revelations.

One reason the Prophet moved so far from Kirtland in September 1831 was to avoid the persecution beginning there. Another reason was to provide a quiet place, more insulated from trivial administrative demands in Kirtland, where he and Sidney could resume serious work on Joseph's translation of the Bible. This work had begun by commandment in 1830, shortly after the Church was organized, and had been interrupted by the move from New York to Ohio in early 1831 and by the mission to Missouri in the summer of that year. Joseph Smith was determined to continue the work of translation as he had been commanded.

Joseph's own brief account of the setting of Doctrine and Covenants 64 reads as follows: "The early part of September was spent in making preparations to remove to the town of Hiram, and renew our work on the translation of the Bible. The brethren who were commanded to go up to Zion were earnestly engaged in getting ready to start in the coming October. On the 11th of September I received the following."[1]

COMMENTARY

2. I will that ye should overcome. God is on our side, and he will do whatever he can to bring us to victory. We must remember that because of our mortal weaknesses, however, we can overcome the world only by the compassion (see v. 2), forgiveness (see v. 3), and mercy (see v. 4) of God. In this mortal sphere, we ultimately overcome all things not by our own efforts or perfection but by relying upon the merits and perfection of Christ (see, for example, 2 Nephi 2:8; 31:19; Alma 22:14; Moroni 6:4). See also Doctrine and Covenants 76:53, where those who inherit the celestial kingdom are not described as overcoming by willpower or by perfect performance but by their faith in Christ.

3. For mine own glory. The salvation of souls *is* the glory of God (see Moses 1:39).

3. I have forgiven you your sins. In a remarkable display of mercy and compassion, the Lord unilaterally declared an amnesty for the elders of the Church. As of 11 September 1831, their slates were wiped clean. In doing this, the Lord provided for the Saints an example of mercy and forgiveness that set the stage for the sweeping commandment that follows in verses 9–10. First the Lord forgave his servants, freely and apparently without exception. Then he commanded the Saints to forgive one another in the same manner, following his example.

4. I have given unto you the kingdom. Note that this is not the promise of a future gift but the assurance of a present possession. When we come to Christ and enter into the covenant of the gospel through faith in Christ, repentance, and baptism, we then receive the gift of the Holy Ghost and so become, conditionally, members of the kingdom of God. The one condition is that we endure. In this life, as long as we keep our gospel covenants, we continue to possess the kingdom of God.

5. The keys of the mysteries of the kingdom. See Doctrine and Covenants 28:7; 35:18. These keys include the right to receive revelation concerning things of the kingdom previously unknown in this dispensation. The Lord informed the Church that while Joseph lived, he, and he alone—not Oliver, not Sidney—would hold these keys on the single condition that he obey the Lord's ordinances.[2] In March 1833, the Lord further declared that Joseph Smith would hold these keys of the kingdom not only during his mortal life, but in eternity as well (see D&C 90:3).

5. The means I have appointed. In Doctrine and Covenants 28:7 the Lord had told Oliver Cowdery that Joseph would hold the keys of the mysteries "until I shall appoint unto them another in his stead." In Doctrine and Covenants 35:18 the Lord told Sidney Rigdon that if Joseph did not "abide in me . . . another will I plant in his stead." Doctrine and Covenants 43:4 also admits the possibility that Joseph could lose his place to another appointed in his stead.

By September 1831, some of the Saints in Kirtland had become antagonistic toward the Prophet (see D&C 64:6), and they could have used the above passages to suggest it was time for another to take Joseph's place. The Lord here made it very clear, however, that while Joseph was obedient he would continue to hold the keys as long as he lived, and this was made explicit eighteen months later in Doctrine and Covenants 90:3. In this verse the Lord informed the Church that Joseph Smith would hold the keys in this world and in the world to come. The same principle holds true today. Barring unfaithfulness, those who hold the keys of the kingdom—the president of the Church individually and members of the Quorum of the Twelve Apostles collectively—hold them for this life and the life to come.

7. He has sinned. Sin is the common lot of all humanity, and it would be impossible for Joseph Smith or any other Church leader before or since *not* to have sinned in some manner or other, even during his career as prophet, seer, and revelator. For all members of the Church, including Church leaders, however, sins of personal weakness can be forgiven through confession, repentance, and the renewal of covenants available in taking the sacrament.

7. Sinned unto death. That is, committed sins that will bring the second death at the last judgment.[3] The willful shedding of innocent blood by a Church member cannot be forgiven in this life despite earnest attempts at confession and repentance, and the sin against the Holy Ghost may not be forgiven even in the life to come (see Matthew 12:31; Hebrews 6:4–6; 10:26–29).

8. My disciples, in days of old. This phrase probably refers to Jesus' disciples in New Testament times. The Lord is not hesitant to let us know that the disciples of that dispensation had trouble getting along with each other, just as the disciples of this dispensation sometimes do (see, for example, Mark 9:33–34;

10:41–42; Acts 15:24, 39; 2 Corinthians 11:12–13; Galatians 2:11; 3 John 1:9–10).

8. Sought occasion against one another. As used here, an *occasion* means an opportunity for taking action (see Daniel 6:4; 2 Corinthians 11:12). Thus, the ancient disciples, like those in Joseph's day and in ours, sometimes sinned by looking for opportunities to accuse, confront, oppose, or antagonize one another.

8. Forgave not one another in their hearts. That is, they still held grudges, even though outwardly they may have appeared to have forgiven one another.

9. He that forgiveth not . . . standeth condemned. The Savior set the stage, so to speak, for verses 9–10 by already forgiving the sins of the Saints in verse 3. Having thus provided the example in his own relationship with the Saints, he now asked the Saints to do the same thing in their relationships with one another. As beneficiaries of the atonement of Christ, we have been forgiven of our sins. If we seek and accept the mercy and forgiveness of God for *our* sins, but then refuse those who seek the same mercy and forgiveness from us, we fall under the condemnation of the unmerciful servant in the Lord's parable (see Matthew 18:21–35, which provides necessary background to vv. 9–10).

9. There remaineth in him the greater sin. Of course, there are worse sins than holding a grudge, but the offender who has truly repented of his sin and truly seeks forgiveness from those he has injured has none of his sin remaining. On the other hand, the grudge holder, unmerciful and unrepentant, has *all* of his or her sin remaining. Our holding a grudge will not keep the repentant individual from receiving God's forgiveness, but it will render *us* unfit for it (see Matthew 6:15).

10. It is required to forgive all men. If we expect to be sons and daughters of God, and if we expect to become like him, then we must be willing, as he is, to forgive all those who sin against us (see Matthew 5:44–48). If we invoke the principle of mercy when we plead for God's forgiveness, how can we reject that same principle when others plead for our forgiveness? At the peril of our souls, we dare not, for we are forgiven *as we forgive* (Matthew 6:12, 14–15).

The forgiveness required of us here is not totally unconditional, however. Even here there are limits, and the implied condition for repeated forgiveness is repeated repentance. Just as God's forgiveness for sins comes only to those who repent, so it is the *repentant* brother we must forgive seven times in a day (see Luke 17:3–4; D&C 98:40).

In addition, the principle of forgiveness does not deprive us of the right to act in our own defense. We are not allowed to hate the aggressor or to hold a grudge against him, but we are not required to suffer preventable injury at his hands either, even on a first offense. The right of self-defense also justifies severing any contact with someone who constitutes a physical, moral, mental, emotional, or spiritual hazard for us.

Moreover, *forgiveness* does not always mean what some people think it means, or what they want it to mean. For example, to forgive an employee who has embezzled does *not* mean one must rehire him or her or even that one must necessarily drop criminal or civil charges. To forgive an errant Church member doesn't mean he or she shouldn't still face a disciplinary council (see D&C 64:12–14). Forgiveness requires that we rid ourselves of all bitterness, hatred, or desire for revenge. It requires that we hold a grudge no longer. But forgiveness does not require that all relations and feelings be restored to what they once were between the forgiver and the forgiven. It is possible to forgive those who have offended us while at the same time preferring not to deal with them again. Forgiveness is about the elimination of negative feelings but not always about the restoration of former relationships and privileges.

11. Let God judge between me and thee. In saying this we decline to judge or to condemn others (see Matthew 7:1). We decline to take things personally but leave it to God to reward or condemn our adversaries. In adopting this attitude in our disagreements with others, we avoid anger, bitterness, hatred, malice, and all the other emotional poisons so dangerous to our own hearts. Suspending judgment about the motives or guilt of those with whom we disagree, however, is not the same as letting them have their way. Once again, this principle does not require us to put ourselves or our stewardship at risk but only to deal with our opposition nonjudgmentally.

12–13. Do with him as the scripture saith . . . that God may be glorified. Many people confuse the issues of forgiveness and justice, suggesting that one excludes the other. Yet the same God who commanded the Saints to forgive one another and all men (verses 9–10) also *commanded* Church leaders to discipline unrepentant sinners (verse 12). Church leaders are to forgive first in their own hearts, and then where appropriate to discipline, and at last, when discipline is complete, to forgive in the name of the Church. There can be no grudge, no desire for revenge, no hatred, no bitterness, and no malice in Church disciplinary proceedings, and, as individuals, Church leaders are required to forgive those who are disciplined.

Nevertheless, reverence for God, the lawgiver, demands that his law be obeyed. Church leaders are expected, as individuals, to forgive sinners. But no local Church leader can, as an individual, extend to an unrepentant sinner the forgiveness of the Church or of God. By commandment, the forgiveness of the Church is obtained through the procedures of the Church—through repentance, through confession, and, for serious sins, through its disciplinary councils.

15. Ezra Booth, and . . . Isaac Morley. These two elders had been missionary companions on the trip to Missouri (see D&C 52:23). Ezra in particular did not do well on that trip, and after returning to Kirtland on 1 September, he began criticizing the Missouri mission and the leadership of the Church, especially Joseph Smith. He was disfellowshipped on 6 September, which is probably why the Lord referred to him here as "him who *was* my servant."[4] Ezra formally rejected the Church on 12 September, the day after this revelation was received.[5]

Isaac Morley had at first refused to consecrate his Kirtland farm to the Lord when commanded to do so, but he soon repented and turned his property over to the Church before going to Missouri as Ezra Booth's companion. Isaac may have been affected somewhat by his companion's attitude or temporarily shared some of his views, but he stayed in Missouri to assist Bishop Partridge, and the Lord noted here that whatever his sins may once have been, he had at this time already been forgiven (see v. 16).

17. Edward Partridge. Edward Partridge and Isaac Morley were still in Missouri when Doctrine and Covenants 64 was received (see D&C 58:24),[6] and they probably did not learn of its contents for weeks. Thus the Lord said of them, "When these things are made known unto them . . . , they shall be forgiven." The specific sins referred to here are not known, but the Lord had warned Edward scarcely a month before to repent of his "unbelief and blindness of heart" or he would fall (D&C 58:15).

18. Sidney Gilbert. Sidney was commanded to go to Missouri and to accept the calling as a Church agent. He took Doctrine and Covenants 63–64 with him to Zion, along with other news, information, and instructions.

20. I gave commandment that his farm should be sold. This commandment was given in Doctrine and Covenants 63:38–39. The Morley farm was already in the hands of the Church when Isaac left for Missouri, and it was being managed by Titus Billings, who received the commandment to sell it. This was partially for the good of Brother Morley, who had some difficulty parting with it, as well as to finance the purchase of more land in Zion (see D&C 63:40). The Morley farm was formally sold a month later on 12 October.

This was the same farm on which "the Morley family" had been living with its system of "common stock" before the missionaries to the Lamanites arrived in Kirtland. Most of the family joined the Church and continued living on the farm after their conversion.

21. Frederick G. Williams. Williams earlier had informally consecrated his farm to the Church, and several members were then living on it, but he still held legal title to it. In May 1834 he deeded this farm to the Church without remuneration.

21. A strong hold . . . five years. The Lord wished to retain Kirtland as a base of operations in the East and as a source of revenue for Zion in the West. The specific mention of five years is important, for just months before these five years were up, the Kirtland Temple was dedicated, the Lord approved the efforts of his Saints, and the keys of previous dispensations and of the sealing power were delivered to the Prophet Joseph Smith (see D&C 109–10). By the fall of 1836, serious problems had begun to develop within the Church and between the Church and non-Latter-day Saint citizens in the area; 1837 was the worst year in the history of the Church in Kirtland, and by the summer of 1838 the faithful members of the Church had left Kirtland for Missouri.

21. I will not overthrow the wicked. With the assurance that the prophesied destructions of the end of the world would not take place for at least five years, the Lord calmed the fears of the Kirtland Saints who wanted to flee to Zion for safety but were told to remain in Ohio.

22. I, the Lord, will not hold any guilty. The Ohio Saints had been commanded to remain in Ohio until called by the Prophet to emigrate to Zion (see D&C 58:56; 63:24, 41). Many disobeyed this commandment and thereby contributed to the failure to establish Zion at that time. Here the Lord declared that after the five years were up, all the Ohio Saints could move to Zion without violating his will, provided they were worthy of Zion.

22. An open heart. This probably refers to the willingness of the Saints to share one another's burdens by living the law of consecration.

23. Now it is called today. See Commentary on Doctrine and Covenants 45:6; see also Psalm 95:7.

23. He that is tithed shall not be burned. This is the first mention of tithing in the Doctrine and Covenants. The burning of the last day will consume only the wicked or those who abide a telestial law (see D&C 76:98, 104–5). Those who are faithful tithe payers are living at least a terrestrial law, and if tithing is understood to mean freely giving of one's financial resources to the Lord, as it was in 1831, then full tithe payers are living the celestial law as well. And those living a terrestrial or celestial law will not be burned at the last day.

24. Any that remain in Babylon. See Doctrine and Covenants 29:9; 45:50; and 3 Nephi 25:1. Babylon is everywhere that is not Zion.

26. Not meet that my servants . . . sell their store. The Whitney store in Kirtland generated revenue for the Church and would be needed as a bishops' storehouse for five or six more years. It was wise, therefore, to keep it.

27. It is . . . forbidden, to get in debt. One of the issues being raised at this time by Ezra Booth and other critics of Joseph Smith was that the Lord had forbidden the Saints to incur debts as individuals, while at the same time the Church was collectively going into debt to acquire property in Kirtland and Zion. Here the Lord explained that while individual members are forbidden to contract debts to their enemies, the Lord will do as he pleases (see vv. 28–29). If the Lord used credit as a means of building his Church, or if he instructed his leaders to do so, this was not in conflict with his instructions for individuals in their own personal conduct. The Lord issues and revokes commandments according to our needs, but he is not himself bound by his commandments to us, nor can his agents go wrong when they obey his instructions. Refer to Doctrine and Covenants 115:13, in which the Lord forbade the Saints to incur debt for the building of temples. Today the Church does not go into debt but rather allocates spending in accordance with the contributions of the members.

31. They shall obtain it. The faithful Saints did obtain their inheritance, and even though they were not allowed to enjoy it very long, it is *still* theirs today, and they will both possess it and enjoy its fruits throughout eternity (see v. 30).

32. But . . . in their time. Once again, the Lord reminded the Saints that they should not expect to see the fulfillment of all things anytime soon.

33. The foundation of a great work. The Lord recognized, as some of the Saints did not, that they were merely planting seeds that would not produce for a long time to come. Ezra Booth was offended at the small things that were accomplished in Missouri. Imagine his thoughts if he could have seen the Church in the twenty-first century.

Some Saints may feel that their services in the Church are "small things," but as the Lord stated here, it is out of such small things that great things proceed.

36. The blood of Ephraim. Ephraim was the second son of Joseph, the son of Jacob, or Israel. Nevertheless, after Reuben, the oldest son of Jacob, lost his birthright through transgression (see 1 Chronicles 5:1–2), Ephraim was declared to be the birthright son through the lineage of his father Joseph (see Jeremiah 31:9) and the "head" of all Israel (Psalm 60:7; 108:8), with the right to preside over his elder brother Manasseh, and also over his uncles. The ancient blessings given the tribe of Ephraim by Jacob and by Moses were, respectively, that Ephraim would "become a multitude of nations" (Genesis 48:19) and that Ephraim, as the son who has responsibility for the family, would "push the people together" in their tens of thousands (Deuteronomy 33:17).

The tribe of Ephraim, however, was also cursed at a later time to become "wanderers among the nations" for their apostasy in making alliances with the gentile nations and for worshiping the gentile gods (Hosea 9:17). In 722 B.C., the Lord scattered Ephraim among the nations, where they eventually intermarried and lost their identity, thus in time becoming Gentiles themselves.

In the latter-day restoration of the family of Israel, Ephraim still holds the right to preside. Thus, the descendants of Ephraim, recognized as Gentiles in the scriptures or "a multitude of nations," were the *first* to be converted in order that they might then "push the people together" from all nations. This fulfills the blessings of both Jacob and Moses upon the head of Ephraim. This is also why the scriptures sometimes refer to the latter-day Church members as Gentiles (see D&C 109:60; 1 Nephi 15:13, 22; 2 Nephi 30:3) and sometimes as "Ephraim" (as here and in D&C 113:4). Most converts *are* Gentiles in terms of ethnicity and national origin, but they are also descended from the house of Israel in at least one ancestral line, or else they are adopted into the house of Israel through the gospel covenant.[7]

36. Shall be plucked out. It is not a certain bloodline that causes obedience nor the lack of it that causes rebellion. The ancient tribe of Ephraim rebelled despite its relatively pure bloodlines. Whatever their genealogy or descent, those who rebel against the Lord are not *counted* as the blood of Ephraim nor do they any longer have a right to Ephraim's blessings. The case of William E. McLellin is instructive on this point (see D&C 66). Although William was designated by Joseph Smith as a "true descendent" of Joseph through Ephraim,[8] and he was commanded to "push many people to Zion," which is Ephraim's calling,[9] he later rebelled against the Lord and was excommunicated from the Church. Therefore, as verse 36 says, he is *not* of the blood of Ephraim—regardless of his biological descent. Just as Ephraim was *declared* the firstborn when biologically he was not, the rebellious can be declared "not of Ephraim" when biologically they are. Obedience or rebellion determines who has the blood of Ephraim, not the other way around (see Romans 9:6–8; Galatians 3:29; Abraham 2:10).

39. They who are not apostles and prophets: The power of revelation and righteousness will be such in Zion that false prophets and apostles will be detected.

40. The bishop . . . and his counselors. That is, Edward Partridge, Isaac Morley, and John Corrill in Independence.

40. Who is a judge. This is the first mention in the Doctrine and Covenants of the bishop's role as a judge in Israel.

42. An ensign. An *ensign* is a standard, banner, or flag by which the identity or location of a people may be known. In the last days, Zion will be seen as the standard that identifies and locates the people of God.

42. The people. The scattered descendants of Israel (see Deuteronomy 33:17).

1. *History of the Church*, 1:211.
2. For the broad meaning of ordinances, see Commentary on D&C 1:15.
3. See Commentary on D&C 63:17.
4. Emphasis added.
5. See Commentary on D&C 63:8; Background to D&C 71.
6. See Cannon and Cook, *Far West Record*, 13–14.
7. See Commentary on D&C 19:27.
8. See Shipps and Welch, *Journals of William E. McLellin*, 46; Smith, *Kirtland Revelation Book*, 97.
9. See previous Commentary on v. 36.

65

BACKGROUND

Very little is known of the circumstances surrounding the reception of Doctrine and Covenants 65 sometime in October 1831. Joseph and Emma Smith had been living with John and Alice Johnson in Hiram, Ohio, for about a month when this revelation was received, and Joseph's short account simply states: "In the fore part of October, I received the following prayer through revelation."[1] Although Joseph later remembered this revelation as being received in early October, the *Kirtland Revelation Book,*[2] *The Evening and the Morning Star,*[3] and the William McLellan manuscript all list the date as 30 October 1831. The McLellan manuscript also adds that this revelation was received in connection with Joseph's study of Matthew 6:10, "Thy kingdom come. Thy will be done in earth, as it is in heaven."[4]

The Prophet Joseph designated Doctrine and Covenants 65 as a prayer received through revelation in which the Lord instructs us to "pray unto the Lord" (v. 4) and "call upon the Lord" (v. 5). It would seem that verses 1 and 3 are divine admonitions for Joseph or for the reader to pay attention to the voice from above that commands humanity to prepare. This divine voice also declares the occurrence of glorious events (see v. 2), predicts yet more glorious events to come (see v. 5), and issues a double exhortation to the reader to pray (see vv. 4–5). This lengthy declaration with its double exhortations to call upon the Lord then elicited from Joseph the inspired prayer found in verse 6: "Wherefore, may the kingdom of God go forth."

The beauty, organization, and literary quality of this divine declaration and its responsive prayer are easy to overlook. The initial call to hearken is followed by two injunctions to "Prepare ye the way of the Lord," the first in verse 1 and the second in verse 3. The former enjoins us to prepare by making "his paths straight." The latter enjoins us to prepare by preparing "the supper of the Lamb" and by making "ready for the Bridegroom." Note that the first "prepare ye" in verse 1 is John the Baptist's description of the Savior's *first* earthly coming, his coming into mortality (see Mark 1:3–4; Revelation 19:7, 9). The second "prepare ye" in verse 3 is linked with themes from the Revelation of John and from the parable of the ten virgins describing the Savior's *second* coming (see Matthew 25:1; compare also D&C 33:17; 133:10, 19).

In perfect balance with these twin exhortations to prepare are two exhortations to pray. The first exhortation to pray, in verse 4, also addresses what the Savior did in his *first* coming, while the second exhortation to pray, in verse 5, addresses what the Savior will do at his *second* coming. The language of the revelation similarly expresses the double destiny of the Church, first in this world (see v. 2) and then in the world to come (see v. 5). In this mortal sphere, the Church will roll forth until it fills the whole earth. In the Millennium, the Church will meet the Savior and glorify him on earth as he is now glorified in heaven.

The balance and symmetry of the three double elements—two exhortations to prepare, two exhortations to pray, and two destinies of the Church—each divided neatly between the world that was and the world that is to come, deserve the appreciation of the reader. Moreover, the power of the declarations ought to call forth from us, as it did from Joseph Smith, the twin responses that the kingdom of God may go forth in this world so that the kingdom of heaven may bring with it the world to come.

COMMENTARY

1. A voice. Perhaps this was an audible voice to Joseph, or perhaps the voice of the Lord came into his mind.

1. As of one sent down. The one who is "sent down from on high, who is mighty and powerful" and whose presence "is unto the ends of the earth," meaning encompasses, can only be Jesus Christ, the Son of God. Joseph heard a voice like the voice of the Savior.

2. Keys of the kingdom of God. Keys imply authority, the ability to unlock and open doors or to lock and shut them; in other words, the ability to seal, or close, and to loose, or open. In ancient courts the chamberlain, who held the keys of the palace and controlled access to the ruler and to his family and possessions, was frequently the most trusted and powerful official in the kingdom. For this reason, Saint Peter, who held the keys of the kingdom of God (see Matthew 16:19), is often depicted in Christian tradition as a chamberlain—one who stands at the door or gate of heaven controlling access to the king and kingdom inside. This great authority to seal or to separate, to open or shut the doors of God's kingdom, to permit or forbid entry into the presence of the King, has been given to apostles and prophets of God upon this fallen, telestial earth.

There is a difference between holding the priesthood and holding the *keys* of the priesthood. Any priest or elder has the authority to baptize, for example, but only those who hold the keys of baptism in any Church unit—a bishop or mission president—may give permission for the ordinance to take place. Priesthood holders have the authority to act for God, but may only do so when directed by those who hold the keys, or the administrative responsibility, for that particular work. Priesthood is authority; keys are the right to direct, control, authorize, or forbid the use of that authority.

2. The stone which is cut out of the mountain. The image is from the dream of Nebuchadnezzar in Daniel 2:34, 45. The stone symbolizes the Church and kingdom of God upon the earth.

Being cut out "without hands" symbolizes its divine origin rather than being something manmade.

3. The supper of the Lamb. This phrase is another term for the Messianic feast when the righteous sit down to eat and drink with Christ in his kingdom (see D&C 58:11;⁵ Revelation 19:7–9).

3. The Bridegroom. As a symbol of complete intimacy and oneness, marriage is frequently used in scripture to represent becoming one with Christ. The faithful Church is the bride, and Christ is the Bridegroom (see D&C 88:92; 133:10, 19). They are joined together in the covenant of the gospel, for which the covenant of marriage is symbolic.

4. His wonderful works. It is natural to think of the many miracles and healings of the Savior during his mortal ministry as "his wonderful works," but by far the most wonderful works of the mortal Messiah were his infinite atonement, his sacrificial death, and his victory over the grave in the resurrection.

5. Clothed in the brightness of his glory. What power, what source of energy, will ignite the world on the last day and burn away anything that cannot abide at least a terrestrial glory? It will be the glory of the Son of Man himself as he descends openly and in full view upon the world.

6. Wherefore. That is, in view of what has been declared in verses 1–5. Our response to these things ought to be the fervent prayer of verse 6, which responds directly to the exhortation of verses 4–5. Verse 5 directs us to pray "that his kingdom may go forth," and this command is *precisely* obeyed in verse 6 with the words, "may the kingdom of God go forth."

6. Kingdom of God . . . kingdom of heaven. The usage here makes a marvelous distinction in beautiful harmony with the balancing of the moral and the millennial events found in verses 1–5. It does this by using "kingdom of God" for the mortal Church and "kingdom of heaven" for the millennial Church. These are not two different Churches; both are the Church of Jesus Christ. The terms refer to the same Church in each of two ages or settings.

6. That the kingdom of heaven may come. When the Savior

comes again to the earth, he will bring with him an entire heavenly kingdom together with its inhabitants—a heavenly New Jerusalem to be joined together with the earthly New Jerusalem built by the Saints. This heavenly kingdom will include, but may not be limited to, the city of Enoch that was taken up anciently (see Moses 7:62–63; Ether 3:3, 10).

1. *History of the Church,* 1:218.
2. See Smith, *Kirtland Revelation Book,* 87.
3. Phelps, "Revelation on Prayer," Sept. 1832, 2.
4. See Shipps and Welch, *Journals of William E. McLellin,* 243.
5. See Commentary on D&C 58:11.

66

BACKGROUND

William E. McLellin was first introduced to the gospel by David Whitmer and Harvey Whitlock in Paris, Illinois, as they traveled to Jackson County in July of 1831 (see D&C 52:25). William was so impressed by their message that he traveled to Independence hoping to see the Prophet Joseph Smith, but he arrived there too late. He was baptized in Jackson County by Hyrum Smith and was soon thereafter ordained an elder. William then traveled to Kirtland with Hyrum and finally met the Prophet at a conference of the Church in Orange, Ohio. During this conference, William McLellin was ordained a high priest, and when the conference was adjourned he accompanied the Prophet to Hiram, Ohio, staying with him there for three weeks.

On 29 October Joseph Smith received Doctrine and Covenants 66 in Hiram, dictating it to William McLellin, who acted as scribe.[1] McLellin's journal specifies that it was received on Saturday, 29 October, after McLellin and the Prophet had returned to Hiram from Orange.

Writing of this experience on another occasion seventeen years later, William McLellin said: "From this conference I went home with *the Prophet,* and on Saturday, the 29th, I received through him, and wrote from his mouth a revelation concerning myself. I had expected and believed that when I saw Bro. Joseph,

I should receive one: and I went before the Lord in secret, and on my knees asked him to reveal the answer to five questions through his Prophet, and that too without his having any knowledge of my having made such request. I now testify in the fear of God, that every question which I had thus lodged in the ears of the Lord of Sabbaoth, were answered to my full and entire satisfaction. I desired it for a testimony of Joseph's inspiration. And I to this day consider it to be an evidence which I cannot refute."[3] The fact that William McLellin wrote this account ten years after his excommunication from the Church lends credibility to its truth.

COMMENTARY

1. Your iniquities. It is pointless to speculate what William McLellin's earlier iniquities may have been. At this time the twenty-five-year-old William was a childless widower. The mention of iniquities here might mean nothing out of the ordinary, for all humans remain in their sins until they accept the gospel.

2. Everlasting covenant.[4] As understood by the Saints in 1831, this phrase described the only covenant then available to the members—the covenant of baptism, or the covenant of the gospel. Strictly speaking, the gospel covenant includes everything required for salvation—but not necessarily for exaltation—in the kingdom of God. The fulness of the gospel that accompanies this covenant is found in the Book of Mormon (see D&C 27:5)[5] and consists of faith in the Lord Jesus Christ, repentance, baptism by immersion for the remission of sins, and receiving the gift of the Holy Ghost. Later on, additional sacred covenants, covenants associated with exaltation in the kingdom of God, would become available to the Saints as they completed construction of the Kirtland and Nauvoo Temples.

In contemporary LDS usage, "the new and everlasting covenant" includes all the doctrines and ordinances presently available to the Saints for both salvation and exaltation in the celestial kingdom of God.

2. Fulness of my gospel.[6] William McLellin was blessed for accepting the new and everlasting covenant, which is the fulness of the gospel. Note that the two are equated here. In October 1831, when this revelation was received, the phrase "fulness of the gospel" was understood to mean those doctrines and ordinances mentioned specifically in the Book of Mormon (see D&C 27:5)[7] and did not include the higher ordinances associated with the temple which had not yet been revealed. Contemporary LDS usage, however, defines "the fulness of the gospel" as everything the Lord has revealed to the Church, including those doctrines and ordinances not mentioned in the Book of Mormon.

3. You are clean, but not all. That is, not altogether. The ordinance of baptism can cleanse an individual of his or her past sins, but old habits of mind are not necessarily removed. Though William McLellin was cleansed at baptism, his thinking and perhaps his private behavior since baptism may not have been entirely pure. It must be emphasized that Christ through baptism remits *all* our sins, but only when baptism follows faith and repentance. The text suggests here that there were sins of mind or deed for which William McLellin was not entirely repentant.

5. Proclaim my gospel. William McLellin was called on a mission to those areas around Kirtland that had not been covered by previous missionaries.

6. Go not up. Like most of the Ohio members, William was concerned about emigrating to Zion. Many of the Saints in Kirtland were anxious to go there, and some needed to be restrained. William McLellin was to send what money he could to Zion and was not to worry about his possessions—apparently he owned no land.[8]

7. Go unto the eastern lands. William McLellin and Samuel Smith traveled and preached in eastern Ohio for six weeks before William got sick and returned to Hiram and Kirtland without his companion. The commandment for William McLellin to go into the eastern lands was revoked by the Lord on 25 January 1832, a month after his return to Hiram (see D&C 75:6).

7. Synagogues. See Commentary on Doctrine and Covenants 63:31.

8. Samuel H. Smith. Samuel was the prophet's younger brother, the third person baptized in this dispensation, one of the original six members of the Church, one of the Eight Witnesses of the Book of Mormon, and the first formal missionary of the modern Church.

8. Give him thine instructions. This verse teaches the responsibility of missionary companions to help each other and to stay together.

8. He that is faithful. This phrase refers to the missionaries, not the investigators.

9. And they shall recover. William McLellin's journal entries for this mission record some remarkable healings.[9]

9. Return not. William McLellin was not given a specific term for his missionary service but was to remain in the field, being patient in his afflictions and not leaving his companion, until the Lord recalled him. William seems to have disregarded all these instructions (see D&C 75:6–8).

10. Seek not to be cumbered. *Cumbered* means hindered or burdened. The command seems to refer to William's lingering unrighteousness and his temptation to sexual sin.

10. Commit not adultery . . . troubled. A remarkably blunt bit of advice, but William McLellin seems to have accepted it with no attempt to refute the allegation, even in his private journals. Indeed, he seems even to have appreciated the warning, since he wrote that this revelation fully answered the specific questions he had asked the Lord and that he was entirely satisfied with the answers.[10] At his excommunication trial on 11 May 1838, William McLellin stated that after he lost confidence in Church leaders he "quit praying and keeping the commandments of God, and indulged himself in his lustful desires."[11] Heber C. Kimball also once reminded the apostate William McLellin that Joseph had foretold he would become a Judas "if you did not forsake your adultery, fornication, lying and abominations."[12]

11. Push many people to Zion.[13] Pushing the people to Zion was the calling of Ephraim (see Deuteronomy 33:17). In an addendum to Doctrine and Covenants 66, as recorded in William McLellin's journal and in the *Kirtland Revelation Book*,[14] William was identified as a "true descendant" of Ephraim. His Ephraimite descent is reflected in the language used here to call him to the latter-day work. Moreover, his calling is not merely to convert the people to the gospel but to help in gathering them to Zion. According to his journal, he was particularly concerned with pushing the Saints to Zion.[15]

11. Songs of everlasting joy. Singing always has been and always will be an important form of worship for the Saints of God. Perhaps refusing to sing is a sin similar to refusing to pray.

12. A crown. The crown is variously described as a crown of righteousness (see D&C 25:15), glory (see D&C 58:4), joy (see D&C 52:43), and eternal life (see D&C 20:14). It is the reward of one who overcomes through Christ and who rules in the kingdom of God (see Revelation 3:11, 21). Even with his weaknesses and temptations, if William McLellin would prove faithful to his covenants "unto the end," he was promised the victor's crown of eternal life.

1. See Shipps and Welch, *Journals of William E. McLellin,* 45–46.
2. See 1:219–20.
3. "Batavia, N. Y.," *Ensign of Liberty, of the Church of Christ,* 61.
4. See Commentary on D&C 1:15; 22:1.
5. See Commentary on D&C 27:5.
6. See Commentary on D&C 1:23; 22:1; previous Commentary on D&C 66:2.
7. See Commentary on D&C 27:5.
8. See Shipps and Welch, *Journals of William E. McLellin,* 46.
9. See Shipps and Welch, *Journals of William E. McLellin,* 66–67.
10. See Background to this section; Shipps and Welch, *Journals of William E. McLellin,* 249–50.
11. Smith, *History of the Church,* 3:31.

12. Shipps and Welch, *Journals of William E. McLellin*, 326.
13. See Commentary on D&C 58:45; 64:36.
14. See *Kirtland Revelation Book*, 97.
15. See Shipps and Welch, *Journals of William E. McLellin*, 271–72.

6 7

BACKGROUND

Oliver Cowdery had been instructed in the summer of 1831 to oversee the work of printing for the Church and to assist the Church printer, W. W. Phelps, in his labors (see D&C 55:4; 57:13). By November of that year it was time for Oliver, who was then in Ohio, to return to Zion with materials for the printer. Chief among these would be the collected revelations of Joseph Smith. Consequently, on 1 November 1831, a conference of ten leading elders was held at the Johnson farm in Hiram to decide the details of publication. During the morning session of this conference it was decided that ten thousand copies of the revelations—to be called the Book of Commandments—should be printed, and that Oliver and John Whitmer should take a printer's copy with them to Zion.[1]

It was also the intention of the Prophet Joseph Smith that the elders present at this conference should bear written testimony to the world of the truth of these revelations in the same manner that the Three Witnesses and the Eight Witnesses had testified to the truth of the Book of Mormon.[2] Such special witnesses as these do not merely testify to what they believe but also of what they have come to know through their own personal experience. For this purpose, the elders present were promised a remarkable blessing from the Lord that would confirm the truth of the revelations to them beyond a reasonable doubt (see v. 3). This blessing would enable them to testify of what they knew from their own personal experience rather than of what they accepted from others on faith.

When the afternoon session of the conference convened, however, there was some disunity among the elders concerning the revelations. Apparently, the problem was threefold. First, the blessing offered to the elders, by which they would know for a surety that the revelations were true, had not been received (see v. 3). Second, without this blessing, at least some of the elders present felt they could not in good conscience testify that they absolutely *knew* that every single revelation was from God (see v. 7). Third, these elders' misgivings were based largely on the style and language of the revelations, which in their estimation was not sophisticated enough to convince others of their divine origin. Some who felt themselves better educated than Joseph wanted to edit his revelations in order to improve upon them (see v. 5).

At that point, in the presence of the nine other elders, Joseph received Doctrine and Covenants 67 with the Lord's explanation of why the offered blessing had not been received (see v. 3), and also with an alternate proposal for establishing the truth of all the revelations to the elders' satisfaction (see vv. 4–8).[3]

It is important to note that the issue here was not whether or not Joseph's writing could be improved. Of course it could; good editors can improve almost any document. The question was whether better educated writers could *on that occasion,* November 1831, unitedly write a more convincing revelation than any of Joseph's. Is the inspired quality of a revelation found in what it says or in how it says it? Is the divinity in the message or in its vocabulary and punctuation? The elders present at the November conference established to their own satisfaction that it was the former. With all their superior education, polish, and literary skills, they could not duplicate the divine element that they sensed in the revelations of the Prophet Joseph Smith. And of that they could bear sure and certain witness.

COMMENTARY

1. Behold and hearken. Both look and listen—a very strong "Pay attention!"

3. Ye endeavored to believe that ye should receive. God had promised the ten elders present at the 1 November conference that they would receive a blessing that would give them personal proof of the revelations. The exact nature of this promised blessing is not stated, but it is strongly implied in verses 10–14.[4] The elders had tried to believe God would give them what he promised, but they were also afraid of what he promised. Apparently, in their hearts they were afraid of receiving the blessing.

3. The blessing which was offered unto you. It appears the Lord had promised a special experience to these elders in connection with the Book of Commandments that would be similar to the experiences granted the Three Witnesses and Eight Witnesses of the Book of Mormon (compare v. 10). Though they did not receive a special manifestation at this time, they would still be eligible in the future to have the veil parted and to see the Lord (see v. 13).

3. There were fears in your hearts. The elders failed to receive the offered blessing not so much because they lacked faith to receive it but because collectively they were afraid of it.

4. I, the Lord, give unto you a testimony. Having failed to receive what was offered in order to make their testimonies of the revelations certain, the Lord proposed an alternative means for accomplishing this. The proposed experiment was simple: If human talent could make a revelation as convincing as one of Joseph's, then prove it. Make one. But if with all your education you can't do it, then testify there is more involved here than mere human talent.

When William McLellin, with the help of the others present, then failed to write anything that sounded convincingly like a revelation from God, the issue was settled. Unaided by the Spirit, not even the brightest among them could write a convincing revelation, even though they knew themselves to be much better writers than Joseph Smith (see v. 5). They could write the words, but they could not put the Spirit into them. Of this they could testify without a doubt.

4. Which are lying before you. Apparently, the collected revelations were there at the conference in manuscript form for these elders to examine.

5. Your eyes have been upon my servant Joseph. They were fully aware of Joseph and his limitations. Joseph had much less education than several of the elders present, and these others apparently were privately embarrassed at the unpolished, frontier quality of Joseph's spelling, punctuation, diction, and such. Note that the Lord basically agreed with their estimate of Joseph's writing skills—but that was not the issue. Some of the elders doubted, on the grounds of Joseph's unsophisticated language, that all the revelations could truly be from God (see v. 7).

5. You have sought . . . that you might express beyond his language. The more educated elders wanted to rewrite or "improve" the revelations to make them sound more impressive to an educated audience. Forgetting that the Lord speaks to humans "in their weakness, after the manner of their language" (D&C 1:24), these elders thought the unlearned language of the Prophet argued against the divine origins of his revelations. They also wanted to say more than Joseph had said—to "express beyond his language."

Latter-day Saints believe that God speaks through prophets. Prophets are not, however, merely scribes taking down divine dictation in a single, pure, perfect, and timeless form. Rather, the precise wording of a revelation can be influenced by the mind, education, and verbal or literary skills of the prophet himself (see D&C 1:24). Therefore, there is actually no reason why a revelation could not, with a prophet's approval, be edited for spelling and punctuation, as long as such changes do not alter the meaning or intent of the original—that is, "express beyond his

[Joseph's] language." Such editorial changes have been frequently authorized in printed editions of the LDS scriptures.

6. The least that is among them. This phrase refers to the least well-written of the revelations in the estimation of the elders present.

6. Appoint him that is the most wise. "After the foregoing was received, William E. M'Lellin, as the wisest man, in his own estimation, having more learning than sense, endeavored to write a commandment like unto one of the least of the Lord's, but failed; it was an awful responsibility to write in the name of the Lord. The Elders and all present that witnessed this vain attempt of a man to imitate the language of Jesus Christ, renewed their faith in the fulness of the Gospel, and in the truth of the commandments and revelations which the Lord had given to the Church through my instrumentality."[5]

It is unlikely that William McLellin intended his actions here as a challenge to the Prophet or to the revelations; likely in his own mind he was simply obeying the instructions in verse 6. McLellin's lack of sense consisted at least in part in putting himself forward as the wisest man in the room and in agreeing so readily, even by invitation, to tempt God.

7. Make one like unto it. Joseph Smith was an uneducated man, so if any of his revelations were not from God, then the educated elders present could surely match it with their combined talents. They were to pick a revelation they were unsure of—one of Joseph's worst, so to speak—and then simply write one that sounded as good. That was all. If any of Joseph's revelations were from Joseph alone, the combined elders would surely be able to match his efforts and duplicate the inspired quality they sensed in his revelations.

The reader should note that the experiment proposed here was not open ended; that is, it was not a test offered to all the world in all times and places. Could the elders at this conference match Joseph's language to the satisfaction of their own consciences? Yes or no? Knowing Joseph's limitations as they did, the doubters would have been certain that they could. But when they tried, they failed. Apparently, there was more to Joseph's revelations than just a frontier education.

7. Then ye are justified. If the elders, without God's help, could match one of Joseph's revelations, then they would be justified in harboring some doubts about some of the revelations.

8. Ye are under condemnation if ye do not bear record. On the other hand, if the combined group of elders with their superior educations could not match Joseph, then they would be obligated to testify of the supernatural quality of these revelations.

Immediately after the vain attempt of William McLellin to write something convincing, Joseph received by revelation the following document, which was then signed by the elders present: "The testimony of the witnesses to the book of the Lord's commandments, which He gave to His Church through Joseph Smith, Jun., who was appointed by the voice of the Church for this purpose; we therefore feel willing to bear testimony to all the world of mankind, to every creature upon the face of all the earth and upon the islands of the sea, that the Lord has borne record to our souls, through the Holy Ghost, shed forth upon us, that these commandments were given by inspiration of God, and are profitable for all men, and are verily true. We give this testimony unto the world, the Lord being our helper; and it is through the grace of God, the Father, and His Son, Jesus Christ, that we are permitted to have this privilege of bearing this testimony unto the world, that the children of men may be profited thereby."[6] A slightly revised version of this testimony, signed by the original Quorum of the Twelve Apostles, is included at the beginning of the present edition of the Doctrine and Covenants.

9. The Father of lights. Compare James 1:17. This title applies appropriately to both the Father and the Son. As the light of Christ lights all things, Jesus Christ is the source of all light and energy in this creation (see D&C 88:7–13). The Eternal Father is the Father of Christ, the light of the world. Also, lights could be understood to mean men and women who shed the light of the gospel around them, in which case the title still might apply to either the Father or the Son, who are both fathers of those who are enlightened—in first and second spiritual birth.

10. The veil shall be rent. The veil of the temple, both under the law of Moses and in the fulness of the gospel, symbolizes the separation that exists between the realm of this life and the spiritual realms of God. In our natural, fallen condition, it is impossible for our minds or senses to perceive or to penetrate this barrier or veil, but as we make and keep sacred covenants and obey the commandments of God, the veil becomes thinner and thinner. When we succeed in receiving the priesthood and its ordinances, when we obey the commandments, and strip ourselves of jealousy, fear, and pride—then the barrier between ourselves and the spiritual realm may be breached, as it was for the brother of Jared (see Ether 3:6–20; see also the parallel experience of the elders of Israel in Exodus 24:9–10 and of Nephi, Jacob, Joseph, etc.). This may have been the blessing promised to these elders of the latter-day Israel in Doctrine and Covenants 67:3.

10. And you shall see me. This is the wonderful promise of the Second Comforter repeated again to disciples in this last dispensation (see John 14:12–27), though not every appearance of Christ necessarily bestows the Second Comforter.

10. And know. When through faithfulness the veil has been parted and individuals receive the Second Comforter, then they no longer testify of Christ through faith, for their faith has become sure and certain knowledge. According to Joseph Smith, the Second Comforter is the resurrected Savior himself, and an individual who receives this blessing "will have the personage of Jesus Christ to attend him, or appear unto him from time to time, and even He will manifest the Father unto him, and they will take up their abode with him, and the visions of the heavens will be opened unto him, and the Lord will teach him face to face, and he may have a perfect knowledge of the mysteries of the Kingdom of God."[7] After a person receives the Second Comforter, *faith* in Christ becomes *knowledge* of Christ. Those who receive the

Second Comforter no longer rely primarily upon the witness of others, or upon the witness of the scriptures, or even upon the witness of the Spirit, for they have come to know of themselves through their own experience and the witness of the Holy Ghost (compare Ether 3:19).

10. Not with the carnal neither natural mind. At present, we are fallen beings and are therefore naturally of the telestial order. It is not possible for what is telestial in nature to interact directly with things of a higher order. In order to interact with celestial beings, we must first be transfigured or translated by the Holy Spirit. In other words, our present, fallen natures must be temporarily raised to a higher state of being by the indwelling of the Holy Spirit and partake momentarily of the nature that will be ours in the resurrection.[9]

The distinction made here between "natural" and "spiritual" is *not* between our spirits and our bodies but between our present fallen bodies and our future glorified bodies. The scriptures frequently use the term *spiritual* to refer to glorified, *physical* bodies (for example, 1 Corinthians 15:44). It is the common error of the world's theologies that "spiritual" must mean "nonphysical."

11. No man has seen God at any time in the flesh. This is a true statement, for God possesses a celestial glory, and all humans from the fall of Adam and Eve to the present have been of the telestial order. In order for the two to interact, either God must veil his glory, as Jesus did during his mortal life, or humans must be temporarily raised to a more-than-human glory.

11. In the flesh, except quickened by the Spirit. No *mere* human may see God, but if our natures are raised by the Spirit to a higher level, if we can be transfigured momentarily by the indwelling of the Spirit, then for a moment we are no longer merely human but raised to a level where like may interact with like. This was the experience of all the prophets who have seen God (see Moses 1:11, 14).

13. Ye are not able . . . now. Though the elders present on this occasion were good men devoted to the kingdom, they were not sufficiently stripped of jealousy, fear, and pride to be transfigured and see God. Indeed, some were not ready at that time for the appearance of an angel, though at least three of them had already enjoyed this blessing—Joseph Smith, Oliver Cowdery, and David Whitmer.

13. Until ye are perfected. The term *perfected* here does not refer to philosophical perfection or absolute unimprovability. This would be an impossible interpretation, given the LDS belief in *eternal* progression or enlargement. Rather, being perfected means becoming mature, complete, or whole by the standards of one's current environment. The elders could become perfected by acquiring the virtues necessary for their offered blessing. Moreover, since *ye* is always plural, it is likely the advice here is collective rather than individual.

14. Let not your minds turn back. That is, don't dwell on the opportunity that was lost here; rather, look forward to the eventual reception of the promised blessing.

14. Conferred upon you by the hands of my servant. The reference here may be figurative, or it may indicate that the elders had received a blessing or some other ministration from the Prophet in preparation for the offered experience.

It should not be assumed that all the elders present on this day had doubts or that they all feared the experience offered to them. After all, as witnesses of the Book of Mormon, Oliver Cowdery and David Whitmer had conversed with angels, and John Whitmer and Peter Whitmer Jr. had seen and handled the gold plates.

1. See Background to D&C 1.
2. See *History of the Church*, 1:226; Cannon and Cook, *Far West Record*, 26–28.
3. See Commentary on v. 8; Shipps and Welch, *Journals of William E. McLellin*, 57–58; Cannon and Cook, *Far West Record*, 26–28; Smith, *History of the Church*, 1:221–26.
4. See Commentary on vv. 4–10.
5. Smith, *History of the Church*, 1:226.

6. *History of the Church,* 1:226.

7. *Teachings,* 151.

8. See Commentary on D&C 76:31, 35, 43.

9. See Ludlow, *Companion to Your Study of the Doctrine and Covenants,* 2:187.

68

BACKGROUND

On 1 November 1831, Joseph Smith had convened a special conference of ten leading elders to discuss publication of the collected revelations in a Book of Commandments. This conference was held at the John Johnson home in Hiram, Ohio.[1] At the end of the second day of this conference, Orson Hyde, Luke Johnson, Lyman Johnson, and William McLellin approached Joseph Smith and asked to know the will of the Lord concerning themselves. The Prophet inquired of the Lord in their behalf and received the revelation known as Doctrine and Covenants 68.[2]

Originally this revelation did not contain verses 15–21, which were added by the Prophet in June 1835 in the Kirtland reprint of *The Evening and the Morning Star* when further information about the structure of the Church, including the organization of the First Presidency, had been revealed.

COMMENTARY

1. Orson Hyde. Two weeks younger than Joseph Smith and orphaned by the age of twelve, Orson Hyde was a clerk in Newel Whitney's store in Kirtland and was a minister in the same

Reformed Baptist movement as Sidney Rigdon and Parley P. Pratt. Brother Hyde had been baptized into the Church by his friend Sidney Rigdon one month before Doctrine and Covenants 68 was received and had been a high priest at this time for only a week. As a new member bearing the responsibilities of the high priesthood, Orson wanted to know the Lord's will concerning him.

1. From land to land. "The prophecy in this verse was literally fulfilled. Orson Hyde proclaimed the gospel 'from people to people, from land to land.' In 1832, he and Samuel H. Smith traveled in the States of New York, Massachusetts, Maine, and Rhode Island—two thousand miles—on foot. In 1835 he was ordained an apostle, and in 1837 he went on a mission to England. In 1840 he was sent on a mission to Jerusalem. He crossed the Ocean, traveled through England and Germany, visited Constantinople, Cairo, and Alexandria, and, finally, reached the Holy City. On October 24th, 1841, he went up on the Mount of Olives and offered a prayer, dedicating Palestine for the gathering of the Jews."[5]

1. Congregations of the wicked. See Commentary on Doctrine and Covenants 60:8.

2. Ensample. An old spelling for *example.*

2. This priesthood. This phrase refers to the office of high priest, to which Orson and several other elders had been ordained a week earlier.[6] At this time the office of high priest was the highest office in the Church, because the offices of general authorities as we understand them were established later. Thus, verses 4–6 were not directed to all Melchizedek Priesthood holders but to the presiding high priesthood of the Church. Today the promises of verses 4–6 apply primarily to the general authorities of the Church, but they may also be extended to high priests who preside over wards, stakes, missions, and such when they are acting within the boundaries of their stewardships.

3. This is the ensample. The call of Orson Hyde is the example for all of those who, like Brother Hyde, have been ordained as high priests. Just as he "was called by his ordination to proclaim the everlasting gospel, by the Spirit of the living God" (v. 1), so they are called by their ordination to "speak as they are moved upon by the Holy Ghost" (v. 3).

4. When moved upon by the Holy Ghost. "The very words of the revelation recognize that the Brethren may speak when they are not 'moved upon by the Holy Ghost,' yet only when they do so speak, as so 'moved upon' is what they say Scripture. No exceptions are given to this rule or principle. It is universal in its application.

"The question is, how shall we know when the things they have spoken were said as they were 'moved upon by the Holy Ghost'?

"I have given some thought to this question, and the answer thereto so far as I can determine, is: We can tell when the speakers are 'moved upon by the Holy Ghost' only when we, ourselves, are 'moved upon by the Holy Ghost.'

"In a way, this completely shifts the responsibility from them to us to determine when they so speak."[7]

4. Shall be scripture. Because the term *scripture* is used in the Church in different ways, care must be taken here to avoid confusion. First and foremost, *scripture* refers to the scriptures, or the standard works of the Church. These are the writings that the Church has collectively agreed to accept as the word of God and by which the Church is collectively bound in doctrine. In this sense of the word, *scripture* includes only the Bible, Book of Mormon, Doctrine and Covenants, and Pearl of Great Price. Nothing else may constitute "the scriptures" for the entire Church.

The term *scripture,* however, is also used in a broader way to mean *anything* said or written under the influence of the Holy Ghost. This is how the term is used in verse 4. Whenever a servant of God speaks by the Spirit of God, then his message is the word of God, or scripture, for those who hear it. The inspiration of a given message in these cases must usually be perceived and accepted individually, whereas the inspiration of the standard works has already been accepted by the Church collectively.

Although a private communication may become "scripture" in this sense for an individual, as in a priesthood blessing, for example, such a communication does not become scripture for the Church simply because it was inspired.

6. Be of good cheer, and do not fear. Among the fruits of the gospel are joy and confidence. Church members who are not in rebellion but who are keeping their covenants have every right to a positive outlook on this life and on the next. When faithful members are not cheerful and confident of their standing before God, something is wrong. Something important has been misunderstood, neglected, ignored, disobeyed, or, perhaps, was just never learned; for a correct understanding of the gospel by faithful members brings joy, peace, confidence, and hope because of the tremendous "good news."

7. Luke Johnson, and . . . Lyman Johnson. Luke and Lyman Johnson were grown sons of John Johnson, with whom the Prophet and his family were living at this time. They later became members of the Quorum of the Twelve Apostles.

7. The word of the Lord . . . unto all the faithful elders. Unlike the promises of verses 4–6, which were given to high priests exclusively, the injunction of verses 7–8 is given to every faithful Melchizedek Priesthood holder. No one capable of fulfilling this obligation is excepted or excused. "All the world" (v. 8) can be understood as our own cities or neighborhoods as well as foreign countries, but every faithful elder must preach the gospel somewhere, in some manner, to someone.

Part of this missionary obligation may be fulfilled by young single elders going on full-time missions. Sisters do not bear the same obligation described in these verses, although they may also serve full-time missions. The *obligation* falls clearly, however, on those who hold the Melchizedek Priesthood. President Spencer W. Kimball has stated: "The question is asked: Should every young man fill a mission? And the answer of the Church is yes, and the answer of the Lord is yes. Enlarging this answer we say: Certainly every male member of the Church *should* fill a mission, like he *should* pay his tithing, like he *should* attend his meetings, like he *should* keep his life clean and free from the ugliness of the world and plan a celestial marriage in the temple of the Lord. . . . Every LDS male who is worthy and able should fill a mission."[8]

10. Even as it is written. Verses 8–10 refer back to the charge of Jesus to his apostles recorded in Mark 16:15–18.

11. The signs of the times. These are the indicators of where we are in the Lord's timetable leading up to the second coming of the Savior. The restoration of the gospel, the preaching of the gospel to all the world, and the establishment of Zion are some examples of such signs. The spread of wars and civil unrest throughout the world and the moral collapse of society are others.

11. Signs of the coming of the Son of Man. No one knows when the Son of Man will come, but faithful Saints will be able to recognize the signs that the time is approaching.

12. The Father shall bear record. See John 6:37; 10:29; 17:11. It is the Father's work (see Moses 1:39), and it is the Father who directs that work through his Son.

12. Power to seal them up. Most of the time the term *sealed*, as it has come to be used in the Church to describe certain temple blessings, means *conditionally* sealed. *If* we are true and faithful, *if* we endure to the end, *if* we keep our covenants, *then*—and only then—certain promises will be kept and certain blessings will be received. Most endowed Church members are sealed with a conditional promise of exaltation. If we meet the condition of faithfulness in this life by faithfully enduring to the end in righteousness, God will exalt us as he has promised.

12. To you shall be given. At this time, November 1831, Elijah had not yet come to restore the keys of sealing. Although Joseph Smith and others sometimes used the language of "sealing" and even "sealed up" whole branches to exaltation on occasion, such "sealings" were conditional or promissory in nature, perhaps awaiting the visit of Elijah in April 1836 (D&C 110).

12. Amen. With this closure, the Lord indicated that his specific response to Orson Hyde and the three high priests inquiring of him was at an end. What follows in verses 13–35 are items of additional instruction for the entire Church.

14. Other bishops to be set apart. At that time Edward Partridge, who was living in Missouri, was the only bishop in the Church. The growth of the Church made ordination of other bishops for specific areas a logistical necessity. One month after this revelation, Newel K. Whitney was ordained the bishop for Kirtland (see D&C 72:2, 8). Neither of these brethren was Presiding Bishop in the modern sense, since neither presided over the other. Rather, they were general bishops each presiding over a specific geographical area of the Church—Bishop Partridge in the West and Bishop Whitney in the East.[9]

15. They shall be high priests. The office of bishop is an office in the Aaronic Priesthood, together with those of deacon, teacher, or priest. When the Aaronic Priesthood was established anciently, however, the right to preside over that priesthood as a bishop does now was designated as a privilege of lineage (see Exodus 28:1; 29:9, 29). Because worthy Levites of the family of Aaron, whose right it was to preside over the Aaronic Priesthood, were not available to the early Church, the Lord directed that high priests should function in that office in their place. Today, a bishop actually presides over the Aaronic Priesthood in his ward and is the presiding high priest in his ward.

15. Appointed by the First Presidency. In 1831, when this revelation was first given, there *was* no First Presidency, and the original text of the revelation read "appointed by a conference of high priests," in other words, by the leadership of the Church as it was then loosely organized. After the First Presidency was organized in 1833, the reading of verse 15 was changed to use the correct terminology. This is also true of verses 22–23. Doctrine and Covenants 107:59–100 gives additional information about the offices of bishop and Presiding Bishop.[10]

16–21. Under the direction of Joseph Smith, these verses were first added to the text of Doctrine and Covenants 68 in *The*

Evening and the Morning Star reprinted at Kirtland in June 1835, and also in the 1835 edition of the Doctrine and Covenants.

16. Descendants of Aaron . . . have a legal right. "The office of Presiding Bishop of the Church is the same as the office which was held by Aaron. It is the highest office, holding the presidency in the Aaronic Priesthood. It was this office which came to John the Baptist, and it was by virtue of the fact that he held the keys of this power and ministry that he was sent to Joseph Smith and Oliver Cowdery to restore that Priesthood, May 15, 1829. . . . Should it be shown by revelation that there is one who is the 'first-born among the sons of Aaron,' and thus entitled by the birthright to this presidency, he could 'claim' his 'anointing' and the right to that office in the Church."[11]

20. Must be designated by this Presidency. "The person spoken of in the revelations as having the right by lineage to the bishopric is the one who is the firstborn. By virtue of his birth he is entitled to hold 'the keys or authority of the same.' This has reference only to the one who *presides over the Aaronic Priesthood. It has no reference whatever to bishops of wards.* Further, such a one must be designated by the First Presidency of the Church and receive his anointing and ordination under their hands. The revelation comes from the Presidency, not from the patriarch, to establish a claim to the right to preside in this office. In the absence of knowledge concerning such a descendant, any high priest, chosen by the Presidency, may hold the office of Presiding Bishop and serve with counselors."[12]

22–23. The provisions of these verses for Church discipline applied only to the general bishops Partridge and Whitney, and later to Presiding Bishops, because their stewardships did not fall under the control of local Church authorities. Local ward bishops may be disciplined by the local authorities under whose jurisdiction they operate—usually a stake president. Additional information on this subject is found in Doctrine and Covenants 107:15–17, 68–69, which clearly illustrates that the office referred to is that of a general or Presiding Bishop and not that of a local ward bishop.

25. Inasmuch as parents have children. Parents—not teachers, bishops, home teachers, or anyone else but *parents*—bear the primary obligation of teaching their children the basics of the gospel, seeing that they are baptized at the proper time, teaching their children to pray, and teaching them to behave properly, to walk uprightly. The Church, through its auxiliaries and programs, will assist in many of these obligations, but the primary responsibility still rests with parents.

25. To understand the doctrine. At eight years of age, children are old enough to be taught the basic doctrines of the kingdom of God (compare Joseph Smith Translation Genesis 17:11). They are old enough to understand sin and repentance. They must be taught the concept of Jesus Christ as the Son of God and the Savior of the world. Faith in Christ cannot be taught without explaining the Savior's divine sonship and his atoning sacrifice. It is not enough that at eight years of age our children are culturally adapted to the Church. They are to understand and willingly enter the covenant of baptism and be prepared to receive the gift of the Holy Ghost. Even at eight years of age, they can and must become obedient members of the Church.

25. The sin be upon the heads of the parents. The key word in this phrase is *sin*. It is not plural but singular, and it refers not to the sins children may subsequently commit but to the sin of the parents in not teaching them better. Some parents, due to their misunderstanding of this verse, try to take responsibility upon themselves for the sins of their children, and shield their children from blame by doing so. But this is not possible. In order to sin at all one must have knowledge and understanding, and even poorly raised children know for the most part what they should and should not do. Parents will be held accountable for not teaching their children the gospel, but parents cannot take the blame for the sins of their children, nor can they protect them from suffering the consequences of those sins.

DOCTRINE AND COVENANTS 68

26. This shall be a law unto the inhabitants of Zion. "We don't wait until they are young adults or till they are nearly grown to teach them these laws. They should know at eight or before eight all about baptism and about confirmation.

"This command was to be a law unto the inhabitants of Zion, not a mere hope or suggestion."[13]

27. When eight years old. "Accountability does not burst full-bloom upon a child at any given moment in his life. Children become accountable gradually, over a number of years. Becoming accountable is a process, not a goal to be attained when a specified number of years, days, and hours have elapsed. . . . There comes a time, however, when accountability is real and actual and sin is attributed in the lives of those who develop normally. It is eight years of age, the age of baptism"[14] (see Joseph Smith Translation Genesis 17:11). This doctrine was first introduced to the Church some seven to ten months previous to the reception of this revelation.

28. Teach their children to pray. Children learn to pray by hearing and watching their parents pray. The most effective way to keep this commandment is to have regular, daily, family prayer in the home, and this ought to be something more than just the habitual blessing of food.

28. And to walk uprightly. The obligation is not just to teach children to understand intellectually what proper behavior is; the full obligation is to teach them to behave properly. In other words, parents in Zion must discipline their children. They must teach them what proper behavior is, and then they must do all they appropriately can to see that their children do, indeed, behave.

29. Observe the Sabbath day. See Doctrine and Covenants 59:9–13.

30. Shall remember their labors. One great obstacle to establishing Zion is the human tendency to do less than our best in the belief that others will make up for our laziness. In Doctrine and Covenants 42:42 the Lord stated the principle of Zion that the idler would "not eat the bread nor wear the garments of the laborer."

31. I, the Lord, am not well pleased. The Saints in Zion—

Jackson County, Missouri—were collectively beset by several sins, which are enumerated here. Some were lazy, some were allowing their children to run out of control, and some had put greed for this world's goods ahead of the spiritual blessings of eternity.

32. These things ought not to be. Such things are below the celestial standard, and certainly Zion could not be established under these conditions.

33. Prayers . . . in the season thereof. There are times when faithful Saints *ought* to pray. These times are not spelled out exactly for us, but they probably ought to include daily personal prayers, daily family prayers, and regular prayers of thanks for specific blessings. To neglect our prayers at their proper times is an offense to God. It is also a proper matter of concern for a bishop in evaluating the faithfulness of his ward members.

35. Alpha and Omega. See Commentary on Doctrine and Covenants 19:1.

---

1. See Background to D&C 1, 67.
2. See *History of the Church,* 1:227.
3. See Cannon and Cook, *Far West Record,* 51, 57; Cook, *Revelations of the Prophet Joseph Smith,* pp. 108–9, 145–46.
4. See Background to D&C 107; Smith, *Kirtland Revelation Book,* 84; Cook, *Revelations of the Prophet Joseph Smith,* 109.
5. Smith and Sjodahl, *Doctrine and Covenants Commentary,* 409.
6. See Cannon and Cook, *Far West Record,* 25.
7. Clark, "When Are the Writings or Sermons of Church Leaders Entitled to the Claim of Scripture?" 7.
8. In *Ensign,* May 1974, 87.
9. See John Taylor, in *Journal of Discourses,* 21:361–62; Orson Pratt, in *Journal of Discourses,* 22:33–34.
10. See Smith, *Kirtland Revelation Book,* 84.
11. Smith, *Church History and Modern Revelation,* 1:259.
12. Smith, *Doctrines of Salvation,* 3:92.
13. Spencer W. Kimball, in *Ensign,* May 1979, 6.
14. McConkie, "Salvation of Little Children," 6.

69

BACKGROUND

It had been decided on 1 November 1831, the first day of the important conferences held in Hiram, Ohio, that Oliver Cowdery would carry a copy of the revelations to Jackson County, Missouri, to be printed. Between sessions on that day, Joseph Smith received "the Lord's Preface" (D&C 1) for the published revelations. Still later in the day, Joseph received Doctrine and Covenants 67, and sometime on that same day or early the next day, 2 November, the testimony of the elders to be published with the Book of Commandments was also received by revelation. On 2 November, Joseph received Doctrine and Covenants 68 after inquiring of the Lord in behalf of Orson Hyde and three others. On 3 November, Joseph received an important revelation that was to complement the preface of section 1; it was received two days earlier and was therefore called an appendix (D&C 133). The reader may want to read section 133 at this point, or both sections 1 and 133, to appreciate them in proper chronological order.[1]

Sometime between 3–12 November 1831, during the series of special conferences and meetings held at the home of John Johnson in Hiram, Joseph also received Doctrine and Covenants 69, which directed John Whitmer to be a traveling companion for Oliver Cowdery. Joseph Smith stated, "The Book of Commandments and Revelations was to be dedicated by prayer to the service of Almighty God by me; and after I had done this, I inquired of the Lord concerning these things, and received the following"[2]—Doctrine and Covenants 69.

Oliver and John left Ohio on 20 November and traveled by way of Winchester, Indiana, where Levi Hancock and Zebedee Coltrin had established a branch of the Church the previous summer. Oliver and John held conference meetings in Winchester and stayed for about a week while they resolved some difficulties in the branch. They arrived in Independence on 5 January 1832.[3]

COMMENTARY

1. For . . . Oliver Cowdery's sake. Note the concern here for Oliver rather than simply for the money he would be carrying.

This was not an issue of whether Oliver could be trusted. It would be foolish to send one man on such a journey alone, when sending two men would lessen the risks both to the couriers and to what they carry.

1. The commandments and the moneys. Oliver was carrying the manuscript of the Book of Commandments that was to be published in Missouri and also the funds collected from the Saints in Ohio and elsewhere for purchasing lands in Jackson County. The manuscript was to be delivered to W. W. Phelps, the Church printer, and the money was to be delivered to Edward Partridge, the bishop in Zion.

2–3. John Whitmer. John Whitmer was one of the Eight Witnesses to the Book of Mormon. He had seen and handled the gold plates and had moved from New York to Ohio in obedience to the command of the Lord. In March 1831, John had been appointed Church historian (see D&C 47). Now he was appointed to travel to Missouri as a companion to Oliver Cowdery. John was not released as Church historian at this time, however, and he was to keep a record of the events and continue his history as best he could.

5–6. Send forth the accounts . . . to the land of Zion. Even though the Prophet lived in Ohio, matters dealing with consecration and stewardship were to be administered from Zion in Jackson County, where Bishop Partridge was still the only bishop in the Church and the only one authorized to receive and disburse under the law of consecration.

7. Let my servant John Whitmer travel. As Church historian in an age before electronic communication, John Whitmer was to travel from place to place in the Church learning and recording what he could for future generations.

8. Preaching and expounding, writing, copying, selecting. The Church historian was not merely to be a clerk or a secretary. Brother Whitmer's office was to bless those whom he visited in his travels by preaching and expounding the gospel, and he was entrusted with selecting and preserving those materials that would bless the whole Church for generations to come.

1. See Background to D&C 1, 133.
2. *History of the Church,* 1:234.
3. See Cannon and Cook, *Far West Record,* 33–38.

70

BACKGROUND

O n the last day of the series of conferences held between 1–12 November 1831 in Hiram, Ohio, the Prophet received the revelation now numbered as Doctrine and Covenants 70. He recorded these events as follows: "My time was occupied closely in reviewing the commandments and sitting in conference, for nearly two weeks; for from the first to the twelfth of November we held four special conferences. In the last which was held at Brother Johnson's, in Hiram, after deliberate consideration, in consequence of the book of revelations, now to be printed, being the foundation of the Church in these last days, and a benefit to the world, showing that the keys of the mysteries of the kingdom of our Savior are again entrusted to man; and the riches of eternity within the compass of those who are willing to live by every word that proceedeth out of the mouth of God—therefore the conference voted that they prize the revelations to be worth to the Church the riches of the whole earth, speaking temporally. The great benefits to the world which result from the Book of Mormon and the revelations which the Lord has seen fit in His infinite wisdom to grant unto us for our salvation, and for the salvation of all that will believe, were duly appreciated; and in answer to an inquiry, I received the following"[1]—Doctrine and Covenants 70.

The business of the conference on 12 November had included

a proposal to provide compensation to the Prophet Joseph Smith and to his scribes Oliver Cowdery, Martin Harris, John Whitmer, and Sidney Rigdon for their labors and sacrifices in receiving, writing, copying, and preparing the revelations of God for the Church in the latter days. This compensation would come out of any proceeds from the sale of the revelations.[2] The conference voted to sustain this proposal, and Joseph's subsequent inquiry of the Lord appears to have been designed to secure divine approval for what the conference had done. That approval was received as Doctrine and Covenants 70.

This revelation established what was essentially the first scripture committee of the Church. It created a joint stewardship over the modern scriptures, which included the Prophet, his scribes, and the Church printer. This joint stewardship or oversight committee was responsible for any plans or decisions involving the revelations. They were responsible for publishing them to the world, and they were to be compensated for their labors from whatever profits the sale of copies generated. This joint stewardship and financial partnership, organized upon the principles of the law of consecration, soon came to be known as the Literary Firm, a term reflecting its stewardship over the media concerns of the Church.[3]

COMMENTARY

1. William W. Phelps. The Hiram conference had originally proposed that only the Prophet and his scribes be included in the joint stewardship over the scriptures. The Lord here added the name of the Church printer, W. W. Phelps, to this list.

3. Stewards over the revelations and commandments. All things related to the modern revelations, both spiritual and temporal in nature, were to be the responsibility of the joint stewards—the Literary Firm. Where other stewards might be given farms or retail stores, the Literary Firm had been given management of the modern revelations and Church publishing. One of their responsibilities was to publish the revelations for the Church and for the world. If the stewards fulfilled this responsibility, they might at the same time generate revenues out of which they could support themselves and their families.

4. An account of this stewardship will I require of them. Every person who receives a calling or has responsibility in the kingdom of God operates under this same condition. God will require an accounting at our hands of all that he has given us, whatever our stewardship may be.

6. They shall not give these things. "These things" refers to the elements of their stewardship, both the responsibilities and the benefits of managing and publishing the scriptures. As faithful workmen, they were worthy of—and may keep—their hire (see v. 12).

7–9. And the benefits shall be consecrated unto the inhabitants of Zion. Even though the Literary Firm received the benefits of their stewardship, it was on the same principles as every other steward in the Church. What they received over and above their personal needs and the expenses of promoting and publishing the scriptures was consecrated to the building of Zion.

10. None are exempt from this law. This expression refers to the law of consecration, which is part of the larger law of the Church (see D&C 42:30–42).

12. Spiritual things, . . . temporal things. It does not matter whether one's stewardship is to manage a farm or to manage publication of the revelations of God for the Church, the principles of consecration remain the same. Working directly with the Spirit in promoting the word of God, however, does pay spiritual benefits beyond those received from managing purely temporal affairs (see v. 13).

14. You shall be equal. Even though a spiritual stewardship might produce more *spiritual* rewards than temporal goods, the temporal resources of Zion must still be distributed equally. Even though temporal stewards might produce more temporal goods and resources than spiritual stewards, the temporal goods must still be distributed equally. Under the law of consecration, neither type of stewardship, temporal on the one hand or spiritual on the other, is valued or rewarded more or less than the other. In the everyday resources of this life, a Zion people must be "equal, and this not grudgingly,"[4] with "no poor among them" (Moses 7:18) to receive the abundance of "the manifestations of the Spirit." Teachers or Church leaders share equally with farmers or laborers the temporal blessings of Zion, just as the latter share with the former in the spiritual blessings of Zion.

15. This commandment. That is, Doctrine and Covenants 70, with its provisions for the support of the faithful brethren in the Literary Firm. One can only imagine how the words of approval and blessing contained here would have been received by the Prophet and his associates who had left all, given all, and suffered much to serve the Lord up to this point. These verses constitute a richly deserved divine commendation for the members of the Literary Firm, and it provides a fitting closure to the labors of the brethren in preparing the revelations for publication, especially between 1–12 November.

1. *History of the Church,* 1:235–36.
2. See Cannon and Cook, *Far West Record,* 31–33.
3. See Cook, *Revelations of the Prophet Joseph Smith,* 112–17.
4. See Commentary on D&C 51:3 for *equal.*

71

BACKGROUND

Oliver Cowdery and John Whitmer had been directed to take a manuscript copy of the revelations to Missouri for publication and also to deliver to Bishop Partridge in Jackson County money raised in Ohio for the purchase of land in Zion. These two brethren left for Independence on 20 November 1831. Joseph Smith recorded that "after Oliver Cowdery and John Whitmer had departed for Jackson county, Missouri, I resumed the translation of the Scriptures, and continued to labor in this branch of my calling with Elder Sidney Rigdon as my scribe, until I received the following"[1]—Doctrine and Covenants 71.

Joseph and Sidney, still living on the Johnson farm in Hiram, had resumed their task of translating the Bible, and had been working at it for just ten days when section 71 was received on 1 December 1831. Once again the Prophet had to interrupt his work on the Joseph Smith Translation for more pressing concerns.

It seems that Ezra Booth and Simonds Ryder, two former members of the Church, had begun to stir up anti-Mormon feelings in northeastern Ohio by speaking in public meetings and writing in local newspapers against the Church. These two were not the first to leave the Church, but they were the most vicious to date, and they were the first to publicly campaign against their former friends.

Ezra Booth was a Methodist minister who had joined the Church in May 1831, after he saw Joseph Smith heal Alice Johnson's arm. A short time later, Joseph successfully rebuked an evil spirit that had overcome Ezra. He was ordained a high priest in June and was one of the missionaries sent to Missouri that month with Isaac Morley (see D&C 52:23). Ezra had apparently expected to experience great miracles in Missouri, but he came home disappointed and disaffected when he did not receive all the spiritual gifts he had expected and when all the Lord's promises about the establishment of Zion in the latter days were not fulfilled at once. Ezra Booth was one of those who aroused the Lord's anger on the Missouri River (see D&C 61:20) and afterward (see D&C 64:15–16). Returning to Kirtland from Missouri on 1 September, Ezra immediately began criticizing the Church and its leaders. He was disfellowshipped on 6 September, and he publicly repudiated any connection with the Church on 12 September. Between October and December, Ezra Booth wrote a series of anti-Mormon letters in the *Ohio Star* newspaper.

Simonds Ryder, like Ezra Booth, had also joined the Church in the spring of 1831, and had been ordained an elder in June. That summer Simonds was called on a mission, but his name was misspelled on the paperwork, and he later referred to this as proof that Joseph Smith was not a true prophet. Like Ezra, Simonds left the Church in the fall of 1831, and he was a member of the mob that tarred and feathered Joseph Smith at Hiram a few months later in March 1832.

These two apostates, Ezra Booth and Simonds Ryder, had been campaigning against the Church since September 1831. They had succeeded in arousing considerable anti-Mormon feeling in Ohio, and for this reason the Lord instructed Joseph and Sidney to discontinue translating for a while in order to preach the gospel and to publicly confront and confound their enemies.

COMMENTARY

1. The time has verily come. The time for Joseph and Sidney personally to preach the gospel in Ohio with the knowledge and power of the revelations from heaven and of the Spirit of God, and to oppose and refute the influence of apostates, which was causing the Church increasing difficulty in that region.

1. The mysteries. See Commentary on Doctrine and Covenants 6:7, 11; 8:11.

2. The regions round about. Northeast Ohio.

2. And in the church also. Unfortunately, some of the Saints appear also to have been affected by the accusations of the apostates and needed to hear the truth from Joseph and Sidney.

3. A mission for a season. This was not a normal proselyting mission. It was a special call to improve public relations and build up the image of the Church in Ohio, which would last until the immediate problems were solved.

4. The commandments and revelations which are to come. Some might have thought that with the publication of the Book of Commandments the revelations were nearly done, but this was not so. There were more to come—many more (see Articles of Faith 1:9).

7. Confound your enemies. It should be pointed out that this was not, and is not, the usual policy of the Church, and this course of action was undertaken at this time only under the explicit command of the Lord. Normally, there is no good reason to include or to invite the enemies of God to participate with us in the work of God. We are commanded to preach the gospel to the pure in heart—not to contend, argue, or debate with the impure in heart (see 3 Nephi 11:29–30).

The Lord may, however, command exceptions as he will. In this case, it was the will of the Lord that Joseph and Sidney confront and confound those who were spreading ill will toward the Church.

7. Call upon them to meet you. Joseph Smith recorded that "from this time until the 8th or 10th of January, 1832, myself and

Elder Rigdon continued to preach in Shalersville, Ravenna, and other places, setting forth the truth, vindicating the cause of our Redeemer; showing that the day of vengeance was coming upon this generation like a thief in the night; that prejudice, blindness and darkness filled the minds of many, and caused them to persecute the true Church, and reject the true light; by which means we did much towards allaying the excited feelings which were growing out of the scandalous letters then being published in the *Ohio Star,* at Ravenna, by the before-mentioned apostate, Ezra Booth."[2]

The 20 December 1831 *Painesville Telegraph* stated that "Sidney Rigdon, the vicegerant and champion of Jo. Smith, has thrown out a challenge, in the Ohio Star, to Mr. Booth and Deacon Rider, who have renounced the Mormon faith, to meet him in mortal combat (of words) on the subject of the Gold Bible." Ryder refused the invitation. Sidney Rigdon wrote a letter, published in the *Ohio Star* on 12 January 1832, in which he charged:

"Simonds, like the worker of iniquity, has sought a hiding place. Let the public remember, when he goes forth again to proclaim his assertions against the book of Mormon, that he has been invited upon honorable principles to investigate its merits, and dare not do it."

9. No weapon that is formed against you shall prosper. "Our enemies have never done anything that has injured this work of God, and they never will. I look around, I read, I reflect, and I ask the question, Where are the men of influence, of power and prestige, who have worked against the Latter-day Saints? Where is the reputation, for honor and courage, of the governors of Missouri and Illinois . . . ? Where are there people to do them honor? They can not be found. . . . Where are the men who have assailed this work? Where is their influence? They have faded away like dew before the sun. We need have no fears, we Latter-day Saints. God will continue to sustain this work; He will sustain the right. If we are loyal, if we are true, if we are worthy of this Gospel, of which God has given us a testimony, there is no danger that the world can ever injure us. We can never be injured, my brethren and sisters, by any mortals, except ourselves."[3]

1. *History of the Church,* 1:238.
2. *History of the Church,* 1:241.
3. Heber J. Grant, in Conference Report, Apr. 1909, 110.

BACKGROUND

After receiving a mission call on 1 December 1831, as recorded in Doctrine and Covenants 71, to preach the gospel and confound the enemies of the Church in Ohio, the Prophet Joseph Smith moved swiftly. "Knowing now the mind of the Lord, that the time had come that the Gospel should be proclaimed in power and demonstration to the world, from the Scriptures, reasoning with men as in days of old, I took a journey to Kirtland, in company with Elder Sidney Rigdon on the 3rd day of December, to fulfil the above revelation. On the 4th, several of the Elders and members assembled together to learn their duty, and for edification, and after some time had been spent in conversing about our temporal and spiritual welfare, I received the following"[1]—Doctrine and Covenants 72.

In Doctrine and Covenants 68:14, which had been received a month before this revelation, the Lord had indicated that "other bishops" besides Edward Partridge would be set apart in the future. The first eight verses of section 72 fulfill that promise by calling Newel K. Whitney to be the bishop of the Church in Kirtland. The second part of this revelation more fully explains the duties of the new bishop and also his relationship with the bishop in Zion. An early manuscript of section 72 in the handwriting of Joseph Smith and Frederick G. Williams indicates that verses 1–8 and 9–26 were revelations received separately on the same day and then joined together.[2]

COMMENTARY

1. The high priests of my church. Although many elders and Church members were present when this revelation was received, these instructions were directed specifically to the leadership of the Church, who alone could call and ordain a bishop in Kirtland.

2. A bishop . . . in this part of the Lord's vineyard. The first bishop of the Church, Edward Partridge (see D&C 41:9), had moved to Jackson County, Missouri, the previous summer, but the majority of the Saints still lived in Ohio and the East. Someone else needed to be called to serve the Church as bishop in the Kirtland area.[3]

3. To render an account of his stewardship. According to the law of the Lord, responsibility for overseeing individual stewards belongs to the bishop (see D&C 42:31–35). Because there were members in Ohio living the principles of consecration, it was necessary to provide a bishop to whom they would be accountable, and a storehouse (see D&C 72:10) for receiving their surpluses or making good their shortfalls.

3. Both in time and in eternity. Each of the Lord's servants is required to account for what he or she has done with his or her stewardship (see Matthew 25:14–30). It is the bishop who receives the accounting, the evaluating and settling up for our stewardship in time or while we live upon the earth. The Lord himself will receive the accounting for our stewardship in eternity, or when our mortal probation is over (see D&C 70:4).

4. Faithful and wise in time is accounted worthy. What we do in time determines what will happen in eternity. This present life is a test or a probationary state. We demonstrate our ability to properly manage an eternal stewardship by what we do here and now with our temporal stewardship (see Alma 34:32).

The various heavenly kingdoms or mansions are prepared, and the Lord desires that we inherit the highest of them. The only question will be what kind of mansions or estates we can be trusted to manage properly. The present test of our faithfulness in mortality will provide the answer to that question.

5–6. Records were to be kept by the bishop in Kirtland, which verified the faithfulness and good standing of individual stewards. These records could then be forwarded to the bishop in Zion when Kirtland Saints moved into his jurisdiction. Once this general pattern had been revealed, it was then possible to appoint as many additional bishops as might be needed to keep up with Church growth, and still keep track of individual stewards even if they moved from place to place.

7. The duty of the bishop shall be made known. Some portions of a bishop's duties had already been revealed.[4] Additional instructions, verses 9–26, were received later on the same day as verses 1–8, and the two portions were joined together as Doctrine and Covenants 72.

8. Newel K. Whitney is the man. A bishop is called by revelation. "Newel K. Whitney, staggering under the weight of the responsibility that was about to be placed upon him, said to the Prophet: 'Brother Joseph, I can't see a Bishop in myself.'

"No, but God could see it in him. He was a natural Bishop— a first class man of affairs. Probably no other incumbent of that important office, the Presiding Bishopric, to which he eventually attained, has been better qualified for it than Newel K. Whitney. But he could not see it, and he shrank from the responsibility. The Prophet answered: 'Go and ask the Lord about it.' And Newel did ask the Lord, and he heard a voice from heaven say: '*Thy strength is in me.*' That was enough. He accepted the office, and served in it faithfully to the end of his days—a period of eighteen years."[5]

8. Amen. This indicates the end of Brother Whitney's actual call. Other instructions concerning the new bishop's duties were added later in the day in verses 9–26.

9. The bishop who has been ordained. Newel K. Whitney.

10–17. Four major responsibilities of a bishop are discussed in these verses. First, the bishop administers the Lord's storehouse, receiving and disbursing Church funds and other resources for his area (see vv. 10–11). Second, he evaluates and keeps track of the financial performance of individual stewards in his ward (see vv. 11, 13, 16). Third, the bishop is responsible for the temporal welfare of the members in his ward, particularly the poor and the needy (see v. 12). Fourth, the bishop serves as a judge in Israel. He has the responsibility of judging and certifying the worthiness of members in his ward (see also D&C 107:68–74).

11. To take an account of the elders. The bishop interviews individual stewards and functions as an accountant or administrator in keeping track of their surpluses or their shortfalls. While the primary focus in this verse is financial, bishops properly monitor and note the progress, successes, and failures of their ward members in matters both temporal and spiritual.

11. Administer to their wants. See Doctrine and Covenants 42:33.

11. Who shall pay for that which they receive. The bishops' storehouse in Kirtland was Newel K. Whitney's store. Financially self-sufficient stewards were expected to purchase their goods at the Whitney store, and the profits from these sales were used for the good of the poor and needy (see v. 12).

13. An account shall be taken. Where local stewards require financial help from the bishops' storehouse, they receive that help from their local bishop and the resources at his disposal. A bill for the debt, however, is then to be forwarded to the bishop in Zion who reimburses the local bishop. Thus, the system of consecration and stewardship was to be a Churchwide system with no local bishop bearing alone the burden of support for needy members.

The present system of fast offerings, which are a type of

consecration, still operates on a pattern similar to that revealed in these verses. First, local needs are met through local offerings. Then net surpluses or net shortfalls are forwarded to the Presiding Bishop of the Church for redistribution or for reimbursement, respectively.

13. The bishop of Zion, who shall pay the debt. How was the bishop in Zion to get the resources to reimburse the debts of local bishops? From what "the Lord shall put into his hands." This would include surpluses forwarded to him from profitable stewards, money sent for purchase of lands in Zion, and profits from other Church enterprises, of which he was the overseer.

The system worked on the premise that on average there would be more profitable stewards or other enterprises in the Church than unprofitable at any given time. Thus, using the local units as collector points, the Presiding Bishop received the cumulative financial resources of the Church and shifted them from place to place as necessary to cover the cumulative financial needs of the Church.

14. The faithful who labor in spiritual things. Who could the bishop in Zion turn to for the resources to pay Church debts? To the leadership of the Church—to Joseph Smith and his associates—whose stewardship was not to farm or to manage stores, but to administer the affairs of the kingdom. Those who held the kingdom's keys were ultimately responsible for the kingdom's finances.

15. It cometh out of the church. And where did Church leaders get the resources to pay Church debts? From the cumulative faithfulness of all the Church's members in paying their tithes and offerings and in otherwise observing the principles of consecration that they covenanted to observe.

15. Must lay all things before the bishop in Zion. It was intended that only those who consecrated all their possessions to the Lord would be called to Zion (compare Acts 4:34–35; 5:1–4). All the Saints in Zion were expected to consecrate all they had to the kingdom, thus providing the resources needed to answer the debts of the Church and to provide the resources needed for the continued growth of Zion.

17. A certificate from the judge. Only those members in good standing with their own local bishop would be commended to the bishop in Zion. In today's Church, membership records are kept to show a member's standing in the Church. A bishop should not call a new member to a position of trust before receiving his or her Church records or by otherwise confirming that member's good standing.

In the early days of the Church, certificates or recommends (see v. 19) were issued by one bishop for the purpose of confirming good standing to another bishop. In this case the certificates or recommends were not used for entering the temples—there were no temples yet—but primarily for being accepted in full fellowship into the community of consecrated Saints in Zion. When followed, this procedure made it difficult for dishonest individuals to receive land and other goods from the Church without first entering the covenant of consecration and otherwise proving worthy.

17. For an inheritance. With a recommend from his local bishop, an individual could emigrate to Zion and receive a stewardship there.

18. Otherwise he shall not be accepted. Going up to Zion was a sacred privilege (see v. 24), and only worthy, profitable stewards with recommends from their local bishop were allowed to go. Without a recommend the Ohio Saints were not supposed to go, and were not to be received into fellowship or receive an inheritance there if they went on their own. The disobedience of many Saints to these and other commandments, however, contributed to the failure to establish Zion in Jackson County.[6]

20. Stewards over the literary concerns. See Doctrine and Covenants 70:3. The obligation of the Literary Firm to consecrate their surplus to the bishops' storehouse is spelled out in Doctrine and Covenants 70:7–8. This verse in section 72 establishes their rights to apply to the same storehouse for their support, if necessary—the same as with any other stewards.

23. This shall be an ensample. That is, the relationship between Edward Partridge and Newel K. Whitney as Presiding Bishops (described in vv. 9–23).

25. A certificate from three elders. Perhaps because of the logistical problems arising from having only one bishop outside Zion (Newel K. Whitney), the Lord amended the instructions given in verses 17–19 to allow certificates to be signed either by the bishop or by three worthy elders.

1. *History of the Church,* 1:239.
2. See Smith, *Kirtland Revelation Book,* 13–15.
3. See Commentary on D&C 68:14.
4. See D&C 41:9–10; 42:31–36, 71–73, 80–83; 46:27–29; 51:3–20; 57:15–16; 58:55; 64:40; 68:15–24.
5. Orson F. Whitney, in Conference Report, June 1919, 47–48.
6. See Cook, *Joseph Smith and the Law of Consecration,* 14–15; Jessee, *Personal Writings of Joseph Smith,* 258–59.

DOCTRINE AND COVENANTS

73

BACKGROUND

On 1 December 1831, the Prophet Joseph Smith and Sidney Rigdon had been commanded to undertake a mission to preach in eastern Ohio, and particularly to confront and confound enemies of the Church who had been spreading lies by word of mouth and in print.[1] By the time Doctrine and Covenants 73 was received, Joseph and Sidney had been on their mission for almost six weeks. They had publicly met their critics and had done much to improve the popular image and perception of the Church.

After successfully completing their mission, the Prophet wrote, "On the 10th of January, I received the following revelation [D&C 73] making known the will of the Lord concerning the Elders of the Church until the convening of the next conference."[2]

The earliest known manuscript of section 73 contains the following notation in the handwriting of Sidney Rigdon: "A Revelation to Joseph and Sidney. The word of the Lord unto them concerning the Elders of the church of the Living God established in the last days, making known the will of the Lord unto the Elders—what they shall do until conference."[3] The conference referred to above was held on 25 January 1832 in Amherst, Ohio, about fifty miles west of Kirtland.[4]

COMMENTARY

1. They should continue preaching the gospel. The elders of the Church were to continue their missionary and Church activities until new assignments were made at the Amherst conference.

2. By the voice of the conference. In the years before the organization of the priesthood quorums, Church business was often conducted and Church assignments made by a process of proposal and sustaining vote in special priesthood conferences like the one in Amherst.

3. It is expedient to translate again. Having achieved the purposes of the mission given them in Doctrine and Covenants 71, Joseph and Sidney were now to resume their work on the Joseph Smith Translation.[5]

4. To preach . . . until conference. Joseph and Sidney were commanded both to translate and to continue their missionary preaching until conference. *After* the Amherst conference, however, they were to devote their full time specifically to translating.

4. Until it be finished. The Prophet continued to work vigorously on the Joseph Smith Translation from this time until 2 July 1833, when the first draft of his work was finished, and he ceased formal labor on the manuscript. He continued making revisions in the text, however, from time to time until his death in 1844.[6] It would be difficult to overestimate the benefits and influence of the Joseph Smith Translation on the doctrinal education of the Prophet and of the Church. The book of Moses and Joseph Smith Translation–Matthew in the Pearl of Great Price, the whole of sections 76–77, 91, and 132, and portions of sections 25–26, 35, 37, 41–42, 45, 73, 90, 93–94, 104, 107, and 124, all resulted directly from the Prophet's translation of the Bible—the Joseph Smith Translation. Many other sections of the Doctrine and Covenants were indirectly influenced by Joseph's work on the Joseph Smith Translation.[7] In particular, the eighteen months between January of 1832—the Amherst conference—and June of 1833 were richly productive. Twenty-three sections of the Doctrine and Covenants were received during that time (see D&C 73–96).

5. Let this be a pattern. From that point on when the elders collectively wonder about the Lord's will for them, let them continue doing their duty and wait to learn his will through the Prophet and other leaders at their scheduled conferences. This remains a pattern for the priesthood holders of the Church today.

1. See Background to D&C 71; Commentary on D&C 71:7.
2. *History of the Church,* 1:241.
3. Cited in Woodford, Historical Development, 1:903; punctuation added.
4. See Background to D&C 75.
5. See Commentary on D&C 35:20; Background to D&C 71.
6. See Ludlow, *Encyclopedia of Mormonism,* 2:763–69.
7. See Millet, "Joseph Smith's Translation of the Bible," 137–41.

DOCTRINE AND COVENANTS

74

BACKGROUND

Afte nearly six weeks of preaching the gospel, confounding their critics, and repairing the Church's image in eastern Ohio (see D&C 71), the Prophet Joseph Smith and Sidney Rigdon were commanded on 10 January 1832 to return to Hiram and resume their work on the translation of the Bible (see D&C 73:3–4). When Joseph and Sidney began translating again in an upstairs room of the Johnson farmhouse, one of the first texts they worked on was Paul's first letter to the Corinthians.

Joseph described his activities of these two weeks as follows: "Upon the reception of the foregoing word of the Lord [D&C 73], I recommenced the translation of the Scriptures, and labored diligently until just before the conference, which was to convene on the 25th of January. During this period, I also received the following [D&C 74], as an explanation of the First Epistle to the Corinthians, 7th chapter, 14th verse."[1] Therefore, Doctrine and Covenants 74 was received sometime between 11–22 January 1832 at the Johnson farm in Hiram, Ohio.

COMMENTARY

1. Doctrine and Covenants 74:1 is an exact quotation of

1 Corinthians 7:14 in the King James Bible. It will be helpful to remember that the setting of this passage in 1 Corinthians is a discussion of part-member families and of the circumstances that would justify the Saints in dissolving marriages to nonmembers. Paul's advice, which remains Church policy today, was that such marriages should be continued if the nonmember would tolerate his or her spouse's activity in the Church (see 1 Corinthians 7:12–13). A second condition for preserving a part-member marriage, implicit in the King James version text and clarified by D&C 74, is that the children of such unions should be reared in the Church as Christians and not in the synagogue as Jews—or today, by extension, in non-Latter-day Saint churches.

It will also be helpful for the reader to remember that the phrases "to be made holy" and "to be sanctified" are exactly equivalent since the Latin word *sanctus,* which is the root of the English word *sanctify,* means "holy."

1. The unbelieving. That is, the nonmember spouse.

1. Is sanctified. Sanctification, or being made sinless and holy, in the fullest sense comes only through the atonement of Christ (see v. 7). Jews of Paul's day, however, tended to divide the world into things clean or unclean, sacred or profane, holy or unholy. They often used these terms in ways that come close to modern distinctions between allowed and not allowed, proper and improper, or tainted and untainted. Therefore, the sense of the terms *sanctified, unclean,* and *holy* in 1 Corinthians 7:14 and in Doctrine and Covenants 74:1 is that where a nonmember spouse allows his or her partner to be active in the Church and agrees that the children will be raised in the Church, then there is no unholiness or impropriety in continuing such a marriage (see also 1 Corinthians 7:13–14), nor is there any taint to the children that may come from it. Such a union constitutes *holy* or acceptable matrimony before God—even though it is an arrangement for time only. There is no unholiness attached to faithful, committed marriages performed outside the temple. They may in truth be a "lesser good," but they are definitely not an evil. The

only thing *wrong* with such marriages for time is their impermanence and the acceptance of their impermanence, with the conse-
quent loss of blessings, by the partners.

1. Else were your children unclean. Adopting the Jewish
perspective addressed by Paul, *unclean* here is equivalent to "not
in the proper relationship to the Lord" or "brought up outside the
Church" (see v. 4). One faithful and active Christian spouse can,
and must, render the home a Christian home. Otherwise children
of part-member families would be brought up outside the Church
and would then, at the age of accountability, become "unclean" or
"unholy"—natural human beings unredeemed by the atonement
of Christ and the covenant of the gospel.

2. The law of circumcision. See Genesis 17:9–14; Joseph
Smith Translation Genesis 17:11–12. Circumcision involved ritu-
ally cutting the foreskin off male children when they were eight
days old, or whenever they converted if they were not born
Israelites. Circumcision on the eighth day was the sign of the
covenant between God and Abraham and was originally instituted
to symbolize, among other things, that children were not accountable before the Lord until they were eight years old. The law of
circumcision of the flesh was done away in Christ (see Moroni
8:8).

2. The Jews. Even though Corinth was a Greek city, there
were during Paul's time a large number of Jews living there. Many
of these were in exile from Rome due to an edict of Claudius
issued in A.D. 41, which banned them from Rome for causing civil
disturbances (see Acts 18:2).

3. A great contention among the people. "The people" here
were the Jews, both Christian and non-Christian Jews. Christian
Jews and non-Christian Jews were irreconcilably opposed over
the law of Moses. The former believed the law was fulfilled, and
the latter believed it was still the perfect statement of God's will
for Israel. One side or the other must be wrong; no compromise
was possible. Naturally, this led to "a great contention" in any relations between Christian and non-Christian Jews, and it would

have been particularly difficult where Christian and non-Christian Jews were already married to each other or were legally obligated to marry.

Many Jews who became Christians would have had legally binding marriage contracts already in force between themselves and non-Christian Jews (today we would say such couples were "engaged"). Should these marriage contracts still be honored now that they had become Christians? Paul said yes—if the non-Christian partner would agree that the spouse and any children from the marriage would be raised as Christians and would not be subjected to the law of Moses, including circumcision. Some Jews were already married when they joined the Church. If their spouse was not also converted, should their marriage be preserved? Again, Paul said yes—on the same terms.

4. They became unholy. If the children of religiously mixed marriages were brought up under the law of Moses, they could not at the same time believe the gospel of Jesus Christ—for the two were often contradictory. Raised under the law of Moses, they would naturally not want to abandon it for the gospel when they reached the age of accountability. Thus, they would *become* unholy—sinful and in need of redemption—when they became accountable if they did not become members of the Church.

5. The apostle wrote unto the church. If this refers to what Paul wrote in 1 Corinthians 7:14, then the present New Testament text has become corrupted, for there is no mention there now of the concerns discussed in Doctrine and Covenants 74:5–6. It is possible that Paul wrote about these things in his earlier, lost letter to the Corinthians[2] and this phrase merely refers to those prior instructions. Thus, by revelation to Joseph Smith, this knowledge was restored.

5. Not of the Lord, but of himself. There is a difference between doctrine and policy. Doctrine is revealed by the Lord through his prophet and never changes. Policy is created and implemented by the Lord's servants and may be adapted or changed from time to time as circumstances warrant. Doctrines are fundamental principles; policies interpret and apply doctrinal principles to broader Church contexts as directed by Church leaders. Though policy may not always come directly from the Lord but rather from his servants, as in this case, where those servants are properly appointed and sustained, the Saints are obligated also to sustain their policies (see D&C 107:30–32).

5. The law of Moses should be done away. Paul's conditions for marriage between Christian Jews and non-Christian Jews were that the home would be a Christian home and that the law of Moses would not be observed there.

6. The tradition . . . that little children are unholy. By Paul's day, Jews had come to believe that infants were born unholy, or outside the covenant, and were in need of circumcision in order to enter the covenant and become holy or clean. Some Nephites had taught that infants need baptism, a doctrine Mormon declared a "gross error" and "solemn mockery before God" (Moroni 8:6, 9). This lie that little children are unredeemed unless some ordinance is performed for them is one of Satan's favorites, for it denies "the mercies of Christ" and would have us trust instead "in dead works" or rituals (Moroni 8:23). Ironically, one reason that circumcision was instituted with Abraham was to show him and his posterity that little children are *not* accountable before the Lord until their eighth year (see Joseph Smith Translation Genesis 17:11) and require no ordinance before that time in order to be sanctified by grace through the atonement of Christ.

7. Little children are holy. Joseph Smith taught elsewhere that "the doctrine of baptizing children, or sprinkling them, or they must welter in hell, is a doctrine not true, not supported in Holy Writ, and is not consistent with the character of God. All children are redeemed by the blood of Jesus Christ, and the moment that children leave this world, they are taken to the bosom of Abraham."[3]

---

1. *History of the Church,* 1:242.

2. See 1 Corinthians 5:9 for evidence of an earlier letter.

3. *History of the Church,* 4:554.

BACKGROUND

O n 10 January 1832, Joseph Smith had received instructions that the elders of the Church were to continue in their various labors for the two weeks remaining until a priesthood conference was held, when they would receive their mission calls and instructions (see D&C 73:1–2). Joseph and Sidney were also told to return home where they translated, preached, and prepared for the coming conference.

This conference was held in Amherst, Ohio, on 25 January 1832 and was a great success. Amherst was the home of Gideon Carter, Sylvester Smith,[1] and others. One reason for holding conferences away from Kirtland or Hiram was to proselytize outlying areas, and Joseph Smith related that "at this conference much harmony prevailed, and considerable business was done to advance the kingdom, *and promulgate the Gospel to the inhabitants of the surrounding country.*"[2]

During the conference itself, Joseph Smith was presented, sustained, and set apart as president of the high priesthood of the Church. It should be remembered that Joseph already possessed the office of apostle and of priesthood authority necessary to organize the Church and preside over all its quorums and auxiliaries. These he had received under the hands of Peter, James, and John. It was still necessary, however, for Joseph to be accepted and set apart within the structure of the Church according to the law of common consent (see D&C 26:2).[3] Orson Pratt related: "At this conference the Prophet Joseph was acknowledged President of the High Priesthood, and hands laid on him by Elder Sidney Rigdon. At this conference, by the request of the Priesthood, the Prophet inquired of the Lord, and a revelation was given and written in the presence of the whole assembly, appointing many of the Elders to missions, among whom Elder Lyman E. Johnson and myself were named and appointed on a mission to the Eastern States."[4]

Joseph Smith's own account of receiving this revelation states that "the Elders seemed anxious for me to inquire of the Lord that they might know His will, or learn what would be most pleasing to Him for them to do, in order to bring men to a sense of their condition; for, as it was written, all men have gone out of the way, so that none doeth good, no, not one. I inquired and received the following"[5]—Doctrine and Covenants 75.

The earliest manuscripts of Doctrine and Covenants 75, including one in the handwriting of Sidney Rigdon that may be the original, indicate that, like Doctrine and Covenants 72, this revelation may have been received in two parts that were subsequently joined together—the first part consisting of verses 1–22 and the second part consisting of verses 23–36.[6]

COMMENTARY

1. Alpha and Omega. See Commentary on Doctrine and Covenants 19:1.

2. Ye who have given your names. Most of the elders present at this conference had already indicated their willingness to serve missions and had been instructed to wait until this conference to receive their specific calls (see D&C 73:2). In contemporary Church terms, they had already "put in their papers."

5. Laden with many sheaves. The proselyting mission of the Church is often compared allegorically to the planting, tending, or harvesting of food crops (compare D&C 4:4; 31:5; 86:5–7). The term *sheaves,* bundles of cut stalks with the grain still on them, is used four times in the Doctrine and Covenants (see D&C 31:5; 33:9; 75:5; 79:3), always in connection with missionary work. Some people may plant the seeds but never see the harvest. Some may water, weed, and tend the fields. Some may gather in what others have planted and nurtured. But all who have shared in the work will be "laden with . . . sheaves" in the day of the harvest.

6. I revoke the commission. William E. McLellin had previously been called to a mission to "the eastern lands" with Samuel Smith (see D&C 66:7–9).[7] Though called on 25 October 1831, he did not actually leave until 16 November, and returned home before the end of December, showing little inclination to go out again. Samuel Smith parted company with William McLellin before Christmas when "because of disobediences our way was hedged up before us [and] Brother William was taken sick."[8]

7. A new commandment. William McLellin was given another mission call, this time to work south of Kirtland, but this mission was as unsuccessful as his first.

7. The murmurings of his heart. There are indications other than this verse that William McLellin's heart was not entirely right. For example, after only three weeks on this second mission, he stopped preaching, claiming ill health and inclement weather. When he took a job working in a store, however, his companion, Luke Johnson, returned home and got another companion. William McLellin himself wrote, "I determined to cease proclaiming until I was satisfied in my own mind."[9]

16. Overcome all things. See Commentary on Doctrine and Covenants 64:2.

16. Lifted up. See Commentary on Doctrine and Covenants 5:35.

20. Shake off the dust of your feet. See Doctrine and Covenants 24:15.[10]

21. You shall be filled with joy. Not because those who

reject the gospel are going to be punished, but because the missionaries themselves will have borne witness of the truth and acquitted themselves of any blame for not warning their neighbors.

22. It shall be more tolerable for the heathen.[11] The heathen are those without a knowledge of Christ, the traditionally non-Christian nations of the world. In the Judgment, those who had no opportunity to live by the light of the gospel will be judged with leniency because of their ignorance. But those who heard the gospel and rejected it, or who knew a portion of it and rejected the fulness, will be judged more harshly. Ignorance in itself is not a sin, unless it is deliberate, and through vicarious work for the dead, ignorance and its consequences can be overcome through the grace of God. Willful rejection of available light, however, *is* a sin and cannot be forgiven without repentance.

24. The duty of the church to assist in supporting. Most of those called on full-time missions in 1832 were married men with families to support. Since the responsibility of supporting one's family in most cases has priority over serving a mission (see vv. 26, 28), most of these men needed some assurance of support for their families before they could accept mission calls. Once individual resources had been exhausted, it was the responsibility of Church members either to assist in supporting or to support entirely, if necessary, the dependents of those called on full-time missions.

25–26. Obtain places for your families. Those who were called on missions were commanded—not merely advised—to find Church members willing to take in and support their families. Once these missionaries had found lodging and support for their families, then, and only then, were they to proceed north, south, east, or west on their missions.

28. Let him provide. When a choice must unavoidably be made between supporting one's family or accepting a mission call, one must meet the higher obligation and support one's family. When such a choice is necessary, the faithful member need not fear losing his place in the kingdom. When resources are not sufficient to do all that is asked of us, we *must* prioritize. According to President Harold B. Lee, "The first priority should be to maintain their own spiritual and physical strength; then comes their family; then the Church and then their professions."[12] Many members set their priorities in exactly the opposite order, usually to the wounding of all parties involved.

28. Let him labor in the church. Where individuals are not able to accept a mission call because lodging and support for their families cannot be obtained, they are to labor in their local wards and branches instead.

29. The idler. Anyone with leisure time who is unwilling to consecrate it to the kingdom. In this context, the idler was one who would neither serve a full-time mission nor accept a local calling or assignment. Idlers may be members of record, and they may even attend their Church meetings, but those who will not work to build the kingdom are not members in good standing and, unless they repent, have forfeited their place in the celestial kingdom.

30. Be united in the ministry. That is, serve as missionary companions.

30. Simeon Carter . . . Emer Harris. Excellent biographical summaries for these and all other individuals mentioned in the Doctrine and Covenants may be found in Lyndon W. Cook's *Revelations of the Prophet Joseph Smith.*[13] It is worthy of note that the first five pairs of missionaries called in this revelation received specific assignments (see vv. 6–17), while the next seven pairs were instructed to ask and to knock and the Comforter would tell them where they should go (see D&C 80:3).

31. Ezra Thayre. Note that Elder Thayre was issued another mission call (see D&C 52:22; 56:5, 8). He accepted this call, and all indications are that he served faithfully.

1. No relation to the Prophet.
2. *History of the Church,* 1:242–43; emphasis added.

3. See also Background to D&C 52.

4. *Journal History of the Church,* 25 Jan. 1832, cited in Woodford, Historical Development, 1:915.

5. *History of the Church,* 1:243.

6. See Manuscripts 1–2, Newel K. Whitney Collection, BYU Special Collections.

7. See also Shipps and Welch, *Journals of William E. McLellin,* 61–78.

8. Shipps and Welch, *Journals of William E. McLellin,* 75; spelling standardized.

9. Shipps and Welch, *Journals of William E. McLellin,* 70–83, esp. 73.

10. See also Commentary on D&C 24:15.

11. See Commentary on D&C 45:54.

12. *Bishop's Training Course and Self-Help Guide,* sec. 2, 7, cited in James E. Faust, Conference Report, Oct. 1973, 18–19.

13. See also Black, *Who's Who in the Doctrine and Covenants.*

76

BACKGROUND

A fter their brief mission to eastern Ohio in December of
1831 and January of 1832 (see D&C 71:1), Joseph Smith
and Sidney Rigdon were living again with their families in borrowed quarters at the John Johnson farm in Hiram, Ohio. There,
according to the Lord's command, they had been working on
Joseph's translation of the Bible since about 10 January (see D&C
73:3). By 16 February, Joseph and Sidney had been translating for
over five weeks, taking only short breaks to preach locally and to
attend the conference in Amherst, Ohio, on 25 January.

As Joseph and Sidney studied the Bible during these weeks of
translation, the Lord revealed to their understanding many things
not contained or not clearly explained in the present biblical text.
Doctrine and Covenants 74, for example, had been received by
the Prophet in January following his study of 1 Corinthians 7:14.
On 16 February 1832, while Joseph and Sidney were in an
upstairs room of the Johnson farmhouse translating John 5:29,
they received a remarkable joint vision now recorded as Doctrine
and Covenants 76. This revelation was so magnificent in scope
and precept and restored such important information on life after
death and other matters that for years afterward the Saints referred
to section 76 simply as "the Vision."[1]

Joseph's own account of receiving this vision reads as follows:

"Upon my return from Amherst conference, I resumed the translation of the Scriptures. From sundry revelations which had been received, it was apparent that many important points touching the salvation of man, had been taken from the Bible, or lost before it was compiled. It appeared self-evident from what truths were left, that if God rewarded every one according to the deeds done in the body the term 'Heaven,' as intended for the Saints' eternal home must include more kingdoms than one. Accordingly, on the 16th of February, 1832, while translating St. John's Gospel, myself and Elder Rigdon saw the following vision."[2]

Several other persons were present at the Johnson farm when Joseph and Sidney received Doctrine and Covenants 76. Sixty years later Philo Dibble, one of those who had been present on that day, shared his recollections of the event: "The vision which is recorded in the Book of Doctrine and Covenants was given at the house of 'Father Johnson,' in Hyrum, Ohio, and during the time that Joseph and Sidney were in the spirit and saw the heavens open, there were other men in the room, perhaps twelve, among whom I was one during a part of the time—probably two-thirds of the time,—I saw the glory and felt the power, but did not see the vision.

"The events and conversation, while they were seeing what is written (and many things were seen and related that are not written,) I will relate as minutely as is necessary.

"Joseph would, at intervals, say: 'What do I see?' as one might say while looking out the window and beholding what all in the room could not see. Then he would relate what he had seen or what he was looking at. Then Sidney replied, 'I see the same.' Presently Sidney would say 'what do I see?' and would repeat what he had seen or was seeing, and Joseph would reply, 'I see the same.'

"This manner of conversation was repeated at short intervals to the end of the vision, and during the whole time not a word was spoken by any other person. Not a sound nor motion made by anyone but Joseph and Sidney, and it seemed to me that they never moved a joint or limb during the time I was there, which I think was over an hour, and to the end of the vision.

"Joseph sat firmly and calmly all the time in the midst of a magnificent glory, but Sidney sat limp and pale, apparently as limber as a rag, observing which, Joseph remarked, smilingly, 'Sidney is not used to it as I am.'"[3]

It should be remembered that Philo Dibble was a very old man when he wrote this account of events that had occurred sixty years before. In an earlier reference to Doctrine and Covenants 76, Brother Dibble had indicated that he was actually present only at the end of the vision.[4] Nevertheless, as a young man he was himself an eyewitness to at least part of the vision and was there at the time to learn from other eyewitnesses exactly what had happened before his own arrival.

Joseph Smith's own summation of the importance of this revelation is instructive: "Nothing could be more pleasing to the Saints upon the order of the kingdom of the Lord, than the light which burst upon the world through the foregoing vision. Every law, every commandment, every promise, every truth, and every point touching the destiny of man, from Genesis to Revelation, where the purity of the scriptures remains unsullied by the folly of men, go to show the perfection of the theory [of different degrees of glory in the future life] and witnesses the fact that that document is a transcript from the records of the eternal world. The sublimity of the ideas; the purity of the language; the scope for action; the continued duration for completion, in order that the heirs of salvation may confess the Lord and bow the knee; the rewards for faithfulness, and the punishments for sins, are so much beyond the narrow-mindedness of men, that every honest man is constrained to exclaim: *'It came from God.'*"[5]

Yet the reaction of the Saints to the doctrines revealed in Doctrine and Covenants 76 was not universally positive. The old orthodox belief that most of humanity would be tortured in hell forever was so ingrained in contemporary religious thinking that Joseph's glorious message of God's inexhaustible love and mercy was unwelcome to some. Brigham Young recalled: "When God revealed to Joseph Smith and Sidney Rigdon that there was a place prepared for all, according to the light they had received and their rejection of evil and practice of good, it was a great trial to many, and some apostatized because God was not going to send to everlasting punishment heathens and infants, but had a place of salvation, in due time, for all, and would bless the honest and virtuous and truthful, whether they ever belonged to any church or not. It was a new doctrine to this generation, and many stumbled at it."[6]

At the close of the vision, Joseph and Sidney were commanded to write down while still "in the Spirit" those portions of it that could be shared with the Church and with the world (see D&C 76:28, 113). Their written account was then forwarded to Independence, Missouri, for Church publication and appeared in *The Evening and the Morning Star* in July 1832.[7] Eleven years later, in Nauvoo, Joseph also penned a poetic version of section 76 in response to a short poem on eternity written by W. W. Phelps entitled "Vade Mecum"—Latin for "Go with Me." Both of these poems were published in the *Times and Seasons* on 1 February 1843.[8] Joseph's poetic treatment of section 76, which is noted in the following commentaries, offers several important additions and insights to the Doctrine and Covenants.

COMMENTARY

1. **Hear, O ye heavens, and give ear, O earth.** Compare Isaiah 1:2; Deuteronomy 32:1. Doctrine and Covenants 76 impacts our knowledge of both heaven and earth, of both the living and the dead, of both this life and the next. Elder Wilford Woodruff stated that this vision "gives more light, more truth, and more principle than any revelation contained in any other book we ever read. It makes plain to our understanding our present

condition, where we came from, why we are here, and where we are going to."⁹

1. The Lord is God. This, of course, refers to the Lord Jesus Christ, who is God the Son. There is no salvation from the Fall and no return to the kingdom of God except through Christ.

3. His purposes fail not. Because of who and what he is, everything Christ undertakes will be successful.

4. From eternity to eternity he is the same. The words usually translated as *eternity* in the Old and New Testaments do not refer to endless time, but rather to distinct "ages" or "eons" of time.¹⁰ "From eternity to eternity means from the spirit existence through the probation which we are in, and then back again to the eternal existence which will follow."¹¹ Jesus Christ is now the same divine being, with the same mind, character, and intent as he was when he created the universe or when he prayed in the Garden of Gethsemane.

4. His years never fail. In his role as Creator and Savior, Jesus Christ never grows too old to achieve his purposes or runs out of time in which to accomplish them. He goes on forever.

5. Gracious. That is, Christ is a source of grace—of gifts and blessings freely and generously given.

5. Fear me. See Commentary on Doctrine and Covenants 10:56.

7. All the hidden mysteries of my kingdom. Whenever the scriptures speak of mysteries, they refer to information that can be learned only through divine revelation. In February of 1832, the knowledge received by Joseph Smith and Sidney Rigdon in Doctrine and Covenants 76 contained what had been until that time "hidden mysteries."¹²

10. For by my Spirit will I enlighten them. The experience of Joseph Smith and Sidney Rigdon in receiving section 76 is just one marvelous example of the fulfillment of the promises made in verses 5–10 to *all* faithful Saints.

"Salvation cannot come without revelation; it is in vain for anyone to minister without it. No man is a minister of Jesus Christ without being a Prophet. No man can be a minister of Jesus Christ except he has a testimony of Jesus; and this is the spirit of prophecy. Whenever salvation has been administered, it has been by testimony. Men of the present time testify of heaven and hell, and have never seen either; and I will say that no man knows these things without this."[13]

11. Being in the Spirit. Being filled with the Holy Ghost.

12. Our eyes were opened. When the power of the Holy Ghost descends directly upon an individual, the mortal veil that normally covers sight and understanding can be temporarily drawn aside, allowing them to see and participate in things beyond this natural world. It is only in this way—through the personal and protective indwelling of the Spirit—that human beings can see God and survive the experience (see vv. 116–18; D&C 67:11; Moses 1:11).

13. Things which were from the beginning. From the pre-mortal state even before the creation of this earth. It is technically incorrect to label section 76 as merely a vision of the afterlife or of the three degrees of glory, for Joseph and Sidney saw much more than this. As promised in verses 7–8, they saw things "from days of old" to "things to come . . . , even the things of many generations." The scope of the vision spanned from the beginning of creation (see v. 13) to the completion of Christ's work (see v. 106) to worlds without number and without end (see vv. 109–12). This vision is similar to the grand panoramic vision of this world from its beginning to its end given to other prophets at the heads of previous dispensations (see Moses 1:1–9, 24–41; 7:21–67; Abraham 3–5). The poetic version of Doctrine and Covenants 76 describes the content of the vision as including "what was, and now is, and yet is to be."[14] The Prophet Joseph once remarked that "I could explain a hundred fold more than I ever have of the glories of the kingdoms manifested to me in the vision, were I permitted, and were the people prepared to receive them"[15] (see also v. 115).

Note also that "the beginning" in this case does not refer to the creation of the earth or even to the creation of the universe, but to the appearance of the Only Begotten in the bosom of the Father. Christ is the beginning of all things (see D&C 19:1).

14. The fulness of the gospel. That is, faith, repentance, baptism, and receiving the Holy Ghost.[16] The "good news" of the gospel, however, can also be summarized as it is in verses 40–42[17] (compare 3 Nephi 27:13–21).

14. The Son, whom we saw and with whom we conversed. Through the power of the Holy Ghost, Joseph Smith and Sidney Rigdon saw and spoke with the Son of God, as had Adam, Enoch, Noah, Abraham, and Moses before them, and as Joseph himself had in his earlier experience in the Sacred Grove.

17. Resurrection of the just; and . . . the unjust: In the King James Version of John 5:29, the two resurrections are called the "resurrection of life" and the "resurrection of damnation" (see also Mosiah 15:24; 3 Nephi 26:5). The change in wording received here agrees with the terminology of Luke 14:14 and Acts 24:15. Neither set of terms, strictly speaking, would be incorrect, since both are found elsewhere in the scriptures. But the change of wording did cause Joseph and Sidney to stop and ponder the nature of the two resurrections (see v. 19).

The first resurrection, the resurrection of life or the resurrection of the just, began with the resurrection of Christ and will extend through the Millennium.[18] It includes all those who receive a celestial or terrestrial glory (see vv. 50–65; D&C 45:54). The second or last resurrection, the resurrection of damnation or the resurrection of the unjust, takes place at the end of the Millennium. It includes those who receive a telestial glory (see D&C 76:85) and those who are sons of perdition.

18. It was given unto us. The full significance of the meaning of John 5:29 was revealed to Joseph and Sidney.

19. And while we meditated upon these things. At first Joseph and Sidney were allowed to understand (see v. 18), and then as they meditated further upon what the Spirit had revealed to them, the Lord caused them not only to understand but to *see*.

"I think we pay too little attention to the value of meditation, a principle of devotion. In our worship there are two elements: One is spiritual communion arising from our own meditation; the other, instruction from others, particularly from those who have authority to guide and instruct us. Of the two, the more profitable introspectively is meditation.

"Meditation is the language of the soul. It is defined as 'a form of private devotion or spiritual exercise, consisting in deep, continued reflection on some religious theme.' . . .

"Meditation is one of the most secret, most sacred doors through which we pass into the presence of the Lord."[19]

20. And we beheld. Although the revelation of section 76 as a whole began with the inspiration of the Holy Ghost leading to an increased understanding of the scriptures, it was at this point that the "vision" proper began. Joseph and Sidney actually experienced several visions, or one vision divided into several parts. The first of these was the vision of the Son on the right hand of the Father and of his eternal glory in verses 20–24. The second was the vision of the premortal life, the fall of Satan, and the sufferings of perdition in verses 25–49. Third was a vision of the celestial glory, which is described in verses 50–70 and is further alluded to in verses 92–96. Fourth was a vision of the terrestrial glory in verses 71–80. Fifth was a vision of the telestial glory in verses 81–113 (except the digression in verses 92–97).

20. And received of his fulness. Most likely this refers to the fulness of God's glory. *Fulness* here probably carries the meaning of "overflowing abundance." The glory that fills the exalted Christ overflows and abounds to fill also those who are his. *Fulness* might also be understood here to mean all that now makes Christ what he is. In the individual process of personally becoming exalted, Christ did not receive his own fulness in the beginning, but was, over time, filled with the glory, attributes, and merits of his Father. As Christ personally experienced and overcame all things, he "continued from grace to grace, until he received a fulness" (D&C 93:13; see also vv. 12–20). Now that he is exalted, he has received as his own all that his Father has, and will share with us all that he now has.

21. Them who are sanctified. Those who are truly and finally "Saints," having been made holy forever through the atonement of Christ and a glorious, celestial resurrection, enter into the Father's kingdom. The poetic version reads, "And sanctified beings from worlds that have been,"[20] thus making clear that these are men and women from other worlds created by Jesus Christ who have already been saved through his atonement and have already been glorified in the Father's kingdom (see v. 24).

22. Last of all. Meaning "the most recent" testimony rather than "the final" testimony.

24. That by him, and through him, and of him. See Doctrine and Covenants 88:41; John 1:3; Colossians 1:16–17. The Creator of the universe and all it contains is Jesus Christ, who acted in behalf of the Father. This is true not only of its finished structures, such as planets and stars, but also of the raw materials themselves, of the elements and atoms and molecules. In a manner more comprehensive than a builder who merely uses preexisting materials, the creative force of Christ is expressed in the very structure or nature of the raw materials themselves. Without Christ, not only would the present structures of the universe collapse into unorganized chaos, but so would the materials out of which they are made, the atoms and molecules, for it is the light of Christ that imposes order and law upon all things—even at the atomic and subatomic levels (see D&C 88:6–13, 41–50).[21]

24. The worlds . . . and the inhabitants thereof. Note that *worlds* is plural, and that there are inhabitants who have lived and who now live upon those many worlds. Is there intelligent life in the universe? Of course there is! There are innumerable inhabitants of countless worlds, all created and saved by the same Jesus Christ who was born in Bethlehem two thousand years ago. The poetic version makes this even more explicit:

By him, of him, and through him, the worlds were all made,
Even all that career in the heavens so broad,
Whose inhabitants, too, from the first to the last,
Are sav'd by the very same Saviour of ours;
And, of course, are begotten God's daughters and sons,
By the very same truths, and the very same pow'rs.[22]

24. Are begotten sons and daughters unto God. Since this verse makes it clear that it is by, through, and of Jesus Christ specifically that all these inhabitants of all these many worlds are begotten sons and daughters of God, this "begetting" cannot refer to our common identity as spirit children of God in premortality. Rather, the reference is to our spiritual rebirth, which is being "born again" as children of Jesus Christ by accepting his atonement and entering his gospel covenant (see D&C 25:1; Mosiah 5:7; 27:24–26; Ether 3:14; Moses 6:6, 62–7:1).[23]

25. An angel . . . in authority. Joseph and Sidney saw events of the premortal life, even before the earth was created. In the premortal world, Satan held a position of great authority in God's very presence. He was one who exercised priesthood power. The poetic version calls him, "an angel of light, in authority great"[24] (see Abraham 3:27–28).

26. Perdition. The Latin root of the word *perdition* (*perditus*) means "lost." The name Perdition is sometimes used specifically for Satan, who is the archetypical "lost one." Perdition is also used more abstractly for the condition of being lost, and thus describes those souls, "sons of perdition," who will not be redeemed and saved in a kingdom of glory (see v. 32).

26. The heavens wept. The inhabitants of the heavens wept over the fall of Satan (compare Moses 7:28).

26. Lucifer, a son of the morning. Besides this verse, the name Lucifer occurs only twice in scripture—in Isaiah 14:12 and 2 Nephi 24:12, which is quoting Isaiah.

It is possible that the Hebrew text made a play on words with the term *ben-shachar,* "son of (the) morning" or "son of dawn." For *shachar* also means "dark" or "black," and thus *ben-shachar* might conceivably be interpreted as something like "son of [outer] darkness" (see also D&C 82:5).

28. Satan, that old serpent, even the devil. The term *Satan* comes from the Hebrew and means "adversary," "enemy," or "accuser" (compare Revelation 12:10). *Devil* on the other hand comes from the Greek word *diabolos,* and means literally "one who separates or divides." This is a particularly apt description, for the devil separated himself and his followers from God in premortal life, he now separates those he deceives from their God, and, where God seeks to make us all one (see D&C 38:27; John 17:21–23), Satan seeks to divide us against one another into factions and parties (see 1 Corinthians 1:10–13). The divine impulse unites; the satanic divides.

Satan is frequently identified with a serpent or dragon and particularly with the serpent in Genesis 3 (see also Revelation 20:2). In the ancient world, the serpent was often a symbol for the forces of chaos and dissolution. Like a poisonous serpent, Satan injects his venom and kills with his mouth, for example by lying, accusing, teaching false doctrine, and so on.

28. To take the kingdom. That is, he attempted a coup—to seize the throne of God by force (see Isaiah 14:12–15).

29. He maketh war. The war in heaven described in Revelation 12:7–10 isn't over yet! The present tense here indicates that Satan is still waging war with the Saints. The only differences are that the battlefield has been moved and that we mortals cannot now remember the war or even recognize our old, common enemy without God's help. Without the gospel in this mortal sphere, we humans are sometimes easy prey for the evil one.

29. Encompasseth. Surrounds or encircles.

30. Those with whom he made war and overcame. Apparently the reference here is not to those who merely succumb to the threats, lies, or temptations of Satan and who become "prisoners" of war, but to those who actually change sides in the war, who knowingly change allegiance, thus becoming traitors to

God, and fight for Satan, thus becoming "sons of perdition" (see vv. 31–32).

31. Those who know my power . . . partakers thereof. The type of person being described in verses 30–38 is not merely disobedient, or even wicked or rebellious. Something much worse is being described here. These persons have experienced the highest blessings of the gospel and the strongest possible manifestations of God's power and glory (see D&C 67:10).[26] Even so—and while they *know* what they are doing—they defy God and subject themselves to Satan.

31. Suffered themselves. They knowingly allow themselves to be overcome. Like Cain, with full knowledge of both lords, they love Satan more than God and deliberately *choose* to follow Satan (see Moses 5:18).

32. Sons of perdition. In the biblical idiom, "sons of" can mean literally "children of," or it can also mean "those who fall in the category of." Sons of perdition, therefore, are (1) those who have made the devil—Perdition—their spiritual father rather than Christ (compare v. 24), and (2) all those whose fate or condition is to be cast off and lost forever—perdition.[27]

According to this revelation there are several characteristics common to sons of perdition (see vv. 31–32). First, they know the Lord's power, which is the priesthood. Second, they have partaken of this power by receiving its ordinances—particularly the ordinances of the temple. Third, having received the power of God, they willingly exchange it for the power of Satan and allow the evil one to bind them to him. Finally, while knowing of a certainty the truth of the gospel and the power of God, they deny the former and defy the latter. Compare these verses with Hebrews 6:4–6.

Those who rebelled in the premortal life, before the mortal veil was drawn, did so with full knowledge of God and of his will and so became perdition. Likewise, in this life only those who, like the devil and his angels, have rebelled after the veil has been parted for them, can become sons of perdition (see v. 35).[28]

32. Better for them never to have been born. This is not just a figure of speech. Before their mortal birth, sons of perdition were spirit children of God who lived with their heavenly parents. Leaving that blessed state for mortality, they have here chosen Satan and have switched sides, and thus they will be cast out from God's presence and influence forever. All the rest of God's mortal children, after meeting the demands of justice, will eventually receive some degree of glory and some relationship with God in the resurrection. Thus, for sons of perdition, and for them alone, it would have been better to have remained premortal spirits and never to have been born into mortality.

33. Vessels of wrath. This metaphor compares sons of perdition to cups or other containers into which the wrath of God is to be poured.

34. No forgiveness in this world nor in the world to come. Forgiveness comes only through the gospel of repentance. For those who refuse to repent, who have crucified Christ within themselves and have ripped his atonement from their souls, there is no other source of forgiveness either now or in all eternity. They have knowingly, intentionally, and irrevocably destroyed their only possible means of salvation (see Hebrews 6:4–6; 10:26; D&C 88:35).

35. Having denied the Holy Spirit. The kind of knowledge that is apparently a prerequisite for perdition—a personal encounter with God (see vv. 43, 118)—can be gained only through the direct intervention of the Holy Ghost (see vv. 116–18). Only when "quickened [made to live] by the Spirit" in some more intimate way than usual can even righteous Saints see God in the flesh and live (D&C 67:11; see also v. 12). Thus, the scriptures correctly tell us that "no man hath seen God" (John 1:18; 1 John 4:12; Joseph Smith Translation parallel scriptures), for no *mere* man ever has. But the Holy Spirit is not a mortal man, nor does he suffer from these mortal limitations. If the Holy Spirit personally descends upon us, filling us with his own divine presence and glory—the state of being fully "in the Spirit" (vv.

11–12)—then we are no longer *merely* human beings, but, becoming one with the Holy Spirit, we are "transfigured" and are thus able to bear contact with the "world of glory" (v. 118).

Because it is the Holy Spirit that comes upon us, changes us, and makes divine contact possible, then denial of this experience and of what one learns by it is also denial of the Holy Spirit. President Spencer W. Kimball indicated the magnitude of this sin when he taught: "The sin against the Holy Ghost requires such knowledge that it is manifestly impossible for the rank and file to commit such a sin."[29] Moreover, the Prophet Joseph Smith taught that this sin can be committed only in the flesh: "No man can commit the unpardonable sin after the dissolution of the body, nor in this life, until he receives the Holy Ghost."[30]

35. Having denied the Only Begotten Son of the Father. "What must a man do to commit the unpardonable sin? He must receive the Holy Ghost, have the heavens opened unto him, and know God, and then sin against Him. After a man has sinned against the Holy Ghost, there is no repentance for him. He has got to say that the sun does not shine while he sees it; he has got to deny Jesus Christ when the heavens have been opened unto him, and to deny the plan of salvation with his eyes open to the truth of it; and from that time he begins to be an enemy. This is the case with many apostates of the Church of Jesus Christ of Latter-day Saints."[31]

35. Having crucified him unto themselves. Through faith, repentance, baptism, and receiving the gift of the Holy Ghost, human beings become one with Christ and with other Saints of God, and Christ becomes their common Father (see v. 24). Jesus Christ and Satan can never become one. Therefore, when one who has partaken of the highest blessings of the gospel rebels and seeks to be one with the devil and his angels, he simultaneously destroys any relationship he may have had with Christ. He becomes like those who first crucified the Savior and murders—crucifies—any part of the Savior that remains within himself. In joining ranks with the murderers of Christ by killing Christ within himself, rendering the Atonement vain in his case, and by seeking to destroy Christ and his work in others, he becomes one with Satan and his angels and thus becomes a child of the devil.

"When a man begins to be an enemy to this work, he hunts me, he seeks to kill me, and never ceases to thirst for my blood. He gets the spirit of the devil—the same spirit that they had who crucified the Lord of Life—the same spirit that sins against the Holy Ghost. You cannot save such persons; you cannot bring them to repentance; they make open war, like the devil, and awful is the consequence."[32]

36. Lake of fire and brimstone. An image used to symbolize the fate of perdition.[33]

37. The only ones on whom the second death shall have any power. One of the greatest truths revealed in this vision is that God eventually saves *all* his children. The only exception to this universal salvation in some degree of glory is the sons of perdition, who by their own choice put themselves beyond God's reach. The redemptive work of Christ saves all who inherit any degree of glory—telestial, terrestrial, or celestial—and the wicked who are not perdition do *not* suffer forever and ever after they have satisfied the demands of justice (see vv. 38, 83–85).[34]

38. The only ones who shall not be redeemed. As plainly as the doctrine is taught in the Doctrine and Covenants (see vv. 39, 42–44, 88–89), it still eludes some of the Saints: *All* our Heavenly Father's children will go to "heaven," that is, they shall inherit heavenly glory in one of its three degrees—telestial, terrestrial, or celestial—except the sons of perdition. *All* humanity is saved from sin, death, and hell at the resurrection—except the sons of perdition. *All* human beings are eventually redeemed from the custody and power of the devil—except the sons of perdition. What a glorious doctrine! Oh, the infinite mercy, love, and grace of God our Father and our Savior Jesus Christ!

Certainly many will be redeemed and saved in a telestial or a terrestrial glory, and many even in the celestial glory will not be *exalted* (see D&C 131:1–5; 132:16–17). But, contrary to the common traditions of the world and with the exception of the sons of perdition, nobody suffers after the resurrection; *nobody burns in hell forever.*

39. All the rest shall be brought forth. This does not mean that the sons of perdition who have lived on this earth and gained mortal bodies will not be resurrected. Every person born of this earth will come forth in the resurrection (see D&C 88:14–16, 95–102; Alma 12:16–18). But the sons of perdition will not be resurrected "through the triumph and the glory of the Lamb" (D&C 76:39), since they have rejected his atonement, are "filthy still" (D&C 88:35, 102), and can receive no glory at all—no heat, no light, no energy (see D&C 88:24; Mosiah 16:11). All the rest of humanity are resurrected and glorified in some degree through the atonement of Christ. The poetic version reads, "While all the rest are, through the triumph of Christ, made partakers of grace, by the power of his word."[35]

40. And this is the gospel. The Greek word translated as *gospel* in the New Testament means literally "glad tidings" or "good news." The capsule statement of the gospel here in verses 40–44 focuses on the role of Jesus in blessing the whole world and all of God's children: Jesus came into the world to die for the world, the *whole* world, and to bear the sins of the world, so that *all* the world, not just the righteous part of it, might eventually be cleansed, sanctified, and saved in some kingdom of glory (compare John 3:16). The poetic version explains that Jesus "lay down his life for his friends and his foes."[36] Other scriptural definitions of the gospel focus on what the gospel requires of us—faith, repentance, and baptism—rather than on the work of Jesus (compare D&C 33:10–11; 39:6; 138:32–35; Articles of Faith 1:3–4). In the fullest sense, any definition of "the gospel" includes *both* a proclamation of Jesus' mission and a clear statement of how humans are to respond to it (see 3 Nephi 27:13–22; Acts 2:22–38).

42. Whom the Father had put into his power. Likely this refers to those who chose Christ and his plan in the premortal world and whom Christ was then given power to save through his atonement. Christ was not given power to save sons of perdition, those who will not repent, because repentance is a condition of receiving the full blessings of the Atonement.

42. And made by him. All the physical laws and processes of the universe depend upon the creative power of Christ, or the light of Christ, in order to work. Thus, while Christ himself does not beget our physical bodies, both the processes of biology and the elements they work with come from Christ the Creator. All physical existence depends upon the light of Christ to remain in an organized state.[37] In this sense he is responsible for all that is— including us (see D&C 88:6–13, 41–42).[38]

The poetic version of Doctrine and Covenants 76:42 here adds two lines to the description of Christ's work, to which there is no parallel in section 76: "And purify earth for the Sabbath of rest, by the agent of fire, as it was by the flood."[39]

43. Saves all the works of his hands. Because the work and the glory of our Father in Heaven are "to bring to pass the immortality and eternal life of man" (Moses 1:39), we may assume that he is very, very good at it. Heavenly Father and Christ lose nothing. Only the sons of perdition are lost, and Christ doesn't lose them; they lose themselves.

Not everyone is saved *at the same time,* however. Speaking in the context of what happens when we die, it is correct to say that some are saved in paradise, or Abraham's bosom, from sin, hell, and the power of the devil, and some are not (see Luke 16:22–23). But in the context of the final resurrection, after our time in the spirit world is over, everyone, *all* of humanity except the sons of perdition, are saved from sin, death, hell, and the power of the devil and receive some degree of glory in the mansions of the Father. It was this glorious doctrine that caused some in the Church in 1832 to stumble, because it so contradicted the traditions they had been taught and had accepted in their former churches.

43. Deny the Son after the Father has revealed him. The

voice of the Father has often been heard revealing the identity of his Only Begotten (see v. 23; Matthew 3:17; 17:5; 2 Peter 1:17; 2 Nephi 31:11, 15; 3 Nephi 11:7; Joseph Smith–History 1:17). Again, it requires more than a loss of testimony to become a son of perdition.[40]

44–48. Everlasting/endless/eternal punishment. See Doctrine and Covenants 19:6–12.[41] It is important to note, however, that the doctrine taught in section 19 does not open the door to a doctrine of redemption for the sons of perdition at some future time. In answer to a letter from W. W. Phelps, Joseph Smith wrote in 1833: "Say to the brothers Hulet and to all others, that the Lord never authorized them to say that the devil, his angels, or the sons of perdition, should ever be restored; for their state of destiny was not revealed to man, is not revealed, nor ever shall be revealed, save to those who are made partakers thereof: consequently those who teach this doctrine have not received it of the Spirit of the Lord. Truly Brother Oliver declared it to be the doctrine of devils. We, therefore, command that this doctrine be taught no more in Zion."[42]

44. To reign with the devil and his angels. Because they progressed further and received resurrected, physical bodies, the sons of perdition who were once mortals upon this earth will rule over the unembodied devil and his angels in eternity (see Moses 5:23).[43]

44. Where their worm dieth not, and the fire is not quenched. The phrasing follows Mark 9:44–48. The ancients believed that a toothache was caused by a worm eating the inside of a tooth just as a worm eats the inside of an apple. A cavity, they believed, marked the place where the worm had entered, and the phrase "the worm turns" described a sudden sharp pain in a bad tooth. When a bad tooth finally stopped aching, it was believed that the worm eating it had died. "Where their worm dieth not," then, described an endless excruciating toothache with no hope of relief. Of course the language is figurative, as is the reference to fire, but the imagery is meant to convey some idea of the unending, inextinguishable, and self-inflicted torments of perdition.

50. The resurrection of the just. Questions about the resurrection of the just had been part of Joseph and Sidney's original inquiry (see vv. 15–19). The resurrection of the just is also called the first resurrection, and this vision, or this part of the vision, extends from verse 50 to verse 80, including both the celestial and the terrestrial worlds—for those who inherit either of these are part of the first resurrection (see D&C 45:54).

There are not three resurrections, one for each kingdom, but only *two*—the resurrection of the just and the resurrection of the unjust. Because the terrestrial beings are part of the just, their resurrection is described here in the same account as that of the celestial beings. Note also that the phrase "this is the end of the vision" (vv. 49, 80, 113), which divides Doctrine and Covenants 76 into its component parts, does not occur between verses 50–80, which should, therefore, be considered a single account dealing with the whole of the first resurrection, or resurrection of the just, in both its aspects.

The two resurrections, the resurrection of the just and the resurrection of the unjust, can each be further divided into their "mornings" and "evenings." Celestial and terrestrial beings will rise in the morning and evening of the first resurrection, respectively; telestial beings and perdition will rise in the morning and evening of the second resurrection, respectively. These four occasions correspond symbolically to the first four trumpets to be blown during the millennial period, according to Doctrine and Covenants 88:97–102.

51. Who received the testimony of Jesus. There is a great difference between having a testimony of Jesus and receiving the gospel. There are many fine and good people of other Christian churches who have received a testimony of Jesus and who know by the Spirit that he is the Son of God, but who still reject the fulness of the gospel as restored in the latter days through the Prophet Joseph Smith.

51–52. And believed . . . and were baptized . . . and receive the Holy Spirit. Those who receive a celestial glory accepted *both* the testimony of Jesus *and* the fulness of his gospel. They received the ordinances of the gospel as administered by the true Church (see vv. 51–52). Accepting the fulness of the gospel and its ordinances as commanded by God is a minimum requirement for celestial glory (see 2 Nephi 31:17–21). In a statement included by the Prophet Joseph Smith in his *History of the Church,* he said: "A man may be saved, after the judgment, in the terrestrial kingdom, or in the telestial kingdom, but he can never see the celestial kingdom of God without being born of the water and the Spirit."[44]

Those who receive celestial glory in the resurrection are they who received *both* a testimony of Jesus *and* the fulness of the gospel. Terrestrial beings received a testimony of Jesus but would not receive the fulness of his gospel, and those who are raised to telestial glory received *neither* the testimony of Jesus nor the fulness of his gospel (compare vv. 51, 74–75, 79, 82, 101).[45]

52. Keeping the commandments. In this context, "keeping the commandments" refers to keeping the specific commandments to have faith, repent, and be baptized (see, for example, D&C 18:19; 29:49; Mosiah 16:12; Alma 9:12; 3 Nephi 27:20; Moses 5:14). By keeping the commandments to have faith, repent, and be baptized, human beings may be washed and cleansed and otherwise be made fit to receive the gift of the Holy Ghost.

53. Who overcome by faith. It is indisputable that those who inherit the celestial kingdom overcome all things (compare v. 60), but the critical question is, "*How* do they do it?" This verse makes it clear that we do *not* overcome by our own magnificent feats of willpower and self-perfection. We do not save ourselves; Jesus saves us. Therefore, we follow the course described in verses 51–52. We receive a testimony of Christ; we believe the gospel of Christ; then we are baptized into Christ and receive the Holy Spirit. We must have faith in Christ and in his ability to save us from our weaknesses. Because it is Christ who overcomes all things, we must have faith in him as our Savior and become one with him through the gospel covenant. Then, as a part of him, we can share in *his* victory (see Romans 8:37), and this is how we overcome by our faith.[46]

While the canonized text emphasizes our ultimate victory through faith in Christ, we must not entirely ignore the role of works in being "faithful." Our work is to come to Christ and to remain faithful to him by keeping his commandments; his work is to perfect and exalt us. This partnership of faith and works is reflected in the text of the poetic version of this text: "For those overcome, by their faith and their works."[47]

53. Sealed by the Holy Spirit of promise. The Holy Spirit of promise is none other than the Holy Ghost. This is a title used for the Holy Ghost when he performs a particular type of function. A covenant is a contract or a mutual promise between two parties, and it becomes valid or binding when it is "sealed." Anciently, contracts were sealed in wax or clay with the impression of a signet ring or an official seal. Today we seal most contracts by signing them, though official seals are sometimes still used. Covenants or contracts made with God are sealed by the power of the Holy Ghost, which testifies to us that all God's promises will be kept. The mere presence of the Holy Spirit in our lives is proof that our covenants with God are valid, while the Spirit itself *promises* that all our covenant blessings will become realities.

Individuals are said to be "sealed" when they are *promised* a certain fate or destination, such as the celestial kingdom or exaltation in that kingdom, although people can also be sealed up to wrath (see D&C 1:8–9; 133:71–73) or even be sealed by the devil (see Alma 34:35). Whether God's promises are conditional, as in the covenants of baptism or the endowment, or unconditional, as when one's calling and election are made sure,[48] on either level it is the power of the Holy Ghost acting as the Holy Spirit of promise that ratifies the contract, guarantees its terms, and testifies or promises that God's word will be kept.

54. The church of the Firstborn. The Firstborn of God the Father is Jesus Christ; therefore, the Church of the Firstborn is the Church of Jesus Christ. "The Church of Jesus Christ" is, however, a term used primarily to describe Jesus' *earthly* Church—the members of which are not always entirely celestial in nature. False or disloyal members are an unpleasant reality in the Church.

Because Firstborn of the Father is one of Jesus' titles in eternity, then Church of the Firstborn can appropriately be used to describe the members of the Church of Jesus Christ who will *still* be members in eternity. The Church of the Firstborn is thus the heavenly church or the eternal church. They are the faithful—the "church within the church"—or those members who keep their covenants, who are faithful and loyal, and who serve God with all their heart, might, mind, and strength. Even though their names may have been upon the rolls of the Church in mortality, those who take their covenants lightly or who will not serve will no longer be members of Jesus' Church in eternity (see vv. 79, 94–95).

55. Into whose hands the Father has given all things. See verses 59–60;[49] Doctrine and Covenants 84:37–38; Romans 8:17; Revelation 21:7. The poetic version adds, "For they hold the keys of the kingdom of heav'n."[50]

56. Priests and kings. They will have all authority, both temporal and spiritual, as kings and priests unto God in eternity. Though kings themselves, they shall still serve him who is the King of Kings.

56. Who have received of his fulness. The antecedent of the pronoun *his* is "the Father," and the fulness spoken of here is the fulness of the Father (see v. 71). The celestial heirs, who are joint-heirs with Christ and follow his example (see Romans 8:17), are made full just as the Father is full and receive the kind of glory the Father gave the Son, thereby becoming like the Father and the Son in glory (see D&C 84:38; 2 Peter 1:3–4). The poetic version specifies, "Receiving a fulness of glory and light."[51]

57. Priests of the Most High. Usually, "the Most High" refers in scripture to Jehovah, who is Jesus Christ (for example, Psalm 83:18). In the fulness of the gospel, however, Jesus introduces us to his Father, who is even greater than himself (see John 14:28). Thus, the title "Most High" may correctly be applied to either the Father or the Son, or even to the Godhead collectively.

57. After the order of. The order or type of priesthood necessary to achieve the kingdom of God, whether as Zion here upon the earth or as the celestial kingdom in eternity, is the priesthood which Jesus Christ himself holds and exercises. Anciently this was called "the Holy Priesthood, after the Order of the Son of God" (D&C 107:3). Because Melchizedek, and before him Enoch, had held this same priesthood and had established Zion with it, the order of the Son also became known as the order of Enoch and the order of Melchizedek. Both anciently and today, out of respect for the sacredness of its full title, this priesthood is called the Melchizedek Priesthood (see D&C 107:4).

58. As it is written. This is probably a reference to Psalm 82:6, which is also cited by Jesus in John 10:34. In John it is clear that Jesus understood the psalm to say that those who receive the "word of God" can be called gods (John 10:35), and in the fullest sense *Christ* is the Word of God (see John 1:1, 12; Revelation 19:13), which must be received to bring this about.

58. They are gods, even the sons of God. Note that the two terms *gods* and *sons of God,* are equated here, for to be one is also to be or to become the other. Children grow up to be what their parents are. If, through the gospel, we have truly become the sons and daughters of God as the scriptures insist (see v. 24; D&C 11:30; 25:1; 50:41; 4 Nephi 1:17),[52] then it follows that as we grow "from grace to grace"—following the example of Jesus himself (D&C 93:13)—we also become more like God (see 2 Peter 1:4; 1 John 3:2; Revelation 3:21).

59. All things are theirs. See 1 Corinthians 3:21–23 (see also D&C 84:37–38; Revelation 21:7). What isn't included in "*all* things"? For the celestial Saints, every righteous desire will be granted; every goal achieved; every need satisfied; every hope fulfilled. It is impossible to adequately describe the gifts and bounties of God toward those who love him. They are truly beyond our present comprehension. Those who receive the celestial kingdom belong to Christ and are in his special care, just as Christ belongs to the Father and is in his special care. And as the Father gives all that he has to the Son, so the Son shares all that he has with us, his children of the covenant (see Romans 8:17; Revelation 3:21). Like a kind and good man who wins a fortune and shares his bounty with needy friends, so Christ overcomes all things and receives all things, and then he invites us to partake with him in his victory.

60. They shall overcome all things. Ultimately, celestial individuals will learn to overcome all things on their own power, but not in this life, or before the Judgment, or for a long time after the resurrection.[53] Until that distant time, those who are celestial do not overcome all things on their own. Rather, they overcome through their faith in the merits of Christ and in their relationship with him (see Romans 8:37). Just as Christ vicariously suffered and paid for sins, so also we, through him, vicariously conquer and overcome all things. In fact, overcoming all things or achieving perfection are not *requirements* for entering the kingdom at all, rather they are some of the *blessings* of doing so (see D&C 76:69). The Book of Mormon in particular reminds us that we must rely wholly upon the merits of Jesus Christ for our salvation and our victory (see 2 Nephi 2:8; 31:19; Alma 22:14; 24:10; Helaman 14:13; Moroni 6:4; D&C 3:20). *Our* job is to come to Christ and to keep his covenants; *his* job is to perfect us and exalt us and bring us to the Father.

61. Let no man glory in man. While we *must,* however imperfectly, keep the commandments in order to remain in the covenant (see D&C 138:4), the righteousness we ultimately rely on for salvation and exaltation is *Jesus'* righteousness. *He* earned it. *He* overcame every temptation and every enemy. *He* had perfect willpower and perfect self-control. *He* led a sinless life. Since we must rely "wholly upon the merits" of Christ for salvation

(2 Nephi 31:19), and upon "the merits, and mercy, and grace of the Holy Messiah" (2 Nephi 2:8), it follows that we cannot—must not—become too proud of our *own* performance (compare Luke 18:9–14), or brag about our *own* merits, or rely upon our *own* strength or righteousness to save us (see Alma 26:11–12, 16; 1 Corinthians 1:31).

62. These shall dwell in the presence of God. "They shall have access to the presence of the Father and the Son. A citizen in a kingdom can have no greater honor than to be a welcome visitor in the palaces of the king. This is the privilege of those who come forth in the resurrection of the just."[54]

63. They whom he shall bring with him. At his second coming, Christ will bring with him the spirits of "the dead in Christ," who have rested in paradise, or Abraham's bosom, since their death (1 Thessalonians 4:16). Before any of those living upon the earth are caught up, these dead in Christ will be resurrected and will join their Savior in the clouds for his descent to the earth. Only then will the righteous mortals upon the earth be caught up—transfigured but not yet resurrected—to meet the Lord in the clouds and will also join him in his glorious descent (see D&C 88:96–98; Acts 1:9–11; 1 Thessalonians 4:14–17).

63. To reign on the earth. This will be the great Millennium, the thousand-year reign of Christ as King of Kings upon the earth. During this period the prayers of the righteous that "thy kingdom come. Thy will be done in earth, as it is in heaven" will finally be answered (Matthew 6:10).

64. The first resurrection. See Doctrine and Covenants 45:54; 63:18.[55]

65. The resurrection of the just. See Commentary on verse 17.

66. Mount Zion. The language of verses 66–69 is paralleled in Hebrews 12:22–24. According to Doctrine and Covenants 84:2–3; 133:56; Moses 7:62, and Articles of Faith 1:10, Mount Zion is the millennial New Jerusalem that is to be built upon the American continent beginning in Independence, Missouri. It was this very city that the Saints in February of 1832 were attempting to build and whose location had been revealed to them barely seven months earlier (see D&C 45:64–71; 57:2–3).[56]

66. The city of the living God, the heavenly place. While Mount Zion, the New Jerusalem, is the millennial city of God, that city itself is symbolic of another, heavenly Jerusalem, a cosmic holy of holies, where the Father dwells in celestial glory. Descriptions of this Mount Zion sometimes blend with descriptions of the New Jerusalem.

67. An innumerable company of angels. Those who inherit the celestial kingdom will find themselves in communion and fellowship with billions upon billions of celestial beings like themselves—the hosts of heaven—from billions upon billions of other worlds all created and glorified by the same Jesus Christ who created our world and who will glorify us.

67. The general assembly and church of Enoch. The English word *church* actually translates from Greek and Hebrew words in the Bible meaning "assembly" or "congregation." Thus, *general assembly* and *church* are parallel terms here meaning roughly the same thing. Because Enoch and his people established Zion and were taken up into heaven, they are a type or symbol for all those later Saints who are worthy of Zion and, therefore, comprise part of the Church of the Firstborn (see v. 54).

68. Whose names are written in heaven. See Luke 10:20; Philippians 4:3; Revelation 3:5; 20:12. There are actually two sets of Church records. One is kept on earth for use by the earthly Church—The Church of Jesus Christ of Latter-day Saints—and one is kept in heaven, where no mistakes are made, for the heavenly Church—the Church of the Firstborn, or the *faithful* Saints who keep their covenants and magnify their callings (see D&C 88:2). Being recorded in the earthly records does not guarantee being recorded in the heavenly.

69. Just men made perfect through Jesus. The moral standard of the celestial kingdom is not goodness or even righteousness. It is perfection, flawless and unblemished. "No unclean thing," no matter how small or inconsequential, "can inherit the kingdom of heaven" (Alma 11:37). Therefore, celestial beings must be sinless and perfect. But how is this possible?

Humans can, through their own agency and willpower, make themselves *just* men and women. That is, by attempting to keep the commandments they can avoid wickedness and make themselves "good" and "righteous" people who keep most of the rules most of the time. And they don't need the Savior to do this; all they need is a conscience and some willpower. This kind of righteousness, however, is not celestial in nature but is characteristic of the *terrestrial* kingdom, for that kingdom will be inhabited by honorable men and women with testimonies of Jesus who will rise in the resurrection of the just (see v. 75; D&C 45:54).

Through our own efforts we can make ourselves relatively good or just human beings, and therefore worthy of terrestrial glory, but only Christ can make us *perfect!* Perfection, that flawless celestial righteousness necessary to dwell in the very presence of God, comes only "through the merits, and mercy, and grace of the Holy Messiah" (2 Nephi 2:8).

Even if we were to so discipline ourselves that one day we managed to live perfectly, there would still be sins in our past that would render us unworthy of celestial glory. Even if we could in this life eventually live flawlessly, when we died we would still be sinners.

No one can perfect himself or herself; it is only Christ who can cleanse our past as well as our present and future, who takes just men and women and *makes* them perfect and celestial by applying *his* merits, *his* mercy, and *his* grace (see Moroni 10:32–33).

The poetic version of this verse reads: "These are they that are perfect through Jesus' own blood."[57] While the hunger and thirst to be clean and righteous and the commitment and drive to do God's will must come from within us, perfection comes only as a gift from our perfect Savior through his perfect atonement.

69. The mediator of the new covenant. When two parties

are at odds or can't deal with each other face to face, a mediator—a negotiator or go-between—is often called. Because sinful, fallen humans are estranged from their perfect, celestial Father (see Romans 8:7; Mosiah 3:19), we also need a mediator to act as a go-between and to work out an agreement.

The "old" covenant arranged between God and Israel was the law of Moses with its preparatory gospel, its carnal commandments, and its lesser priesthood (see D&C 84:23–27; Joseph Smith Translation Exodus 34:1–2). Because of Israel's iniquity at Sinai, knowledge of the Father and access to him were severely limited under this old or lesser covenant, because these are exclusive privileges of the fulness of the gospel and of the Melchizedek Priesthood, which had both been taken away (see D&C 84:25). Under the old covenant of Moses, Jehovah or Jesus Christ represented the Godhead, and his Father, the Father of spirits, remained largely unknown to Israel. The Prophet Moses became the mediator or go-between between the Godhead—represented by Jehovah, the Son—and Israel, and this lesser covenant was named after its mediator "the law of *Moses.*"

In the "new" and everlasting covenant, which is the fulness of the gospel, Jesus Christ once again reveals his Father to Israel and once again seeks to bring us into his Father's presence, as he once did with Adam, Enoch, Noah, and Abraham. In so doing, the Son himself now replaces Moses as mediator between the Godhead—now represented by Elohim, the Father—and Israel or the Church. This new and better covenant, which once again brings us a knowledge of and access to God the Father, is also named after its mediator "the gospel of *Jesus Christ.*"

69. Shedding of his own blood. Jesus' blood was shed both in his agony in the Garden of Gethsemane (see D&C 19:18; Luke 22:44; Mosiah 3:7) and in his scourging, crucifixion, and death upon the cross (see Colossians 1:20).

70. Whose bodies are celestial. Bodies resurrected to the celestial kingdom are qualitatively different from those resurrected to a lesser kingdom in that they possess greater *glory.* Glory is divine energy. Celestial bodies possess and are able to withstand a higher level of this energy. Just as some elements, such as gold or copper, can carry more electric current than other elements, so celestial bodies can bear a more intense glory than terrestrial or telestial bodies. Thus, a celestial body can tolerate or "abide" the very presence of God and the fulness of his glory when a terrestrial or telestial body could not stand the full intensity of that glory.

In the resurrection, our bodies will receive glory appropriate to those principles by which we lived during our probation. If we pursue celestial principles here and attempt to live by them upon the earth, then our bodies will receive celestial glory in the resurrection. What we seek to live here, we will receive there (see D&C 88:20–24). This is one aspect of the law of the harvest.

70. Whose glory is that of the sun. The full glory of God is much, much greater than the energy of the sun. The relative glories of the sun, moon, and stars are only symbolic of the differences between the heavenly kingdoms. It is in this sense, as "symbolic" rather than as "a representative sample," that the word *typical* is used at the end of this verse. The sun is a type or symbol of celestial glory. Bear in mind that even the telestial glory is beyond our present powers of perception and appreciation (see v. 89), and that the actual glory of the celestial kingdom is infinitely greater than the brightness of the sun that symbolizes it.

71. The terrestrial world. Joseph and Sidney saw the terrestrial portion of the first resurrection. The difference between the brightness of our sun and moon symbolizes the difference between the glory of the celestial and terrestrial worlds.

Outside sections 76 and 88, the word *terrestrial* occurs in scripture only in 1 Corinthians 15:40, where it is used to mean "of the earth" in contrast to *celestial,* which means "of the heavens." The root of *terrestrial* is the Latin *terra,* which means "earth." This derivation has troubled some students who associate the earth with Babylon, or the fallen, telestial world. But Paul made it clear he was speaking of the earth from which Adam was originally made (see 1 Corinthians 15:45, 47), that is, the earth as Eden, or paradise. And the Eden state, or paradisiacal glory, is what this earth will receive again during the Millennium, when it will be returned to the terrestrial glory in which it was first created (see Articles of Faith 1:10).

72. These are they who died without law. The different degrees of glory that one may receive in the resurrection will be positively or negatively influenced by the amount of knowledge a person was faithful to on the one hand, or against which a person sinned on the other. There will be different standards of accountability for those who (a) knew the fulness of the gospel, (b) had a portion of the gospel through the teachings of the New Testament and of traditional Christianity, (c) had the preparatory gospel of the law of Moses,[58] or (d) had no revealed principles of gospel or law at all. This last category will consist mainly of the heathen nations of the world (see D&C 45:54),[59] as the poetic version confirms: "The heathen of ages that never had hope."[60] When the ignorant heathen sin, they do not sin against the revealed word of God, for they never had it. Thus, they are judged more leniently and have greater cause for hope in the resurrection than those who may have had a revealed law of some kind, but who sinned against it.

Merely being a heathen, however, does not guarantee a person terrestrial glory nor does it limit them to that kingdom. For, "all who have died without a knowledge of this gospel [including the heathens], *who would have received it* if they had been permitted to tarry, shall be heirs of the *celestial* kingdom of God" (D&C 137:7).[61] Many such heathens will accept the gospel in the spirit world and will ultimately receive celestial glory (compare Matthew 8:11).

On the other hand, the *wicked* heathen, while they may not have violated revealed laws and commandments, can still sin against their own consciences and against whatever light they do have (see D&C 84:46–47; John 1:9). And the unrepentant wicked of all nations, heathen or not, LDS or not, will receive *telestial* glory (see D&C 76:102–6). These wicked are those who in violation of the law given them, on whatever level, seek to become their own law instead (see D&C 88:35). They make their own rules.

In the resurrection, a large portion of those who inherit the terrestrial world will be righteous heathens who were not wicked, but who also would not have accepted the gospel and joined the Church even if they had had the chance, and who did not accept the gospel in the spirit world.

73. And also. In addition to the category of righteous heathens, there are other categories of persons who also inherit terrestrial glory.

73. The spirits of men. The term *men* is used here, as elsewhere, for human beings of both sexes.

73. Kept in prison. A prison is any place you can't leave when you want to, and in the spirit world even the righteous are held captive by the chains of death (see D&C 138:16–18). The spirits of the righteous cannot leave paradise. Rather, they wait for deliverance from death, and they look upon absence from their bodies as bondage (see D&C 138:15, 49–50). Thus, the phrase "spirit prison" applies to the entire spirit world, *including* "paradise," and not merely to that part of the spirit world where the wicked suffer in hell. "Spirit world" and "spirit prison" are synonymous terms.[62] The spirit prison includes both paradise, where the spirits of the righteous rest and wait in pleasant surroundings for their glorious resurrection, and hell (see D&C 76:84), where the spirits of the wicked suffer for their sins until their resurrection.

73. Whom the Son visited. See the remarkable account of President Joseph F. Smith concerning his vision of this great event in Doctrine and Covenants 138.

73. Be judged according to men in the flesh. The spirit world allows people a continuation of their probationary state, so that they may learn, repent, and possibly receive a greater reward in eternity than their performance in mortality would otherwise merit. Joseph Smith praised this "continued duration for completion, in order that the heirs of salvation may confess the Lord and bow the knee."[63] Any additional progress made in the spirit world, including acceptance of vicarious ordinances, may then be credited to an individual just as though it had been achieved while still in the flesh. The poetic version reads, "And then were the living baptiz'd for their dead, That they might be judg'd as if men in the flesh."[64]

74. Who received not the testimony of Jesus. This revelation distinguishes between a full knowledge of the gospel on the one hand and a more generic testimony of Jesus Christ on the other.[65] Many good non-LDS Christians in the world have firm testimonies of Jesus Christ as the Son of God and Savior of the world, but will not accept baptism and the fulness of the gospel. Knowledge and acceptance of the fulness of the gospel is not necessary for having a testimony of the divinity of Jesus Christ. From before the Restoration and to the present day, thousands of righteous Christian missionaries, armed only with the Bible, have spread their testimony of Jesus throughout the world. Those who accepted or "received" the testimony of Jesus when they heard it in the flesh will have the further opportunity of accepting the fulness of the gospel in the spirit world, and may eventually receive celestial glory.

Those honorable men and women of the earth, however, who rejected the testimony of Jesus Christ when they heard it in the flesh may still repent of their error and accept the lordship of Christ in the spirit world. If they do this much but will not accept baptism and the fulness of the gospel, they will receive at least a terrestrial glory in the resurrection. On the other hand, no one who has a testimony of Jesus but is not valiant in that testimony may obtain celestial glory (see v. 79).

"Received not" here evidently means "rejected it when they heard it" rather than "didn't have a chance to hear it." This is supported by the reading of the poetic version: "They receiv'd not the truth of the Savior at first; But did, when they heard it in prison, again."[66] Thus, it would seem that those honorable people who reject the basic testimony of Jesus when they hear it in the flesh but later accept it in the spirit world, will inherit eternal glory, generally terrestrial glory wherein they may enjoy the presence of Jesus forever as he administers that kingdom (see v. 77; D&C 88:32–33; 138:32–33, 58–59).

75. Honorable men of the earth. The terrestrial kingdom is inhabited by good people, people who were good neighbors and who lived according to the light they had. At some point, whether in this life or in the spirit world, these people accept the testimony of Jesus, and as a result they will rise in the first resurrection. They are worthy of enjoying the presence of Jesus in eternity. These terrestrial beings, basically good though they may be, would not either in this life or in the spirit world accept the fulness of the gospel, having allowed themselves to be misled by human arguments and reasoning. For this reason they will not receive celestial glory.

76. Receive of his glory. Terrestrial beings will bask in the glory of Jesus Christ, but they will never be able to make his glory their own. They will enjoy the presence of Christ, but they will never become like him.

77. The presence of the Son. The terrestrial kingdom is not hell. Neither is it a place of sadness or of deprivation, for those who receive terrestrial glory rise in the first resurrection, the resurrection of the just. In fact, the usual non-LDS concept of heaven pretty closely matches the LDS understanding of the terrestrial kingdom—a place where good people dwell in joy with Jesus forever but without family ties and without the possibility of actually becoming what Jesus is. In order to receive more than the terrestrial, to return to the presence of the Father and to receive as joint-heirs with Christ all that the Father has, it is necessary to accept the fulness of the gospel. The poetic version reads, "They are they, that come into the presence of Christ, But not to the fulness of God, on his throne."[67]

78. Bodies terrestrial. Terrestrial bodies cannot handle or "abide" the full glory of God. Like a too-thin wire receiving too much electrical power, they would burn up. Therefore, they are given as much glory as they can handle, but a *lesser* glory than the celestial, just as the moon is less bright than the sun.

79. Not valiant in the testimony of Jesus. Just as ignorance of the gospel presents no permanent obstacle to the righteous who always pursue more light (see D&C 137:7), even so a testimony of Jesus or of his gospel is no advantage for the slacker. There is a difference between merely *having* a testimony and actually *living* by it. If what we know doesn't move us to make appropriate choices in life, then we are not living up to our testimony; we are not valiant. Many Christians believe in Jesus, but do not act according to their belief by serving him and keeping his commandments. Many Latter-day Saints have testimonies of the gospel, but will not accept callings in their wards or keep the commandments in their personal lives. Whether members or nonmembers, those who are not valiant, whose commitment does not match their testimony, need not expect more than terrestrial glory. Those who receive the terrestrial kingdom have a testimony of Jesus but were not sufficiently motivated by that testimony either to accept the gospel when the Spirit bore witness (non-LDS) or to live it conscientiously thereafter (LDS).

81. The telestial. The term *telestial* occurs in scripture only in Doctrine and Covenants 76 and 88. It is not found in the Bible or anywhere else before 1831. Joseph Smith here added a new word to the English language. It is possible that the term was derived from the Greek prefix *tele,* which means "at a distance" or "far away," as the word *telephone* means "a faraway voice," or *television* means "distant viewing." That would make the *telestial* kingdom mean something like "the farthest or most distant" kingdom of glory. This etymology is only speculative, however.

82. Received not the gospel of Christ. Again, "received not" here probably means "rejected" or "*would not* receive," that is, when they had the chance. Those who inherit the telestial kingdom reject *both* the fulness of the gospel as found in The

Church of Jesus Christ of Latter-day Saints *and also* the more basic testimony of Jesus. Terrestrial glory requires at least a basic testimony of Jesus, but telestial beings won't accept even that. The poetic version reads, "These are they that receiv'd not the gospel of Christ, Or evidence, either, that he ever was."[68]

83. Who deny not the Holy Spirit. Though the telestial beings have been wicked, there is one sin they do not commit. They do not deny the Holy Ghost.[69]

84. Who are thrust down to hell. The word *hell* has more than one meaning in the scriptures and in contemporary LDS usage. In this context it refers to the spiritual state of the wicked, rebellious, and unbelieving between their death and resurrection. During that time their spirits are subject in the spirit world to the power of Satan and his angels, for this was their demonstrated preference while still in the flesh. If one chooses Satan's path in life, it leads one into Satan's power at death. "What is the damnation of hell? To go with that society who have not obeyed His commands."[70]

Fortunately, this hell does not last forever (see the "until" in vv. 85, 106)[71] but will eventually give up its captive spirits at the resurrection (see D&C 19:6; 2 Nephi 9:12; Revelation 20:13). Hell is a temporary state of intense but appropriate suffering for one's own sins, which is usually experienced between death and resurrection. In many cases, however, the pains of hell may begin in this life (see Alma 14:6; 36:13–16). Yet it is possible even for the wicked, after they have suffered appropriately for their sins— or "paid the uttermost farthing" (Matthew 5:26)—to repent, to bow the knee, to accept redemption through Christ, and finally to receive telestial glory (see LDS Bible Dictionary, s.v. "hell").

Thus, a loving God does not—as the religions of men insisted in Joseph's day—torture the wicked and the unbaptized forever and ever. Eventually, Christ redeems all human beings, including the wicked, rebellious, and unbelieving, from death and from hell, upon the condition of repentance. "Hell . . . is a place prepared for the teaching, the disciplining of those who failed to learn here upon the earth what they should have learned. . . . No man will be kept in hell longer than is necessary to bring him to a fitness for something better. When he reaches that stage, the prison doors will open and there will be rejoicing among the hosts who welcome him into a better state"[72] (see also D&C 29:38).

85. Who shall not be redeemed from the devil. In hell, between death and resurrection, those who chose Satan in life are delivered into his power. By their own choice, they have sold themselves as slaves to the devil who has become their lord and master. God respects the agency he has given us, and if we freely choose the lordship of Satan during life, then at death our choice must be respected, and we must be given into the power of the evil one we have chosen.

The wicked who are delivered to Satan in hell cannot be raised up in the first resurrection, the resurrection of the just, which takes place at the beginning of the Millennium. Rather, their bodies will remain in the graves and their spirits will continue to suffer enslavement to Satan in hell until the second resurrection (see D&C 88:101). Only then, at the end of the Millennium, will Christ finally redeem the wicked who have repented of their poor choices and who seek deliverance from their former master, the devil.

The word *redeem* means "to buy back." In the second resurrection, even the wicked are finally bought back from the power of the devil by the atonement of Christ. Even though the wicked have suffered in hell for their own sins, still they must turn to Christ and accept his sacrifice in order to change masters, in order to be bought back, or redeemed, from Satan's ownership. Thus, there is no degree of glory, not even that of the faintest and most distant star, that does not depend entirely upon the infinite atonement of the Lord Jesus Christ.

86. Who receive not of his fulness . . . but of the Holy Spirit: Telestial beings will never really know the Son. Though they will finally acknowledge Jesus' lordship, they will not enjoy his direct presence in eternity, as will terrestrial beings. The

Godhead will administer the affairs of the telestial world through the person of the Holy Spirit and through ministering angels sent to them from the terrestrial world. The logic of this is impeccable. The telestial beings rejected both the fulness of the Father, which is accessible through the gospel, and the fulness of the Son, which comes through the testimony of Jesus (see v. 82). They did *not,* however, deny the Holy Spirit (see v. 83). Thus, they may receive "of the Holy Spirit," but not the presence or power of the Father or the Son.

This does not mean that the Son or the Holy Spirit will permanently inhabit the terrestrial and telestial kingdoms. Both these members of the Godhead will be exalted, celestial beings in eternity, and will enjoy all the blessings of exaltation, including the company and fellowship of other exalted beings. It is likely, however, that the Son and the Holy Spirit will administer the affairs of the terrestrial and telestial kingdoms, respectively, just as they administer affairs upon the earth right now, through chosen intermediaries and perhaps, at times, through personal contact.

87. The terrestrial through the ministration of the celestial: The many kingdoms of our Father's house will be governed and will enjoy communication with their presiding authorities in ways very much like the present priesthood government of the Church upon the earth. As the Lord reveals his will to the prophets, and they to the General Authorities, and they to area authorities, and they to stake and mission authorities, and so on, so in heaven lower kingdoms will be governed by communication and instruction from higher kingdoms in an orderly manner from the top to the bottom. And the will of God will be done in all things and in all kingdoms.

Elder Melvin J. Ballard has written, "We must not overlook the fact that those who attain to the higher glories may minister unto and visit and associate with those of the lesser kingdoms. While the lesser may not come up, they may still enjoy the companionship of their loved ones who are in higher stations."[73]

88. For they shall be heirs of salvation. Once again: the telestial kingdom is not hell. Neither is it a place of sadness or of deprivation, for those who inherit the telestial kingdom rise in the resurrection to a heavenly glory. They are saved from all their enemies, including physical and spiritual death, sin, hell, and the devil. They receive as much divine glory as their natures can stand, and their joy will be *full* (see D&C 88:31), though it will be the fulness of thimbles or of teacups rather than the fulness of barrels or of oceans or of the infinity of space.

89. Surpasses all understanding. Even the least glory in the lowest of God's kingdoms is beyond our mortal comprehension. First, imagine what the glory of the celestial kingdom must be like; then realize that what you have imagined falls far, far below the reality of the faintest degree of *telestial* glory. "It is a doctrine fundamental in Mormonism that the meanest sinner, in the final judgment, will receive a glory which is beyond human understanding, which is so great that we are unable to describe it adequately. Those who do well will receive an even more glorious place. . . .

"The Gospel is a gospel of tremendous love. Love is at the bottom of it. The meanest child is loved so dearly that his reward will be beyond the understanding of mortal man."[74] The poetic version refers to the three heavenly kingdoms as "great, greater, greatest."[75]

90. No man knows it. Among mortals, no one can know the glory of even the telestial kingdom except through direct revelation.

91. In might, and in dominion. "'Might' refers to the ability to do, or perform whatever must be done; 'dominion' refers to the extent of the field of action. The terrestrials have more intelligence, more authority, more strength, and a larger expanse in which to operate, than the telestials."[76]

92. Where God, even the Father, reigns upon his throne. The God who presides over the celestial kingdom is God the Father. All who attain that kingdom, even the Son, will give all glory and reverence to the Father (see vv. 93, 107). This, it will be recalled, is something that Satan was unwilling to do (see Moses

4:1–3). We, who are the offspring of God, have the ability to add to the glory of God through our achievements and accomplishments, just as mortal parents can be built up by the achievements of their children. As God enlarges us, he himself is glorified (see Moses 1:39).[77] Then, if we can avoid the satanic impulse to glorify *ourselves* for the progress we make (see Moses 4:1), and rather give all glory to the God who made all things possible and through whom all things are accomplished (see D&C 76:61),[78] then we will in turn *be* glorified by God himself with all the powers, dominion, and privileges of his own kingdom. As we in humility give God all praise, honor, laud, and glory, he in turn exalts us to sit upon the throne of his glory.[79]

94. Church of the Firstborn. See verse 54.[80]

94. They see as they are seen. Because God through his grace has given these individuals his fulness and has brought them into his very presence, they interact with him there directly—not as equals, for he still reigns over them, but on equal terms, face to face. It would also seem that celestial beings interact with one another on the same terms, knowing as they are known, without guile or hidden agendas.

95. He makes them equal. All the sons and daughters of God who are exalted in the celestial kingdom are equal with each other and with Christ in receiving *all* the power and might and dominion of that kingdom (see D&C 88:107). This is the celestial principle upon which the law of consecration rests. In order to establish Zion upon the earth, "every man [must be] *equal* according to his family, according to his circumstances and his wants and needs" (D&C 51:3[81]; see also D&C 70:14; 78:5–6; 82:17–19). This celestial principle is the same in eternity.

This does not necessarily mean that celestial beings will all be the same or that their situations in eternity will be identical, for there, as here, one individual's family, wants, needs, and other circumstances may differ from another's. Consequently, their individual, celestial stewardships or kingdoms may likewise be different.[82] All will have, however, equal access to all the corporate resources of the exalted family.

The Lord Jesus Christ also observes the eternal principles of the law of consecration. His eternal consecration is essentially himself—his own perfection, his own merits, his own righteousness. In sharing these, his "earnings," with us, he raises us to his level, thus making us equal to himself as well as to each other, and making us joint-heirs with him of all that the Father has (see D&C 88:107; Romans 8:17). In consecrating ourselves and our resources for the establishment of Zion here in mortality, we are following the example of Jesus Christ in consecrating himself and the "earnings" of his infinite atonement for the good of all in eternity.

96–98. The glory of the celestial/terrestrial/telestial is one. That is, celestial glory is one distinct level or class of glory. Terrestrial glory is another distinct type of glory, and telestial glory is yet a third distinct type. Even though individuals within the telestial kingdom may differ from one another in glory as much as one star differs from another in size or brightness, they are all still of the same order, class, or type of glory (see 1 Corinthians 15:39–41). No one mistakes a star for the moon or the moon for the noonday sun.

99–100. These are they who are of Paul, and of Apollos, . . . and some of another. The divine impulse is unity; the satanic impulse is division (compare D&C 38:27).[83] Zion is established when the Saints are of *one* heart and *one* mind (see Moses 7:18), and Zion is lost when the Saints divide up into individual special interests.

In the New Testament Church this wicked impulse for division was manifested by those in Corinth who accepted some Church leaders while rejecting others or who accepted some doctrines while resisting others as they pursued their own individual agendas (see 1 Corinthians 1:10–13; 3:3–9). Thus, they divided the unity of the Church and of the gospel into rival factions and parties—of Paul, of Apollos, of Cephas, and such. The Old

Testament names in Doctrine and Covenants 76:100 witness to the same wicked impulse toward factionalism among the members in earlier dispensations. Similarly, there are some in the Church today who will sustain some leaders but not others and who treat the restored gospel as though it were a buffet lunch—accepting the leaders, doctrines, and policies they like and rejecting the ones they do not. But if the Saints cannot learn to become one in Jesus' Church upon the earth, we need not suppose we will do so in eternity.

101. Received not the gospel. There are some telestial persons in the LDS Church and in other Christian churches who do not really have testimonies of the fulness of the gospel or even of Jesus Christ as the Son of God, though they would appear to. In reality, these persons are followers of men and believe in the teachings of men. They strive to turn the Church to the prevailing views of Babylon. Such persons merely use the church membership as a mask while they pursue their own individual ends in the service of a different master. The poetic version of the vision says of them, "They went their own way, and they have their reward," and "In darkness they worshipp'd; to darkness they go."[84]

102. See verses 63–67; Doctrine and Covenants 45:45; 78:21.

103. These are they who. In a parallel list of characters, the book of Revelation adds: the fearful, the unbelieving, the abominable, murderers, and idolaters (see Revelation 21:8; 22:15).

104–5. Who suffer the wrath of God on earth . . . eternal fire. The reference here is to the wicked who will be living on the earth and who will be burned to death at the second coming of Christ (see also v. 106). Their physical suffering from this very real and very literal fire will last, however, only until they are dead. It is called "eternal" fire because it is the just punishment of an eternal God (see D&C 19:6–12). Additionally, once the wicked are dead, their spirits will be consigned to hell, and "eternal fire" is also used as a *figurative* expression for the spiritual suffering they will experience in hell between their death and their resurrection.

This hell is also located "on earth" now, though separated by a veil from the mortal and temporal world of our experience.

106. Until the fulness of times. Once again, this verse teaches us that there is an eventual exit from hell. When Christ has completed all his work, the captives in hell will be set free and will be resurrected to the telestial kingdom. This will take place only after the great Millennium and after Satan has been put in chains and cast out forever.

106. Perfected his work. *Perfected* is used in its biblical sense to mean "completed." The Greek and Hebrew words sometimes translated as *perfect* in the Bible usually mean "complete," "whole," or "mature."

106–7. Compare 1 Corinthians 15:24–28.

107. He shall deliver up the kingdom. When Jesus Christ has completed his stewardship assignment and has redeemed all that was fallen and has redeemed and reconciled it all to God, he will then turn all things over to his Father and render the glory of his accomplishments to the Father (see D&C 19:19; Moses 4:2; Revelation 1:6). The Father will thus be further glorified and enlarged by the immortality and eternal life brought to pass for so many of his children (see Moses 1:39). Christ will be installed upon the throne of his Father, where the righteous will reign with him as joint-heirs, and the glorified Father will assume an even more glorious state.[85]

107. Have trodden the wine-press alone. The winepress is a double symbol representing the dual roles of Christ as both Savior and as judge. As a symbol of divine justice, the winepress represents Christ's work in crushing all his enemies beneath his feet as if they were grapes in a vat and directing them to drink the wine or the results of his victory over them. The poetic version says, "Till Christ shall have trodden all enemies down."[86] In this role as conqueror and judge, the redness of Jesus' garments (see Isaiah 63:1–4; D&C 133:48, 50) comes from the blood of the wicked whom he justly tramples down at his second coming "like him that treadeth in the winefat" (Isaiah 63:2) and who are forced to drink the bitter wine of his victory and his justice by suffering for their sins in hell.

As a symbol of Christ's saving atonement, however, the winepress represents the Savior *himself* being pressed therein until his blood is shed in the Garden of Gethsemane. *Gath* in Hebrew means "winepress," and *semane* means "oil" or "richness." Thus, Gethsemane means "winepress of richness." Jesus as the "true vine" (John 15:1, 5; 1 Nephi 15:15; Alma 16:17) enters the garden of the winepress, Gethsemane, and there is pressed like grapes in a vat with the hideous weight of the sins and pains of the world. Under that tremendous load, his blood, like the juice pressed from grapes, is squeezed through his very skin, and he bleeds at every pore (see D&C 19:18; Mosiah 3:7; Luke 22:44). In his role as Savior, the redness of Jesus' garments comes from his *own* blood shed in the garden and on the cross in our behalf so that we might not suffer (see D&C 133:48). In partaking of the sacrament, the early Saints drank wine squeezed in a press in remembrance of the symbolic wine of his blood that was squeezed from his body and shed for us in the press of Gethsemane.[87]

Further, Jesus is described as having "trodden the wine-press *alone*" because on the one hand he *alone* conquers all things as victor, and because on the other hand he *alone* suffered all things as victim. Beyond this, we must remember that the Savior endured his infinite agony in the garden alone. When the worst came, there was no one to help him or comfort him—the Spirit left him, and even his Father withdrew from him, to leave him utterly and horribly alone in his infinite agony (see Matthew 27:46).

109. Innumerable as the stars in the firmament: It is sad to note that the number of individuals who receive telestial glory will be so great that it will be hard to number them. Still, they will be heirs of salvation, and will praise God forever for raising them beyond what they once were and for bringing them glory and joy beyond mortal comprehension (see v. 89).

110. These all shall bow . . . confess. *These* seems here to refer specifically to the heirs of the telestial kingdom, a view supported by the poetic version. All those in the celestial and terrestrial kingdoms would by this time have been raised in the first resurrection and would have already acknowledged Jesus as their Lord by their previous acceptance of the gospel or the testimony of Jesus. Of those who will be saved, all that are left at this point, at the second resurrection, the resurrection of the unjust, are these telestial rebels—who *must* accept Christ as their ruler and acknowledge his power in order to be redeemed at last from the power of the devil.

Among all the innumerable hosts of the saved in all the kingdoms of glory, every knee will bow and every tongue confess that Jesus is the Christ and that his is the only name in eternity through which they may be saved. Such bowing and confessing is not the same as having a testimony of Jesus; it merely recognizes the practical necessity of submission to his power. The celestial and terrestrial heirs will have made their confession and obeisance before or at the first resurrection. The telestial beings will do it before or at the second resurrection. Note how radical this doctrine would have seemed in 1832. When the Christian world insisted that the wicked would burn in hell forever, Joseph Smith revealed that they will all finally bend the knee and confess the Savior and then be redeemed in heavenly glory.

110. Him who sits upon the throne. This is Jesus Christ.

112. And they shall be servants. All those saved in any degree of glory, including the telestial, will be servants of God in eternity and will be faithfully employed in his work.

112. Where God and Christ dwell they cannot come. Resurrected bodies are not all of one type. There are distinctly different types or kinds of bodies (see 1 Corinthians 15:40–41).[88] Once a person has been resurrected as a celestial, terrestrial, or telestial body, they are inseparably connected to it. While they may make eternal progress as one type of body or another, it would seem problematic for them to escape from being one type to be changed into another type—for the differences between the types of resurrected bodies may be as eternal as the resurrection itself.

Human beings have the potential to receive any type of resurrected body they desire and will work for—until the resurrection. But once that event takes place, there is no indication that changes can be made from one type of body or of glory to another. Just as resurrected plants or fish remain in their own class and will never progress to become exalted human beings, so those resurrected in lesser kingdoms will remain in their own class and never progress to become exalted.

President George Albert Smith observed: "There are some people who have supposed that if we are quickened telestial bodies, that eventually, throughout the ages of eternity, we will continue to progress until we will find our place in the celestial kingdom, but the scriptures and revelations of God have said that those who are quickened telestial bodies cannot come where God and Christ dwell, worlds without end."[89] Elder Spencer W. Kimball agreed with this when he declared: "After a person has been assigned to his place in the kingdom, either in the telestial, the terrestrial or the celestial, or to his exaltation, he will never advance from his assigned glory to another glory. That is eternal!"[90]

112. Worlds without end. In both the Old and New Testaments the same Hebrew and Greek words are used for *eternity, age,* and *world.*[91] Thus, "worlds without end" also means "eternities without end" or "forever and ever." In the idiom of the ancient scriptures, a "world" is as much, if not more, a period of time as it is a place.

114. The mysteries of his kingdom. See verse 7.

115. Not lawful for man to utter. Joseph and Sidney saw much, much more in this great vision than is recorded in Doctrine and Covenants 76, and much of what they saw was not to be published to the world or even to the membership of the Church. A later comment of Joseph's to this effect is recorded in *History of the Church:* "Paul ascended into the third heavens, and he could understand the three principal rounds of Jacob's ladder—the telestial, the terrestrial, and the celestial glories or kingdoms, where Paul saw and heard things which were not lawful for him to utter. I could explain a hundred fold more than I ever have of the glories of the kingdoms manifested to me in the vision, were I permitted, and were the people prepared to receive them. The Lord deals with this people as a tender parent with a child, communicating light and intelligence and the knowledge of his ways as they can bear it."[92]

"Not *lawful* . . . to utter" indicates knowledge received by one individual that he or she is then prevented by covenant or by commandment from revealing to others, even if they are also faithful members of the Church. In 1832 this would have included, but would not be limited to, most of the information Latter-day Saints now receive lawfully in the temples of God.

"Could we read and comprehend all that has been written from the days of Adam, on the relation of man to God and angels in a future state, we should know very little about it. Reading the experience of others, or the revelation given to *them,* can never give *us* a comprehensive view of our condition and true relation to God. Knowledge of these things can only be obtained by experience through the ordinances of God set forth for that purpose. Could you gaze into heaven five minutes, you would know more than you would by reading all that ever was written on the subject."[93]

117–18. This privilege of seeing and knowing . . . while in the flesh. This is refering to the privilege granted here to Joseph and Sidney. This passage refers to receiving first-person experience of God rather than only having faith in the words or experiences of others. It is knowing the Father and the Son directly, personally, and empirically through the mediation of the Holy Spirit.[94] This is the great privilege of those for whom the veil is parted because of their faith, that they may see God and come into his presence while yet in the flesh. For this experience it is necessary to be filled with the Holy Spirit, whose indwelling presence changes our nature and preserves our mortal bodies in their contact with divine glory (compare D&C 130:22).

1. See Delbert L. Stapley, in Conference Report, Sept.-Oct. 1967, 73–74.
2. *History of the Church,* 1:245.
3. In *Juvenile Instructor,* 15 May 1892, 303–4.
4. See "Philo Dibble's Narrative," 81.
5. *History of the Church,* 1:252–53.
6. In *Journal of Discourses,* 16:42.
7. See Phelps, "A Vision," 2.
8. See "Ancient Poetry," 81–85.
9. In *Journal of Discourses,* 22:146–47.
10. See Commentary on D&C 19:3, 6; 76:112.
11. Smith, *Doctrines of Salvation,* 1:12.
12. See Commentary on D&C 6:7, 11; 8:11.
13. Smith, *History of the Church,* 3:389–90.
14. Smith, "Ancient Poetry," 82 (v. 11).
15. Smith, *History of the Church,* 5:402.
16. See Commentary on D&C 1:23.
17. See Commentary on v. 40.
18. See Commentary on D&C 63:18.
19. David O. McKay, in Conference Report, Apr. 1967, 85.
20. Smith, "Ancient Poetry," 82 (v. 17).
21. See also Commentary on D&C 88:6–13, 41–50.
22. Smith, "Ancient Poetry," 83 (vv. 19–20).
23. See also Commentary on D&C 25:1.
24. Smith, "Ancient Poetry," 83 (v. 21).
25. Cannon, "Discourse by President George Q. Cannon," 563–64.
26. See also Commentary on D&C 67:10.
27. See Commentary on v. 26.
28. See also Commentary on v. 35.
29. *Teachings of Spencer W. Kimball,* 23.
30. *Teachings,* 357.
31. Smith, *Teachings,* 358.
32. Smith, *Teachings,* 358.
33. See Commentary on D&C 63:17; compare also *Teachings,* 357.
34. See Commentary on D&C 29:41; 63:17.
35. Smith, "Ancient Poetry," 83 (v. 31).
36. Smith, "Ancient Poetry," 83 (v. 33).

37. See Commentary on v. 24.
38. See Commentary on D&C 88:6–13, 41–42.
39. Smith, "Ancient Poetry," 83 (v. 34).
40. See Commentary on vv. 32, 35.
41. See Commentary on 19:6–7, 10–12.
42. *Teachings*, 24.
43. See Smith, *Teachings*, 181.
44. 1:283.
45. See Commentary on vv. 51, 74–75.
46. See Commentary on vv. 60–61, 69; D&C 20:30; Maxwell, *All These Things Shall Give Thee Experience*, 34–35.
47. Smith, "Ancient Poetry," 84 (v. 43).
48. See Commentary on D&C 68:12.
49. See also Commentary on vv. 59–60.
50. Smith, "Ancient Poetry," 84 (v. 44).
51. Smith, "Ancient Poetry," 84 (v. 45).
52. See also Mosiah 5:7; 27:25; Ether 3:14; Moroni 7:19; Moses 6:68; 7:1; Matthew 5:9, 45; John 1:12; Romans 8:16–17, 21; 9:8, 26; Galatians 3:26; 1 John 3:9–10.
53. See Smith, *Teachings*, 348; Commentary on v. 53; D&C 20:30.
54. Smith and Sjodahl, *Doctrine and Covenants Commentary*, 458.
55. See also Commentary on D&C 63:18.
56. See Commentary on D&C 88:2–3.
57. Smith, "Ancient Poetry," 84 (v. 52).
58. See Commentary on v. 69.
59. See also Commentary on D&C 45:54.
60. Smith, "Ancient Poetry," 84 (v. 54).
61. Emphasis added.
62. See Smith, *Teachings*, 310.
63. *History of the Church*, 1:252.
64. Smith, "Ancient Poetry," 84 (v. 55).
65. See Commentary on vv. 51–52, 82, 101.
66. Smith, "Ancient Poetry," 84 (v. 56).
67. Smith, "Ancient Poetry," 84 (v. 57).
68. Smith, "Ancient Poetry," 84 (v. 59).
69. See Commentary on vv. 35, 86.
70. Smith, *History of the Church*, 4:555.
71. See also Commentary on D&C 19:6.
72. James E. Talmage, in Conference Report, Apr. 1930, 97.
73. Hinckley, *Sermons and Missionary Services of Melvin Joseph Ballard*, 257.

74. Widtsoe, Message of the Doctrine and Covenants, p. 167.

75. Smith, "Ancient Poetry," 85 (v. 63).

76. Smith and Sjodahl, *Doctrine and Covenants Commentary,* 468.

77. See Smith, *Teachings,* 348.

78. See also Commentary on v. 61.

79. See Smith, *Teachings,* 347–48.

80. See also Commentary on v. 54.

81. Emphasis added.

82. See Commentary on D&C 51:3.

83. See Commentary on D&C 76:28.

84. Smith, "Ancient Poetry," 85 (vv. 71–72).

85. See Smith, *Teachings,* 347–48.

86. Smith, "Ancient Poetry," 85 (v. 74).

87. Neal A. Maxwell, *Ensign,* August 1987, 72.

88. See Commentary on D&C 76:96–98.

89. In Conference Report, Oct. 1945, 172.

90. *Miracle of Forgiveness,* 243–44.

91. See Commentary on D&C 19:3, 6.

92. 5:402.

93. Smith, *History of the Church,* 6:50.

94. See Commentary on v. 35.

77

BACKGROUND

By March 1832 Joseph Smith and his scribe Sidney Rigdon had been working on the translation of the Bible—the Joseph Smith Translation—for about two months at John Johnson's home in Hiram, Ohio. During that period of time the Lord had revealed much additional information to them concerning the New Testament, and the Prophet had received Doctrine and Covenants 74 and 76 in connection with his work on 1 Corinthians and the Gospel of John, respectively.

Doctrine and Covenants 77 answers certain questions about the Revelation of John in the New Testament. It is not a commentary on the book of Revelation so much as it is an example to the student of the scriptures about how certain terms and images are used in Revelation 4–11. The focus of section 77 is not on the overall meaning of the biblical text; rather it provides a key by which the reader can search the meaning out for himself or herself. The brief interpretive example provided in Doctrine and Covenants 77 illustrates a method of prophetic composition that is subjective, figurative, and symbolic rather than strictly objective, literal, and historical. This mode of prophetic writing is not the usual way prophets write. It is a distinctively different way of communicating divine revelation, and it is common enough in the scriptures that readers must be aware of its occurrence and of its different interpretive keys.

Scholars refer to the unusual method of composition found in the book of Revelation and elsewhere in the scriptures as *apocalyptic* prophecy, which is from the Greek *apokalypsis,* meaning "revelation." The use of apocalyptic writing accounts for the difference in character between such scriptures as the books of Daniel and Revelation, portions of Ezekiel, or Lehi's dream on the one hand, and nonapocalyptic gospels, or narrative books like Judges, Acts, and Alma, or epistles like Romans or James, on the other hand. Both apocalyptic and nonapocalyptic, or "regular," scriptures are inspired, but each type follows its own rules. In most apocalyptic scriptures the seer is caught up, or taken up, or caught away in the Spirit, thus and the perspective of the revelation that follows is changed from a human perspective on earth to a divine perspective in the heavens. Consequently, the mortal limitations of time, space, and logic do not always apply, meanings are clothed in symbols, and a symbol can and often does have more than one correct meaning or interpretation.

In many ways apocalyptic revelation is similar to parables. Like the parables, apocalyptic passages of scripture are not best understood as literal descriptions of historical events, but as "figurative expressions" (D&C 77:2). As with parables, this use of symbols is designed to conceal as much as to reveal deeper meanings (compare Matthew 13:10–13). As with parables, sometimes apocalyptic passages are interpreted in scripture for the reader, but often they are not. Section 77 provides the Saints with an example of certain figures and symbols characteristic of the apocalyptic revelation seen by John and of how these are to be interpreted. Nephi's lengthy explanation of Lehi's dream in the Book of Mormon provides us with another good example of how apocalyptic revelation has been received and interpreted (compare 1 Nephi 11–14).

The Prophet Joseph Smith himself seldom preached either from or about the book of Revelation; however, in a conference sermon delivered in Nauvoo on 8 April 1843, Joseph did expound on some of the symbols earlier discussed in Doctrine and Covenants 77, and on the use of the book of Revelation by the Church in general. He did this primarily to diminish a disproportionate interest in the book among the members—a fault that continues to plague many Saints today. On that occasion Joseph did say, "The book of Revelation is one of the plainest books God ever caused to be written." In the same sermon he also said, "we never can comprehend the things of God and of heaven, but by revelation," meaning the principle, not the book. The intent of his remarks on this occasion, taken all together, was to discourage speculation on the book of Revelation, and his advice to the Church was to leave its mysteries alone: "I have seldom spoken from the revelations [of John]. . . . It is not very essential for the elders to have knowledge in relation to the meaning of beasts, and heads and horns, and other figures made use of in the revelations." "Declare the first principles, and let mysteries alone, lest ye be overthrown. Never meddle with the visions of beasts and subjects you do not understand. Elder Brown, when you go to Palmyra, say nothing about the four beasts, but preach those things the Lord has told you to preach about—repentance and baptism for the remission of sins."[1] Mature Saints today continue to heed the Prophet's advice.

Very few details have been preserved concerning the reception of Doctrine and Covenants 77. This revelation did not appear in the 1833 Book of Commandments nor in the 1835 edition of the Doctrine and Covenants. Although it was included in the first edition of the Pearl of Great Price in 1851, section 77 did not appear in the Doctrine and Covenants until 1876, where it was included under the direction of President Brigham Young. The oldest manuscript of section 77, indeed, the earliest evidence of its existence, is a copy in the handwriting of Willard Richards that dates to 1840. Doctrine and Covenants 77 was, however, included as one of the Prophet's revelations in the *History of the Church,* written sometime between 27 August 1841 and 24 August 1843, and it was printed in the *Times and Seasons* on 1 August 1844.[2]

The exact date Doctrine and Covenants 77 was received is somewhat problematic, but *History of the Church* and the *Kirtland Revelation Book* each provide some information that help clarify matters. The *Kirtland Revelation Book* contains a notation from Joseph Smith in the handwriting of Frederick G. Williams dated 8 March 1832, which states that "from the 16th of February [when D&C 76 was received] up to this date have been at home except a journey to Kirtland on the 29 February and returned home on the 4th of March. We received a revelation in Kirtland and one since I returned home." Since the *Kirtland Revelation Book* also records the dates of Doctrine and Covenants 78 as 1 March and Doctrine and Covenants 80 as 7 March, it is likely that these are the two revelations referred to here.[3]

Moreover, in *History of the Church* the brief introduction to Doctrine and Covenants 78–81 chronologically follows the references to Doctrine and Covenants 77. Here Joseph also noted that "previous to the 20th of March, I received the four following revelations." The four revelations mentioned are section 78 received on 1 March, section 79 on 12 March, section 80 on 7 March, and section 81 on 15 March.[4] All of this indicates that Doctrine and Covenants 77 was likely received on or before 1 March, when Doctrine and Covenants 78 was received.

Since Joseph was not scheduled to be translating from the book of Revelation in his work on the Joseph Smith Translation at that time, it is possible that the questions found in section 77 were put to him by the brethren in Kirtland upon his arrival there late on 29 February or early the next day before section 78 was received.[5] The informality of an impromptu question and answer session might explain why Joseph's inspired responses were not included among his published revelations until later.[6] Joseph's brief note simply stated, "About the first of March, in connection with the translation of the Scriptures, I received the following explanation of the Revelation of St. John."[7]

COMMENTARY

Q. What is the sea of glass: When John the Revelator was taken up to the throne of God in heaven, he saw in front of the throne a sea of glass like rock-crystal (see Revelation 4:6).

A. It is the earth, in its sanctified, immortal, and eternal state: The sea or lake of glass symbolizes the future celestialized earth. The earth is elsewhere described as God's "footstool" (Matthew 5:35) and therefore logically sits "before the throne" (Revelation 4:6). This is the earth as it *will* appear after the last resurrection when it will be raised to a celestial glory. In a note concerning his activities on 18 February 1843, Joseph further recorded: "While at dinner, I remarked to my family and friends present, that when the earth was sanctified and became like a sea of glass, it would be one great urim and thummim, and the Saints could look in it and see as they are seen."[8]

Note that the sea of glass symbolizes the *future* earth, for Joseph also wrote: "There is a grand difference and distinction between the visions and figures spoken of by the ancient prophets, and those spoken of in the revelations of John. The things which John saw had no allusion to the scenes of the days of Adam, Enoch, Abraham or Jesus, only so far as is plainly represented by John, and clearly set forth by him. John saw that only which was lying in futurity and which was shortly to come to pass. . . .

"Now, I make this declaration, that those things which John saw in heaven had no allusion to anything that had been on the earth previous to that time."[9]

2. The four beasts: John's description of the beasts worshiping before the throne of God is very similar to the vision of Ezekiel in the Old Testament (see Ezekiel 1:5–25). In Ezekiel, the four beasts are described as each having four faces, one face on each of four sides—man, lion, bull, and eagle. There are many parallels between Ezekiel 1–7 and Revelation 4–11. In Ezekiel's vision, God's throne is described as both a throne and a chariot and is called in Hebrew a *merkabah* (chariot). In later times, the *merkabah,* or throne/chariot of God was associated with the deepest mysteries of rabbinic lore.

2. They are figurative expressions: Just as the Lamb that John saw in vision was not an actual lamb, but a symbolic image representing Jesus Christ, the Lamb of God, so also John saw four strange creatures in his vision that are similarly not actual animals, but figurative expressions or images meant to represent other entities or ideas—in this case, heaven, paradise, and the future happiness of human beings and of all God's other creatures. John was shown several figurative beasts in order to represent the several different glories of different types or classes of creatures in eternity. Even the many eyes and wings of these figurative images are symbols, representing respectively the abstract concepts of knowledge and power or mobility (see v. 4).

The figurative nature of the elements described in John's Revelation is a critically important consideration in coming to the meaning of his vision. If we try to interpret his descriptions literally instead of figuratively, we will miss the symbolic meanings of the elements described. The Prophet Joseph wrote, "There is a grand distinction between the actual meaning of the prophets and the present translation. The prophets do not declare that they saw a beast or beasts, but that they saw the *image* or *figure* of a beast. Daniel did not see an actual bear or a lion, but the images or figures of those beasts. The translation should have been rendered 'image' instead of 'beast,' in every instance where beasts are mentioned by the prophets."[10]

The four "images" of beasts that John describes, however, do symbolize both the multitude and the eternal nature of the many animals God has created. According to Joseph Smith, what John saw was intended to *symbolize* the many beasts that *actually* do exist in heaven: "I suppose John saw beings there of a thousand forms, that had been saved from ten thousand times ten thousand earths like this,—strange beasts of which we have no conception: all might be seen in heaven. . . . John learned that God glorified Himself by saving all that His hands had made, whether beasts, fowls, fishes or men"[11] (see also D&C 29:24). Are there animals in heaven? Yes.

2. The spirit of man in the likeness of his person: There is a similarity of form between the spirit of a living thing and the body it inhabits. This similarity may not be exact, however, as in the case of birth defects and other mortal deformities, and the precise degree to which individual spirits correspond to the appearance of their mortal bodies has not been revealed. Certainly, spirits *can* look exactly like their deceased bodies when necessary, but whether they *always* do so is open to question. It is not necessary to insist that genetic and environmental influences on mortal, physical bodies are coincidentally shared by their inhabiting spirits.

3. Limited to individual beasts, or . . . classes: The question being asked is whether the four beasts seen in vision just represent themselves or whether they represent types of living things. The answer is that the beasts represent four, but only four, examples of the glory enjoyed by different kinds of beings—both of men and of animals (see v. 2)—in eternity. In another place, Joseph Smith wrote, "The four beasts [the four *types* of creatures represented figuratively in Revelation 4:6] were four of the most noble animals that had filled the measure of their creation, and had been saved from other worlds, because they were perfect: they were like angels in their sphere. We are not told where they came from, and I do not know; but they were seen and heard by John praising and glorifying God."[12]

3. In their destined order or sphere of creation: There is no revealed doctrine explaining this phrase.

3. Their eternal felicity: All forms of living things, and not just human beings, will, through the work of Christ, receive eternal joy—except perdition. Whether this means, however, every *individual* virus, microbe, plant, or insect, or only representatives of each class, has not been revealed. It certainly *does* mean every individual human being.

4. Eyes and wings: Again, these beasts are not real, but figurative. Their physical description is symbolic of a deeper meaning: in this case, their eyes and wings represent knowledge and power, or the omniscience and omnipotence of God.

5. The four and twenty elders: John saw in his vision twenty-four elders who, along with the four beasts, had harps and little bottles of perfume—symbolizing their singing and praying to God as acts of worship (see Revelation 5:8–9). John may have known some of these men personally, for they had lived in the seven churches of western Turkey addressed in the book of Revelation among which John had labored (see Revelation 1:11). Though John saw in his vision twenty-four specific individuals, these twenty-four symbolically represented all the faithful elders who will be exalted through Christ out of every nation of the earth[13] (see Revelation 5:9). Again, in an apocalyptic vision it is critical to distinguish between what is seen—in this case, twenty-four elders from western Turkey—and what is represented—the joy of all faithful elders in paradise.

5. The paradise of God: This is speaking of the pleasant portion of the spirit world, or their happy state between death and resurrection.

6. The book which John saw: Compare Revelation 5:1. John saw in vision a scroll with writing on both sides, sealed with seven seals.

6. The revealed will, mysteries, and the works of God: The book symbolizes the comprehensive plan of God for this earth and its inhabitants from beginning to end.[14]

6. The seven thousand years of its continuance: The seven thousand years refers to the period of time between the fall of Adam and the end of the Millennium. Just as the earth was created in seven "days," so it will experience its temporal existence for seven "days"—a thousand years being as one day with the Lord (see Abraham 3:4; facsimile 2, figure 1; 2 Peter 3:8). Just as the seven "days" of the earth's creation are *figurative* days representing undefined periods of time, even so it is possible that the seven parallel "days" of the earth's temporal existence are also figurative days representing undefined periods of time. Nevertheless, many of the modern apostles and prophets have alluded to these "days" as being literally of one thousand years each.[15] Whether the days are understood as literal thousand-year periods or as figurative periods of time, the first six of these periods will cover the earth's telestial history, while in the seventh period the earth will be restored to a terrestrial or paradisiacal state (see Articles of Faith 1:10).

7. The seven seals: The seals described here are bits of wax or clay, imprinted with God's identifying mark, which keep the scroll mentioned in verse 6 tightly rolled up. For ancient Jews the number seven symbolized perfection or completeness. Since the scroll represents the comprehensive plan of God (see v. 6), the sequential opening of the seven seals likely represents the full unfolding or implementation of the divine plan for this earth from beginning to end. With the opening of the seventh seal, God's plan for the temporal earth will reach its final stage in a glorious Millennium.[16]

8. The four angels: In another similarity between apocalyptic revelation and parables, these four angels and their supervisor (see Revelation 7:1–2) may be the same angels referred to in the parable of the wheat and the tares (see D&C 86:5–7; Matthew 13:24–30, 36–43). In both cases, the angels with the power to save or to destroy were instructed by their leader to wait—until the wheat has been gathered (see Matthew 13) or until the Saints have been sealed (see Revelation 7). In the meantime their work is to prepare the nations of the world to receive the restored gospel and to bring the world to repentance, even by the use of natural disasters if need be.

According to President Wilford Woodruff, "These angels that have been held for many years in the temple of our God have got their liberty to go out and commence their mission and their work in the earth, and they are here to-day in the earth."[17] At the end of the world, when both the wheat and the tares have had a chance to exercise their agency and reveal their true character, these angels will save the wheat—the righteous Saints—while "the tares are bound in bundles, and the field remaineth to be burned" (D&C 86:7).

The number *four* is symbolic of the entire earth with its four cardinal directions, and thus might here be intended figuratively. Whatever their number, however, the great work of God is being performed by his servants on both sides of the veil, by men and by angels.

9. The angel ascending from the east: This "angel" ascends or rises from the East. He personally possesses the great seal of God and may bind or loose with divine authority. He presides over and directs the work of the other angels. He gathers Israel, and he restores all things.[18]

9. Sealed the servants of our God: Literally, this would mean using the great seal of God to imprint his identifying mark on their foreheads. The mark put upon them that seals them is the name of God (see Revelation 22:4). Figuratively, it probably refers to binding the Saints to Christ and to one another in the name of Jesus Christ. In this case the seal would be the stamp of God's authority—the priesthood power—performing the ordinances of salvation and, perhaps, actually sealing the Saints up to eternal life in the manner described in Doctrine and Covenants 68:12.[19] Only when the servants of God—the wheat—have been gathered out from among the tares can the residue of chaff be burned.

9. This is Elias: There has been more than one Elias according to the scriptures.[20] Among these Eliases are John the Baptist (see Matthew 17:10–13), John the Revelator (see D&C 77:14), the prophet Elijah (see Malachi 4:5; D&C 110:13–14), and the ancient patriarch Noah, who holds the keys of restoring all things (see D&C 27:6–7; Luke 1:19).[21] In fact, any or all of those heavenly beings who appeared to the Prophet Joseph Smith to prepare him for his mission or to restore knowledge and authority might rightly be called Elias, for *Elias* is a function and a title in addition to being a personal name.[22]

Elias in this verse, however, does not refer to the prophet

Elijah, nor to John the Revelator, nor to John the Baptist. This Elias is none other than Jesus Christ himself. John the Baptist testified that Jesus was the Elias of restoration while the Baptist was an Elias of preparation (see JST John 1:20–28). In the context of the earth's existence in the first six thousand years, restoring all things perhaps means restoring the fulness of the gospel and the keys of the priesthood to a telestial world, and the Eliases listed above have done this. In the context of the seventh thousand years, restoring all things includes restoring the earth itself to a terrestrial state and bringing to pass the redemption and resurrection of the dead. This is the mighty work of Jesus Christ alone, who will be at his Second Coming the great and final Elias or restorer. It is Jesus Christ himself who ultimately will restore *all* things and who will finally gather *all* of Israel together "as a hen gathereth her chickens" (3 Nephi 10:4–6).[23]

10. In the sixth thousand years: The work of spreading the gospel throughout the world to every nation, kindred, tongue, and people is the work of the latter-day Church. We now live in the sixth time period, or day, or thousand years—the period of time immediately before the glorious Millennium, which is the seventh time period or the sabbath day of the earth's temporal existence.

11. One hundred and forty-four thousand: The number *twelve* is associated symbolically with Israel (such as twelve tribes and twelve Apostles). Twelve times twelve, or twelve squared, thus represents the idea of Israel raised to a higher order of magnitude—perhaps something like the essence of Israel or the millennial Israel.

According to this passage, these one hundred and forty-four thousand, whether the number is taken literally or figuratively, represent not the total number of the saved but the number of high priests designated from every nation of the world to bring people to Christ. "Will not that be a great work? Imagine one hundred and forty-four thousand High Priests going forth among the nations, and gathering out as many as will come to the Church of the first-born. All that will be done, probably, in the morning of the seventh thousand years. The work is of great magnitude, Latter-day Saints, and we are living almost upon the eve of it."[24]

The book of Revelation explains that these hundred and forty-four thousand high priests will be constituted "of all the tribes of the children of Israel" (Revelation 7:4). There is a certain ambiguity in scriptural terminology, however, that should suggest caution in trying to draw any further conclusions from this distribution (for example, that the end can't come until we find and baptize a lot more people from the "lost" ten tribes). The ambiguity is this: In the Old Testament the term *Ephraim* usually refers to the younger son of Joseph and his posterity, but sometimes *Ephraim* is used as a synonym for Israel and refers to all ten of the northern tribes collectively (see Hosea 11:8, 12). Thus, someone might be from the tribe of Asher or Zebulon genealogically, and yet at the same time be an Ephraimite politically. In much the same way, Paul often called himself a Jew (of Judah) in the New Testament (see Acts 21:39; 22:3), even though his actual lineage was from the tribe of Benjamin (see Romans 11:1; Philippians 3:5).

11. The church of the Firstborn: See Commentary on Doctrine and Covenants 76:54.

12. The sounding of the trumpets: After the opening of the seventh seal in his Revelation, John saw a series of seven angels, who sounded their seven trumpets one after the other in another symbolic series. Doctrine and Covenants 77 informs us that the events symbolized by the seven trumpets are mighty works that Jesus Christ will perform after the beginning of the Millennium but before his Second Coming (see v. 13)—works of judgment, redemption, and resurrection. These works, on the seventh day of the earth's temporal existence, will be part of sanctifying the earth and raising it to a paradisiacal glory, just as Christ sanctified the earth and gave it the glory of paradise, or Eden, once before—on the seventh day of its creation. This is the same series of trumpet blasts described in Doctrine and Covenants 88:96–106.

There seems to be an intentional parallel between the seven

days of the earth's creation and the seven days of its temporal existence. The soundings of the trumpets mark the events and
changes that must take place in the seventh thousand years for the
earth to be raised to terrestrial glory. The seventh trumpet
announces the completion of all preparations and the coming of
the glorious Christ himself to the earth (see Exodus 19:16–20,
where the descent of Jehovah, or Christ, to the earth was also
marked by the sounding of a trumpet).

**12. On the seventh day he finished his work, . . . and also
formed man**: The language here has sometimes been interpreted
to indicate that Adam and Eve were created on the seventh day
rather than on the sixth day as in as in the accounts of Genesis,
Moses, Abraham, and elsewhere. Granted, this would seem to be
the sense of the passage; however, there is a grammatical ambiguity. The phrase "and also formed man" can be understood as one
event during the "week" of creation mentioned earlier in the same
sentence, rather than as occurring specifically on the seventh day.

The creation of Adam on the seventh day would require
rejecting the specific testimony of Genesis 1:31; Moses 2:31; and
Abraham 4:31 that Adam was created on the sixth day or time,
and the latter two sources were translated by the Prophet Joseph
Smith. It would also require interpreting Genesis 1:27; Moses
2:26; and Abraham 4:27—the so-called "first" creation—as referring exclusively to Adam's spiritual creation, thus leaving Genesis
2:7; Moses 3:7; and Abraham 5:7 to describe Adam's physical creation. But this is impossible; for Adam, as Michael, already existed
before the creation of the world as described in Genesis 1, Moses
2, and Abraham 4. Adam was one of its creators. Adam could not
be created spiritually after he already existed as a spirit. The
account in the book of Abraham reports chronologically that
Abraham saw the noble and great spirits, presumptively including Adam, or Michael (see Abraham 3:22–23). Then, he saw the
council in heaven and the rebellion of Satan (see Abraham
3:24–28), and only then does he describe the creation of the
world and of Adam and Eve (Abraham 4:1, 27). Thus, Abraham

4:27 cannot be describing the *spiritual* creation of Adam, who already existed at the council as Michael, unless Adam/Michael were created spiritually twice.

Moreover, the command to "be fruitful, and multiply" clearly recorded in Moses 2:22, 28 (and paralleled in Moses 2:12, 20–21, 24; Abraham 4:28; Genesis 1:28) is an absurdity if given to spiritual beings without even the means or power of obeying it. Moses 2 and Abraham 4 can only be describing the creation of physical beings with the power to multiply, and Abraham 4:27 and Moses 2:26 can only be describing the *physical* creation of Adam and Eve on the sixth day of creation (see also Moses 2:31; Abraham 4:31). While it is true that all things were created spiritually in heaven before they were created physically (see Moses 3:5), both the so-called "first" and "second" creation accounts in Genesis, Moses, and Abraham are describing the physical creation. And all three of these books specifically place that creation on the sixth day.

It follows, therefore, that since there is a slight grammatical ambiguity in Doctrine and Covenants 77:12, this passage should not be interpreted as contradictorily describing the physical creation of Adam on the seventh day, as plausible as this might seem, without further revelation on the subject.

13. After the opening . . . , before the coming: Note that the seventh period of the earth's existence started *before* the second coming of Christ and that there was a space of time "after the opening of the seventh seal, before the coming of Christ." The two events are not simultaneous, nor does the opening of the seventh seal initiate the Millennium. According to John's Revelation, there was silence in heaven for the space of half an hour after the opening of the seventh seal before the events symbolized by the seven trumpets—the final preparations for the coming of Christ—began to take place.[25] If we interpret literally the formula of one day with God being a thousand years with man, which is by no means certain that we must so interpret (see the different formula in D&C 88:44), a half hour would amount to a little less than twenty-one years separating the opening of the seventh seal and the beginning of the seven trumpets. No indication is given of how much additional time the events associated with the seven trumpets will take, although it seems that all will be completed in less than one generation (see JST Matthew 1:34).

14. The little book: In his vision John saw an angel holding a little book or scroll. John was instructed to take the book and eat it. When he did so, according to the book of Revelation, he found that it was delicious but that it upset his stomach. The experience of John in this regard is an almost exact repetition of the experience of Ezekiel (see Ezekiel 2:9—3:4).

14. It was a mission: The interpretation offered here is supported by the similar experience of Ezekiel, who with the same visionary imagery was also called on a mission to preach and minister to the house of Israel. John the Beloved Apostle is here identified as one who will assist in the restoration and gathering of Israel in the latter days.[26] This mission of preparation and restoration makes John *an* Elias, along with Noah, Elijah, John the Baptist, and others.

15. The two witnesses: In Greek the words for *witness* and *martyr* are the same. This is appropriate, since being one often leads to becoming the other. John saw in his vision two servants of the Lord who testify of the truth and who suffer martyrdom for it. These two witnesses have the power to shut the heavens and to smite the earth with plagues. These witnesses will not be casual elders who just happen to be in Jerusalem when war breaks out; they will likely be General Authorities of the Church—prophets specifically called on this mission to the Jewish nation (compare Zechariah 4:12–14; Revelation 11:1–4).

15. The Jewish nation: It is intriguing that at the time Joseph Smith wrote this revelation, there was no Jewish nation upon the face of the earth. The existence of the nation of Israel in the Holy Land since 1948 constitutes just one more prophecy of Joseph Smith that has come to pass since the Restoration.

---

1. *History of the Church*, 5:340, 342, 344.

2. See Woodford, Historical Development, 2:975–76.
3. *Kirtland Revelation Book,* 11, 15, 18; spelling and punctuation standardized.
4. *History of the Church,* 1:255; for the dates see *Kirtland Revelation Book,* 12, 15–18.
5. See Dahl, "Joseph Smith Translation and the Doctrine and Covenants," 123.
6. Note the parallel question and answer format in D&C 113, in *Journal of Discourses,* 2:342, and in two unpublished revelations dated 7 January and 20 March 1832 located in the Newel K. Whitney collection at the Harold B. Lee Library.
7. *History of the Church,* 1:253.
8. *History of the Church,* 5:279; see Commentary on D&C 130:9.
9. *History of the Church,* 5:341–42.
10. *History of the Church,* 5:343.
11. *History of the Church,* 5:343.
12. *History of the Church,* 5:343–44; see Commentary on v. 4.
13. See *History of the Church,* 5:342.
14. Compare the record of John in D&C 93:6, 18 and Commentary.
15. See Smith, *Teachings of the Prophet Joseph Smith,* p. 252; Spencer W. Kimball, *Ensign,* May 1978, 102.
16. See Commentary on D&C 88:108–10.
17. *Millennial Star,* 8 Oct. 1894, 643.
18. See Commentary on D&C 38:12.
19. See Commentary on D&C 68:12.
20. See Commentary on D&C 27:6.
21. See *History of the Church,* 3:386.
22. See Smith, *Teachings of the Prophet Joseph Smith,* 159.
23. See Commentary on D&C 10:64–65; 29:2.
24. Orson Pratt, in *Journal of Discourses,* 16:325–26.
25. See Commentary on D&C 88:95.
26. See Commentary on D&C 7:1–3.

78

BACKGROUND

In the two weeks between 1 and 15 March 1832, as the Prophet Joseph Smith continued the work of translating the Bible, he received four revelations now known as sections 78–81. Joseph's own account concerning these revelations is brief: "Besides the work of translating, previous to the 20th of March, I received the four following revelations."[1] According to the *Kirtland Revelation Book,* Joseph, who was living in Hiram, Ohio, at the time, traveled to Kirtland between 29 February and 4 March and received Doctrine and Covenants 78 on 1 March while in Kirtland.[2] The earliest manuscript copy of section 78, in the handwriting of Frederick G. Williams, also gives the date of this revelation as 1 March.[3] In addition to information on Doctrine and Covenants 78, the *Kirtland Revelation Book* also lists the dates of Doctrine and Covenants 79 as 12 March, Doctrine and Covenants 80 as 7 March, and Doctrine and Covenants 81 as 15 March 1832.[4]

In March 1832 it had been a little over a year since the Lord had revealed his law to the Church, including the law of consecration (see D&C 42). The publishing interests of the Church and those leaders involved in them had subsequently organized a consecrated "order" known as the Literary Firm (see D&C 70). By March 1832, however, the Saints had not yet organized a storehouse either in Kirtland or in Missouri, even though an important part of the Lord's plan for the consecration of his Saints was the establishment of a bishops' storehouse, and some instruction concerning the storehouse had already been received by the Church (see D&C 51:13). Therefore, in order to help the Church take this necessary step in implementing the principles of consecration, the Lord directed in this revelation that Joseph Smith, Sidney Rigdon, and Newel K. Whitney form a business partnership for the purpose of generating revenue for the Church and establishing a bishops' storehouse in Kirtland. This partnership was called the united firm—also known as the united order or the order of Enoch—and it would operate on many of the same principles as the previously established literary firm.

Within three months of receiving section 78, Bishop Whitney's mercantile store was fully consecrated as the bishops' storehouse in Kirtland. This united firm operated like a Church-owned corporation with the managers Joseph Smith, Sidney Rigdon, and Newel Whitney taking out a salary sufficient for their needs while the corporate profits went toward providing for "the poor of my people" (D&C 78:3). In Kirtland the united firm also purchased building lots, businesses, and the eventual site of the Kirtland Temple.[5] Thus, the united firm gives us one example of how the principles of consecration might be applied in a business, mercantile, or manufacturing situation rather than in farming or agriculture, just as the literary firm provides an example for consecration in the business of publishing.

The three members of the united firm in Kirtland were further instructed in Doctrine and Covenants 78 to travel to Zion to strengthen the Church there and also to create a branch of the united firm there and provide for a bishops' storehouse.[6] It must be understood that the united firm, or united order, never included the general membership of the Church, and there were never more than twelve individuals included in the partnership. Members of the united firm were generally Church leaders with property or businesses to be consecrated toward the establishment or continuation of the storehouse and the pursuit of other Church financial projects. In a period before the leading quorums of the Church were fully organized, the united firm was intended for a limited time to provide financial leadership and accountability for the Church, and its members dealt with matters of Church financial policy that would later be the responsibility of General Authorities. Modern analogues to the united and literary firms can be seen in the corporation of the First Presidency, the corporation of the Presiding Bishopric, and the various financial, publishing, welfare, and other committees of the Church.

Although the term *united order* is often used as an equivalent for "the law of consecration," this usage is technically incorrect, since the united firm was specifically the consecrated business partnership between Joseph Smith and other Church leaders in Kirtland and Missouri between March 1832 and April 1834 (compare D&C 104). The law of consecration is the broader term and the eternal principle; the united order was merely one example of how the law of consecration was implemented in the business affairs of the Church during the Kirtland period.

COMMENTARY

1. The Lord spake unto Joseph Smith, Jun.: When section 78 was first published in the 1835 Doctrine and Covenants, the Church was under attack on many fronts. At that time it was decided that it was unwise to reveal details of the Church's financial structure and the identity of its financial officers to the world. Code names were therefore used for the individuals mentioned in section 78 and some other revelations. Joseph Smith was variously referred to as Enoch, Gazelam, or Barauk Ale. Sidney Rigdon was Pelagoram or Baneemy, and Newel Whitney was Ahashdah. Since these names were not part of the original revelation,[7] and since there is no longer any need for secrecy in these matters, the code names have been removed from recent editions of the Doctrine and Covenants.

1. The high priesthood of my church: Although no historical information is available for the setting of section 78, the wording here indicates a meeting with the Church leadership in Kirtland.

2. In that thing which you have presented before me: It is clear that Doctrine and Covenants 78 was received in answer to a request of the Lord by the assembled leaders in Kirtland. Although we do not know the exact wording of their petition, it would seem likely that it dealt with the financial problems of the Church and the difficulty in establishing the bishops' storehouse. This pattern of actively seeking guidance from the Lord concerning the difficulties of our lives and then listening to and following his advice continues to be instructive for modern Saints.

3. The time has come: More than a year had passed since the Lord commanded that the poor and needy be provided for under the law of consecration (see D&C 42:30–44). Further instruction had been given to Bishop Edward Partridge and the Church ten months earlier in Doctrine and Covenants 51. But by March 1832 very little had actually been done to organize and administer the commanded program.

4. For a permanent and everlasting establishment and order: What was to be permanent and everlasting was the establishment and regulation of a storehouse for the poor. The specific means of creating and funding the storehouse, in this case the united firm, was not necessarily permanent. Today bishops' storehouses are administered through the Presiding Bishopric.

4. To the salvation . . . , and to the glory: Whatever contributes to the salvation of human beings also contributes to the glory of God, for the work and the glory of God *is* the immortality and eternal life of man (see Moses 1:39).

5. That you may be equal: The purpose of the law of consecration is to make the Saints equal in earthly blessings now so that they might become equal in the enjoyment of heavenly or celestial blessings later.[9] Where the Saints are not equal temporally, it is because someone will not live the law of consecration. Since consecration is a celestial law, those who will not live it cannot be equal in their heavenly blessings with those who do live it.

Therefore those who would enjoy the celestial kingdom in the Resurrection must be willing to abide by its laws here upon the earth—including the law of consecration.

9. Sit in council with the saints which are in Zion: Obedient to this command, the three brethren mentioned in this revelation, accompanied by Jesse Gause, traveled to Independence, Missouri, met with the members and the leaders, and inducted Oliver Cowdery, Edward Partridge, Sidney Gilbert, John Whitmer, and William Phelps into the united firm. Martin Harris, Jesse Gause, and eventually Frederick G. Williams and John Johnson were also members of the united firm. The retail store that had been established in Independence by Sidney Gilbert, Newel K. Whitney's former associate in Kirtland, became the bishops' storehouse in Zion (see D&C 57:8).

10. Satan seeketh to turn their hearts: Apparently the Saints in Zion were having as much difficulty implementing the principles of consecration and establishing a viable storehouse as the Saints in Kirtland. If Satan could divert the Saints from living this law, then he could destroy their opportunity of gaining the blessings of eternity. Firm measures were required in both Kirtland and Zion to get the Saints over the hurdle of consecration.

11. Organize yourselves by a bond or everlasting covenant: Entrance into the united firm was by sacred covenant, just as those who accept the burden of consecration today do so by sacred covenant in the temples of God. As President Ezra Taft Benson declared: "We covenant to live the law of consecration. This law is that we consecrate our time, talents, strength, property, and money for the upbuilding of the kingdom of God on this earth and the establishment of Zion.

"Until one abides by the laws of obedience, sacrifice, the gospel, and chastity, he cannot abide the law of consecration, which is the law pertaining to the celestial kingdom. 'For if you will that I give you a place in the celestial world, you must prepare yourselves by doing the things which I have commanded you and required of you' (D&C 78:7)."[10]

11. That cannot be broken: As long as people have their moral agency, they can indeed break this covenant if they wish— as verse 12 indicates. The meaning seems to be that since the covenant of consecration is an eternal and a celestial covenant, it cannot be broken without the loss of celestial glory.

12. Shall lose his office and standing: Because Zion can only be established upon the principle of consecration, those who reject that principle cannot lead others to Zion. Therefore, they must not hold Church leadership positions. Worse than this, however, since they have rejected the avowed destination of the Church, they cannot even be counted as members "in good standing." An extreme example is provided in the New Testament in the case of Ananias and Sapphira (see Acts 5:1–11).

12. The buffetings of Satan: According to the 1828 edition of Webster's Dictionary, "to buffet" means "to strike with the hand or fist; to box; to beat." The war in heaven is not yet over, and Satan, our implacable enemy, remembers very clearly our opposition to him in the premortal state. Those who choose Satan's plan in this life must be handed over to him. We are free agents, and we must be given what we choose. Like prisoners of war who have fallen into the hands of a hideously sadistic enemy, these unfortunates will be completely in Satan's power and must endure his full hatred, torture, and abuse. This will, indeed, be hell.

12. Until the day of redemption: Even hell has an end, and even those who find themselves in Satan's power can repent and eventually be redeemed from Satan by the power of the Atonement. Jesus Christ, the Savior, saves. That is what he does. He saves those who will listen to him from the pit of hell by showing them how to avoid it. He saves the stubborn who wouldn't listen to him by descending into the pit himself and pulling them out—if only they will repent. Eventually, all of those who will repent and accept the atonement and lordship of Christ will be redeemed from the power of Satan (see D&C 76:42–43).

13. The preparation . . . and the ensample: The creation of the united firm was not the ultimate fulfillment of the law of consecration, but it was a beginning and an example of how the principle could be implemented and the commandment obeyed. The commandment will only be fulfilled when the Saints have collectively established Zion in preparation for the second coming of the Lord by living the law of consecration and becoming equal in temporal things.

14. The tribulation which shall descend upon you: Once again the Lord clearly informs the Saints of the persecutions and trials that are waiting for them in the future.[11] Nor should modern Church members think that trials and tribulations are necessarily a thing of the past: "We can certainly anticipate some exciting and wonderful opportunities in the years ahead. But it will be more and more difficult to remain a committed follower of Jesus Christ. I believe future followers of Christ will face adversity and persecution that is much more intense than anything we see today."[12]

14. The church may stand independent: Implementation of the law of consecration through the united firm and other means will, with the blessings of God, give the Church the ability to survive on its own resources without being forced to compromise its principles or to ally itself with or rely upon the institutions of the world. From time to time the Church may choose to cooperate with other entities in matters of mutual concern, but never in a manner that would infringe upon its sovereignty and self-determination.

14. Creatures: This refers to institutions or entities.

15. The crown prepared for you:[13] The eternal destiny of faithful Saints, those who make and keep the covenant of consecration, is not to serve, but to rule—and not over one kingdom alone, but over many.

15. The foundations of Adam-ondi-Ahman: Adam-ondi-Ahman is the name of the place where Adam and Eve settled after they were expelled from the Garden of Eden (see D&C 117:8).[14] It was there that the Lord appeared to Adam and his righteous posterity three years before Adam's death, and it is there that another great meeting with the Savior will take place before his second coming.[15]

The last clause in verse 15 and all of verse 16 were not in the original revelation of Doctrine and Covenants 78, but were added to the text by the Prophet Joseph in the first printed edition in 1835. By that time the name and the significance of Adam-ondi-Ahman had apparently been revealed to the Prophet, and three years later in May 1838, Joseph indicated that Adam-ondi-Ahman had been located at a place the Saints called Spring Hill in Daviess County, about sixty miles north of Independence.[16]

16. Michael your prince: Michael, or Adam,[17] is not the king, for Christ is King (see Revelation 19:16). But Michael is the next in authority, and having been "born again" as a son of Christ (see Mosiah 5:7), he is now the prince of the kingdom of God. In this role he represents all of us as heirs to the kingdom. Adam still stands at the head of his posterity, the human family, but in subjection to Christ his King. Next to Christ, Adam holds the keys of salvation and works for the benefit of his posterity. According to Joseph Smith, "The Priesthood was first given to Adam; he obtained the First Presidency, and held the keys of it from generation to generation. . . .

" . . . The keys have to be brought from heaven whenever the Gospel is sent. When they are revealed from heaven, it is by Adam's authority."[18]

17. Little children: Our present understanding, compared with what we will understand when we reach our eternal "adulthood," is like that of little children. Though we may be mortal adults, we have been "born again" and are in the infancy of our eternal lives. By eternal standards we are still naive and without understanding. At present we lack the maturity even to comprehend the full blessings of God, let alone to receive them. Despite the tribulations we must experience in this life, our destiny is happiness and joy beyond our present comprehension.

18. Ye cannot bear all things now: The present limitations of mortality make it impossible for us to receive now or even to understand now all that we will receive from God in the future. The blessings of eternity are so great that only resurrected beings can bear them. For now we must follow the leadership of the Lord and trust in his assurances that we are going to be all right—that the kingdom and its blessings and the riches of eternity are truly going to be ours—assuming, of course, that we remain faithful.

19. He who receiveth all things with thankfulness: Compare Doctrine and Covenants 59:21.[19]

20. Son Ahman: Doctrine and Covenants 95:17 declares that this is Jesus Christ, the son of God. Orson Pratt once expressed the opinion that Ahman was the name of God in the pure, Adamic language and that Son Ahman was the name of the Son, Jesus Christ.[20] Joseph Smith is recorded to have taught the Nauvoo lyceum on 9 March 1841, however, that "the Great God has a name by which he will be called which is Ahman."[21] Smith and Sjodahl additionally observe that "the word is possibly akin to 'Amen.' In Isaiah (65:16) the Almighty is called 'God of Amen,' but the translators have made it, 'God of truth.' In Rev. 3:14, our Lord calls Himself by that name: 'These things saith the *Amen*, the faithful and true witness.' There is also the word *Amon*, the name which Egyptians gave a Deity, in whose honor the magnificent temple at Karnak was reared."[22]

21. The church of the Firstborn: Compare Doctrine and Covenants 76:54.[23]

21. He will take you up in a cloud: On the last day, the righteous will be lifted off the earth and caught up to meet the Lord in the clouds while the earth is cleansed by fire (see D&C 45:44–45; 88:96–97; 1 Thessalonians 4:17).

1. *History of the Church*, 1:255.
2. *Kirtland Revelation Book*, 11, 15.
3. See Newel K. Whitney papers, in Brigham Young University Archives, Harold B. Lee Library.
4. *Kirtland Revelation Book*, 12, 17–18.
5. See Anderson, *Joseph Smith's Kirtland*, 132–33.
6. See Cannon and Cook, *Far West Record*, 47–48.

7. See *Kirtland Revelation Book,* 15–17; Orson Pratt, in *Journal of Discourses,* 16:156.

8. See *Journal of Discourses,* 16:156.

9. See Commentary on D&C 51:3; 56:16–18; 82:17–18.

10. *Teachings of Ezra Taft Benson,* 121.

11. See Commentary on D&C 58:3–4.

12. M. Russell Ballard, *Ensign,* July 1995, 15.

13. See Commentary on D&C 20:14; 66:12.

14. See Orson Pratt, in *Journal of Discourses,* 18:343.

15. See Commentary on D&C 107:53–57; 116:1.

16. See *History of the Church,* 3:35; Brown, Cannon, and Jackson, *Historical Atlas,* 42–43.

17. See Commentary on D&C 27:11; 29:26.

18. *History of the Church,* 3:385–86.

19. See Commentary on D&C 59:21.

20. See *Journal of Discourses,* 2:342.

21. Ehat and Cook, *Words of Joseph Smith,* 64; spelling and capitalization standardized.

22. *Doctrine and Covenants Commentary,* 484.

23. See Commentary on D&C 76:54.

79

BACKGROUND

J ared Carter was one of the Colesville Saints and had joined the Church in New York sometime in February 1831. The following Spring he left his farm in Chenango, New York, near Colesville and moved with the Saints to Ohio. Settling first in Thompson, Ohio, he later moved to Amherst, about fifty miles west of Kirtland, to be near his brother Simeon. In June 1831 the Lord directed that Carter be ordained a priest (see D&C 52:38), and he was ordained an elder sometime before September of that year.[1]

Doctrine and Covenants 79 records a call from the Lord for Jared Carter to serve a mission in the Eastern states. The revelation was received by the Prophet Joseph Smith on 12 March 1832 in Hiram, Ohio.[2] Joseph left no comments specifically concerning section 79, but Jared Carter did record the following details in his journal: "I at length went to Hiram to the Seer to inquire the will of the Lord concerning my ministry the ensuing season and the word of the Lord came forth that showed that it was his will that I should go forth to the Eastern countries in the power of the ordinance wherewith I had been ordained which was to the high privilege of administering in the name of Jesus Christ even to seal on earth and to build up the Church of Christ and to work miracles in the name of Christ."[3] Jared Carter served on this mission for just over six months and contributed to the conversion of nearly one hundred persons.

COMMENTARY

1. Should go again into the eastern countries: Jared Carter had just gone to Ohio the previous year from Chenango, New York, in obedience to the commandment of the Lord (see D&C 37:3). Now he was to return to the east as a missionary to his former neighbors and others as directed by the Spirit.

1. In the power of the ordination: Those who hold the priesthood are God's agents and have been given his power. They are expected to use that power as God would to bless, preach, perform ordinances, and on. When a priesthood holder is asked to give a blessing, he should not merely pray that God will bestow a blessing. The appointed agent having the necessary power should bestow the blessing in the name of Jesus Christ. That which God has delegated to his servants, they should perform in confidence and power, and not delegate back to him by merely praying that God will do something. There is a critical difference between blessing "in the power of the ordination" and merely praying for a blessing.

2. The way whither he shall go: Jared Carter was to keep moving and to travel as directed by the Spirit. His journal shows great determination on his part to travel to the major cities in New York, as directed in verse 1, "from city to city."

3. Crown him again with sheaves: See Commentary on Doctrine and Covenants 75:5 Notes.

---

1. See Cook, *Revelations of the Prophet,* 73–74; Black, *Who's Who in the Doctrine and Covenants,* 51–54.
2. See *Kirtland Revelation Book,* 12; Background to D&C 78.
3. Cited in Woodford, *Historical Development,* 2:1005; spelling and capitalization standardized.

DOCTRINE AND COVENANTS

80

BACKGROUND

Doctrine and Covenants 80 is a revelation directing
Stephen Burnett, a high priest, to serve a mission for the
Church, taking Elder Eden Smith with him as a companion.
Joseph Smith left no information in the *History of the Church* on
the reception of section 80 other than the comment previously
cited in the background to section 78 that four revelations were
received between 1–20 March 1832. According to an entry in the
Kirtland Revelation Book in the handwriting of Joseph Smith and
Frederick G. Williams, however, this revelation was received in
Hiram, Ohio, on 7 March 1832.[1] Chronologically this would actu-
ally place Doctrine and Covenants 80 five days earlier than
Doctrine and Covenants 79, which was received on 12 March.
Section 80 was first published in the 1835 Doctrine and
Covenants.

COMMENTARY

1. Stephen Burnett: Stephen Burnett was converted to the
Church by late November 1830 in Orange, Ohio, by John
Murdock, who had himself been a member of the Church at that
time less than one month. The important Church conference held
on 25–26 October 1831, at which the first high priests were
ordained, met at the Burnett home in Orange, Ohio. Among the

high priests ordained there was seventeen-year-old Stephen Burnett.

On 25 January 1832, Burnett was called to serve a mission with Ruggles Eames, although that mission either did not take place or was of very short duration, since Burnett is called here two months later to serve a mission with Eden Smith. Burnett also preached for awhile in New Hampshire with Horace Cowan during the summer of 1833. By 1837, however, Burnett had come out in opposition to the Prophet Joseph and was excommunicated on 3 December 1838.[2]

1. Preach the gospel to every creature: Missionaries are called to preach to any individual who will listen. Neither social status, nor education, nor nationality, nor financial status, nor any other factor should cause us to ignore our Heavenly Father's children when we have been called to teach the gospel of Jesus Christ. Without restriction, all who will hear are invited, all who will repent are called, and all who will obey are chosen.

2. Eden Smith: Eden Smith was also an Ohio resident who joined the Church in 1831 at the age of twenty-four. He served several short missions in 1831 and 1832, but his style was to preach for a short period of time and then return home to work and be with his family.[3]

3. It mattereth not: Stephen Burnett and Eden Smith were given no revelation concerning where they were to preach on their mission. The Lord assured them that wherever they went it would be right. Once again the Lord stated that there are some decisions that just do not matter in the great scheme of things. There are some decisions in life for which there is no right answer and no wrong answer.[4] It might additionally be noted that the opportunities to preach the gospel are so abundant that one cannot go amiss wherever one chooses to labor. Both the righteous and the wicked in all the earth must be warned.

4. Declare the things which ye . . . know to be true: The power of the Spirit can work through our testimonies only when we actually have spiritual testimonies ourselves. When one heart testifies what it knows by the Spirit to another honest heart, that is when the miracle of spiritual witness takes place. It is also why such confirmations seldom take place when we merely repeat what we have learned intellectually or when we merely state what is culturally expected of us in a testimony. Rumors, speculation, family tradition, and secular learning have no place in the spiritual transaction of preaching and hearing the gospel. The most effective missionaries are those who testify by the power of the Spirit what they themselves have learned to be true through the confirmation of the Spirit.

1. See *Kirtland Revelation Book*, p. 18.
2. See Cook, *Revelations of the Prophet*, pp. 153–54, 170; Black, *Who's Who in the Doctrine and Covenants*, pp. 39–40.
3. See Black, *Who's Who in the Doctrine and Covenants*, pp. 271–72.
4. See Commentary on D&C 60:5.

SOURCES

Ahlstrom, Sydney A. *A Religious History of the American People.* New Haven: Yale University Press, 1972.

Anderson, Karl Ricks. *Joseph Smith's Kirtland: Eyewitness Accounts.* Salt Lake City: Deseret Book, 1989.

Backman, Milton V., Jr. *The Heavens Resound: A History of the Latter-day Saints in Ohio 1830–1838.* Salt Lake City: Deseret Book, 1983.

Backman, Milton V., Jr., and Keith W. Perkins. "United under the Laws of the Celestial Kingdom: Consecration, Stewardship, and the United Order, 1830–1838 (D&C 42, 51, 78, 82, 83, 104, etc.)." In Robert L. Millet and Kent P. Jackson, eds. *Studies in Scripture: Volume One, the Doctrine and Covenants.* Salt Lake City: Randall Book, 1989, pp. 170–85.

Benson, Ezra Taft. *The Teachings of Ezra Taft Benson.* Salt Lake City: Bookcraft, 1988.

———. "Prepare Yourselves for the Great Day of the Lord." *Brigham Young University 1981 Fireside and Devotional Speeches.* Provo: Brigham Young University, 1981, pp. 64–69.

Black, Susan Easton. *Who's Who in the Doctrine and Covenants.* Salt Lake City: Bookcraft, 1997.

Booth, Ezra. "Mormonism No. VIII." *Painesville Telegraph,* 20 Dec. 1831, pp. 2–3.

Cannon, Donald Q. and Lyndon W. Cook, eds. *Far West Record: Minutes of The Church of Jesus Christ of Latter-day Saints, 1830–1844.* Salt Lake City: Deseret Book, 1983.

Cannon, George Q. "Discourse by President George Q. Cannon." *Millennial Star,* 5 Sept. 1895, pp. 561–66.

———. *Gospel Truth: Discourses and Writings of President George Q. Cannon.* Selected by Jerreld L. Newquist, 2 vols. Salt Lake City: Deseret Book, 1957–74.

———. *Life of Joseph Smith the Prophet.* Salt Lake City: Deseret Book, 1958.

Carter, Jared. Journal. MSS SC 547. Harold B. Lee Library, Special Collections, Brigham Young University, Provo, Utah.

Clark, James R., comp. *Messages of the First Presidency of The Church of Jesus Christ of Latter-day Saints.* 6 vols. Salt Lake City: Bookcraft, 1965–75.

Clark, J. Reuben, Jr. "When Are the Writings or Sermons of Church Leaders Entitled to the Claim of Scripture." Address to seminary and institute personnel, 7 July 1954.

Conference Report of The Church of Jesus Christ of Latter-day Saints. Salt Lake City: The Church of Jesus Christ of Latter-day Saints, 1900–1995.

Cook, Lyndon W. *Joseph Smith and the Law of Consecration.* Provo: Grandin Book, 1985.

———. *The Revelations of the Prophet Joseph Smith: A Historical and Biographical Commentary of the Doctrine and Covenants.* Salt Lake City: Deseret Book, 1985.

Dahl, Larry E. "The Joseph Smith Translation and the Doctrine and Covenants." In Robert L. Millet and Robert J. Matthews, eds. *Plain and Precious Truths Restored: The Doctrinal and Historical Significance of the Joseph Smith Translation.* Salt Lake City: Bookcraft, 1995, pp. 104–33.

Dibble, Philo. "Philo Dibble's Narrative." In *Early Scenes in Church History: Eighth Book of the Faith-Promoting Series.* Salt Lake City: Juvenile Instructor Office, 1882, pp. 74–81.

The Doctrine and Covenants Student Manual. Church Educational System Religion 324–325 student manual, 1981.

Dunn, Loren C. "Teaching by the Power of the Spirit." *Ensign,* Sept. 1984, pp. 8–12.

Ehat, Andrew F., and Cook, Lyndon W., comps. *The Words of Joseph Smith: The Contemporary Accounts of the Nauvoo Discourses of the Prophet Joseph.* Provo, Utah: Brigham Young University Religious Studies Center, 1980.

Flake, Lawrence R. "A Shaker View of a Mormon Mission." *Brigham Young University Studies.* Fall 1979, pp. 94–98.

Garrett, H. Dean. *Great Teachings from the Doctrine and Covenants.* Salt Lake City: Bookcraft, 1972.

Gentry, Leland H. "Light on the 'Mission to the Lamanites.'" *Brigham Young University Studies* 36, no. 2 (1996–97), pp. 226–30.

Hinckley, Bryant S. *Sermons and Missionary Services of Melvin Joseph Ballard.* Salt Lake City: Deseret Book, 1949.

Jessee, Dean C., comp. *The Personal Writings of Joseph Smith.* Salt Lake City: Deseret Book, 1984.

Josephus, Flavius. *Josephus, the Jewish War.* Edited by Gaalya Cornfeld. Grand Rapids: Zondervan, 1982. Preferred over the older translation of William Whiston.

Journal of Discourses. 26 vols. London: Latter-day Saints' Book Depot, 1854–86.

Kimball, Spencer W. *The Miracle of Forgiveness.* Salt Lake City: Bookcraft, 1969.

———. *The Teachings of Spencer W. Kimball.* Edited by Edward L. Kimball. Salt Lake City: Bookcraft, 1982.

———. *Tragedy or Destiny.* Salt Lake City: Deseret Book, 1977.

Ludlow, Daniel H. *A Companion to Your Study of the Doctrine and Covenants.* 2 vols. Salt Lake City: Deseret Book, 1978.

———. *Encyclopedia of Mormonism.* 5 vols. New York: Macmillan Publishing, 1992.

Lundwall, N. B., comp. *Masterful Discourses and Writings of Orson Pratt.* Salt Lake City: N. B. Lundwall, 1946.

Matthews, Robert J. "Joseph Smith's Efforts to Publish His Bible Translation." *Ensign,* Jan. 1983, pp. 57–64.

Maxwell, Neal A. *All These Things Shall Give Thee Experience.* Salt Lake City: Deseret Book, 1979.

McConkie, Bruce R. *Doctrinal New Testament Commentary.* 3 vols. Salt Lake City: Bookcraft, 1965–73.

————. *The Millennial Messiah: The Second Coming of the Son of Man.* Salt Lake City: Deseret Book, 1982.

————. *Mormon Doctrine.* 2d ed. Salt Lake City: Bookcraft, 1966.

————. "The Salvation of Little Children." *Ensign,* Apr. 1977, pp. 2–7.

McLellin, William E. "Batavia, N. Y.," *The Ensign of Liberty, of the Church of Christ,* Jan. 1848, p. 60–62.

Millet, Robert L. "Joseph Smith's Translation of the Bible and the Doctrine and Covenants." In Robert L. Millet and Kent P. Jackson, eds. *Studies in Scripture: Volume One, the Doctrine and Covenants.* Salt Lake City: Randall Book, 1989, pp. 132–43.

————. "The Joseph Smith Translation, the Pearl of Great Price, and the Book of Mormon." In Robert L. Millet and Robert J. Matthews, eds. *Plain and Precious Truths Restored: The Doctrinal and Historical Significance of the Joseph Smith Translation.* Salt Lake City: Bookcraft, 1995, pp. 134–46.

————. *Life in Christ.* Salt Lake City: Bookcraft, 1990.

Murdock, John. Autobiography. Typescript. Special Collections, Harold B. Lee Library, Brigham Young University, Provo, Utah.

Oaks, Dallin H. "Speaking Today: Criticism." *Ensign,* Feb. 1987, pp. 68–73.

Perkins, Keith W. "The Ministry to the Shakers." In Robert L. Millet and Kent P. Jackson, eds. *Studies in Scripture: Volume One, the Doctrine and Covenants.* Salt Lake City: Randall Book, 1989, pp. 211–24.

Phelps, W. W. "Commandment, Given May 9, 1831." *The Evening and the Morning Star.* Independence, Missouri, Oct. 1832, p. 1.

————. "Common Schools." *The Evening and the Morning Star.* Independence, Missouri, June 1832, p. 6.

————. "A Revelation on Prayer, Given October 30, 1831." *The Evening and the Morning Star.* Independence, Missouri, Sept. 1832, p. 2.

————. "A Vision." *The Evening and the Morning Star.* Independence, Missouri, July 1832, p. 2.

————. "The Way of Journeying for the Saints of the Church of Christ." *The Evening and the Morning Star.* Independence, Missouri, Dec. 1832, p. 5.

Porter, Larry C. "The Colesville Branch in Kaw Township, Jackson County, Missouri, 1831 to 1833." In Arnold K. Garr and Clark V.

Johnson, eds. *Regional Studies in Latter-day Saint Church History: Missouri.* Provo: Brigham Young University, 1994, pp. 281–311.

Pratt, Parley P., ed. *Autobiography of Parley P. Pratt.* Classics in Mormon Literature series. Salt Lake City: Deseret Book, 1985.

Roberts, B. H. *A Comprehensive History of The Church of Jesus Christ of Latter-day Saints. Century One.* 6 vols. Salt Lake City: The Church of Jesus Christ of Latter-day Saints, 1930.

Shipps, Jan and John W. Welch, eds. *The Journals of William E. McLellin, 1831–1836.* Provo: Brigham Young University, 1994.

Smith, Hyrum M. and Janne M. Sjodahl. *The Doctrine and Covenants Commentary.* Rev. ed. 1972.

Smith, Joseph. "Ancient Poetry." *Times and Seasons,* 1 Feb. 1843, pp. 81–85.

———. "History of Joseph Smith." *Times and Seasons,* 15 Mar. 1844, p. 464.

———. *History of The Church of Jesus Christ of Latter-day Saints.* 7 vols. 2d ed. rev. Edited by B. H. Roberts. Salt Lake City: The Church of Jesus Christ of Latter-day Saints, 1932–51.

———. *Kirtland Revelation Book.* Salt Lake City: Modern Microfilm, 1979.

———. *Teachings of the Prophet Joseph Smith.* Selected by Joseph Fielding Smith. Salt Lake City: Deseret Book, 1976.

Smith, Joseph F. *Church History and Modern Revelation.* 2 vols. Salt Lake City: Deseret Book, 1953.

———. *Doctrines of Salvation.* 3 vols. Compiled by Bruce R. McConkie. Salt Lake City: Bookcraft, 1954–56.

———. *Gospel Doctrine.* 5th ed. Salt Lake City: Deseret Book Co., 1939.

Smith, Joseph Fielding. *The Predicted Judgments.* Brigham Young University Speeches of the Year. Provo, 21 Mar. 1967.

Sperry, Sidney B. *Doctrine and Covenants Compendium.* Salt Lake City: Bookcraft, 1960.

Talmage, James E. *The Articles of Faith.* 12th ed. Salt Lake City: The Church of Jesus Christ of Latter-day Saints, 1924.

Van Wagoner, Richard S. *Sidney Rigdon: A Portrait of Religious Excess.* Salt Lake City: Signature Books, 1994.

Whitmer, John. *An Early Latter Day Saint History: The Book of John Whitmer, Kept by Commandment.* Edited by F. Mark McKiernan and

Roger D. Launius. Independence, Mo.: Herald Publishing House, 1980.

Whitney, Newel K. Manuscripts 1 and 2. Newel K. Whitney Collection. Special Collections, Harold B. Lee Library, Brigham Young University, Provo, Utah.

Widtsoe, John A. *The Message of the Doctrine and Covenants.* Edited by G. Homer Durham. Salt Lake City: Bookcraft, 1969.

Woodford, Robert J. 1974. "The Historical Development of the Doctrine and Covenants." 2 vols. Ph.D. dissertation, Brigham Young University.

INDEX

Aaron: gift of, 1:63–64; Oliver Cowdery even as, 1:190–91; descendants of, 2:247–48

Aaronic Priesthood, 1:30, 48, 89; conferred on Joseph and Oliver, 1:90–91, 103; bishop an office in, 2:247

Abilities, as gifts of Spirit, 2:78

Abortion, 2:17, 96, 164

Abortion industry, 1:240

Abraham: book of, 1:66–67; seed of, 1:121; Jehovah's covenant with, 2:51, 54

Abundance, 2:140

Abuse, of spouses and children, 2:59

Accountability, 1:39, 71, 108, 142; and knowledge of good and evil, 1:209; of Church members, 2:3; personal and collective, 2:196; age of, 2:250; for Church callings, 2:257; of Church leaders, 2:265

Acquittal, 2:50

Activity, Church, 2:275

Adam: and Eve, 1:134, 205, 207; as Michael, 1:183, 203, 206; 2:346, 357

Adam-ondi-Ahman, 1:180; 2:356–57; location of, 2:357

Adoption, into house of Israel, 2:95

Adultery, 2:20–21, 30; sign seeking and, 2:191–92; results of, 2:192–93; William McLellan commanded not to commit, 2:229–30

Adversary, 1:38. See also Satan and Devil

Adversity, in last days, 2:356

Advocate, Jesus Christ as, 1:196. See also Jesus Christ

Agency, 1:74, 205–6, 252, 261; 2:153–54; law of, 1:20; unwise use of, 2:27, 137

Agent, for Church, 2:124–26

AIDS, as scourge, 2:60

Allowance, least degree of, 1:26

Alpha and Omega, 1:112

American continent, 1:75

Amherst, Ohio, conference held in, 2:271

Ananias and Sapphira, 1:120

Ancestors, Israelite, 1:121

Angel, restoring, 2:343

Angel Moroni, 1:29–30, 39, 102, 130; vision of, 1:101–2

Angels, 1:198, 204; ministering of, 1:91; 2:320–21; as messengers, 1:185; visitations by, 2:240;

company of, 2:310; in
Revelation, 2:342
Anger, 1:73
Animals, ordained for man, 2:97, 98;
in Revelation, 2:339–40
Anointing, oil of, 1:77
Anthon, Charles, 1:34, 46
Anti-Mormons, 1:122–23, 261
Apostasy, 1:21; Great, 1:227;
2:56–57; due to D&C 76, 2:288
Apostates, 2:3, 32; anti-Mormon
claims of, 2:261–62
Apostles: voice of, 1:27–28; keys
held by, 1:140; 2:211, 223; as
witnesses, 1:150; judgment by
the, 1:199; authority of, 2:36–37,
117–18
Archangel, 1:203
Arm: of flesh, 1:23; of God, 1:96,
239
Armor, 1:184
Articles and covenants of the
Church, 1:127, 154–55
Asking in faith, 1:64
Assembly, solemn, 1:9
Atchison, David R., 1:216
Atonement, the, 1:112, 152; 2:50,
224, 300; becoming like Christ
through, 1:37; 2:172; faith in,
1:43; and exaltation, 1:94; and
true nature, 1:134; infinite,
1:135; as cure for corruption,
1:260; becoming innocent
through, 2:17–18,185; death
overcome through, 2:194–95;
our rebirth through, 2:294;
denial of, by sons of perdition,
2:298–99; all degrees of glory
dependent on, 2:320
Authority: obedience to, of Jehovah,
1:19; priesthood, 1:25, 153, 233;
apostolic, 1:105–6, 165;
legitimate Church, 1:171; line of,
1:213; 2:37; false claims of, 2:13,
34; civil, murderers subject to,
2:18

Authorization, divine priesthood,
1:157

Babylon, 1:22, 27, 239–40;
deliverance from, 2:62
Backbiting, 2:21
Ballard, Melvin J.: on teaching
gospel, 2:41; on kingdoms of
glory, 2:321
Baptism, 2:74; by immersion, 1:24,
130, 133, 142–43, 228;
ordinance of, 1:48, 267; Joseph
and Oliver's inquiry regarding,
1:90; authority to perform, 1:91;
and repentance, 1:119; manner
of, 1:138; new and everlasting
covenant of, 1:155; 2:227; as
gateway, 1:157, 169; becoming
heirs of the kingdom through,
1:261; necessary to salvation,
2:95; of children, 2:249–50; of
infants, 2:278
Baptists, 1:107, 154, 237–38, 269
Basset, Heman, 2:2, 121
Beasts, four, meaning of, 2:338–39
Beings: terrestrial, 2:313–18; eternal,
represented by four beasts, 2:339
Belief, action and, 2:4
Benson, Ezra Taft, 1:19, 27, 151; on
holy places, 2:61; on sexual
immorality, 2:164; on law of
consecration, 2:354
"Beware of False Prophets" (anti-
Mormon tract), 1:6–7
Bible, 1:83; as testimony of Jews,
1:39; Book of Mormon proves,
true, 1:132–33; truths lost from,
2:286
Bible, New Translation of the:
printing of, 1:8; Joseph Smith's
labors on, 1:17, 149; differences
in KJV and, 1:31. See also Joseph
Smith Translation
Billings, Titus, 2:201
Birthright, of Ephraim, 2:218–19
Bishop: calling and sustaining of,

Disciples of Christ, 1:235
Discipleship, determined by actions, not beliefs, 2:4
Discipline, Church, 2:31–32
Discord, in last days, 2:59–60
Discussions, missionary, 1:142
Disease, desolation by, 2:59–60
Dishonesty, 2:21; intentional, 2:193
Disputes, settling of, 2:31–32
Dissention: over Church indebtedness, 2:217; among elders at Hiram, Ohio, 2:233
Diversity, 2:5; of gifts of the Spirit, 2:76–77
Divisiveness, 2:324–25
Divorce, 2:30, 96
Doctrine and Covenants: as capstone of Restoration, 1:1–2; funds for printing, 1:8; as title of revelations, 1:8; contents of, 1:10–11; as missionary tool, 1:12; editions of, 1:12–13; acceptance of, as revelations, 1:13; chronological order of, 1:36, 69, 81; study of revelations in, 1:83–84; preface to, 2:252; influence of Joseph Smith Translation on, 2:272–73
Doctrine, 2:277–78; false, 1:226; interpretation of, 2:x
Doctrines, influence of Joseph Smith Translation on, 2:272
Dogberry, O., 1:110
Doubts, of Hiram Saints, based on language of revelations, 2:233
Drug industry, 1:240
Dust, casting off, 1:166
Duty, of priesthood holders, 2:273
Dyer, Alvin R., 1:189

Eames, Ruggles, 2:363
Earth, 1:21, 23; wasting of the, 1:32–33; cleansing of, 1:185; 2:42, 301, 358; ripe in iniquity of inhabitants of, 1:198; renewal of, 1:203; celestialized, 1:263; righteous to inherit, 2:67; purpose of, 2:96; fatness of, 2:140; resources of, 2:167; cursed for Adam's sake, 2:179; as terrestrial place, 2:196; as telestial place, 2:196–97; baptism of, 2:196–97; paradisiacal glory of, 2:197, 202, 313–14; sanctified, 2:338; creation and temporal existence of, 2: 341–42, 345–46
Earthquakes, 2:61
Ebola virus, 2:60
Edify, meaning of term, 2:38
Edom, 1:27
Education, value of, 2:133
Eight Witnesses to the Book of Mormon, 1:47, 81, 132, 160; 2:84, 229
Elder, 1:150; first, 1:130; second, 1:133; and apostles, 1:140
Elders: willingness of, to serve, 2:280; four and twenty, 2:341
Elect: Emma as, lady, 1:169–70; gathering of, 1:196; promise to the, 1:243
Elias, 1:181–82; meaning of, 2:343–44
Elijah, 1:30–33, 182, 238; keys restored by, 2:246
End of the world, signs of, 2:57
End, enduring to the, 1:78, 94, 107, 135, 169; 2:26, 50, 126
Endowment, 1:266
Enemies: to Church, 2:122; confounding, 2:261
Enoch, 1:253; Zion of, 1:258; city of, 2:53, 225; order of, 2:307; church of, 2:310
Ensign: meaning of term, 2:52; Zion to serve as, 2:219–20
Ephraim: stick of, 1:180–81; descendants of, 2:58; tribe of, 2:158, 345; right of, to preside, 2:218; blood of, 2:218–19; losing the blessings of, 2:219; calling of, 2:230

2:213; repentance prerequisite to, 2:297

Fornication, "wine of the wrath of [Babylon's]," 1:239

Fraud, 1:224–25

Fulness of the gospel, 1:22, 25, 42, 75, 233; and principles of celestial kingdom, 1:23–24, 95; and children of Israel, 1:89; in Book of Mormon, 1:130–31; restoration of, 1:150–51. *See also* Gospel

Fulness of times, telestial beings receive degree of glory in, 2:326

Funds, Church, 2:267–68

Gabriel, 1:182

Garments, unclean, 1:248

Gate: strait, 1:156; of baptism, 1:157

Gathering, 1:54, 251, 253; of Israel, 1:42, 60–61, 77, 217, 227, 255; in Ohio, 1:261–62; spirit of, 2:46–47

Gause, Jesse, 2:354

General Authorities, 1:150, 196; support of, 1:164; promises pertaining to, 2:243; as two witnesses, 2:348

Generation, possible meanings of, 2:57–58

Gentile nations, 2:24; gospel taken to, 2:40, 59

Gentiles: taking the gospel to, 1:105–6, 121; Book of Mormon written to, 1:132; times of the, 1:238–39; 2:40, 52, 58–59; Church members as, 2:218–19

Gethsemane, agony of Jesus Christ in, 1:106, 118

Gift: of revelation, 1:63; of translation, 1:62, 67; of Aaron, 1:63–64; promised to Hyrum Smith, 1:81–82; of the Son, 1:232; Pentecostal, of the Spirit, 1:266

Gifts of the Spirit, 2:75; purpose of, 2:75; distribution of, 2:76, 78

Gilbert and Whitney store, 2:124–25, 144

Gilbert, [Algernon] Sidney, 2:124–26, 143–44; as Church's agent, 2:177–78; commanded to go to Missouri, 2:215

Gird up loins, 1:184

Glory: degrees of, 1:208, 237; 2:287, 290, 299, 324; paradisiacal, of earth, 2:179; Jesus Christ to come in, 2:224; fulness of God's, 2:292, 306; sons of perdition to receive no degree of, 2:297; terrestrial degree of, 2:317

God:

Characteristics and power of:
love of, 1:24–25; 2:287–88; omniscience of, 1:55–56, 74–75; as living God, 1:95, 134; arm of, 1:96; nature of, 1:134; 2:98; voice of, 2:40–41; glory of, 2:50, 322–23; wrath of, 2:61; Jesus Christ speaks for, 2:94; light and influence of, 2:105; as only reliable source of inspiration, 2:74–75; power of, over life and death, 2:189

Man's relationship with:
fear of, 1:76; entering into presence of, 1:97; 2:309, 322; closeness to, 1:137, 139, 232; 2:238–39, 292; seeking not to counsel, 1:157; 2:138; sons of, 1:232, 270; mankind not commanded by, in all things, 2:171, 363; tempting, 2:191; victory of Saints through, 2:209–10; leaving judgment to, 2:213–14; God's will, acting contrary to, 2:27; seeing, 2:239

Works and purposes of:

of D&C 42, 2:22–23; on Martin Harris's character, 2:156; on sustaining and setting Joseph Smith apart, 2:280

Pratt, Parley, 1:192, 213, 219; conversion of, 1:221; as missionary, 1:223, 231; mission of, to Shakers, 2:92–93; on spiritual excesses, 2:101–2

Prayer, 1:71, 172, 217–18, 222; 2:221; vocal, 1:122, 160; importance of, 1:229; for further knowledge, 2:3; for Church leaders, 2:39; as guard against deception, 2:75; frequent, 2:206; for God's kingdom to go forth, 2:224; parental responsibility to teach, 2:250; private and public, 2:205, 251

Preachers: self-appointed, 1:82; called by authority, 1:83

Preaching, 1:77–78, 119

Preface, the Lord's, 2:252

Prejudice, against Church, 2:48

Premortal life, 1:206; choices made during, 2:300–301

Preparation, 1:265; 2:354; lack of, 2:49; of five wise virgins, 2:67

Preparedness, oil of, 1:229

Presidency, 1:130; keys of the, of the Church, 1:61; power of, in Aaronic Priesthood, 1:90

Presiding bishop, 2:152–53, 247; responsibility of, for funds, 2:268

Pretenders, spiritual, 2:103–4

Pride, 1:159, 267; 2:32, 308–9; Ezra Thayre rebuked for, 2:135; overcoming, 2:323

Priestcraft, 1:76, 202, 226

Priesthood: restoration of the, 1:24, 42; keys of the, 1:25, 30–31, 61, 244; 2:223; duties of the, 1:140; ordination to the, 1:140; line of authority, 1:213; false claims of, 2:13; authority of, 2:35; quorums, 2:272; eternal nature of, 2:307. *See also* Aaronic

Priesthood; Melchizedek Priesthood

Priesthood leaders, as instruments, 2:107

Priesthood power, 2:343, 361; Satan to be bound by, 2:42

Priests of the Most High, 2:306–7

Prince of Peace, 1:77. *See also* Jesus Christ

Printing, of Book of Commandments, 1:6

Printing press, purchase of, 2:145

Priorities, 2:282–83; in marriage, 2:19–20

Prison, spirit, 1:32; 2:315

Privileges, 1:38

Probation: days of, 1:208; mortal, 2:51

Problems, everyday, 2:206–7

Procrastination, 2:49–50

Profanity, 2:205

Promise: children of the, 2:54; Holy Spirit of, 2:305

Promises, 1:39–40, 183, 271; sealed up to righteous, 2:246

Property: communal, of Ohio sect, 2:2; excess, 2:23; sharing of, 2:87

Property, consecrated, 2:11, 22, 138; stewardship of, 2:23; bishop's responsibility for, 2:268–69

Prophecy, 1:149; spirit of, 2:290; apocalyptic, 2:335

Prophets, 1:149–50; voice of, 1:27–28; and signs of Second Coming, 1:274; role of, 2:35; authority of, to speak for God, 2:36–37; keys held by, 2:211, 223; false, 2:219

Protection, of Saints, 2:99

Pseudonyms, Church leaders given, due to persecution, 2:352

Publishing, or revelations, 1:17–18; 2:132–33

Punishment, 1:48; unbelieving are sealed to, 1:20; eternal, of sons of perdition, 2:302

Pure Church of Christ, the, 1:223

2:174; called to raise funds for Zion, 2:202; persecution of, by Kirtland Saints, 2:211; lack of education of, 2:235; called to refute anti-Mormon accusations, 2:260; sustained as president of Church, 2:279–80; unrecorded visions of, 2:290, 329–30

Missionary labors of:
missions of, 1:105; 2:119, 141–42, 271

Teachings of:
on the spirit of revelation, 1:63; on love, 1:87; on sacrifice, 1:92; on the end of the world, 1:113; on preaching the gospel, 1:123; on organizing the Church, 1:126, 127; on reference to years, 1:128; on the Millennium, 1:185; on gathering, 1:197; on signs of Second Coming, 1:200; on knowledge of Jehovah, 1:256–57; on sin of murder, 2:18; on JST, 2:28; on false prophetess, 2:35; on enemies of the Church, 2:48, 261–62; on city of Enoch, 2:53; on discerning false spirits, 2:79; on misuse of spiritual gifts, 2:80–81; on beliefs of Shaker sect, 2:91; on brethren in Missouri, 2:142, 183; on sign seeking and adultery, 2:191–92; on suffering of the Saints, 2:200; on Second Comforter, 2:238; on infant baptism, 2:278; on everlasting punishment of sons of perdition, 2:298, 302; on necessity of baptism for celestial glory, 2:304; on postmortal progression, 2:316; on gaining spiritual knowledge, 2:330; on dwelling on mysteries, 2:336; on appearance of celestialized earth, 2:338; on book of Revelation,

2:336, 340; on Adam's authority, 2:357; on God as Ahman, 2:358
Smith, Joseph, Sr., 1:42, 52; called to manage Williams farm, 2:134
Smith, Joseph F., 2:315; and the Doctrine and Covenants, 1:1; on Church as legal entity, 2:46–47; on diverse religions during Millennium, 2:63
Smith, Joseph Fielding, 1:54, 92; on Oliver Cowdery, 1:159; on Emma Smith, 1:170; on Elias, 1:182; on D&C 29, 1:195; on mentally handicapped, 1:209–10; on priesthood succession, 2:38
Smith, Lucy Mack, 1:36, 41, 236; on Emma Smith, 1:53; on meeting with Edward Partridge, 1:245–46
Smith, Samuel, 1:52, 80, 195; 2:229; and organization of the Church of Christ, 1:127; revelation to, 1:158–60; death of, 1:160
Smith, Sylvester, 2:279
Son Ahman, 2:358
Son of the morning, Satan as, 2:294
Sons of perdition, 1:117, 204, 206–7; 2:295–300; characteristics of, 2:296; false speculation about, 2:302. *See also* Perdition
Sorcery, 2:194
Spirit: striving of the, 1:26; confirmation of the, 1:67–68; 2:364; recognizing the, of God, 1:82; denying the, 1:84; of world, 1:90, 116, 206–8; contrite, 1:138–39; of Christ, 1:139; that quickens, 1:228; teaching by the, 2:14–15, 38; gifts of the, 2:27, 75
Spirit body, likeness of, to mortal body, 2:340
Spirits, counterfeit, 2:2, 8, 72, 103; discerning, 2:79, 81; subject to power of priesthood, 2:106–7
Spiritual experience, purposes of, 2:104

ABOUT THE AUTHORS

STEPHEN E. ROBINSON was a professor of ancient scripture at Brigham Young University. He received a BA in English literature and studied for a master's degree in ancient scripture at BYU, and received a PhD in Biblical studies from Duke University. Brother Robinson's articles appeared in Church publications, as well as in respected scholarly publications such as *The Anchor Bible Dictionary, The Coptic Encyclopedia*, and *The Old Testament Pseudepigrapha*. A popular speaker and author, he wrote the bestselling book, *Believing Christ*, and a sequel entitled *Following Christ*, as well as *Are Mormons Christians?* He and his wife, Janet, are the parents of six children. Dr. Robinson passed away on June 17, 2018.

H. DEAN GARRETT retired in 2006 from teaching Church history and doctrine at BYU. He received bachelor's and master's degrees from Utah State University and an EdD in secondary curriculum and instruction from BYU. Prior to teaching at BYU, he taught in the Church Educational System as a seminary and institute teacher, and served as an institute director. A widely respected scholar on the Doctrine and Covenants, Brother Garrett contributed to the Church's institute manual on the Doctrine and Covenants, and he is the author of *Great Teachings from the Doctrine and Covenants*. He is also a former president of the Canada Calgary Mission. He and his wife, Patsy, are the parents of five children.